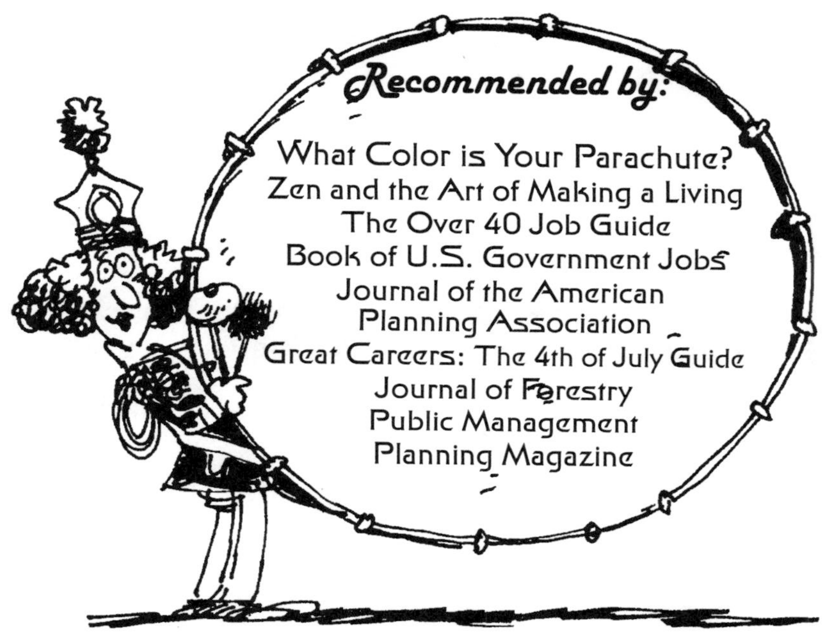

"**Everything you wanted to know about locating government vacancies** (and possibly a few things you never even thought about)...**unlocks** seemingly limitless (and sometimes obscure) data about finding positions in local, state, and federal government agencies. **Easy–to–use**, compact guide to a broad subject."

— *Journal of Career Planning and Placement*

"It steers you to ...**where you can actually find job openings**...it will **help you find a job.**"

— *Job Training and Placement Report*

"**Outstanding** book...**jammed packed** with useful resources to aid those interested in government work...and overseas employment.

— *Career Opportunities News*

"**Useful sourcebook chockablock**...suggestions for handling obviously sexist or otherwise illegal interview questions are **well worth noting**."

— *Booklist*

"Expanded, more thorough ...**outstanding**...compendium of resources for local, state, and federal government job seekers....**recommended**... worthy, **affordable**..."

— *Library Journal*

Career titles by Daniel Lauber

- ***The Ultimate Job Finder*** *(computer software)*
- ***Non–Profits' Job Finder***
- ***Professional's Private Sector Job Finder***
- ***Government Job Finder***
- ***Professional's Job Finder ****
- ***The Compleat Guide to Finding Jobs in Government ****
- ***The Compleat Guide to Jobs in Planning and Public Administration ****
- ***The Compleat Guide to Jobs in Planning ****

* These titles are out of print and have been superseded by the titles at the top of the list.

GOVERNMENT JOB FINDER

DANIEL LAUBER

SECOND EDITION

1994—1995

For quantity discounts and permissions, contact the publisher:
Planning/Communications, 7215 Oak Avenue
River Forest, Illinois 60305-1935; phone: 708/366-5200

Distribution to the trade by
National Book Network
4720-A Boston Way, Lanham, MD 20706; phone: 301/459-8696

Front cover design by Salvatore Concialdi

Graphics used by permission from *Megatoons* by Phil Frank, *Presentation Task Force*, and *PC/Graphics Deluxe*.

Library of Congress Cataloging–in–Publication Data

Lauber, Daniel.

Government Job Finder / Daniel Lauber. — 2nd edition
p. cm.
Includes bibliographical references and index.
ISBN: 1–884587–01–1 (hard cover): $32.95 — 0–9622019–7–9 (paperback): $16.95

1. Civil service positions—United States—Handbooks, manuals, etc. 2. Civil service positions—Handbooks, manuals, etc. 3. Job hunting—Handbooks, manuals, etc. I. Title. II Title: Job finder.

JK692.L39 1994

353.001'03—dc20 93–45780
CIP

Table of contents

Preface

Just trying to fill a void in the job-search game, that's all! Back in 1975 when I left my first job as a city planner, I discovered a whole lot more sources of job vacancies besides the local paper and our professional association's job bulletin. So I published the 16-page *Compleat Guide to Jobs in Planning* in 1976 to provide a reliable, one-stop shopping center for job vacancies for planners. Six years later I looked around and saw that nobody had done the same for public administration. The result was the 44-page *Compleat Guide to Jobs in Planning and Public Administration* (1982, 1984).

And in 1989 when I was running out of copies of that booklet, I looked around and realized that all the rest of government lacked a similar **one-stop shopping center for government job vacancies.** The result was the 183-page *Compleat Guide to Finding Jobs in Government*.

In 1992, my assistants and I replaced that book with the first edition of the *Government Job Finder* which greatly expanded and updated the 1989 volume with 33 percent more job sources. This new second edition is a whole new book. It goes far beyond the 1992 volume to provide details on several hundred more job sources, especially job hotlines and computerized online job services — most of which did not exist a few years ago. But it still achieves the goal of the 1989 volume: to give you enough reliable information about each source of local, state, and federal government job vacancies so you can use them to find the government job where *you* want to live.

Today, with over 25,000 "Compleat Guides" sold, this new edition covers the whole gamut of government positions — professional, trades, labor, technical, and office support — in local, state, and the federal government, both in the U.S. and abroad. In addition, we've added illustrations and cartoons to bring a little liveliness to a dry subject (there really isn't much of a plot). And I've continued to including dozens of references and puns on the musical and cultural "icons" of our age in the sample resumes and cover letters.

No single book, however, could possibly tell you everything about every aspect of getting government work. The *Government Job Finder* concentrates on getting you to the job vacancies — for most people this is the only book you'll need for your job search. But for those who want more information on other aspects of the government job hunt, the *Government Job Finder* refers you to the best sources of that information. Since so many of these other books are hard to find in bookstores, we've made them available in Planning/Communications' catalog that begins on page 321 just in case you can't find them at your local bookstore.

This book could not have been prepared without the very kind cooperation of the thousands of people who publish and operate the job sources enumerated in these pages. I offer my deepest thanks to them for providing the information needed to determine if the job–quest aides they produce and operate would really help people seeking government work.

A project of this size is impossible for one individual to undertake. I cannot heap enough praise upon my research associate Laura Southwick for the dedicated effort she contributed to this book and its companion volumes: the ***Professional's Private Sector Job Finder*** and the ***Non–Profits' Job Finder,*** as well as the computer software version of these books, ***The Ultimate Job Finder***. Aside from having to tolerate my demands and eccentricities, she mastered the very complicated process through which we found and verified the job sources included in these three books.

Most of all, I would like to thank my wife, Diana, for not only putting up with me during the past year (during which I did a fairly effective impersonation of an obsessed workaholic), but for also offering invaluable advice on the manuscript as well as moral support when the going got tough.

These companion volumes just mentioned grew out of the fact that when I started working on the first edition of the *Government Job Finder* in November 1990, I noticed that there was no one–stop shopping center for private sector nor non–profit sector jobs. As the research on the *Government Job Finder* progressed, I decided to expand our work to produce these two other books to cover job sources for the private and non–profit sectors. Since many job sources include a good number of positions in two or more sectors of the economy, there is some overlap between the three books. However, the vast majority of the job sources each one presents are very different.

As several reviewers have noted, we "leave the motivation babble to other authors." You'll get just the facts in these three books without useless filler. Heck, just to fit everything in we had to reduce the size of the type.

Finally, for those readers who have written or called during the past 17 years about the "misspelling" in the title of the three predecessor books: "compleat" in the title was not a mistake! That's just the old–fashioned way to spell "complete." I stumbled upon that spelling in a used–record bin where I spotted "The Compleat Tom Paxton." I thought this spelling might attract more attention than the conventional modern spelling. Obviously it did! However, I certainly do appreciate your well–intentioned concern.

But the title had to change with this edition. The editor of *Career Opportunities News* wrote about *The Compleat Guide to Finding Jobs in Government*: "An outstanding book, our only complaint is that the title is so passive it fails to reflect the terrific book which follows." The real nail on the coffin was a call I got from a fifth grade English teacher who asked how we can expect her to teach her pupils to spell correctly when we misspell "complete." I guess her fifth graders are mighty precocious to look at job books at their age. Frankly, I just don't want to get those kinds of phone calls anymore.

We've tried to make this book as "compleat" as possible. But between the time I write this and the time you read it, some new sources of government jobs have been initiated and some have closed, moved, or changed their fee structure. As explained in Chapter 1, many job sources are highly mobile and often change their phone numbers and addresses.

You can keep on top of these changes by sending for free updated information on those job sources which have changed since this book went to press. See page 313 for instructions on how to obtain our **free *Update Sheet*** with new information on any job sources in this book that have changed. Please follow the instructions on page 313.

The *Update Sheet* is only as good as the information you send us. There's a ***Reader Feedback Form*** on page 311 to help you send us information about any job source in this book that has changed— or let us know about new job sources. If you can't track down a job source, tell us. The chances are pretty good that we've already found its new address or phone number and can tell you what it is. Please let us know about these changes as soon as you come upon them so we can include them in the *Update Sheet*.

Thanks for purchasing the *Government Job Finder*. If you follow the suggestions in Chapter 1 on how to use this book effectively, it will help you find the government job you want, in the locale in which you wish to live.

Daniel Lauber

Daniel Lauber
February, 1994

Chapter 1

How to get the most out of the Government Job Finder

Read this chapter first!

With 17 million government jobs, there are always thousands of vacant positions waiting to be filled. The *Government Job Finder* guides you through the quick and easy way to find these vacancies, the vast majority of which never make it into the classifieds section of your local newspaper.

That's because local, state, and federal government employers have become smart, just like many private sector businesses and non–profit organizations. When they advertise in the local newspaper, they get a lot of responses from people who are not even remotely qualified for the job, many of whom think their political connections can get them the job. In addition, ads in the local paper don't reach top–notch professionals' from out of town who don't read the local paper. Government personnel directors don't want to spend time and money reading lots of cover letters and resumes from applicants whose resumes are prime candidates for the circular file. So most local, state, and federal government agencies that hire by merit rather than patronage advertise job openings where the qualified job candidates will see them: in specialty and trade periodicals, on job hotlines, on computerized job databases and online services, and in unique directories. A growing number of government agencies, particularly federal, also use resume databases to fill slots with qualified employees.

The *Government Job Finder* goes boldly where no other book has gone to tell you exactly where to find the job vacancies in local, state, and federal government — it's a quick and easy **one–stop shopping center for government job vacancies**! It also introduces you to the almost metaphysical exercise of applying for federal government jobs, and to the less onerous, but still mysterious task of applying for government jobs in Canada and overseas. Sources of government internships are also identified. In addition, the *Government Job Finder* offers solid, no–nonsense advice for both seasoned professionals and entry–level workers on writing effective cover letters and resumes as well as preparing for job interviews.

The *Government Job Finder* is the place to start your search for a government job. It is **essential that you read this chapter before you go any further in this book so you will be able to find all the job sources that will help you.** If you follow the suggestions this chapter presents for using the *Government Job Finder*, job openings at all levels of government will soon be at your fingertips in both the so–called "non–professional" technical, labor, trades, and office support (clerical, secretarial, etc.) fields, as well as in the government professional specialities listed on page 3.

One of the most difficult parts of job hunting involves finding out what jobs are available in the geographic area in which you wish to ply your skills. Most people in government are aware of only one or two publications that advertise government positions in their field and maybe a job hotline with a tape recording that names job openings. Yet, every month, there are many more government jobs in the same field that are advertised in the now legendary "hidden" job market.

The *Government Job Finder* unlocks the secrets of the hidden job market as it leads you to the specialty and trade periodicals, job banks, job–matching services, computerized job and resume databases, online services, and job hotlines that government agencies use to fill vacancies in your specialty. Because it is often necessary to contact an agency directly to learn about job openings, this book also identifies over 250 directories of local, state, and federal government officials, agencies, and departments to get you to the right person the first time you try. You'll also find details on salary surveys for different government professions which will enable you to negotiate your salary more effectively.

For each job source, the *Government Job Finder* tells you everything you need to know to decide whether to use the job source. You won't have to make any long distance calls or write letters for more information, except where directed to do so.

Occupations included in the Government Job Finder

Accounting
Aerospace
Agriculture
Airport operations
Animal control
Aquariums
Architecture
Archival services
Arts
Code enforcement
Communications
Community development
Correctional services
Court administration
Court reporting
Data processing and computers
Economic development
Emergency management
Employee relations
Engineering
Environment
Finance
Fire protection
Fleet/facilities management
Forestry
Grounds management
Horticulture
Housing
Human services
Labor relations
Landscape architecture
Law enforcement
Legal services
Library services
Media
Mental health
Museum services
Parking
Parks and recreation
Personnel
Planning
Political industry
Port management
Property management
Public administration
Public health
Public safety
Public works
Purchasing
Real estate appraisal
Real estate management
Records management
Risk management/insurance
Sanitation services
Social services
Solid waste management
Tax assessment
Trades
Traffic engineering and parking
Transit management
Transportation planning
Urban design
Utilities management
Water/wastewater operations
Zoos

In addition, this volume offers concise advice to help you prepare more effective cover letters and resumes. It also suggests techniques for preparing for a job interview so you can present the best possible portrait of yourself to the interviewer. Not only does this information clear up common misconceptions held by many entry–level job seekers, but it also serves as a refresher course for long–employed practitioners who have been out of the job market for years.

The *Government Job Finder* provides all the information you need to find and be hired for the government job you want, in the location you desire.

Job search strategies

There are at least two basic ways to find job openings in government. One is the direct approach, in which you find actual job openings. The second is more circumspect, where you write, almost blindly, to possible employers to learn if there are any job openings, or if there are any expected in the near future. The *Government Job Finder* furnishes information for both techniques.

Using the direct approach

Periodicals

Newspapers. Generally speaking, fewer than 20 percent of job vacancies are advertised in local newspapers. But that doesn't mean you should ignore them altogether. If you want to work in the same location as you live, you should still start your job search each week by perusing the local classifieds, just in case something turns up. Then turn to the other, more productive job sources presented in this book. If you want to see classified ads from newspapers in other cities, see *Classifacts,* a job service described on page 32 that compiles job ads from dozens of local newspapers from across the country.

In a few locales, the Sunday edition of the local newspaper may be the only accessible source for jobs openings with cities and counties. State and federal positions rarely make it into the local newspaper. In some states, a major newspaper is the best source for government job ads for locations throughout the state, and in areas like New England, throughout the region. The *Government Job Finder* identifies these newspapers in the state–by–state listings that appear in Chapter 3.

Be forewarned that it is sometimes a bit difficult to locate government job ads thanks to the unfathomable job categories classified sections use. Many government jobs simply wind up under "Administration." Federal positions often appear in the business section. There is no national nor rational pattern. You'll have to rely on your wits to determine what categories to peruse.

Specialty and trade periodicals. Most government positions, however, don't make it into the local newspaper. Among the best sources for government job openings are the specialty and trade periodicals that a professional association or private publisher produces. These appear in Chapter 2 of the *Government Job Finder*.

Most state municipal leagues include ads for local government positions in their newsletters or magazines. Many of these periodicals devote a portion of their classified advertising to job ads or announcements. Some publish display ads for jobs, while still others print both types of ads. Some of these periodicals publish just one or two job ads an issue while others print scores of ads.

The vast majority of the specialty magazines are available to the general public, usually at higher subscription rates than for association members. Some of these are available only to organization members. The *Government Job Finder* presents full information on these periodicals so you can focus on those most likely to carry ads for jobs for which you are qualified and in which you are interested.

Job listing periodicals. The best source of jobs for a particular government specialty is usually a periodical devoted primarily or entirely to job ads or announcements. The number of job ads in a typical issue ranges from about a dozen to 100, although a few go higher and several run announcements for thousands of government jobs.

Sometimes a periodical is available only to members of the organization that publishes it. Most, however, are available to nonmembers as well, although members often receive the job magazine for a reduced fee or free as part of their membership package.

The Quick & Easy Job Finder

If you just can't wait to read all of Chapter 1 first, follow the steps shown below to find sources of job vacancies in local, state, or federal government in the U.S. or abroad. But, be advised, you won't get the most out of this book if you don't read all of Chapter 1 first.

Local and state government jobs: Look up the general sources at the beginning of Chapter 2, then go to your specialty in Chapter 2.

↓

To find job sources for a region, go to the beginning of Chapter 3. For job sources for a specific state, see that state's section in Chapter 3.

↓

Look in the Index for additional job sources for your specialty that are not located where you would intuitively expect to find them.

Federal jobs: For sources of jobs with the federal government, first read Chapter 4.

↓

To find job sources in Chapter 2 that include federal positions, look under "Federal jobs" in the Index.

↓

To locate the Federal Job Information Center for your state, look under your state's section in Chapter 3.

Jobs outside the U.S.: For sources of job openings with governments outside the U.S., read Chapter 5.

↓

For sources of jobs with U.S. possessions, see the entries for each possession at the end of Chapter 3.

↓

To find job sources in Chapters 2 and 4 that include jobs outside the U.S., look under "Foreign jobs" in the Index.

Since so many professional organizations publish job ads in their periodicals, the ***Government Job Finder*** also tells you about several directories of associations so you can track down any job listing periodicals or job services that escaped our attention. If you find any, please use the *Reader Feedback Form* on page 311 to tell us about them so we can include them in the free *Update Sheet* (see page 313 for details) and the next edition. As you read this book, you'll find that some job listing periodicals are also published by private businesses rather than non–profit professional or trade associations.

State chapters of professional or trade associations. Many of the associations that publish periodicals with ads for government positions have state or regional chapters that also announce job openings in their chapter newsletters. Unfortunately, few of these national federations can provide information on which chapters publish job ads. You will have to contact an organization's national office to obtain the proper addresses and phone numbers to reach the chapter president or newsletter editor who can tell you if their newsletter features job openings. The address and phone number given for a publication or job service issued by an association is almost always that for the association's headquarters.

Positions wanted. In addition to listing positions which are available, many of these periodicals let job seekers advertise themselves under a category like "Positions Wanted." Many of these are identified in the *Government Job Finder*. Before seeking to place a "Positions Sought" ad, you'd be prudent to first examine the periodical. Try to get a sample copy from the publisher or examine one in a library. After you've identified the periodicals in which you want to advertise yourself, contact them directly to learn if they publish "Position Wanted" ads, any restrictions that limit such self–advertising to members only, the rates charged, and whether you can publish a "blind" ad without your name in it that uses a box number to identify responses (a useful tool if you don't want your current employer to know you're looking for a new job).

Inspect some periodicals first. The *Government Job Finder's* descriptions of each periodical will give you a good idea whether it's worth the price of a subscription. But in a few cases you can't really decide without seeing a sample copy. Many publishers will be happy to send you a complimentary sample copy to help you decide if you want to subscribe. Others charge a few dollars for a single issue. If the entry for a periodical includes its single–issue price, you can be sure the the publisher will *not* give you a free sample copy. You'll just have to buy a single issue to check it out.

In addition, you can inspect many of the periodicals listed in the *Government Job Finder* at your local public library. Municipal reference libraries and university libraries are even better sources for the periodicals named here. The libraries of professional associations are also likely to carry relevant periodicals. However, it is usually worth the subscription price to get the periodical delivered to you rather than rely on library copies since subscribers invariably receive their periodicals at least a few days before they are available at any library.

Internships. Throughout the next three chapters, you'll come upon some directories of internships and a few periodicals that carry internship announcements. Unlike the vast majority of directories described in the *Government Job Finder*, these internship directories actually present openings, albeit for internships and not permanent jobs. Also be sure to consult the Index to find job sources that include internships.

Listings for periodicals

The ***Government Job Finder*** tells you everything you need to know about each periodical so you can make an informed decision whether to subscribe without having to call or write the publisher for more information. Periodicals are listed under the heading "Job ads in print." Included in each periodical's entry is the following information:

- ***Periodical's title*.**
- ***Address for subscriptions*.**
- ***Publisher's phone number.*** Toll–free "800" numbers are given when available.
- ***Frequency of publication.*** To clear up the confusion, "biweekly" means every two weeks; "bimonthly" means every two months. "Semi-monthly" is twice a month.
- ***Subscription rates*.** Both rates are given when a professional or trade association charges different rates for nonmembers and members. Contact the association for membership dues. Sometimes annual dues don't cost much more than the price of an annual subscription.

  Prices given are for surface mail delivery to addresses in the United States and its possessions. Entries note when different rates are charged for Canada, Mexico, and/or other foreign countries. Most subscription rates are annual rates. Rates for shorter periods of time are noted. Contact a periodical if you wish to subscribe for more than 12 months since many offer discounts for two– or three–year subscriptions. Although prices are accurate as of the date on which we obtained them, they are certainly subject to change without notice at any time.
- ***Special information about the periodical*.** If a periodical is regional in scope, the states within its region are noted. Also provided is any other pertinent information that will help you decide if the periodical is worth your attention.
- ***Heading under which job openings appear*.** For the periodicals that contain articles as well as job listings, the heading under which job ads appear is given.
- ***Number of job openings in a typical issue*.** "Few job ads" means no more than two or three appear in the average issue. Generally each entry will tell you how many jobs were advertised in a typical issue during 1993. If the economy remains in stasis in 1994, then you can figure the same number of jobs will be advertised in 1994. If the economy should miraculously boom, anticipate more job ads in each issue in 1994.

Job–matching services and job banks

Many trade and professional organizations, private companies, and state governments operate services in which the resumes of job candidates are matched with positions for which they qualify. These services can be quite effective for government professionals as well as individuals seeking support, technical, trades, or labor positions in government.

Some job–matching services supply a form for the job candidate to complete, while others allow you to submit your regular resume. Most place the information you submit in a computer database while others operate manually. Some charge job candidates for their services, while others do not (they will usually charge employers a fee to search the candidates' database). The job–matching services operated by state Job Service Offices are free.

Many colleges and universities participate in job–matching services designed for their alumna's use. Because you can simply check with your school's alumni association or placement office to learn if your school participates in one, we left these out of the *Government Job Finder*.

Attractive as these sound, you should be aware that they can be agonizingly slow in getting you a job interview. Despite all the hype that surrounds them, most are relatively new services without proven track records. If you are the sort of person who is likely to quickly find a job using conventional methods, you may also be matched to a job pretty quickly using one of these services. But if you've been having trouble getting hired using conventional job search methods, you should probably not expect instantaneous results using a job–matching service.

Job–matching services and job banks are listed under the heading "Job services." Entries that describe these services provide the following information:

- ***Name of service***.
- ***Operator of service***.
- ***Operator's address and phone number***.
- ***Type of resume used***. Does the service require job seekers to fill out the service's own resume data form or do you submit your own resume?
- ***How the service operates***. Is the service computer–based or manually operated? Are you able to be identified by number so your current employer doesn't accidentally stumble upon your resume?
- ***Who contacts whom?*** Does the job service tell the job candidate that an employer would like to contact her for an interview, or does the potential employer contact selected candidates directly?
- ***Length of time resume is kept on file***.
- ***Fees for applicants, if any***. Fees are accurate as of 1993. These fees, though, are no exception to the adage "things change."
- ***Other pertinent information***. Some job services may be available only to members of the organization that operates the service. A few privately–operated job services attempt to compensate for past and continuing discrimination against minorities or women and, therefore, serve only members of the discriminated–against group.

Online job databases

This decade has witnessed an explosion in the number of online job databases which anybody can access using a personal computer and modem. This electronic job search revolution enables you, from your armchair, to see the growing number of job ads that appear on many of the nation's electronic bulletin boards. These online services enable you to read ads for the latest job openings and, if you wish, download them onto your own computer where you can print them out.

Generally speaking, it is well worth your while to contact the operator of any online job database you wish to use to learn the details of how to hook up and what the costs are. Many of these online job databases tend to be a bit ephemeral. Only a few of those operating in 1989 still exist. Charges are subject to frequent changes.

Many colleges and universities participate in online job services specifically for their alumna's use. Because you can easily check with your school's alumni association or placement office, we left these out of the *Government Job Finder*.

Online job databases appear under the heading "Job services." The *Government Job Finder* offers the following information on each of the online job databases it describes:

- ***Name of online job database service***.
- ***Name of the association or private business that operates the online job database service***.
- ***Operator's address and regular telephone number***.
- ***Online job database service phone number.*** Each listing will give you the voice phone number of the company that operates the service. The entry will also give you the phone number to dial with your modem to access the service when there are no charges to use the service other than the cost of a phone call, frequently long distance, or the entry tells you what the charges are.
- ***Costs***. If there are any costs required to use an online job database service, we'll tell you about them. These include a monthly subscription fee, connection charge, telecommunications charge for each minute you're connected, and a software starter kit which is usually inexpensive or free. If the entry gives the phone number for your modem to call, be sure to note if it begins with "900." There is a per minute charge in addition to normal phone line charges to numbers that begin with a 900 area code.
- ***Hours the online job database service operates***. You can assume that you can access each of these any time you want unless operating hours are provided.

Mr. Boffo reprinted by permission of Tribune Media Services. Copyright 1992. All rights reserved.

- ***When job listings are changed***. So you don't waste time calling too often, most of the entries note when job listings are updated.
- ***Types of jobs included***. When an online job database is for specific types of jobs that may not be readily apparent from its name, we'll tell you the types of jobs featured.
- ***Membership requirements, if any***. The description of a online job database service notes when it is available only to subscribers or to a sponsoring association's members.

Job hotlines

Many professional and trade associations, and governments, operate job hotlines which often offer recordings that describe available jobs and how to apply. These hotlines have become much more sophisticated than just two years ago thanks to the wonders of the "automated attendant" device. You will almost certainly need a touch-tone phone to call these hotlines because the recorded voice at the other end will give you instructions that can be implemented only with a touch-tone phone. The most sophisticated job hotlines allow you to specify the geographic area(s) in which you are interested and the types of jobs about which you want to hear.

Some of the less high-tech hotlines simply give you a recording that lists jobs. You have no control over what you hear. Often you will first hear a list of all the job titles available. If you want to hear a detailed description and how to apply for a particular position that was just listed, keep listening because that information is often conveyed next.

When you call a few of these hotlines, a live person will answer and read job openings to you. Other job hotlines can be accessed by computer (via a modem) to generate printed listings. Those that are accessible by computer modem are noted in chapters 2 and 3. Some of these job hotlines offer very extensive listings.

The main personnel offices of many federal departments operate tape recorded, 24–hour job hotlines. These phone numbers are listed by agency in Chapter 4.

Pay attention to the area code of the job hotline you are about to call. If the area code is "900," the call not only isn't free, but you will be charged an additional fee directly on your phone bill. When a 900 number is listed here, the charges are generally identified.

Job hotlines appear under the heading "Job services." If a job hotline operated by a local, state, or federal government is free, the *Government Job Finder* simply gives you the phone number to call. But for job hotlines operated by a business or association that charges for use of the hotline, the following information is presented:

- ***Name of the job hotline***.
- ***Name of the entity that operates the hotline***.
- ***Operator's address and regular voice telephone number***.
- ***Hotline's phone number***. A small, but growing number of hotline operators offer a "Telecommunications for the Deaf" number as well. These are identified in bold face type as **TDD** phone numbers.
- ***Hours the hotline operates***. Most of these recordings can be called 24–hours a day, eight days a week. Operating hours are listed if they are limited.
- ***When job listings are changed***. So you don't waste time calling too often, most of the listings note when recordings are updated.
- ***Types of jobs included***. Some job hotlines are for specific types of government jobs that may not be readily apparent from the name of the hotline. In addition, some operators of job hotlines like the State of California, have different hotline numbers for different types of state jobs.
- ***Membership requirements, if any***. The description of a hotline notes when a hotline is available only to subscribers or only to the sponsoring association's members.

Using the indirect approach

Unfortunately, many public agencies are less than aggressive when announcing job openings. In a few extremely popular locales, like the San Francisco Bay Area, many agencies merely post announcements of open positions in obscure, albeit, legal places. Some governments don't advertise widely so they can keep the jobs in the "family." Others, like the City of Chicago, not only rarely advertise vacancies, but they post them only at the

Mother Goose and Grimm reprinted by permission of Tribune Media Services.

city personnel office and won't even let you apply for a job unless you already live in the city. Generally speaking, jurisdictions that do not allow nonresidents to apply are not good places to work. There is often a fear of fresh ideas that an "outsider" may bring in that could upset the apple–cart of the powers that be.

Many local and state government agencies and departments, will, upon request, place job candidates on a mailing list to receive announcements of certain types of job openings. Others will tell you about jobs available at the time you contact them. And in some instances, you just get lucky by contacting the right person at the right time.

You can also use these directories and computer databases to learn more about the jurisdiction before your interview so you can answer interview questions more effectively and ask intelligent questions about that government.

Using directories and computer databases

National directories. The *Government Job Finder* includes hundreds of directories of officials and government departments to steer job seekers to the right person concerning possible job openings. Speaking directly to the right person can give you a genuine competitive edge. It tells her that you've done your homework. Also, you can learn a lot more about the nature of vacant jobs and the character of the hiring agency by talking to someone in the know than just by reading job ads. As noted in Chapter 7 on interviewing, you would be most prudent to know something about the jurisdiction for which you are applying for a job when you step into that interview.

Directories are also useful for networking purposes. They give you an opportunity to identify people who already work for the jurisdiction to which you want to apply. By knowing who they are when you meet them at professional gatherings, you can "network" with them and place yourself in a position to hear about vacancies even before they are officially open. For details on the networking game, see *The New Network Your Way to Job and Career Success* by Ron and Caryl Krannich ($12.95, 1993, 168 pages; for your convenience, it's available from the catalog at the end of this book).

State Directories. Most state municipal leagues publish directories of municipal and county officials. A number of state governments publish directories as well. In addition, some state chapters of specialty associations publish directories of relevant local and state government departments and agencies. To learn if a state chapter publishes such a directory, contact the national organization to get the name, address, and phone number of the chapter president in each state in which you are interested.

Libraries. Some of the directories listed in the *Government Job Finder* are rather lengthy tomes that cost the proverbial arm and a leg. No rational individual would spend the hundreds of dollars some of these cost. Fortunately, most of them are available at well–stocked public libraries and can also be found through inter–library loan systems. Municipal reference libraries and libraries at colleges and universities are even more likely to carry the directories described in the next three chapters. The libraries of professional associations are also likely to carry relevant directories.

Directories are listed throughout this book under the heading "Directories." The following details are furnished for each of the directories of government agencies and/or officials:

- ***Title***.
- ***Publisher***.
- ***Publisher's address and phone number***.
- ***Price***. Members of an association that publishes a directory usually can purchase it at a lower price than nonmembers, or receive it free as part of their membership package. The price of the most recent edition is given. Subsequent editions may cost more. When a directory is available only to association members, this restriction is noted.
- ***Frequency of publication.*** Most of these directories are published annually or less frequently. The handful that are updated and republished several times a year are sold by subscription. The date of the most recent edition is usually given as is when the directory is published.
- ***Description of contents.*** Information on the subjects a directory covers is provided when the directory's title doesn't adequately describe its contents. When it's helpful, indexing information is presented. The number of entries and pages is usually provided, especially for the really large and expensive directories.

There is a growing number of databases that are essentially directories of government agencies and officials. Their big advantage is that you can often set specific search criteria to find the governments or agencies that interest you. Some of these databases are available through the types of online services described earlier in this chapter. Others are available on computer disks. Still others come on CD-ROMs (compact disk, read-only memory) which require you to have a CD-ROM player attached to a personal computer.

As with the directories discussed immediately above, you can use computer databases to construct a list of governments for which you may wish to work. You can also use them to learn more about governmental entities with which you have an interview coming up.

All three types of these databases are listed under "Directories" in the *Government Job Finder*. The same sort of information that is furnished about directories is provided for these databases. However, for online database services, we'll also give you details on how to access the database by computer modem.

Salary surveys

As Chapter 7 of the *Government Job Finder* explains, the more a job applicant knows about the wage scales in the locale or region for a particular type of position, the better he can negotiate salary and meet the employer's expectations in the job interview. In addition, knowing differences in salary between states and regions can help you decide where to look for a government job.

Consequently, the next three chapters include books, monographs, and articles that report the results of salary surveys. Many trade and professional associations collect salary data but do not publicize their findings very widely. To obtain salary information on the professions for which salary survey information is not listed, contact the appropriate professional or trade association directly. To find associations not mentioned in this book, see the directories of associations cited herein.

Salary surveys appear under the heading "Salary surveys." The descriptions of salary surveys include:

- ***Title***.
- ***Publisher.***
- ***Publisher's address and phone number***.
- ***Price.***
- ***Most recent publication date or frequency of publication***.
- ***Survey coverage.*** Entries often include details of how data is presented (by size of city, type of city, region, etc.).
- ***Types of positions included***.

How to use this book effectively

Nationwide job–hunting helpers. The periodicals, job hotlines, job–matching services, and directories described in the *Government Job Finder* can be divided into two classes based on the geographic area they cover. The periodicals and other job–hunting aides that feature job openings for the entire country are listed in Chapter 2. These are divided again into two groups based on the scope of their subject matter. Those that provide information on jobs for a broad range of government specialties are listed first. Next, those that focus on a particular field such as fire protection, social services, or utility management, are listed under the appropriate category of job specialties. When one or more specialities are closely related, a cross reference is provided to alert you to examine the job sources for the related specialities as well. When just one or two job sources listed under a different specialty are relevant, a cross reference to them is given.

Local sources of state and local vacancies. The other set of job–search aides present information on jobs available within a multi–state region or in just one state. Nearly all these job sources include the broad range of government job specialties. Chapter 3 identifies these periodicals, job hotlines, job databases, job–matching services, and directories.

Federal jobs. Chapter 4 guides you to the sources of federal job openings and through the unique maze job hunters encounter when seeking employment with the federal government. Also be sure to see the Index listing for "Federal jobs" because it guides you to the job sources in chapters 2 and 3 that include federal positions in addition to the local and state positions on which they primarily focus.

Jobs in Canada and abroad. Chapter 5 identifies periodicals, job–matching services, job hotlines, and directories that help job hopefuls find government positions in Canada and abroad. This chapter also introduces you to the the world of working, and finding work overseas.

Cover letters, resumes, and interviews. Chapter 6 presents succinct guidelines for writing cover letters and for preparing and designing resumes. Two sample cover letters and resumes are presented. They illustrate effective formats and writing styles. But to lighten things up a bit (and who doesn't need a few laughs when looking for work?), they are filled with references to rock music, movies, and P.D.Q. Bach. See how many references to them you can find. Chapter 7 explains how to prepare for job interviews, what to wear, and how to perform at the interview. It addresses some of the many myths regarding interviews for government jobs.

How to find technical, labor, trades, and office support positions

Local and state government jobs

Although they tend to concentrate on professional positions, many of the periodicals in the "Government jobs in general" section of Chapter 2 carry advertisements for technical, trades, labor, and office support positions with local and state governments. Most of the periodicals and job hotlines listed under the categories of government specialties in Chapter 2 also list openings for these types of positions. Be sure to also look in the Index under "Trades" and other relevant entries.

Local newspapers. A fairly good source of advertisements for these types of state and local government positions is the classified advertising section in a local newspaper. Many libraries and newspaper vendors carry newspapers from around the country.

Civil Service. Many cities and states hire technical, trades, labor, and support personnel through their civil service systems. Contact local personnel departments directly to learn about job openings. Many of the directories of municipal officials described in Chapter 3 furnish the addresses and phone numbers of local government personnel departments. Each state–by–state listing explains how to find openings in that state's government.

Job Service Offices. One of your best bets is to examine the job sources available in the state–by–state listings in Chapter 3. These include Job Service or Employment Security offices which generally operate a computer–based system that matches applicants with the local and/or state government jobs for which they qualify. Since all government jobs are supposed to be listed with these services, you stand a very good chance of finding local and state positions at Job Service Offices. See the discussion of them in Chapter 3. For state government positions, read the specific sections on state jobs for each state in Chapter 3.

Mr. *Boffo* reprinted by permission of Tribune Media Services. Copyright 1992. All rights reserved.

Federal government jobs

Chapter 4 brings you descriptions of a number of periodicals that carry lists or announcements of jobs with the federal government. Unless otherwise indicated, these periodicals list job openings for technical, trades, labor, and office support jobs, as well as for professional positions. ***Be sure to also look in the Index under "Federal jobs" for entries in other chapters that include federal positions.***

Chapter 4 also explains how to find job openings directly from the federal government. It provides the telephone number for the main personnel office for over 200 federal departments and agencies as well as their job hotlines. In addition, it describes several guides to federal jobs including one specifically directed to technical, trades, support, and labor positions and one solely devoted to the U.S. Postal Service. For more details, see the discussion below on finding professional positions in the federal government.

Federal Job Information Centers. The Federal Job Information Centers (FJICs) located throughout the country are an excellent source of non–professional positions with the national government. These are discussed in detail in Chapter 4. Each center has information on federal jobs located in a specific geographic area. To find the FJIC closest to you, see the state–by–state listings in Chapter 3. Also note that many federal openings are listed in each state's Job Service Offices which are also identified in the state–by–state part of Chapter 3.

Government jobs in Canada and abroad

While most of the periodicals listed in Chapter 5 won't help nonprofessionals very much, the directories will enable you to determine where to find job openings and to whom to apply for jobs with foreign governments. In addition, a number of the general books on overseas employment will be very helpful.

You should be aware, though, that many foreign governments hire only their own citizens. Before applying for a job with a foreign government, you would be prudent to first learn if it hires foreigners and learn the visa and work permit rules.

While Chapter 5 includes sources of overseas jobs with the United States government, you should also examine the job sources in Chapter 4. The periodicals that list U.S. government jobs include both domestic and foreign positions for technical, trades, labor, and office support employees. For more details, see the discussion below on overseas hiring for professional positions.

How to find professional positions

Local and state government jobs

Start with the nationwide job–quest aides identified in Chapter 2. First look under the heading "Government jobs in general" for the job sources that cover more than just one government job specialty. These job helpers are quite broad in coverage. Each issue of these periodicals is almost certain to include ads for professional positions in most, if not all, of the classifications into which job specialities are divided later in Chapter 2. The job sources in this section focus largely on local government jobs, although some state jobs and even federal positions creep in.

Next, turn to the section headed "Jobs by specialty" to find the job category or categories that are most related to the sort of work you seek. These categories are cross–referenced so periodicals, job–matching services, job hotlines, and directories that serve more than one discipline can be easily found. Virtually all of the job–search aides identified here are nationwide in scope. Regional and state job sources for a specific occupation are generally listed here with the nationwide job sources, rather than in the state–by–state listings of Chapter 3.

You'll find that the number of items presented in each category varies significantly. There are simply more job sources available for some specialties than for others. For those specialities with few nationwide job sources, you will have to rely more heavily on the job sources in the "Government jobs in general" section of Chapter 2 and in the state–by–state listings in Chapter 3. *Be sure to also look in the Index to find job sources for an occupation that are placed somewhere other than where you would intuitively expect to find them.*

Finally, turn to Chapter 3 for job–search aides that cover multi–state regions and individual states. You'll first come upon a catalog of nationwide directories of local government officials and departments, followed by a list of nationwide directories of state agencies and officials. These can be used to contact the appropriate officials for local or state government jobs.

Reprinted by permission from *Which Niche?* by Jack Shingleton, illustrated by Phil Frank. Copyright 1989. All rights reserved.

For job sources in a particular state, refer to the section headed "Job sources: State–by–state." Be sure to read the material that precedes the state listings. Job sources identified include periodicals, usually state municipal league magazines, that carry local government job announcements; job–matching services; directories of local and/or state officials; and job hotlines. In addition, information specific to finding state jobs is provided. The state agency locator telephone number is provided for each state as is the address and phone of the pertinent Federal Job Information Center or centers.

Federal government positions

Federal positions rarely appear in the periodicals, job hotlines, and job–matching services that handle state and local government jobs. Most federal jobs are announced in periodicals and on job hotlines.

Chapter 4 walks you through the most effective ways to find jobs with the federal government. After explaining the federal hiring system (which could very well be in transition when you read this), it presents the periodicals that list job openings in the federal government. Cross references are made to the relevant periodicals or job services listed earlier in Chapter 2. Be sure to also look in the Index under "Federal jobs" for entries in other chapters that include federal positions.

Next, you are introduced to the unique world of the federal government's own job sources. Using them is definitely not for the faint of heart. However, job seekers are often best off contacting an agency's personnel department directly to learn of job openings, obtain job announcements, and procure an application. You will be introduced to the directories that get you to the appropriate officials in each federal agency. An extensive list of job hotlines and main personnel office telephone numbers is furnished for federal agencies, commissions, and departments.

The chapter ends with descriptions of several books that help you apply for a federal job. Some of these proffer detailed information on federal job classifications, which agencies hire which classifications, where the jobs are located, which jobs, departments, and agencies are exempt from using the Office of Personnel Management's hiring procedures, and how to complete the dread SF 171 application form.

Government jobs in Canada and abroad

Start with Chapter 5, which describes the periodicals, job services, and directories of foreign regimes and officials that guide you to government positions overseas and in Canada. Since job hunting outside the U.S. requires adapting to procedural and cultural differences, several books on the overseas job search game are recommended. You should also examine the entries in Chapter 2 because many of them include advertisements for jobs overseas. Look in the Index under "Foreign jobs" to find these. Those that frequently sport such announcements are so noted in their Chapter 2 listings. Chapter 5 also refers you directly to several periodicals in Chapter 2 that carry an extensive number of foreign job openings.

Just as only U.S. citizens can work for the United States government, many other countries also restrict government employment to their own citizens. Before applying for a position with a foreign government, be sure to find out if it hires aliens and learn what its visa and work permit regulations are.

Because the United States government is a major overseas employer, you should also consult Chapter 4 where several of the job–hunting aides described supply information on finding overseas employment with the federal government.

Canada. There are many fewer job services available in Canada than one might intuitively expect. Consequently, the listings for Canada are relatively slim. Also, many Canadian jurisdictions have hiring freezes. Job sources that serve a specific province are so identified.

Be sure to examine the periodicals listed in Chapter 2 because some of them contain job ads for positions in Canada. These are noted in the Index under "Canadian jobs." Those that have frequent announcements for government positions outside the U.S. are noted.

Great Britain and New Zealand. Several sources for government jobs in Great Britain and New Zealand are also presented. Information on government jobs was not forthcoming from other individual countries.

Directories. The directories presented in Chapter 5 furnish valuable information on foreign countries that is relevant to the job seeker. Use these directories to contact the relevant foreign professional associations not listed in this book to learn if they offer job–hunting services.

Patronage: Government at its worst

Patronage continues to be the bane around the neck of cost–effective and fair local and state government. Hiring on the basis of *whom* you know rather than *what* you know has consistently led to wasteful, ineffective government employees. Bloated patronage armies continue to be one of the major reasons some state and local governments face a constant fiscal crisis.

Patronage is not limited to "non–professional" positions. By practicing "pin–stripe patronage," political bosses have been able to steer excessively lucrative consulting contracts to favored law and accounting firms, suppliers, and consultants who contribute heavily come election time.

Fortunately, most government hiring in this country appears to be based on merit. But far too much patronage remains. Rather than rant and rave further about the dimensions of the problem, let's give the last word to retired University of Pittsburgh public administration professor Christine Altenberger with the following article of hers from the November 1, 1990 issue of *PA Times*, published by the American Society for Public Administration. The article is reprinted with Ms. Altenberger's permission.

Is patronage an ethical "No–No?"

Like other cities around the country, the City of Pittsburgh is in the process of drafting a Code of Ethics. It is fairly predictable that the debate over what, if anything, to say about patronage will be lively, and may generate more heat than light. It is a difficult area, but I hope that Code drafters will speak in a very restrictive way to patronage — for our purposes here, the awarding of public jobs to friends, relatives and political supporters. (I will beg the question of merit. Those practicing patronage almost always will assert the high qualifications of their appointees.)

The Buckets reprinted by permission of Tribune Media Services.

What's wrong with patronage? The U.S. Supreme Court pondered that question in 1976 (*Elrod v. Burns,* 427 U.S. 347). Here, in the time–honored fashion, after local elections, the Republican sheriff of Cook County, Illinois, and other Republicans were replaced by Democrats. In a close decision, the Court held the dismissals unconstitutional: "The cost of the practice of patronage is the restraint it places on the freedoms of belief and association. It breeds inefficiency, corruption and ineffective administration." The majority felt that accountability could be achieved by limiting patronage to policy–making positions — not the case in Cook County. In a stirring dissent, Justice Powell countered by saying, "The history and long prevailing practice across the country support the view that patronage hiring practices make a sufficiently substantial contribution to the practical functioning of our democratic system to support their relatively modest intrusion on first amendment interests...." The majority was not convinced.

The Court, in 1980, expanded and strengthened its holding in *Elrod,* saying that the ultimate inquiry is not whether the label "policy–maker" or "confidential" fits a particular position; rather, the question is whether the hiring authority can demonstrate that party affiliation is an appropriate requirement for effective performance of the public office involved. (*Branti v Finkel,* 445 U.S. 507.) The Court, then, in these two cases ... has placed significant restrictions on patronage practices. Nevertheless, there is still plenty of room for creative posturing and drafting of job descriptions.

But there is more to the ethical dimensions of patronage than has been addressed by the Court. There is more than questions of efficiency and good administration. There are larger issues and they have to do with the whole image of government and its ability to command the respect and trust of the people. This point is well illustrated in an article in the *New York Times,* March 27, 1986, headline: "The Power of Patronage."

> Federal indictments, in addition to listing extortion and bribery counts, charged that a city official and a former official used their ability to place people in city jobs as a tool to turn a city agency into a money–making machine. These officials controlled the City Park-

> ing Violations Bureau from the outside, because they used the power of political patronage to put their associates into key jobs.... They turned the P.V.B. into their own private property, and it doesn't belong to them.

The very essence of a free government must be grounded in the belief that public offices are public trusts, bestowed for the good of the country and not for the benefit of friends, relatives, and political supporters of those in public office. The intricate web that is forged by patronage in governments across the country, in School Districts, and in authorities and special districts, is not only unfair, not only leads to corruption and inefficiency — it tears at the whole fabric of government. Is it wide–spread? You bet, if my clipping file is any indication. Is it an ethical "no–no?" Absolutely.

But wait. Is the answer really so easy and absolute? Consider the following case:

> You are a member of a city council. There are two vacancies in your police department, and the city proceeds to hire two new officers. Under civil service the positions are publicly advertised, there is a competitive examination, and the top three names are certified to council. Your son takes the test and achieves the top score. He is hired by a unanimous vote of council.

Should there be a rule prohibiting relatives of elected officials from competing for city jobs?

❑ Yes ❑ No

Should you have discouraged your son from applying for the police job in the first place?

❑ Yes ❑ No

Should you have voted on his appointment?

❑ Yes ❑ No

Interestingly, where this case has been "tossed out" for discussion with elected officials and others, there is strong disagreement, particularly with respect to the first two questions. A big concern is perception — how does this action look when it becomes public? How much should perception count in formulating a rule for the ethical code?

Since there is really not an easy answer to the patronage issue, is there help for those charged with pondering whether or not to restrict or prohibit its practice? Perhaps the best we can do is to keep before us a conceptual framework which provides the basis for evaluating every moral system. That framework has as its foundation the elements of human welfare, human dignity, and human justice. We are enjoined to:

☒ Serve the well–being of people: Do good, or at least do no harm. Ask what will provide the greatest good for the greatest number?

☒ Respect the rights and dignity of individuals. An individual's freedom should not be violated.

☒ Observe the canons of justice. Construct a political and legal system which will distribute fairly the burdens and benefits of life.

If one examines patronage within the context of this framework, does it give support to the proposition that it is ethically wrong? Going back to the illustration of the New York City Parking Violations Bureau, I think clearly it does. Here, the use of patronage did harm — to the bureau, the city, and the public. It would be hard to argue that a greater good was served. It would be hard to argue that it was fair. ***Public jobs belong to the public, not the friends, relatives and supporters of a few.*** What happened with the Parking Violations Bureau was also an affront to the dignity and freedom of all of us, and diminished the image and luster of government.

On the other hand, how about the second case — the son/police officer? It seems to me that the elements of human freedom and rights, and of fairness and justice look quite different.

In deciding the ethical dimensions of patronage, and what, if any, regulation might be appropriate, it becomes a question of balancing the interests exposed in the three elements above, and each of us might balance differently. For me, the "greater good" is overriding, and is not served by the traditional practice of patronage. The practice of patronage is government teaching a bad lesson about public service.

Chapter 2

Nationwide sources of local and state government jobs

This chapter presents the periodicals, job services (job hotlines and job–matching services), and directories that will help you find jobs in municipal, township, county, regional, and state government throughout the country. Aides that focus on a single state or a multi–state region appear in Chapter 3. Job sources solely for federal government positions are presented in Chapter 4.

In this chapter, the job–hunting aides that cover the wide gamut of government specialities are presented first. For additional job sources that focus on individual government specialties such as accounting, engineering, law enforcement, library services, planning, public administration, and waste water management — and their related technical, trades, labor, and office support positions—see the "Job sources by specialty" entries in this chapter, where periodicals, job–matching services, job hotlines, and directories are identified for each of over 50 different government disciplines. Because so many of these specialities overlap, cross references are made to related fields and to specific periodicals, job services, and directories listed

Job sources are presented in groups under the labels:

- ***Job ads in print,***
- ***Job services,***
- ***Directories, and***
- ***Salary surveys***

Within each classification, sources are listed in this order: first come those with the broadest coverage which are the most helpful, followed by those with a more narrow focus.

Every job source has been verified unless expressly noted in its description.

elsewhere in the *Government Job Finder*. For the government specialties which do not have helpful job aides that focus on them alone, job openings can be found in the periodicals and other job aides listed under "Government jobs in general" as well as in the state–by–state listings in Chapter 3. Also, be sure to consult the Index for references to these specialties. However, some of these specialties really don't have many good sources for job vacancies that focus primarily on government positions. In those instances, you will be referred to one or both of the companion books to this volume, the *Professional's Private Sector Job Finder* or the *Non-Profits' Job Finder*. The job sources in those books include the relatively few local and state government positions that get advertised.

Federal job seekers should be aware that federal positions sometimes appear in a number of the periodicals itemized in this chapter. The publication descriptions note when federal jobs are frequently listed. Also see "Federal jobs" in the Index.

Similarly, positions in Canada or abroad are included in some of the periodicals included in this chapter. A publication's description notes when ads for foreign positions appear in it on a regular basis. See "Canadian jobs" and "Foreign jobs" in the Index.

Government jobs in general

How to proceed. The periodicals, job services (primarily job–matching placement services and job hotlines), and directories listed in this section will help government professionals find positions in virtually all of the fields itemized in the "Jobs by specialty" section that follows.

First, identify any items in this section that would help your job search. Then, be sure to check the applicable categories in the "Jobs by specialty" section. Many of the positions advertised in the periodicals detailed below may not appear in the more specialized periodicals, and vice versa. Ads for office support jobs, labor, trades, and technical positions often appear in many of the periodicals listed by specialty. Be sure to also check the Index if you can't easily find your specialty.

Few periodicals that present job openings in higher education are included here. See the *Non-Profits' Job Finder* for those job sources.

Job ads in print

Jobs Available: A Listing of Employment Opportunities in the Public Sector (P.O. Box 1040, Modesto, CA 95353–1040; phone: 209/571–2120) biweekly, $25/annual subscription. Serves mainly the states from Colorado westward, although a growing number of jobs east of the Rockies are advertised here. A typical issue features 100 to 200 job openings in all facets of local government.

Public Sector Job Bulletin (P.O. Box 1222, Newton, IA 50208–1222; phone: 515/791–9019) biweekly, $19/annual subscription, $12/six months. Features 30 to 75 ads for local government jobs throughout the nation.

J.O.B. The Job Opportunities Bulletin for Minorities and Women in Local Government (International City/County Management Association, 777 N. Capitol St., NE, Washington, DC 20002; phone: 202/289–4262) biweekly, $12/annual subscription. Thirty to 50 ads for all phases of local and regional government appear throughout this newsletter.

Job Recorded Bulletin (Job Opportunities for the Blind, 1800 Johnston St., Baltimore, MD 21230; phones: 410/659–9314, 800/638–7518) six issues/year, free to individuals who are legally blind and who live in the United States. Subscribers receive a voice tape that describes 70 to 130 government and private sector jobs per issue.

Affirmative Action Register (Warren H. Green, Inc., 8356 Olive Blvd., St. Louis, MO 63132; phones: 800/537–0655, 314/991–1335) monthly, individuals: $15/annual subscription, $8/six–month subscription; free to institutional and organizational minority, female, or disabled candidate sources. Dozens of positions in all phases of government appear throughout this publication.

Careers and the disABLED (Equal Opportunity Publications, 150 Motor Parkway, Suite 420, Hauppauge, NY 11788–5145; phone: 516/273–8743) quarterly, $8/annual prepaid subscription. Over 40 display ads throughout this magazine feature positions in all areas of government (and the private sector) for college graduates from employers who certify they are equal opportunity employers who will hire people who have disabilities. Readers can submit their resume to the magazine which then forwards it to advertising employers the job seeker specifies—for free.

Nation's Cities Weekly (National League of Cities, 1301 Pennsylvania Avenue, NW, Washington, DC 20004; phone: 202/626–3040) weekly, $80/annual subscription. Five to 10 jobs appear under "Classifieds" for city government jobs such as city managers, finance directors, public works directors, police chiefs, fire chiefs, city attorneys, city clerks, and more.

Equal Opportunity (Equal Opportunity Publications, 150 Motor Parkway, Suite 420, Hauppauge, NY 11788–5145; phone: 516/273–0066) three issues/year, $13/annual subscription, free to minority college graduates and professionals. Over 25 display ads throughout this magazine feature positions in all areas.

Career/#1 WOMAN (Equal Opportunity Publications, 150 Motor Parkway, Suite 420, Hauppauge, NY 11788–5145; phone: 516/273–8743) three issues/year, $13/annual subscription, free to female college graduates and female students within two years of graduation (request application form). Around a dozen or so job ads appear throughout the magazine, including federal positions. A reader can submit her resume to the magazine which then forwards it to advertising employers she specifies—for free.

The Part–Time Professional (Association of Part–Time Professionals, 7700 Leesburg Pike, Suite 216, Falls Church, VA 22043; phone: 703/734–7975) free/members only. The typical issue includes about five positions under "Part–Time Job Leads Fed./State/Local Government."

The National Directory of Internships (National Society for Experiential Education, Suite 207, 3509 Haworth Dr., Raleigh, NC 27609–7229; phone: 919/787–3263) biannual, $24/nonmember, $20/member. Lists 28,000 internship opportunities in 75 different fields with chapters on government, the arts, business, clearinghouses, communications, consumer affairs, education, environment, health, human services, international affairs, museums and history, public interest, sciences, women's issues, and resources for international internships.

1994 Internships (Peterson's Guides; for your convenience, this book is available from Planning/Communications; see the catalog at the end of this book) $29.95, published every October. This 422–page book provides detailed descriptions and application instructions for paid and unpaid internships with over 1,700 organizations and companies. It includes geographic and alphabetical indexes, and details on regional and national internship clearinghouses.

Summer Jobs '94 (Peterson's Guides, available from Planning/Communications; see the catalog at the end of this book) $15.95, 344 pages, annual. Describes over 20,000 summer job openings in the U.S. and Canada at resorts, camps, amusement parks, environmental programs, national parks, expeditions, theaters, and in government. Each detailed employer description includes salary and benefits, employer background, profile of employees, and whom to contact to apply. Includes category, employer, and job title indexes.

Job services

Career Placement Registry (Career Placement Registry, Inc., 302 Swann Ave., Alexandria, VA 22301; phones: 800/368–3093, 703/683–1085) registration fees: $15/students, others by salary sought: $25/through $20,000 salary, $35/$20,001–$40,000 salary, $45/$40,001+. Complete detailed data entry form. Resume information kept in database for six months. Database updated weekly. Maintains resume database that employers access through DIALOG Information Services computer network. Employers contact registrant directly. Over 11,000 governments and non–profit organizations — all potential employers — have access to CPR's database.

CU Career Connection (University of Colorado, Campus Box 133, Boulder, CO 80309–0133; phone: 303/492–4127) $30/two–month fee entitles you to a "passcode" which unlocks this job hotline. You need a touch–tone phone to call and request the field in which you are interested in hearing job openings. The hotline is turned off Monday through Friday, 2 to 4 p.m. for daily updating.

ACCESS Resumé Bank for Staff/Board Diversity (ACCESS: Networking in the Public Interest, 50 Beacon St., Boston, MA 02108; phone: 617/720–5627), $5. The purpose of this resume database is to give employers who wish to conduct a more inclusive job search that includes people of all races and levels of physical abilities, access to the resumes of individuals of color or with physical disabilities. Call or write to obtain the resume application form. Submit it and your resume both of which will be placed in this computerized job bank. When a government employer sends in a "Candidate Request Form," the computer spews out the resumes of job candidates who match the job's requirements. A hard copy of these resumes is sent to the employer who is then responsible for contacting the job candidate for an interview. The vast majority of the 4,000 employers who use this service are in the non–profit sector. But a growing number of governments are also using it to identify qualified job candidates.

Non–Profit Organization Search (ACCESS: Networking in the Public Interest, 50 Beacon St., Boston, MA 02108; phone: 617/720–5627) $25. While the vast majority of agencies in this database are non–profits, it does include government agencies, public policy, and consumer protection among the categories it covers. You specify up to four regions, states, or cities you prefer and which of 23 job categories interest you. ACCESS searches its extensive database to find up to 100 agencies that meet your criteria. The report you get gives the name, address and phone number for each organization along with a description of it. While this service doesn't direct you to agencies that necessarily have current job openings, it does enable you to identify agencies for which you may wish to work so you can set up informational interviews and contact them to learn about future openings.

Here's everything you need to know to use this service. Send ACCESS your check and the following information: your name, address, and phone number; and the geographic areas you want searched: up to four cities, regions, and/or states. Then specify that you want your search to cover the following organizational focus category: W–Public policy, government agencies, consumer protection. For a complete list of all 23 categories of non–profits, see Chapter 2 in the *Non–Profits' Job Finder*.

National Resume Bank (Suite 330, 3637 4th St., North, St. Petersburg, FL 33704; phone: 813/896–3694) $25/three–month resume listing, $40/six months; to update your resume listing, send five copies of your resume with the $5 update fee. To get on this resume database, you must send in your check along with five copies of your resume. Unless you request your name, address, and phone number to be hidden from prospective employers' view, you will be contacted directly

Chapter 1 told you to be sure to *also* examine the classified ads in your local newspaper. Here's a new job service that lets you see classified ads taken from newspapers across the country.

Classifacts (North American Classifacts, Suite 305, 2821 S. Parker Rd., Aurora, CO 80014; phone: 303/745–1011) $29.95/four–week subscription plus $4.95/shipping, $4.95/each additional week (includes shipping), extra charges to receive material via fax, modem, or overnight mail. When it started in September 1993, 54 newspapers were participating. By the end of 1994, it expects to have over 100 newspapers take part. Participating newspapers place all their classified job ads in *Classifacts'* job database. You can have *Classifacts* search this database for up to three job titles, nationally, by state, or by city. The results of the search are then sent to you by mail, or if you choose to pay an additional charge, by fax, modem, or overnight mail.

Call 303/745–1011 in Denver to get the toll–free number for your region of the country. Call that "800" number to subscribe to this service. The live operator (no recordings) will help you decide which job titles to have them search for. Currently operators are on hand every day except Saturday, from 8 a.m. to 10 p.m. Eastern Standard Time. As business builds, they expect to become a 24–hour service.

by employers interested in you. Includes jobs in government and public service.

Resume Service (Air Force Association, 1501 Lee Highway, Arlington, VA 22209–1198; phones: 800/727–3337, 703/247–5800) $160/complete resume written, $50/resume critique. Includes copy of AFA's resume writer's book. They say they specialize in helping people make the transition from military life to civilian life.

Directories

National Trade and Professional Associations of the United States (Columbia Books, 1212 New York Ave., NW, Suite 300, Washington, DC 20005; phone: 202/898–0662) $55. With information on over 6,450 trade and professional associations, this annual volume enables you to identify any government professional associations beyond those included in this volume.

Associations Yellow Book (Monitor Publishing Co., 104 Fifth Ave., 2nd Floor, New York, NY 10011; phone: 212/627–4140) semiannual, $165/annual subscription, 900 pages. Being published twice a year makes this volume perhaps the most accurate directory of professional associations for government employees.

Encyclopedia of Associations (Gale Research, Inc., 835 Penobscot Bldg., Detroit, MI 48226; phone: 800/877–4253) Volume 1: *National Organizations of the U.S.* $340/set of three parts, published each July, includes entries on over 22,000 associations including hundreds for government professionals. Usually available at public libraries. Volume 2: *Geographic and Executive Indexes*, $275, published each July, enables you to locate organizations in a particular city and state to identify association executives. Volume 3: *Supplement,* $295, published every November, provides full entries on associations not listed in Volume 1.

The *Encyclopedia of Associations* is available on the DIALOG online computer service (File number 114) on which records can be accessed by name, key word, description, publications, and other fields. For information on online subscriptions, contact DIALOG Information Services (3460 Hillview Ave., Palo Alto, CA 94304; phone: 800/334–2564)

The *Encyclopedia of Associations* is also available on CD–ROM ($995/annual single–user subscription) Issued every June and December, this offer also includes one updated replacement disc after six months.

Reprinted by permission from *Which Niche?* by Jack Shingleton, illustrated by Phil Frank. Copyright 1989. All rights reserved.

Salary surveys

Available Pay Survey Reports: An Annotated Bibliography (Abbott, Langer & Associates, 548 First St., Crete, IL 60417; phone: 708/672–4200) Part 1: U.S. surveys, $350; Part 2: Non–U.S. surveys, $125. Covers over 1,100 individual pay survey reports. Heavily indexed to help you find the specialities that interest you.

American Salaries and Wages Survey (Gale Research, available from Planning/Communications as a special order, phone: 800/829–5220) $95, 1,125 pages, 1993. Covers more than 4,500 occupational classifications with salary ranges, entry level, highest paid. Figures are derived from more than 300 publications issued by federal, state, and local governments, and professional organizations.

Salary Budget Survey Report (American Compensation Association, 14040 N. Northsight Blvd., Scottsdale, AZ 85260; phone: 602/951–9191) $80/nonmembers, $55/members, published each September. This survey is broken down into 45 industry groups nationally in four regions.

Governing (Congressional Quarterly, Inc., 2300 N St., NW, Washington, DC 20037; phones: 800/829–9105, 202/867–8802) monthly, $29.95/annual subscription, $59.95/foreign. The December issue usually contains an annual survey reporting the salaries of major city and county officials. *Note: Sometimes* several government job ads appear in the "Bulletin Board" section near the back of the magazine.

The American Almanac of Jobs and Salaries 1994–1995 (Avon Books, 105 Madison Ave., New York, NY 10016; phone: 800/762–0779) $17, 638 pages, 1993. This is a good *general* source on salaries. It covers a broad spectrum of careers, including federal jobs, and salaries for very general categories of state and local government jobs. However, it is not nearly as detailed as the salary studies conducted by trade and professional organizations.

Job sources by specialty

In this section, job–quest aides are presented by government specialty. To avoid unnecessary repetition, when a job–hunt aide provides job information for more than one discipline, a cross reference guides you to the page where a full description is given. When two specialties are very closely related, one category is cross referenced to the other where the job–search aides for both are described. When two disciplines are related, but not as closely, they are cross–referenced because many of the job–quest aides for one also encompasses the other discipline, although not as thoroughly.

Accounting

See listings under "Finance/accounting."

Agriculture

Also see listings under "Environment."

Job ads in print

Phytopathological News (American Phytopathological Society, 3340 Pilot Knob Rd., St. Paul, MN 55121; phone: 612/454–7250) monthly, free/members only. About ten positions in plant pathology, genetics, or pesticides with the Department of Agriculture and extension services appear under "Classified."

FMRA News (American Society of Farm Managers and Rural Appraisers, Inc., 950 S. Cherry Street, Suite 508, Denver, CO 80222; phone: 303/758–3513) bimonthly, $15/annual subscription, free/members. Jobs listed under "Career Corner." Usually two to four job ads per issue, but some issues have no ads.

Agronomy News (American Society of Agronomy, 677 S. Segoe Rd., Madison, WI 53711; phone: 608/273–8080) monthly, $11/annual nonmember subscription, free/members. About 25 openings for agronomists and crop and soil scientists are described under "Personnel."

Alternative Agriculture News (Henry A. Wallace Institute for Alternative Agriculture, Suite 117, 9200 Edmonston Rd., Greenbelt, MD 20770; phone: 301/441–8777) monthly, $16/annual membership includes subscription. Few ads in typical issue.

Women in Agribusiness Bulletin (WIA, P.O. Box 10241, Kansas City, MO 64111; phone: 816/361–5846) quarterly, annual subscriptions: $15/U.S., $20/elsewhere. Four or five jobs appear under "Classifieds."

Farm Chemicals (37733 Euclid Ave., Wiloughby, OH 44094; phone: 216/942–2000) monthly, free to qualified professionals. One to five display ads include jobs in agricultural chemicals, fertilizers, seed, and related regulatory and research positions.

Job services

Career Development and Placement Service (American Society of Agronomy, 677 S. Segoe Rd., Madison, WI 53711; phone: 608/273–8080) $15/annual fee, free to members. Job seeker submits resume which is matched with jobs. The potential employer contacts the job seeker. Resume kept on file for 12 months; $7.50 fee to update resume during that time.

APS Placement Service (American Phytopathological Society, 3340 Pilot Knob Rd., St. Paul, MN 55121; phone: 612/454–7250) free/members only. This service sends job announcements to participating members who then contact employers. At the annual meeting, current resumes are available to employers to examine. Positions are generally in plant pathology, genetics, or pesticides with the U.S. Department of Agriculture and extension services.

Directories

Accredited and General Membership Directory (American Society of Farm Managers and Rural Appraisers, Inc., 950 S. Cherry Street, Suite 508, Denver, CO 80222; phone: 303/758–3513) free, published each February.

Directory of Pesticide Control Officials (Association of American Pesticide Officials, c/o Mike Fresvik, Agronomy Services Division, Minnesota Department of Agriculture, 90 W. Plato Blvd., St. Paul, MN 55107; phone: 612/296–8547) $30/nonmembers, free/members, issued each March. Includes names, addresses, and phone numbers for each state's administrative official in charge of pesticide and related programs, the primary contact person for programs in each state, registration officials, certification officials, and laboratory officials.

Airport operations and aerospace

Also see listings under "Engineering."

Job ads in print

Air Jobs Digest (P.O. Box 70127, Dept. JF, Washington, DC 20088; phone: 301/984–0002 ext. 215) monthly, $96/annual subscription (U.S. and Canada), $59/six–month subscription, $39/three–month subscription, $18/single issue, $153.24/foreign annual subscription (air mail). Among the 64 pages of job vacancies in each issue are dozens of government positions in aviation and aerospace with the FAA, NASA, Defense Department, NOAA, and air traffic controllers and other federal positions for Pilots, ATC, Mechanics, accident investigators, aviation safety instructors, technicians, engineers, management and administration.

Aviation Employment Monthly (P.O. Box 8058, Saddle Brook, NJ 07662; phones: 800/543–5201, 201/794–3820) monthly, $99.95/annual subscription, $79.95/six–month subscription, $49.95/three–month subscription. Each issue contains ads for over 300 pilots, aviation and aerospace technicians and engineers.

Airport Highlights (Airports Council International-North America, 1220 19th St., NW, Suite 200, Washington, DC 20036; phone: 202/293–8500) 26 issues/year, available to members only. Six to ten positions are listed under "Employment Opportunities."

Airport Report (American Association of Airport Executives, 4212 King St., Alexandria, VA 22302; phone: 703/824–0500) bimonthly, $100/annual subscription. Jobs listed under "Positions Open." Typical issue carries announcements of about 10 positions for airport managers, airport operations, and support staff (noise abatement, public affairs, engineers).

Airport Report Express (American Association of Airport Executives, 4212 King St., Alexandria, VA 22302; phone: 703/824–0500) biweekly, subscription price depends on size of subscribing airport. Entire issue consists of job openings for airport managers, airport operations, and support staff (noise abatement, public affairs, engineers). This newsletter, which usually features about five job openings, is delivered by fax rather than mail.

Aviation Week & Space Technology (McGraw Hill, P.O. Box 503, Hightstown, NJ 08520; phone: 800/257–9402) 51 issues/year, $72/annual subscription. About six ads appear under "Classified–Recruitment."

Plane and Pilot (Warner Publications, P.O. Box 57218, Boulder, CO 80322; phone: 800/283–4330) monthly, $16.95/annual subscription. Among the six ads under "Help Wanted" are aviation–related positions in law enforcement.

Air Traffic Control Journal (Air Traffic Control Association, 2300 Clarendon Blvd., Suite 711, Arlington, VA 22201; phone: 703/522–5717) every three months, $36/nonmember annual subscription, free/members. Very few positions are scattered throughout the magazine, although not in every issue, primarily for air traffic controllers in the U.S. and abroad, and for system engineers.

Directory

ACI-NA Membership Directory (Airports Council International-North America, 1220 19th St., NW, Suite 200, Washington, DC 20036; phone: 202/293–8500) $35/members only, published annually.

Animal control, aquariums, and zoos

Job ads in print

Shoptalk (American Humane Association, 63 Inverness Dr. East, Englewood, CO 80112; phone: 303/792–9900) bimonthly, $10/year annual subscription (U.S.), $25/elsewhere. As many as six jobs for animal care and control professionals (including administrative) appear in a typical issue under "Employment."

Animal Keepers Forum (American Association of Zoo Keepers, 635 SW Gage Blvd., Topeka, KS 60606–2066; phones: 800/242–4519, 913/272–5821) available only to members, annual dues: $30/fulltime zookeeper, $25/affiliates and associates, $20/libraries. Six to eight vacancies for animal keepers, veterinary technicians, and education specialists appear under "Opportunity Knocks."

NACA News (National Animal Control Association, P.O. Box 1600, Indianola, WA 98342; phone: 800/828–6474) bimonthly, $20/nonmember annual subscription, free/members. Jobs listed under "Classified–Help Wanted." Four or five job ads for management and supervisory positions appear in the typical issue. For non–supervisory animal control officer positions, contact local government personnel offices and the state Job Service offices identified in Chapter 3.

Communique Magazine (American Association of Zoological Parks and Aquariums, Oglebay Park, Route 88, Wheeling, WV 26003; phone: 304/242–2160) monthly, available only to members; annual dues range from $35 to $110; write for dues schedule. Jobs are listed under "Position Directory."

Mother Goose & Grimm reprinted with permission of Tribune Media Services.

Journal of the American Veterinary Medical Association (American Veterinary Medical Association, 1931 N. Meacham Rd., Suite 100, Schaumburg, IL 60173; phone: 708/925–8070) biweekly, $100/annual nonmember subscription (U.S.), $120/foreign, free/members. Among the 300 to 450 "Classifieds" are many positions for veterinarians and veterinary technicians.

Veterinary and Human Toxicology (c/o Comparative Toxicology Laboratories, Kansas State University, Manhattan, KS 66506–5606; phone: 913/532–4334) bimonthly, $50/annual subscription (U.S.), $60/Canada, $70/elsewhere. Forty to 50 openings, including positions for veterinarians, toxicologists, biologists, and health professionals appear under "Job Opportunities." A membership directory of related organizations is published once a year in this journal.

Veterinary Surgery (J. B. Lippincott, P.O. Box 1590, Hagerstown, MD 21741; phone: 800/777–2295) bimonthly, $75/annual nonmember subscription, free/members of the American College of Veterinary Anesthesiologists. About two ads for government positions for veterinary surgeons and anesthesiologists appear in the "Classified Ad Section."

Job service

AVMA Job Placement Service (American Veterinary Medical Association, 1931 N. Meacham Rd., Suite 100, Schaumburg, IL 60173; phone: 708/925–8070) free/AVMA members only. Complete an application form and this service will match you with vacancies in government, clinical practice, private industry or college universities.

Directories

Directory of Animal Care and Control Agencies (American Humane Association, 63 Inverness Dr. East, Englewood, CO 80112; phone: 303/792–9900) $50 (or $2 per state listing) for non–profit agencies, $500 (or $10 per state listing) for individuals and profit–making organizations. This 200+ page directory of over 3,600 animal care and control agencies in the U.S. and Canada is maintained on computer and is published in a binder. Agencies are listed alphabetically by state and city. This directory is also available as cheshire or pressure sensitive labels.

Zoological Parks and Aquariums in the Americas (American Association of Zoological Parks and Aquariums, Oglebay Park, Route 88, Wheeling, WV 26003; phone: 304/242–2160) $63/nonmembers, $33/members, published in the summer of even–numbered years.

ACVS Directory of Diplomates (American College of Veterinary Surgeons, 4330 East West Highway, Suite 1117, Bethesda, MD 20814; phone: 301/718–6504) $15, published in late autumn of odd–numbered years. Lists veterinary surgeons.

California Museum Directory: A Guide to Museums, Zoos, Botanic Gardens, and Historic Buildings Open to the Public (California Institute of Public Affairs, P.O. Box 189040, Sacramento, CA 95818; phone: 916/442–2472) $25, 1992, 192 pages. Includes name, location, mailing address, telephone, hours open, tours available, whether admission is charged, publications issued, and descriptions of collections of 1,200 institutions. Listings are by location, with indexes of names, subjects, and counties.

Architecture/Urban Design

*Also see listings under "Engineering" and "Planning." See the **Professional's Private Sector Job Finder** for a larger collection of job sources that sometimes have government job vacancies in them.*

Job ads in print

Progressive Architecture (Penton Publishing, 1100 Superior, Cleveland, OH 44114–2543; phone: 216/696–7000) monthly; annual subscription: $48/professional architects, designers, engineers, and draft persons (U.S.), $48/students (U.S.), $65/Canada, $130/elsewhere. Jobs listed under "Job Mart." Very extensive list of job openings in good times (you vaguely remember those, don't you?). During recessions there are only about ten job openings listed plus "Situations wanted." Largely architecture and engineering positions. Some federal positions.

Job service

AIA Employment Referrals (American Institute of Architects, 1735 New York Ave., NW, Washington, DC 20006; phones: 800/864–7753, 202/626–7364). This service is part of the *AIAOnline* computer network which can be accessed by a modem (1,200, 2,400, or 9,600 baud) attached to a Macintosh or IBM–compatible computer. There are two parts to the *AIA Employment Referrals*. The ***Positions Available Bulletin Board*** has about 40 to 50 job openings for architects and related fields described on it at any one time. While most of the jobs are private sector, they do include some government positions. Since this service started in the summer of 1993, there are probably many more job vacancies on it now. You can access these job openings *only* by subscribing to *AIAOnline*. Call 800/864–7753 to ask for *AIAOnline* brochure and subscriber application form. There's an initial one–time $50 setup charge plus a monthly fee and online charges of 25 cents per minute. If you don't need everything the service provides, and just want to access to the Employment Referral bulletin boards, choose the Reduced Access Rate Plus plan which will cost just $20 per month — it's the lowest cost plan.

If you can't afford the cost of this service or don't have a modem, the folks at the AIA tell us that you can go to your local AIA chapter or an academic institution that subscribes to *AIAOnline,* and ask them to print out the current job listings from the *Positions Available Bulletin Board*.

If you want to advertise your availability for a job in architecture and related fields, you can place your cover letter and resume on the ***Positions Wanted Bulletin Board*** for six months for $25, even without subscribing to *AIAOnline* as long as you belong to AIA. For instructions, contact Dorothy Degennaro at the AIA. However, if you subscribe to *AIAOnline*, you can place your cover letter and resume on the *Positions Wanted Bulletin Board* by sending a disk with them on it in ASCII format or by using E–mail. Once you subscribe to *AIAOnline* you'll be told how to do this.

Directory

Profile: 1993–1994 (American Institute of Architects, 1735 New York Ave., NW, Washington, DC 20006; phones: 800/365-2724, 202/626–7364) $145/nonmembers, $138.50/members, add $8/shipping, issued in July of odd–numbered years. For each of the 30,000 architects and 15,000 firms, this directory lists the kinds of projects they work on, awards they've received, as well as the basic address and phone information.

Salary survey

Careers in Architecture: A Salary Survey of Architects Working in Settings Other Than Private Practice (American Institute of Architects Order Department, P.O. Box 753, Waldorf, MD 20604; phones: 800/365–2724, 410/626–7509) $20/nonmembers, $19/AIA members, plus $5/shipping, 15 pages, 1993. Reports on compensation and benefits for architects who work for local, state, and federal government as well as for corporations, developers, builders or contractors, colleges, and universities.

Archivists

See listings under "Records management and archival services" and "Library services."

Code Administration and Enforcement

Also see listings under "Engineering" and "Public Administration."

Job ads in print

BOCA–The Building Official and Code Administrator Magazine (BOCA, International, 4051 W. Flossmoor Rd., Country Club Hills, IL 60478; 708/799–2300) bimonthly, $18/nonmember annual subscription, add $3/year for postage outside U.S., free/members. Jobs listed under "Classified Ads." Typical issue has about three to six job ads.

BOCA Bulletin (BOCA, International, 4051 W. Flossmoor Rd., Country Club Hills, IL 60478; 708/799–2300) bimonthly, free/members only. Write for membership information. Jobs listed under "Classified Ads." Typical issue sports about eight job ads.

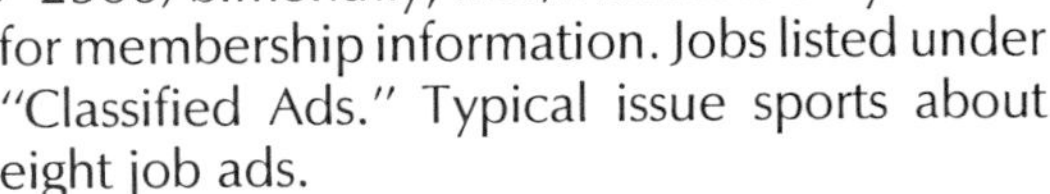

Building Standards Magazine and ***Building Standards Newsletter*** (International Conference of Building Officials, 5360 Workman Mill Road, Whittier, CA 90601–2298; phone: 310/699–0541) bimonthly, each periodical is published in alternating months, $21/nonmember annual subscription to the magazine, the newsletter is available only to members. Jobs are listed under "Job Opportunities." About four to seven job ads appear in the usual issue.

Southern Building and ***SBCCI Newsletter*** (Southern Building Code Congress, International, 900 Montclair Rd., Birmingham, AL 35213–1206; phone: 205/591–1853) bimonthly in alternating months, $15/nonmember annual subscription to the pair, $12/member. Jobs listed under "Positions Available." Ranges from zero to ten jobs an issue. Includes architect and engineering positions.

Directories

SBCCI Membership Directory (Southern Building Code Congress, International, 900 Montclair Rd., Birmingham, AL 35213–1206; phone: 205/591–1853) $15, published each January.

Directory of Building Codes and Regulations (National Conference of States on Building Codes and Standards, Suite 210, 505 Huntmar Park Dr., Herndon, VA 22070; phones: 800/362–2633, 703/437–0100) both volumes: $150/nonmembers, $120/members, plus $4.58/shipping, December 1993. You can use these directories (***State Directory of Building Codes and Regulations***, $95/nonmembers, $76/members, plus $4.23/shipping; and ***City Directory of Building Codes and Regulations***, $75/nonmembers, $60/members, plus $4.23/shipping) to help you decide where to seek a code enforcement position. They tell you which codes each jurisdiction uses so you can identify jurisdictions that use the building codes with which you have experience. Also included are the names and addresses of state or city code officials so you can send blind job application letters.

IAEI Membership Directory (International Association of Electrical Inspectors, 901 Waterfall Way, Richardson, TX 75080; phone: 214/235–1455) $10, published annually. This is a list of over 27,000 members.

Communications

See listings under "Media and the arts." Also see the ***Professional's Private Sector Job Finder*** *for a very extensive set of job sources which sometimes have government positions in addition to private sector jobs.*

Community and economic development

Also see listings under "Planning" and "Public administration." Also consult the job sources described in the "Housing, planning, and development" chapter in the ***Non–Profits' Job Finder***.

Job ads in print

Economic Developments (National Council for Urban Economic Development, 1730 K St., NW, Suite 915, Washington, DC 20006; phone: 202/223–4735) 24 issues/year, available only to members; membership costs $275/year). Jobs listed under "Job Mart." Typical issue sports three to ten job ads.

Council News (American Economic Development Council, 9801 W. Higgins, Suite 540, Rosemont, IL 60018; phone: 708/692–9944) ten issues/year, available to members only, annual membership: $265, plus $15 processing fee first year only; $140, plus $15 processing fee first year only, when another person in your office is already a member. Jobs listed under "Career Opportunities." About six job ads per issue.

Resources for Community–Based Economic Development (National Congress for Community Economic Development, Suite 523, 1875 Connecticut Ave., Washington, DC 20009; phone: 202/659–8411) quarterly, $39/annual subscription. Two to five jobs are listed under "The Checklist."

Job services

Resume Referral Service (American Economic Development Council, 9801 W. Higgins, Suite 540, Rosemont, IL 60018; phone: 708/692–9944) $100/nonmembers for 12 months, free to members. Return form with 10 copies of your resume. AEDC lets you know when it matches your qualifications with a potential employer, but it is up to the employer to contact you for the interview. Once you are in the resume referral service you will be sent by first class mail job listings from hiring organizations as they come into the AEDC office. You are responsible for contacting prospective employers. Ads will be mailed within a week of receipt.

NAHRO–Net (National Association of Housing and Redevelopment Officials, 1320 18th St., NW, Washington, DC 20036–1803; phone: 202/429–2960, ext. 237) $150/annual subscription, $20/hour monthly online charge whether you use it or not. Using your computer and modem you can access announcements of job vacancies in the housing and community development field, as well as a vast world of information you can use on the job. Currently, 10 to 20 jobs which also appear in the NAHRO Monitor, described above under "Job ads in print," are listed. NAHRO expects to expand the job listings sometime in 1994.

Directories

CUED Directory (National Council for Urban Economic Development, 1730 K St., NW, Suite 915, Washington, DC 20006; phone: 202/223–4735) free/members only, published annually. Lists all private corporate members of National Council for Urban Economic Development.

Trends & Economic Development Organizations: A Directory (National Council for Urban Economic Development, 1730 K St., NW, Suite 915, Washington, DC 20006; phone: 202/223–4735) $225/nonmembers, $145/members. Profiles 114 economic development organizations from 35 metropolitan areas

Who's Who in Economic Development (American Economic Development Council, 9801 W. Higgins, Suite 540, Rosemont, IL 60018; phone: 708/692–9944) free/members only, published each August. Geographical and alphabetical listings of members throughout the world. Also includes geographical and alphabetical lists of certified economic developers.

NCCED Membership Directory (National Congress for Community Economic Development, Suite 523, 1875 Connecticut Ave., Washington, DC 20009; phone: 202/659–8411) $25, last issued April 1993.

NAHRO Directory of Local Agencies (National Association of Housing and Redevelopment Officials, 1320 18th St., NW, Washington, DC 20036–1803; phone: 202/429–2960) $80/nonmembers, $65/members, published in September 1991 and every three years thereafter. Includes national listings of 7,000 city and county public agencies that administer public housing, Section 8, community development, urban renewal and development, neighborhood revitalization, housing rehabilitation, housing code enforcement, and other housing assistance programs. For each entry, you'll get the agency name, address, and phone number; executive director's name; population served; and number and type of housing and community development programs administered.

Salary surveys

CUED Salary Survey (National Council for Urban Economic Development, 1730 K St., Suite 915, NW, Washington, DC 20006; phone: 202/223–4735) $75/nonmembers, $45/members, published every two years.

1992–1993 Compensation and Benefits Survey (American Economic Development Council, 9801 W. Higgins Rd., Suite 540, Rosemont, IL 60018; phone: 708/692–9944) $75/nonmembers, $50/members, issued every three years. Profiles organization background, base salary, and benefits for economic development professionals.

Correctional services

See listings under "Law enforcement" and "Public safety."

Court administration

See entries under "Legal services and court administration."

Data processing and computers

Job ads in print

ASIS Jobline (American Society for Information Science, Suite 501, 8720 Georgia Ave., Silver Springs, MD 20910–3602; phone: 301/495–0900) monthly, free. About 15 jobs appear in the typical issue.

Computer (IEEE Computer Society, 10662 Los Vaqueros Cr., Los Alamitos, CA 90720–1264; phone: 714/821–8380) available only to members. Two to 15 pages of "Career Opportunities" can be listed.

Journal of Systems Management (Association of Systems Management, P.O. Box 38370, Cleveland, OH 44138; phone: 216/243–6900) monthly, $60/annual subscription, included in dues. About five positions are listed under "Joblink."

Government Computer News (Cahners Publishing, 44 Cook St., Denver, CO 80206; phone: 303/388–4511) biweekly or 20 issues/year, $79.95/annual subscription (U.S.), $117.65/Canada, $144.95/elsewhere. Although "Career Opportunities" do not appear in every issue, when they do, there are about ten positions for software engineers, programmers, and analysts, including federal positions.

*See also **APCO Bulletin** listed under "Public safety."*

*See also **NELS** listed under "Law enforcement."*

Job service

CU Career Connection (University of Colorado, Campus Box 133, Boulder, CO 80309–0133; phone: 303/492–4127) $30/two–month fee entitles you to a "passcode" which unlocks this job hotline. You need a touch–tone phone to call and request the field in which you are interested in hearing job openings. The hotline is turned off Monday through Friday, 2 to 4 p.m. for daily updating.

Directory

ASIS Handbook and Directory (American Society for Information Science, Suite 501, 8720 Georgia Ave., Silver Springs, MD 20910–3602; phone: 301/495–0900) $100/nonmembers, free/members, published each March.

Salary surveys

Computer Salary Survey and Career Planning Guide (Source edp, P.O. Box 152109, Irving, TX 75015–9831; phones: 214/387–1600, 214/387–0795) free, published annually by this computer recruiting firm.

1992 National Association of State Information Resource Executives Salary and Classification Report for State Information Resource Management (The Council of State Governments, 3560 Iron Works Pike, P.O. Box 11910, Lexington, KY 40578–1910; phone: 800/800–1910) $40 plus $3.75 shipping and handling, 52 pages.

Economic development

See listings under "Community and economic development" and listings in Chapter 5 on overseas employment.

Emergency management

Also see listings under "Environment," "Public administration," and "Public health." See the listings in the state–by–state section of Chapter 3. See the information on state jobs sources for each state.

Job ads in print

The NCCEM Bulletin (National Coordinating Council on Emergency Management, Unit N, 7297 Lee Highway, Falls Church, VA 22042; phone: 703/533–7672) monthly, free/members only ($75/annual dues, membership open to anyone). Jobs listed under "Personnel Corner." About one job ad every three months.

See also ***APCO Bulletin*** *listed under "Public safety."*

Directory

The NCCEM Membership Directory (National Coordinating Council on Emergency Management, Unit N, 7297 Lee Highway, Falls Church, VA 22042; phone: 703/533–7672) $10, published each January.

Employee relations

See listings under "Personnel/human resources."

Engineering

Also see listings under "Architecture/urban design," "Planning," "Public safety," "Public works," "Sanitation/solid waste management," "Utilities management," and "Water/wastewater operations."

Job ads in print

Civil Engineering–ASCE (American Society of Civil Engineers, 345 E. 47th St., New York, NY 10017; phones: 212/705–7288, 212/705–7276) monthly, $81/nonmember annual subscription, $116/foreign, free/members. About 100 job ads are listed under "Engineering Market Place."

Dilbert reprinted with permission of Tribune Media Services. Copyright 1993. All rights reserved.

ASCE News (American Society of Civil Engineers, 345 E. 47th St., New York, NY 10017; phones: 212/705–7288, 202/705–7276) monthly, $36/nonmember annual subscription, $54/foreign, free/members. About 100 jobs are advertised under "Engineering Market Place."

NSBE Magazine (National Society of Black Engineers, 1454 Duke St., P.O. Box 25588, Alexandria, VA 22313–5588; phone: 703/549–2207) five issues/year; $10/nonmember annual subscription, free/ members. 40 engineering positions are advertised in every issue.

Mechanical Engineering (American Society of Mechanical Engineers, 22 Law Drive, Fairfield, NJ 07007; phones: 800/843–2763, 212/705–7722) monthly, $45/nonmember annual subscription, $24/member annual subscription. Jobs listed under "Jobs Open." About 50 job ads appear in the average issue.

Woman Engineer (Equal Opportunity Publications, 150 Motor Parkway, Suite 420, Hauppauge, NY 11788–5145; phone: 516/273–0066) three issues/year, $17/annual subscription. Over 20 display ads throughout this magazine feature positions in all areas of engineering, including federal positions.

Engineering Times (National Society of Professional Engineers, 1420 King St., Alexandria, VA 22314–2794; phone: 703/684–2800) monthly, $30/nonmember annual subscription, $48/foreign, free/members. Jobs listed under "Engineering Times Career Mart." A typical issue carries about ten to 15 job ads.

Consulting–Specifying Engineer (Cahners Publishing, 44 Cook St., Denver, CO 80206–5800; phone: 303/388–4511) 15 issues/year, $74.95/annual subscription, $112.30/Canada and Mexico, $134.95/elsewhere (surface mail), $150/elsewhere (air mail). Jobs listed under "Job Opportunities." Typical issue includes about three job ads.

ENR—Engineering News Record (McGraw–Hill, P.O. Box 516, Hightstown, NJ 08520; phones: 800/257–9402, 212/512–3549) weekly; $69/annual subscription (U.S. and possessions), $75/Canada, $160/Europe,

$210/Japan, $180/elsewhere. Jobs listed under "Positions Vacant." Typical issue prints 50 to 100 display ads and job ads plus "Positions Wanted." There are also three issues a year specifically geared towards careers that include job ads: *Minority & Women Careers* (March), *Environment Career Survey* (September), and *Environment Career Opportunities* (November). If you don't need a subscription, you can purchase any of these for the $5 price of a single issue.

Journal of the Air & Waste Management Association (1 Gateway Center, 3rd Floor, Pittsburgh, PA 15222; phone: 412/232–3444) monthly, annual subscription: $90/non–profit libraries and institutions, $200/others, add $5 Canada and Mexico, add $15/Europe, add $20/Asia. Ten job ads listed under "Classified."

The Environmental Engineer (American Academy of Environmental Engineers, Suite 100, 130 Holiday Ct., Annapolis, MD 21401; phone: 410/266–3311) quarterly, $20/annual subscription (U.S. and Canada), $30/elsewhere. Typical issue features two to four display ads for jobs.

Graduating Engineer (16030 Ventura Blvd., Suite 560, Encino, CA 91436; phone: 818/789–5293) eight issues/per school year, $5/copy. About 30 or so display ads for all disciplines of engineers are in the typical issue.

See also ***ITE Journal*** *listed under "Traffic engineering and parking."*

See also ***Airport Report*** *listed under "Airport services."*

Job services

On–line Career Fair (Response Technologies Corp., 2 Campton Commons, Campton, NH 03223–0968; phone: 603/726–4800) free. Use your PC and modem to access local, national, and international positions in software, computers, engineering, sales/marketing, and finance. Apply for these positions by faxing, mailing, or uploading your resume on the computer. Claims confidentiality. To access dial 603/726–3344, press ENTER twice and key in the password "NEW JOB" (1200/2400 baud).

CU Career Connection (University of Colorado, Campus Box 133, Boulder, CO 80309–0133; phone: 303/492–4127) $30/two–month fee entitles you to a "passcode" which unlocks this job hotline. You need a touch–tone phone to call and request the field in which you are interested in hearing job openings. The hotline is turned off Monday through Friday, 2 to 4 p.m. for daily updating.

SOLE Electronic Job Referral Service (Society of Logistics Engineers, 8100 Professional Pl., Suite 211, New Carrollton, MD 20785; phone: 301/459–8446) free. Armed with a modem and communications software, use your computer to call 203/464–0457 (settings: 2400 Baud will go up to 9600, 8–N–1) and you'll be connected to a national bulletin board. If you run into difficulty, call Femi Bajomo at 203/440–0827 X4481. A free printout of the job listings is available from Sam Hahn (PO Box 597, Palm Harbor, FL 34682–0597; phone: 813/736–6299).

Directories

ASCE Membership Directory (American Society of Civil Engineers, 345 E. 47th St., New York, NY 10017; phones: 212/705–7288, 212/705–7276) $100/nonmembers, $25/members.

SOLE Membership Directory and Handbook (Society of Logistics Engineers, 8100 Professional Pl., Suite 211, New Carrollton, MD 20785; phones: 800/695–7653, 301/459–8446) free/members only, printed each April.

Who's Who in Engineering (American Association of Engineering Societies, 1111 19th St., NW, Suite 608, Washington, DC 20036–3690; phones: 800/658–8897, 202/296–2237) $200/nonmembers, $120/members, 1,026 pages, 1993. Gives names, addresses, specializations, and biographies of more than 15,000 engineers.

International Directory of Engineering Societies and Related Organizations (American Association of Engineering Societies, 1111 19th St., NW, Suite 608, Washington, DC 20036–3690; phones: 800/658–8897, 202/296–2237) $185/nonmembers, $115/members, 327 pages, 1993. Provides information on over 950 organizations in the U.S. and overseas.

International Directory of Engineering Societies and Related Organizations, 1994 Supplement (American Association of Engineering Societies, 1111 19th St., NW, Suite 608, Washington, DC 20036–3690; phones: 800/658–8897, 202/296–2237) $85/nonmembers, $48/members. Adds over 200 organizations to the 1993 edition. If purchasing both the 1993 edition (described immediately above) and this supplement, the total cost is $200/nonmembers, $125/members.

The Biotechnology Directory (Stockton Press, 257 Park Avenue South, New York, NY 10010; phones: 800/221–2123, within New York State call 212/673–4400) $235 plus $5 shipping. Includes the often hard–to–find government departments engaged in biotechnology as well as over 10,000 companies, research centers, and academic institutions involved in the field. The most recent edition was released in 1993.

Salary surveys

Professional Income of Engineers (American Association of Engineering Societies, 1111 19th St., NW, Suite 608, Washington, DC 20036–3690; phones: 800/658–8897, 202/296–2237) $115/nonmembers, $70/members, published annually in July, 190+ pages. Includes data for federal, state, and local government engineers as well as broad industry groups.

Engineers' Salaries: Special Industry Report (American Association of Engineering Societies, 1111 19th St., NW, Suite 608, Washington, DC 20036–3690; phones: 800/658–8897, 202/296–2237) $287.50/nonmembers, $169/members, published each July, 330 pages. Extremely detailed breakdown of engineering salaries according to industry type and geographic location, company size, years of experience, highest degree held, and supervisory status.

Environment

Also see "Engineering," "Forestry and horticulture," "Parks and recreation," and "Planning." Additional job sources that occasionally include government positions appear in the ***Professional's Private Sector Job Finder*** *and the* ***Non–Profits' Job Finder.***

Job ads in print

The Job Seeker (Route 2, Box 16, Warrens, WI 54666; phone: 608/378–4290) biweekly, $60/annual subscription, $36/six–month subscription, $19.50/three–month subscription. Lists 200 environmental and natural resource vacancies in every aspect of these fields, including environmental education. $10/nine special supplement issues, December through April, feature summer jobs not listed in the Job Seeker.

Environmental Opportunities (P.O. Box 747, Mendocino, CA 95460; phone: 707/937–1529) monthly, $44/annual subscription (U.S.), $24/six–month subscription (U.S.), $50/annual subscription (Canada), $55/annual subscription/elsewhere. Over 125 jobs, internships, seasonal work, educational offerings, and conferences. Includes administrative positions, fisheries, wildlife, forestry, research, parks, outdoor recreation, and ecology. Write for free sample copy.

Environmental Career Opportunities (Brubach Publishing Company, P.O. Box 15629, Chevy Chase, MD 20825) $29/two–month subscription, $49/four months, $69/six months, $129/annual, $7.95/single issue. You'll find announcements of over 300 positions in all aspects of the environmental field: government agencies; legislative assistants; advocacy, communications, and fundraising; environmental policy, legislation, and regulation; conservation and resource management; environmental engineering, risk assessment, and impact analysis; research and education; and internships. The job announcements include jobs advertised exclusively in this periodical as well as jobs advertised elsewhere.

Environmental Careers Bulletin (11693 San Vicente Blvd., Suite 327, Los Angeles, CA 90047; phone: 213/399–3533, no phone orders) monthly, free, but when you write for a subscription you must provide your job title, college major, college degree, and year received. From 150 to 200 display ads for environmental positions, largely private sector, appear in the typical issue.

Journal of the National Technical Association (Black Collegiate Services, Inc., 1240 S. Broad St., New Orleans, LA 70125; phone: 504/821–5694) biannually, $30/annual subscription, $15/qualified professionals, $35/foreign. Among the 40 or so positions in display ads and listed under "Job Opportunities Bulletin," are a handful of government jobs, sometimes with the U.S. Department of Agriculture's Forest Service. Most positions, though, are for health physicists, biologists, and environmental scientists.

EarthWorks includes *Job Scan* (Student Conservation Association, P.O. Box 550, Charlestown, NH 03603; phone: 603/543--1700) monthly, $29.95/nonmember annual subscription, $24.95/member annual subscription. About 70 jobs in a typical issue plus 20 to 30 internships.

Fisheries (American Fisheries Society, 5410 Grosvenor Ln., Suite 110, Bethesda, MD 20814–2199; phone: 301/897–8616) monthly, $66.50/annual nonmember subscription, $70.50/Canada, $70.50/elsewhere, included in dues which, coincidentally are $66.50/U.S. and $70.50/foreign, $32.25/students. "Jobs Bulletin" sports ten to 15 ads including one or two for government positions, usually federal.

The Caretaker Gazette (P.O. Box 342, Carpentersville, IL 60110; quarterly, $8/three issues. Among its 60 job announcements are jobs and internships in forestry, fisheries, environment, and caretaking.

Opportunities (Natural Science for Youth Foundation, 130 Azalea Dr., Roswell, GA 30075; phones: 800/992–6793, 404/594–9367) bimonthly, $35/annual subscription, $10/single issue, free/ members. "Positions available " lists details on 45 to 70 jobs for naturalists, curators, raptor rehabilitators, and administrative positions, largely at nature centers.

Employment Opportunity Service (National Association for Interpretation, P.O. Box 1892, Ft. Collins, CO 80522; 303/491–6434) $3.00/week. This is a printout of the *Dial–a–Job* and *Dial–an–Internship* jobs listed by phone as described below under "Job services." Be sure to indicate the week or weeks for which you want a printout.

The Wildlifer (The Wildlife Society, 5410 Grosvenor Ln. Bethesda, MD 20814; phone: 301/897–9770) bimonthly, available only to members: $36/annual dues, $18/student dues. About 20 positions in conservation, wildlife, and natural resources appear under "Positions Available."

Environmental Science & Technology (American Chemical Society, P.O. Box 3337, Columbus, OH 43210; phone: 614/447–3776) monthly, $90/nonmember annual subscription, $44/members. The "Classified Section" carries between five and ten job vacancies, mostly in the private sector.

Employment Announcements (American Meteorological Society, 45 Beacon St., Boston, MA 02108–3693) monthly, $30/annual nonmember subscription, $15/members, $7.50/students. About 20 to 30 jobs for weather forecasters and meteorologists grace these pages.

Jobs Clearinghouse (Association for Experiential Education, 2885 Aurora Ave., Suite 28, Boulder, CO 80303–2252; phone: 303/440–8844) monthly, $40/annual nonmember subscription, $25/members. Lists mostly internships and outdoor education instructorships, counselors, camp staff, program directors, and environmental educators, with an emphasis on wilderness experience, under "Job Openings." From 60 to 125 job vacancies per issue.

National Technical News (Black Collegiate Services, Inc., 1240 Broad St., New Orleans, LA 70125; phone: 504/821–5694) biweekly; $26/annual subscription. Eleven job ads appear in "Job Opportunities Bulletin" for health physicists, biologists, and environmental scientists.

Environmental Action (Environmental Action, Inc., 6930 Carroll Ave., Suite 600, Takoma Park, MD 20912; phone: 301/891–1100) quarterly; annual subscription: $35/institutions, $25/annual subscription for individuals. There are a few job vacancies listed under "Eco–Exchange."

Journal of Soil and Water Conservation (Soil and Water Conservation Society, 7515 NE Ankeny Rd., Ankeny, IA 50021–9764; phone: 515/232–1080) bimonthly, $39/annual subscription (U.S. and Canada), $45/elsewhere. Jobs listed under "Classified Advertising." About five job ads per issue.

Journal of Air and Waste Management (Air Pollution Control Association, P.O. Box 2861, Pittsburgh, PA 15230; phone: 412/232–3444) monthly, $200/nonmember annual subscription, $90/annual subscription for non–profit libraries and institutions, free/members. About three vacancies are listed under "Manpower."

Newsletter of the Ecological Society of America (ESA, 2010 Massachusetts Ave., Suite 420, NW, Washington, DC 20036; phone: 202/833–8773) five issues/year, free. Ten to 15 ads for ecotoxicologists, plant ecologists, and ecologists appear under "Job Announcements." Most positions are with universities or other institutions. Some positions with the U.S. Department of the Interior appear.

*See also **Journal of Environmental Health** listed under "Public safety."*

Job services

Dial–a–Job and ***Dial–an–Internship*** (National Association of Interpretation, P.O. Box 1892, Ft. Collins, CO 80522; 303/491–6434) Call 303/491–7410 24–hours a day for a recording of full–time, seasonal, and temporary jobs in environmental education, interpretation, and related fields: naturalists, park rangers, outdoor education, biologists, historians, archaeologists, museum personnel, and publication designers. The tape runs from 10 to 30 minutes. Updated each Wednesday. For internships, call 303/491–6784 24–hours a day. The tape runs from 5 to 20 minutes. Updated every Wednesday.

Environmental Careers Organization Placement Service (286 Congress St., Boston, MA 02218-1009; phone: 617/426-4375) $15/one region, $25/more than one region. Geared towards college graduates (you must be at least a junior in college) and career changers, this service finds you temporary employment that ranges from six months to a year. There is also a possibility of permanent placement. Send in their completed application form to the national office in Boston. The national office sends it to a regional office where you are placed into the applicant pool. This service claims to place at least one out of every seven registrants. Positions are with government agencies, non-profit organizations, corporations, and consulting firms.

Diversity Initiative Program Placement Service (Environmental Careers Organization, 286 Congress St., Boston, MA 02218-1009; phone: 617/426-4375) free/one year. This service places minority college students and graduates in permanent positions. Send in a completed application form to the national office in Boston. The national office sends it to a regional office where you are placed into the applicant pool. This service claims to place at least one out of every seven registrants. Positions are with government agencies, non-profit organizations, corporations, and consulting firms.

Environmental Action Job Book (Environmental Action, Inc., 6930 Carroll Ave., Suite 600, Takoma Park, MD 20912; phone: 301/891–1100) free. Includes more than 15 job ads. This up–to–date book of environmental jobs and internships can be seen only at the Environmental Action office.

Directories

Job Opps '94: Job Opportunities in the Environment (Peterson's Guides, available from Planning/Communications' catalog at the end of this book) $16.95, 229 pages, published each September. Among its brief descriptions of 1,200 high–growth companies in the environmental field are many state and regional environmental government agencies. Briefly describes each government agency, number of employees, expertise needed, and person to contact about job vacancies. Many of these agencies need civil engineers, biologists, and air quality control experts. Actual vacancies cannot be guaranteed, but this serves as a good directory of government agency descriptions.

Summer Jobs '94 (Peterson's Guides, available from Planning/Communications' catalog at the end of this book) $15.95, 344 pages, annual. Describes over 20,000 summer job openings in the United States and Canada with environmental programs, resorts, camps, amusement parks, expeditions, theaters, national parks, and government. Each detailed employer description includes salary and benefits, employer background, profile of employees, and whom to contact to apply. Includes category, employer, and job title indexes.

World Directory of Environmental Organizations (California Institute of Public Affairs, P.O. Box 189040, Sacramento, CA 95818; phone: 916/442–2472) $63 plus 7.25 percent sales tax for California residents, foreign: $45/surface mail, $70/air mail; most recent edition published in 1992, 232 pages. Includes government agencies, research institutes, and citizens' and professional associations in the U.S. and around the globe. Divided into 50 topics with index, glossary, and bibliography of related directories and databases.

Environmental Information Directory (Gale Research, Inc., 835 Penobscot Bldg., Detroit, MI 48226; phone: 800/877–4253) last published in 1991; currently out of print, you may be able to find this at your local library. Divided into 20 chapters, this directory includes information on federal government and state agencies that deal with the environment in addition to private and non–profit players in the environmental field.

NAI Membership Directory (National Association of Interpretation, P.O. Box 1892, Ft. Collins, CO 80522; 303/491–6434) free/members only, published each spring. Lists members and institutional members.

Directory of Natural Science Centers (Natural Science for Youth Foundation, 130 Azalea Dr., Roswell, GA 30075; phones: 800/992–6793, 404/594–9367) $78.50/nonmembers, $43.45/members, published in 1991 and next in 1996. This 600 page tome gives details on over 1,350 nature centers.

Environmental Telephone Directory (Government Institutes, 4 Research Place, Suite 200, Rockville, MD 20850; phone: 301/921–2355) $59, published in odd–numbered years. Detailed information on government agencies that deal with the environment, identifies the environmental aides of U.S. Senators and Representatives.

Directory of Environmental Information Sources (Government Institutes, 4 Research Place, Suite 200, Rockville, MD 20850; phone: 301/921–2355) $74, published in November of even–numbered years. Includes federal and state government resources, professional, scientific, and trade organizations; newsletters, magazines, and databases.

The Wildlife Society Membership Directory and Certification Registry (The Wildlife Society, 5410 Grosvenor Ln. Bethesda, MD 20814; phone: 301/897–9770) $3/nonmembers, free/members, published each September.

The Northeast Directory of Programs (Association for Experiential Education, 2885 Aurora Ave., Suite 28, Boulder, CO 80303–2252; phone: 303/440–8844) $7.50/nonmembers, $5/members (add $2.50 shipping). This 35–page index lists over 100 experiential education programs and agencies in the northeast.

The Northwest Directory of Experiential Programs (Association for Experiential Education, 2885 Aurora Ave., Suite 28, Boulder, CO 80303–2252; phone: 303/440–8844) $7.50/nonmembers, $5/members (add $2.50 shipping). This directory lists 36 programs in seven states and British Columbia.

The New Careers Directory: Internships and Professional Opportunities in Technology and Social Change (Student Pugwash USA, 1638 R St., NW, Suite 32, Washington, DC 20009; phone: 202/328–6555) $18, $10/students (add $3 shipping), last published in 1993. Offers full details on where and how to apply for internships and entry–level jobs with non–profits and government agencies in environment and energy, development, communications, peace/security, health, law, and general science.

The Intermountain Referral Service Guide to Western States Indoor/Outdoor Summer Employment with the United States Federal Government (Intermountain Publishing, 311–B0 14th St., Glenwood Springs, CO 81601–3949; phone: 303/945–8991) $9, $5/subscribers to any edition of the *Rocky Mountain Employment Newsletter* described under "Job sources for multi–state regions" near the beginning of Chapter 3. This four–page guide is chock full of small print that explains how to find and apply for summer positions with the Forest Service, Department of Energy, Bureau of Mines, Bureau of Land Management, Geological Survey, Fish and Wildlife Service, and the National Park Service.

California Environmental Directory: A Guide to Organizations and Resources (California Institute of Public Affairs, P.O. Box 189040, Sacramento, CA 95818; phone: 916/442–2472) $40, May 1993, 128 pages. A guide to nearly 1,000 government agencies, university programs, and major associations concerned with air quality, soil, law, health, the desert, the coast, and much more.

Films—motion pictures and television

See listings under "Media." Also see the ***Professional's Private Sector Job Finder*** *for a very extensive set of job sources which sometimes have government positions in addition to private sector jobs.*

Finance/accounting

Also see listings under "Public Administration."

Job ads in print

GFOA Newsletter (Government Finance Officers Association, Suite 800, 180 N. Michigan Ave., Chicago, IL 60601–7476; phone: 312/977–9700) biweekly, $50/annual nonmember subscription to both *GFOA Newsletter* and *Government Finance Review* (does not include job ads), free/members. Jobs listed under "Employment Opportunities." Very extensive listing of finance/accounting positions in the *GFOA Newsletter.*

Internal Auditor (Institute of Internal Auditors, 249 Maitland Ave., Altamonte Springs, FL 32701–4201; phone: 407/830–7600) bimonthly, $36/nonmember annual subscription (U.S.), $56/elsewhere (air mail), $42/elsewhere (surface mail), free/members. Typical issue features four to eight job ads plus ads from recruitment agencies. Includes ads for positions overseas.

In Search Of (American Academy of Actuaries, 1720 I St., NW, Washington, DC 20006; phone: 202/223–8196) monthly, free/members only. Three to five state and federal positions for actuaries fill this one or two page newsletter.

The Insight (Society of Financial Examiners, 4101 Lake Boone Trail, Suite 201, Raleigh, NC 27607; phone: 919/787–5181) monthly, free/members only. The few job ads that appear under "Classifieds" are for state insurance, financial institutions, and banking departments.

CA Magazine (277 Wellington St., West, Toronto, Quebec M5V 3H2 Canada; phone: 416/204–3257) monthly, $46/annual subscription, $4.75/single issue. About 2 to 3 jobs for tax specialists, auditors, lecturers, tax managers, and professors appear under "Positions Vacant."

Job services

Job Hotline (American Association for Budget and Program Analysis, P.O. Box 1157, Falls Church, VA 22041; phone: 703/941–4300) $30/members only. Call 703/941–4300 between 9 a.m. and 5 p.m. *only on Thursdays.* Tell the operator the location(s) in which you are interested and the type of position. She will read to you one–line listings with the job title, location, series, grade level (if federal), closing date, and, upon request, where to apply. Nearly all the 75 jobs on the list are federal positions, including military; some local and state positions occasionally show up and two to three overseas jobs.

Employment Referral Program (Institute of Internal Auditors, 249 Maitland Ave., Altamonte Springs, FL 32701–4201; phone: 407/830–7600) free/members only. Call for an application to be included in this services referral program. As many as 150 jobs come into their office at a time.

Directories

American Academy of Actuaries Yearbook (American Academy of Actuaries, 1720 I St., NW, Washington, DC 20006; phone: 202/223–8196) $50/nonmembers, free/members, published each January.

American Bankruptcy Institute Membership Directory (American Bankruptcy Institute, 510 C St., NE, Washington, DC 20002; phone: 202/543–1234) members only, published annually. Includes bankruptcy judges and clerks.

Institute of Internal Auditors Membership Directory (249 Maitland Ave., Altamonte Springs, FL 32701–4201; phone: 407/830–7600) free/members only, 1994. Gives names and addresses of auditors who belong to the Institute of Internal Auditors.

AWSCPA Roster (American Women's Society of Certified Public Accountants, 401 N. Michigan, Chicago, IL 60611; phone: 312/644–6610) free/members only, published annually.

Salary survey

Compensation in the Accounting/Financial Field (Abbott, Langer & Associates, 548 First St., Crete, IL 60417; phone: 708/672–4200) $450, annual. In–depth analysis of salary and benefits for 18 different positions from junior accountants to department heads in government as well as private and non–profit sectors.

Fire protection

Also see listings under "Public safety."

Job ads in print

NFPA Journal (National Fire Protection Association, 1 Batterymarch Park, Quincy, MA 02269; phone: 617/770–3000) published in alternating months with ***Fire News***, members only. Write for membership information. Jobs listed under "Classifieds." About ten ads appear in a typical issue.

Fire News (National Fire Protection Association, 1 Batterymarch Park, Quincy, MA 02269; phone: 617/770–3000) published in alternating months with NFPA Journal, available only to members. Write for membership information. Jobs listed under "Job Mart." Few job ads.

Fire Chief (Argus Business, 6151 Powers Ferry Rd., NW, Atlanta, GA 30339; phone: 404/955–2500) monthly, $52/annual subscription (U.S.), $72/overseas surface mail, $123/overseas air mail, free/qualified professionals. The classifieds section usually contains ads for five or more fire chief, deputy chief, and fire department administrator positions.

IAFC On Scene (International Association of Fire Chiefs, 4025 Fair Ridge Drive, Fairfax, VA 22033; phone: 703/273–0911) biweekly, $60/nonmember annual subscription. Jobs listed under "Classifieds." Generally two to six job ads per issue.

See also ***APCO Bulletin*** *listed under "Public safety."*

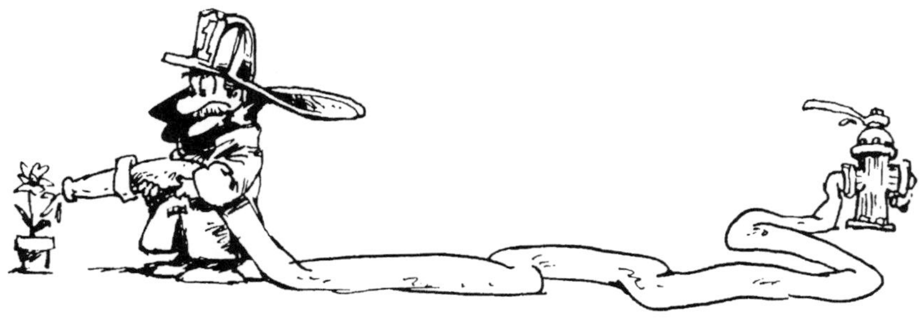

See also ***Law Enforcement News*** *listed under "Law enforcement."*

Directory

Fire and Emergency Services Leadership Directory (International Association of Fire Chiefs, 4025 Fair Ridge Drive, Fairfax, VA 22033; phone: 703/273–0911) free/members only, published each winter.

Salary surveys

Fire Salaries (International City/County Management Association, 777 N. Capitol St., NE, Washington, DC 20002; phone: 202/289–4262) $29.75 (add $3.50 shipping and handling if not prepaid), published every September. State–by–state listings of minimum and maximum salaries each jurisdiction pays to firefighters, paramedics, engineers, arson investigators, medical technicians, fire captains, fire lieutenants, fire prevention officers, fire code inspectors, deputy chiefs, assistant chiefs, fire chiefs, and fire commissioners.

Police, Fire, and Refuse Collection Personnel and Expenditures (International City/County Management Association, 777 N. Capitol St., NE, Washington, DC 20002; phone: 202/289–4262) $16.50 (add $2.50 shipping and handling if not prepaid), 1992. A comparative study depicting trends in salary and expenditures data from police, fire, and refuse collection and disposal services.

Fleet/facilities management

Job ads in print

Automotive Fleet (Bobit Publishing, 2512 Artesia Blvd., Redondo Beach, CA 90278; phone: 310/376–8788) monthly, $24/annual subscription. Jobs listed under "Classifieds." About one to two job ads in typical issue. Many more "Positions Wanted" ads appear in each issue.

NAFA Newsletter (National Association of Fleet Managers, Suite 615, 120 Wood Ave. South, Iselin, NJ 08830; phone: 908/494–8100) monthly, free/members only. The ***Newsletter, The NAFA Fleet Executive*** (which does not contain job ads), and an annual reference book, are included in membership package. Jobs listed under "Jobs Available." About five job ads in the typical issue. Many more "Positions Wanted" ads are run.

IFMA News (International Facility Management Association, 1 E. Greenway Place, 11th Floor, Houston, TX 77046–0194; phone: 713/623–4362) monthly, available only to members. Two or three positions in facilities management appear under "FM Jobs."

Also see ***Community Transportation Reporter*** *listed under "Transit management."*

Job service

IFMA Job Referral Service (International Facility Management Association, 1 E. Greenway Plaza, 11th Floor, Houston, TX 77046–0194; phone: 713/623–4362) free/members only. You complete the service's resume form and your resume is kept on file in their database for a year. When a match is made, your resume is sent to the employer who is responsible for contacting you for an interview.

Directories

State Fleet Managers Information Register (Council of State Governments, 3560 Iron Works Pike, P.O. Box 11910, Lexington, KY 40578–1910; phones: 800/800–1910, 606/231–1939) $20 plus $3.75/shipping, last published in 1989. Compilation of state fleet administrators and the types of vehicles each state uses. Although this directory is clearly out–of–date, the Council of State Governments still keeps track of this information and may be able to give you specifics over the phone on the state fleet managers for one or two states.

IFMA Membership Directory (International Facility Management Association, 1 E. Greenway Place, 11th Floor, Houston, TX 77046–0194; phone: 713/623–4362) free/members only, published each August.

Forestry and horticulture

Also see listings under "Environment" and "Parks and recreation."

Job ads in print

Journal of Forestry (Society of American Foresters, 5400 Grosvernor Lane, Bethesda, MD 20814–2198; phone: 301/897–8720) monthly; $55/nonmember individuals annual subscription (U.S. and Canada), $85/individuals elsewhere (surface mail), free/members. Jobs listed under "Classifieds." About 12 job ads per issue.

Ferrell's Jobs in Horticulture (154 E. Chapel Ave., Carlisle, PA 17013–3435; phone: 800/428–2474) $19.95/six issues, $36/twelve issues, $60/twenty–four issues, residents of Pennsylvania add 6 percent sales tax. Twenty or so job ads in arboretum administration, greenhouse production, horticulture education, golf course maintenance, landscaping, grounds maintenance, horticultural science, floral, nursery and garden center, sports arena supervision, cemetery management and more.

City Trees (Society of Municipal Arborists, c/o Leonard Phillips, Editor, P.O. Box 364, Wellesley Hills, MA 02181; phone: 617/235–7600, ext. 330) bimonthly, $20/annual subscription, included in $40 annual dues. Typical issue has one or two ads for arborists, horticulturalists, or urban foresters.

American Forests (American Forestry Association, P.O. Box 2000, Washington, DC 20013; phones: 800/368–5748, 202/667–3300) bimonthly, $24/annual subscription. Jobs as foresters, resource managers, arborists, and environmental policy directors appear under "The Green Pages."

AABGA Newsletter (American Association of Botanical Gardens and Arboreta, 786 Church Rd., Wayne, PA 19087; phone: 215/688–1120) monthly, members only (annual dues: $50, $25/students). About 15 positions in public horticulture ranging from gardener to director appear under "Positions Available."

Forest Products Journal (Forest Product Society, 2801 Marshall Ct., Madison, WI 53705; 608/231–1361) ten issues/year, $115/annual nonmember subscription, included in dues. Three to six positions are listed under "Employment Referral Service."

Internship Directory (American Association of Botanical Gardens and Arboreta, 786 Church Rd., Wayne, PA 19087; phone: 215/688–1120) $5/nonmember, $4/members, published each October. This is a very extensive state–by–state listing of summer internships available in public horticulture and private estates.

Association of Zoological Horticulture Newsletter (Jim Martin, Riverbanks Zoo, P.O. Box 1060, Columbia, SC 29202–1060; phone: 803/779–8717) quarterly, available only to members, $25/annual professional dues, $15/annual student dues. A few positions for zoo horticulturists and gardeners are listed under "Positions Available." "Positions Wanted" listings included.

Job services

Jobs Hotline (American Association of Botanical Gardens and Arboreta, 786 Church Rd., Wayne, PA 19087; phone: 215/688–1120) free. Call 215/688–9127 weekdays 5 p.m. to 8 a.m. (eastern time) and 24 hours on weekends for a tape recording that lists four to eight jobs in public horticulture.

Florapersonnel (2180 W. State Rd. 434, Suite 6152, Longwood, FL 32779–5008; phone: 407/682–5151) free. The job seeker completes Florapersonnel's form and submits it along with her resume. Resumes are kept on file indefinitely. When a match is made, Florapersonnel contacts the job seeker and, if the job seeker gives the okay, Florapersonnel gives her name and resume to the potential employer who then contacts the employer. (Normally, we don't list "headhunters" in this book, but the horticulture field has so few job sources that it seems reasonable to include this entry.) Jobs range from greenhouse growers to directors. Includes nursery, floral, landscape, and irrigation.

Directories

AABGA Membership Directory (American Association of Botanical Gardens and Arboreta, 786 Church Rd., Wayne, PA 19087; phone: 215/688–1120) free/members only (annual dues: $50, $25/students). Lists institutional members of AABGA.

The FPS Membership Directory (Forest Product Society, 2801 Marshall Ct., Madison, WI 53705; 608/231–1361) free/members only, issued annually. Lists association members job titles, addresses, and fax and phone numbers.

Salary survey

1992 AABGA Salary Survey (American Association of Botanical Gardens and Arboreta, 786 Church Rd., Wayne, PA 19087; phone: 215/688–1120) $38/nonmembers, $28/members. Contains salary information for 22 job categories in botanical gardens in the U.S. and Canada.

Housing

See also listings under "Community and Economic Development," "Planning," and "Public Administration." Also see the ***Non–Profits' Job Finder.***

Job ads in print

NAHRO Monitor (National Association of Housing and Redevelopment Officials, 1320 18th St., NW, Washington, DC 20036–1803; phone: 202/429–2960) biweekly, available only to members. Jobs listed under "Jobs Available." Typical issue features ten or more job openings generally in housing administration, planning, and community or neighborhood development.

Trends in Housing (Trends, Inc., 1629 K St., NW, Suite 802, Washington, DC 20006; phone: 202/833–4456) bimonthly, $20/annual subscription. A few ads appear under "Job Opportunities Available in Housing."

Job service

NAHRO–Net (National Association of Housing and Redevelopment Officials, 1320 18th St., NW, Washington, DC 20036–1803; phone: 202/429–2960, ext. 237) $150/annual subscription, $20/hour monthly online charge whether you use it or not. Using your computer and modem you can access announcements of job vacancies in the housing and community development field, as well as a vast world of information you can use on the job. Currently, 10 to 20 jobs which also appear in the NAHRO Monitor, described above under "Job ads in print," are listed. NAHRO expects to expand the job listings sometime in 1994.

Directories

NAHRO Directory of Local Agencies (National Association of Housing and Redevelopment Officials, 1320 18th St., NW, Washington, DC 20036–1803; phone: 202/429–2960) $80/nonmembers, $65/members, published in September 1991 and every three years thereafter. Includes national listings of 7,000 city and county public agencies that administer public housing, Section 8, community development, urban renewal and development, neighborhood revitalization, housing rehabilitation, housing code enforcement, and other housing assistance programs. For each entry, you'll get the agency name, address, and phone number; executive director's name; population served; and number and type of housing and community development programs administered.

Directory of State Housing Finance Agencies (National Council of State Housing Agencies, Suite 438, 444 North Capitol St., NW, Washington, DC 20001; phone: 202/624–7710) $150/nonmembers, $5/member Housing Finance Authorities, $10/affiliates, published each January, 55 pages. Provides names, addresses, and phone numbers for key staff and affiliated individuals.

State Housing Finance Agency Program Catalog (National Council of State Housing Agencies, Suite 438, 444 North Capitol St., NW, Washington, DC 20001; phone: 202/624–7710) $150/full set plus $10/shipping or $36.95/volume plus $3/each shipping, 1991. This five–volume tome gives excruciating detail on over 600 housing finance agencies including a fact sheet describing each program, funding source, participants, beneficiaries, and housing produced. It is also available as individual volumes: 1–Home ownership Programs, 2–Rental Housing Programs, 3–Special Needs Programs, 4–Economic Development Programs, and 5–Technical/Financial Assistance Initiatives and Financing Tools.

Directory of Housing Attorneys (Low and Moderate Income Housing and Community Development) (American Bar Association, Order Fulfillment 1391–5720, 750 N. Lake Shore Dr., Chicago, IL 60611; phone: 312/988–5000) $20 plus $3.95/shipping, most recent edition: 1990–91. Extensive listing of lawyers who practice in the housing field.

Human services

See listings under "Public administration" and "Social services."

Labor relations

See listings under "Personnel" and under "Public administration."

Landscape architecture

Also see listings under "Parks and recreation" and "Planning."

Job ads in print

Landscape Architecture (American Society of Landscape Architects, 5th floor, 4401 Connecticut Ave., NW, Washington, DC 20008–2302; phone: 202/686–2752) bimonthly; $42/annual subscription (U.S.), $32/students (U.S.), foreign: $70/surface mail, $125/air mail. Two to five jobs for landscape architects and horticulturists are listed under "Classifieds" in the "Buyers Guide" section.

*See also the **Employment Referral Service** of the Golf Course Superintendents Association of America listed under "Parks and recreation."*

Directory

ASLA Membership Handbook (American Society of Landscape Architects, 4401 Connecticut Ave., NW, Washington, DC 20008–2302; phone: 202/686–2752) $129.95/nonmembers, free/members, 396 pages, published each October. The "In Practice" section includes a directory of member firms by state with their addresses and phone numbers.

Law enforcement

*Also see listings under "Public administration" and "Public safety." Sources of positions in the private sector security industry appear in the **Professional's Private Sector Job Finder.***

Job ads in print

NELS—National Employment Listing Service (Criminal Justice Center, Sam Houston State University, Huntsville, TX 77341–2296; phone: 409/294–1692, 1690) monthly, individuals: $30/annual subscription, $37.50/foreign, $17.50/six–month subscription; institutions and agencies: $65/annual subscription (U.S.), $85/foreign; Texas residents must include 8.25 percent sales tax; tax–exempt institutions must include proof of tax exempt status. Each issue describes 100 to 200+ positions in four categories: Law enforcement and security (police officers, document examiners, print examiners, criminologists, public service aides, jailers); Community services and corrections (correctional trainees, psychologists, social workers, physicians, speech pathologists, communications, clerical, counselors, probation officers); Institutional corrections (correctional officers, psychologists, nurses, chaplains, cooks, therapists, pharmacists, trades and laborers); and Academics and research.

Police Career Digest and Express Jobs Newsletter (Police Career Digest, P.O. Box 7772, Winter Park, FL 33883; phones: 800/359–6260, 813/666–3184) published in alternating months, $34/annual subscription, $26/six–month subscription. Jobs listed in *Police Career Digest* under "Law Enforcement Opportunities." *Express Jobs Newsletter* is all job announcements. Twenty to 40 ads for police personnel are in the typical issue of *Police Career Digest* while *Express Jobs Newsletter* has approximately the same amount.

PSIC Listing (Protective Services Information Center, P.O. Box 3831, Springfield, IL 62708) monthly, $57.95/annual subscription, $21.95/four–month subscription. Forty to 50 position for entry–level to supervisory security in law enforcement and private security found in each issue.

The Police Chief (International Association of Chiefs of Police, Inc., 515 N. Washington St., 4th Floor, Alexandria, VA 22314; phone: 703/836–6767) monthly, $25/nonmember annual subscription, free/members. About eight police chief and public safety director jobs under "Classified" and advertised in display ads throughout the magazine.

NBPA Advocate (National Black Police Association, 3251 Mt. Pleasant St., NW, Washington, DC 20010–2103; phone: 202/986–2070) quarterly, free. Two or three openings appear under "Positions Available."

The Criminologist (American Society of Criminology, 1314 Kinnear Rd., Suite 212, Columbus, OH, 43212; phone: 614/292–9207) bimonthly, $7.50/annual nonmember subscription (U.S.), $10/foreign, free/members. Ten to 12 jobs for probation officers, police, and faculty are listed under "Positions Announcements."

American Jails (American Jail Association, Suite 100, 2053 Day Rd., Hagerstown, MD 21740; phone: 301/790–3930) bimonthly, $4.50/annual subscription, included in membership package ($25/annual dues). Five to eight job ads in typical issue.

Law Enforcement News (John Jay College of Criminal Justice, Suite 438, 899 Tenth Ave., New York, NY 10019; phone: 212/237–8442) bimonthly, $18/annual subscription (U.S.), $28/foreign. Vacancies are offered under "Jobs."

Law and Order (Hendon, Inc., 1000 Skokie Blvd., Wilmette, IL 60091; phone: 708/256–8555) monthly, $20/annual subscription. Jobs listed under "Classified Ads." About five job ads per issue.

The ASLET Journal (American Society of Law Enforcement Trainers, P.O. Box 361, Lewes, DE 19958; phone: 302/645–4080) bimonthly, available only as part of membership package. Few job ads; job ads not in every issue.

NARC Officer (International Narcotic Enforcement Officers Association, Inc., Suite 1200, 112 State St., Albany, NY 12207; phone: 518/463–6232) semimonthly, $35/nonmember annual subscription, $30/members, (add $35 for surface mail to foreign countries; for air mail, add: $40/Canada and Mexico, $45/Caribbean, $60/Europe, $85/Asia). Publishes a limited number of job ads plus position wanted ads for free.

Food Service Director (355 Park Avenue South, New York, NY 10010; phone: 212/592–6200) monthly, $40/annual subscription, free to qualified food service personnel. Among the eight job ads under "Classifieds" you'll often find a prison system food service management or cook position.

Employment Bulletin (American Sociological Association, 1722 N St., NW, Washington, DC 20036; phone: 202/833–3410) monthly, $23/nonmember annual subscription, $8/members. This newsletter features around 70 positions in academic applied and fellowship settings. Most positions are in sociology, but related areas such as anthropology and criminology are included.

The Federal Network (American Sociological Association, 1722 N St., NW, Washington, DC 20036; phone: 202/833–3410) weekly, $75/nonmember six–month subscription, $60/members, $35/students and low–income ASA members ($15,000 or less annual income), $100/annual subscription for institutions; any subscription can be extended for six months for $10. Each issue features announcements of new federal government administrative and research positions in the sociology, anthropology, and criminology fields.

Forum Newsletter (Criminal Justice Statistics Association, 444 N. Capitol St., NW, Suite 606, Washington, DC 20001) quarterly, $25/annual nonmember subscription, free/members. One or two jobs for analysts, programmers, researchers, and administrative positions in criminal justice statistics appear in the typical issue.

Laboratory Medicine (American Society of Clinical Pathologists, 2100 W. Harrison St., Chicago, IL 60612; phone: 312/738–1336) monthly, $40/annual nonmember subscription (U.S.), $55/foreign, free/members. About 45 openings for pathologists, technicians, and other laboratory–related positions are listed under "Professional Exchange."

American Journal of Clinical Pathology (J. B. Lippincott Company, P.O. Box 1590, Hagerstown, MD 21741; phone: 800/777–2295) monthly with 2 supplements, $135/annual subscription (U.S.), $195/foreign. Ten to 12 "Classifieds" appear for pathologists in government and private practice.

Job services

Law Enforcement and Security Hot Line (National Association of Chiefs of Police, 3801 Biscayne Blvd., Miami, FL 33137; phone: 305/573–0202) $36/year. Calls are accepted weekdays from 9 a.m. to 4 p.m. The list of positions as peace officers, correctional staff, private security in government agencies, and private firms is updated monthly. When you call you get a live person, not a recording. Vacancies are available by geographical area and qualifications.

Employment Hotline (American Federation of Police, 3801 Biscayne Blvd., Miami, FL 33137; phone: 305/573–0070) free, but available only to "active" members, $36/annual active membership. Member calls the hotline number (available from the federation) and hears brief job descriptions of 20 to 30 police positions. The job seeker contacts each hiring agency directly.

ACA Job Advisory Service (American Correctional Association, 8025 Laurel Lakes Ct., Laurel, MD 20707–5075; phone: 301/206–5048) $5/per state; available only to members. The job seeker identifies the state(s) he/she is interested in finding a job in and is sent a list of job vacancies for those states.

Directories

National Directory of Law Enforcement (National Police Chiefs & Sheriffs Information Bureau, P.O. Box 365, Stevens Point, WI 54481–0365; phone: 715/345–2772) $55, 600 pages. This annual directory includes chiefs of police; sheriffs; county and district prosecutors; state police and highway patrols; state criminal investigation units; state correctional agencies; college and university security and police departments; 57 federal agencies; U.S. military; airport, harbor, and railroad police departments; and more. It is also available on computer disks and as mailing labels.

International Association of Chiefs of Police Membership Directory (International Association of Chiefs of Police, Inc., 515 N. Washington St., 4th Floor, Alexandria, VA 22314; phone: 703/836–6767) $77.50/nonmembers, free/members, published each October.

Law Enforcement Career Guide (Police Career Digest, P.O. Box 7772, Winter Haven, FL 33883; phones: 800/359–6260, 813/666–3184) $30 plus $3/shipping, Florida residents add 6 percent sales tax, 1993. Provides information on over 100 municipal, county, state, and federal law enforcement agencies: basic qualifications, selection process, salary, benefits, and contact information.

Directory of Juvenile and Adult Correctional Institutions and Agencies (American Correctional Association, 8025 Laurel Lakes Ct., Laurel, MD 20707–5075; phone: 301/206–5048) $75, published each January.

American Society of Criminology Membership Directory (American Society of Criminology, 1314 Kinnear Rd., Suite 212, Columbus, OH, 43212; phone: 614/292–9207) free/members only, published every other year, most recent edition published in 1992.

Salary surveys

Police Personnel Salaries (International City/County Management Association, 777 N. Capitol St., NE, Washington, DC 20002; phone: 202/289–4262) $29.75 plus $3.50 shipping and handling if not prepaid, published every October. This report gives state–by–state data on minimum and maximum salaries that jurisdictions pay to: police private, motorcycle officer, police corporal, detective, sergeant, lieutenant, captain, inspector, deputy chief, assistant chief, police chief, and police commissioner.

Vital Statistics in Corrections (American Correctional Association, 8025 Laurel Lakes Ct., Laurel, MD 20707–5075; phones: 301/206–5059, 800/825–2665) $18.95/nonmembers, $15/members. Usually published every two years. Last edition published fall of 1991, new edition will come out fall 1994. Salaries, education, benefits, training, budgets, unions, employee groups, institutional populations, and recidivism rates for jails, prisons, probation, and parole.

Police, Fire, and Refuse Collection Personnel and Expenditures (International City/County Management Association, 777 N. Capitol St., NE, Washington, DC 20002; phone: 202/289–4262) $16.50 plus $2.50 shipping and handling if not prepaid, 1992. A comparative study depicting trends in salary and expenditures data from police, fire, and refuse collection and disposal services.

Legal services and the courts

Also see listings under "Library services." Extensive listings of sources for private sector job openings appear in the ***Professional's Private Sector Job Finder****.*

Job ads in print

National and Federal Legal Employment Report (Federal Reports, Inc., Suite 408, 1010 Vermont Ave., NW, Washington, DC 20005; phone: 202/393–3311) monthly. Subscription rates for individuals: $34/three–month, $58/six–month, $104/annual subscription; rates for institutions: $45, $80, $140, respectively. Typical issues contain descriptions of 500 to 600 attorney and law–related positions primarily in the federal government, state and local government, and private employers in government–related fields, including legal aid offices. Includes legal positions in the Washington D.C. area, throughout the U.S., and abroad.

Opportunities in Public Interest Law (ACCESS: Networking in the Public Interest, 50 Beacon St., Boston, MA 02108; phone: 617/720–5627) biannually (February and October), $42.90/February edition, $42.90/October edition. Hundreds of jobs are listed for positions in nonprofit and government public interest law. Subscribers can also receive an annual *Public Interest Law Employer Directory* listed below under "directories." $113.70/both editions including directory (individuals), $175/both editions including directory (institutions).

Job Announcements (National Center for State Courts, Publications Coordinator, 300 Newport Ave., Williamsburg, VA 23185; phone: 804/253–2000 ext. 390) biweekly, $30/annual subscription, $15/six–month subscription. Thirty to 50 announcements for all levels of employment appear in a typical issue.

Lawyers Job Bulletin Board (Federal Bar Association, Publications Department, Suite 408, 1815 H St., NW, Washington, DC 20006; phone: 202/638–0252) monthly, $30/nonmember annual subscription, $20/members,

$20/students. Typical issue features 25 job openings primarily with the federal government, although about 10 percent of the ads are for positions with District of Columbia area courts, private firms, and non–profits.

Clearinghouse Review (National Clearinghouse for Legal Services, 205 W. Monroe, 2nd Floor, Chicago, IL 60606; phones: 800/621–3256, 312/263–3830) monthly, $75/annual subscription (U.S.), $95/foreign. About 25 ads for attorneys, paralegals, and faculty appear under "Job Market."

Job Market Preview (National Clearinghouse for Legal Services, 205 W. Monroe, 2nd Floor, Chicago, IL 60606; phones: 800/621–3256, 312/263–3830) monthly, $35/annual subscription. About 30 jobs ads fill this newsletter, often the same jobs that appear in *Clearinghouse Review*.

Position Report (David J. White & Associates, Suite 200, 809 Ridge Rd., Wilmette, IL 60091; phone: 708/256–8826) weekly, $43.50/four week subscription, $115/12 weeks, $226/24 weeks, $452/48 weeks. This is a collection of 500+ job ads for attorneys taken from over 100 newspapers and periodicals nationwide, including government and institutional positions.

Legal Times (1730 M St., NW, Suite 802, Washington, DC 20036; phone: 202/457–0686) weekly, $525/annual law firm subscription, contact for individual subscription rate. "Classified Advertising–Employment for Attorneys" includes 10 to 15 positions from around the country in addition to local positions in the Washington DC area. Jobs include attorneys (firm, corporate, government), paralegals, and legal secretaries offered directly and through legal recruiters. Also includes a "Positions Wanted" section.

The NLADA Cornerstone (National Legal Aid and Defender Association, 8th Floor, 1625 K St., NW, Washington, DC 20006; phone: 202/452–0620) quarterly, $20/nonmember subscription, included in membership package. "Job Listings" usually includes 15 to 20 job announcements.

ALA Management Connections Bulletin (Association of Legal Administrators, Suite 325, 175 E. Hawthorn Pkwy, Vernon Hills, IL 60061–1428; phone: 708/816–1212) weekly, $150/nonmember six–month subscription, $100/members. This is the print version of the *ALA Management Connection* job hotline described below under "Job services." In it you will find job ads for law office managers with government agencies and in the court system, although the vast majority of positions advertised are with private firms. You can place a "Position Wanted" ad of your own for $75/nonmembers, $50/members. This ad will be recorded on *ALA Management Connections* and appear in the *ALA Management Connections Bulletin*. Contact the Association of Legal Administrators for details.

The Update (Food and Drug Law Institute, 1000 Vermont Ave., NW, Suite 1200, Washington, DC 20005; phone: 202/371–1420) quarterly, $25/annual nonmember subscription, free/members. One to three job ads appear under "Positions Available–Job Exchange." Also included is a "Positions Wanted" section.

NCRA Employment Referral Service Bulletin (National Court Reporters Association, 8224 Old Courthouse Rd., Vienna, VA 22182; phone: 703/281–4677) monthly, $24/nonmember annual subscription, $12/members. Typical issue features 20 to 30 job announcements for both freelance and more formal court reporter positions.

Summer Legal Employment Guide (Federal Reports, Inc., Suite 408, 1010 Vermont Ave., NW, Washington, DC 20005; phone: 202/393–3311) $16 plus $2 shipping, published annually, 36 pages. Describes federal summer legal intern and clerkship programs for law students. Since these internships go quickly, get your copy by mid–autumn of the year before you want the summer internship.

Internships for College Students Interested in Law, Medicine and Politics (Graduate Group, 86 Norwood Rd., West Hartford, CT 06117; phones: 203/232–3100, 203/236–5570) $27.50, published annually. Includes information on hundreds of actual internship opportunities with government law offices.

Job services

NCRA Employment Referral Service (National Court Reporters Association, 8224 Old Courthouse Rd., Vienna, VA 22182; phone: 703/281–4677) $6/six–month nonmember registration, free/members. Obtain the "Employment Referral Data Sheet." Completed data sheets are kept on file for six–month period. A copy of this data sheet is furnished to potential employers. NCRA recommends that you also contact your state court reporters association to see if it has a referral service. Contact NCRA for the address and phone of the association in your state.

CU Career Connection (University of Colorado, Campus Box 133, Boulder, CO 80309–0133; phone: 303/492–4127) $30/two–month fee entitles you to a "passcode" which unlocks this job hotline. You need a touch–tone phone to call and request the field in which you are interested in hearing job openings. The hotline is turned off Monday through Friday, 2 to 4 p.m. for daily updating.

ALA Management Connections (Association of Legal Administrators, Suite 325, 175 E. Hawthorn Pkwy, Vernon Hills, IL 60061–1428; phone: 708/816–1212) free, updated weekly. To hear job descriptions for law office managers with government agencies or in the court system (as well as mostly private sector positions), call 708/810–4333 anytime. You'll need a touch–tone phone. Press "3" after the message starts so you can hear the instructions. You can place a "Position Wanted" ad of your own for $75/nonmembers,

$50/members. This ad will be recorded on *ALA Management Connections* and appear in the *ALA Management Connections Bulletin* described above under "Job ads in print." Contact the Association of Legal Administrators for details.

Local Women's Bar Associations. A number of these operate job services. Contact the National Conference of Women's Bar Associations (P.O. Box 77, Edenton, NC 27932–0077; phone: 919/482–8202) for information.

Directories

Directory of Legal Aid and Defender Offices in the U.S. and Territories (National Legal Aid and Defender Association, 8th Floor, 1625 K St., NW, Washington, DC 20006; phone: 202/452–0620) $30/nonmember, $15/member, published biannually.

NDAA Membership Directory (National District Attorneys Association, 99 Canal Center Plaza, Suite 510, Alexandria, VA 22314; phone: 703/549–9222) $15/nonmembers, $10/members, most recent edition 1992, next edition will be published May 1994.

Public Interest Law Employer Directory (ACCESS: Networking in the Public Interest, 50 Beacon St., Boston, MA 02108; phone: 617/720–5627) $27.90, annual.

Federal Careers for Attorneys (Federal Reports, Inc., Suite 408, 1010 Vermont Ave., NW, Washington, DC 20005; phone: 202/393–3311) $21.95 plus $2 shipping, most recent edition published in March 1991, 170 pages. Comprehensive guide to legal careers with over 300 U.S. government general counsel and other federal legal offices throughout the country and abroad. Each entry specifies attorney hiring procedures, special recruitment programs, where to apply, and type of legal work. Includes Subject Matter Index with over 80 major areas of government legal practice and Geographic Index of about 400 cities in the U.S. and abroad.

Federal Law–Related Careers (Federal Reports, Inc., Suite 408, 1010 Vermont Ave., NW, Washington, DC 20005; phone: 202/393–3311) $14.95 plus $2 shipping, 86 pages. Describes over 80 law–related careers and identifies the primary federal agency employer in each field. Includes addresses for over 1,000 federal recruiting offices.

Directory of Lawyers and Consultants (Food and Drug Law Institute, 1000 Vermont Ave., NW, Suite 1200, Washington, DC 20005; phone: 202/371–1420) $75/nonmembers, $60/members, 1992. Gives biographies, names, addresses, and phones of law firms, sole practitioners, consultants, public relations firms, and professional services by specialty and alphabetic listing.

The ALJ Handbook: An Insider's Guide to Becoming a Federal Administrative Law Judge (Federal Reports, Inc., Suite 408, 1010 Vermont Ave., NW, Washington, DC 20005; phone: 202/393–3311) $20 plus $2/shipping. In addition to teaching you the hoops you have to leap through, this valuable guide tells you which federal agencies hire administrative law judges, which agencies "borrow" administrative law judges, and where ALJs are currently located.

Paralegal's Guide to U.S. Government Jobs (Federal Reports, Inc., Suite 408, 1010 Vermont Ave., NW, Washington, DC 20005; phone: 202/393–3311) $14.00 plus $2 shipping. Designed for both entry–level and experienced paralegals, this book explains federal hiring procedures, describes 70 law–related careers for which paralegals qualify, outlines special hiring programs, and includes a directory of over 1,000 federal agency personnel offices that hire the most paralegal talent.

Judicial Staff Directory (Staff Directories, Ltd., P.O. Box 62, Mt. Vernon, VA 22121; phone: 703/739–0900) $69, published every November, 865 pages. Over 11,000 individuals listed for the 207 federal courts, 13,000 cities and their courts, court administration, U.S. marshals, U.S. attorneys, and the U.S. Department of Justice. Includes 1,800 biographies.

Salary survey

Legal Salary Survey (David J. White & Associates, 809 Ridge Rd., Wilmette, IL 60091; phone: 800/962–4947) $190, last issued in 1993. Covers attorney positions.

Library services

*Also see listings under "Records management and archival services" and see the **Non–Profits' Job Finder** listings under "Museums and library services." Most of the job sources listed below include positions in private sector libraries as well as public sector. Since so much library hiring is done through state and regional job sources, we've included those here as well as the job sources that are national in scope.*

Nationwide job sources

Job ads in print

American Libraries (American Library Association, 50 E. Huron St., Chicago, IL 60611; phones: 800/545–2433 [outside Illinois], 800/545–2444 [Illinois only], 800/545–2455 [Canada only], 312/280–4211) 11 issues/year; $50/annual subscription for libraries, free/members. Jobs listed under "Career Leads." Typical issue features 75 to 100 job ads.

Job notices can be obtained three weeks prior to publication in *American Libraries* in **Career Leads Express** which is a copy of the uncorrected galleys of job notices that will appear in the next issue of *American Libraries*. *Career Leads Express* is available to nonmembers and members alike for $1/issue, prepaid only. With your check, send a self–addressed stamped (two ounces postage) #10 envelope to AL Leads Express, 50 E. Huron, Chicago, IL 60611. Typical issue includes 75 or more positions.

Library Journal (Cahners Publishing Company, P.O. Box 6457, Torrance, CA 90504; phone: 800/278–2991) 20 issues/year, $79/annual subscription (U.S.), $99/Canada, $138/elsewhere (air mail). Jobs listed under "Classified Advertising." Fifty to 70 ads for librarian positions grace the pages of a typical issue.

Library Hotline (P.O. Box 713, Brewster, NY 10509; phone: 800/722–2346) 50 issues/year, $74/annual subscription. Forty percent of the 25 to 30 job vacancies listed in each issue are for government jobs.

Information Today (Learned Information, Inc., 143 Old Marlton Pike, Medford, NJ 08055; phone: 609/654–6266) 11 issues/year, $43.95/annual subscription, $53.95/Canada and Mexico, $59/elsewhere. About ten ads for library positions appear under "Classified Today."

School Library Journal (Cahners Publishing, 44 Cook St., Denver, CO 80206; phone: 303/388–4511) monthly, $67/annual subscription (U.S.), $91/Canada, $110/elsewhere. About 15 librarian positions with public libraries and university, elementary, and secondary school libraries appear under "Classifieds."

Journal of Academic Librarianship (Mountainside Publishing Co., 321 S. Main St., Suite 300, Ann Arbor, MI 48107; phone: 313/662–3925) bimonthly, $29/annual subscription (individuals), $65/institutions. Two or three ads for university librarians appear under "Classified Ads."

Institutional Library Mail Jobline (c/o Gloria Spooner, Library Consultant, State Library of Louisiana, P.O. Box 131, Baton Rouge, LA 70821–0131; phone: 504/342–4931) monthly, free. Send self–addressed stamped #10 envelope for copy. Lists institutional library positions in U.S. and its territories.

ASIS Jobline (American Society for Information Science, 8720 Georgia Ave., Suite 501, Silver Spring, MD 20910–3602; phone: 301/495–0900) monthly, free. About 15 vacancies are announced in a typical issue.

Rural Libraries Jobline (Center for the Study of Rural Librarianship, Department of Library Science, Clarion University of Pennsylvania, Clarion, PA 16214; phone: 814/226–2383) monthly, $1/issue.

Specialist (Special Libraries Association, 1700 18th St., NW, Washington, DC 20009; 202/234–4700) monthly, $60/annual subscription, $65/foreign. From five to ten jobs are listed under "Positions Open."

Newsletter (American Association of Law Libraries, Suite 940, 53 W. Jackson, Chicago, IL 60604; phone: 312/939–4764) ten issues/year, $50/nonmember annual subscription, free/members. Jobs listed under "Career Hotline." Over 20 job ads appear in the typical issue. Advance copies of job ads are available for $2.50/month prepaid. The advance copies include job ads two to four weeks before they are published in the *Newsletter* plus several ads not published in the *Newsletter*.

Job Database (American Association of Law Libraries, Dept. 77–6021, Chicago, IL 60678–6021; phone: 312/939–4764) monthly, $25/annual subscription. This is a monthly compilation of all jobs listed on the AALA's *Job Database Service* and *Career Hotline* described below under "Job services." Expect to see 10 to 25 positions advertised in an issue.

MLA News (Medical Library Association, 6 N. Michigan Ave., Suite 300, Chicago, IL 60602; phone: 312/419–9094) ten issues/year, $48.50/nonmember annual subscription (U.S.), $61.50/foreign, free/members. From 10 to 15 ads appear in the "Employment Opportunities" for librarian posts in the health sciences. These ads may also be purchased two weeks before they are published through the service *Advanced Employment Opportunities* listed directly below.

Advanced Employment Opportunities (Medical Library Association, 6 N. Michigan Ave., Suite 300, Chicago, IL 60602; phone: 312/419–9094) $25/nonmembers, $15/members. Over a six–month period you are sent a listing of job ads from *MLA News*, listed directly above, two weeks before it is published and sold.

Veterans Administration Librarian Register. For printed job list, write to: Diane Wiesenthal, Library Division (143B), Virginia Control Office, 810 Vermont Ave., NW, Washington, DC 20420, Atten: Vacancy List; phone: 202/535–7360. Most listings are for medical librarian positions with the Department of Veterans Affairs. Only for persons eligible for inclusion on Veterans Administration Licensed Register of Professional Librarians.

Job services

Career Hotline (American Association of Law Libraries, Suite 940, 53 W. Jackson, Chicago, IL 60604). Call 312/939–7877 for a tape of job listings for law libraries. Recording is updated every Friday. Five or more jobs on each recording.

Infoline (Medical Library Association, 6 N. Michigan Ave., Suite 300, Chicago, IL 60602; phone: 312/419–9094) free, call 312/553–4636 for a 24–hour recording of job openings in *MLA News* listed above under "Job Openings." On your touch–tone phone, be ready to select type of job, part of the country, and salary range desired.

SpeciaLine Employment Clearinghouse Job Hotline (Special Libraries Association, 1700 18th St., NW, Washington, DC 20009; 202/234–4700). Call 202/234–3632 for 24–hour tape recording of jobs with special libraries.

MLA Job Line (Medical Library Association, 6 N. Michigan Ave., Suite 300, Chicago, IL 60602–4805; phone: 312/419–9094) Call 312/553–4636 for a 24 hour tape–recording of 15 or more jobs in the medical library field. Updated weekly.

American Library Association Job Hotline (American Library Association, 50 E. Huron St., Chicago, IL 60611; phones: 800/545–2433 [outside Illinois], 800/545–2444 [Illinois only], 800/545–2455 [Canada only], 312/280–4211). If you want to work for the ALA, call 312/280–2464 anytime to hear a recording of job openings at the ALA.

Career Hotline/Job Database Service (American Association of Law Libraries, Suite 940, 53 W. Jackson, Chicago, IL 60604; phone: 312/939–4764). Call the 24–hour Career Hotline, 312/939–7877, for a recording of brief job descriptions of law librarian positions and where to apply. This is the index to the AALL's *Job Database Service* which is updated weekly by Friday noon. AALL members can request a free printout of all job listings by calling 312/939–4764 or faxing a request to 312/431–1097. Nonmembers can obtain a printout for $5 (send to: AALL, Dept. 77–602, Chicago, IL 60678–6021). There are typically 10 to 25 jobs listed at any one time.

Canadian Association of Special Libraries and Information Services, Ottawa Chapter Jobline (Job Bank Coordinator, CASLIS, 266 Sherwood Drive, Ottawa, Ontario, K1Y3W4 Canada). Call 613/728–9982 for a recording of job openings.

See also ***ASIS Jobline*** *listed under "Data processing and computers."*

Directories

AALL Directory and Handbook (American Association of Law Libraries, Suite 940, 53 W. Jackson, Chicago, IL 60604; phone: 312/939–4764). This annual directory of government and private law libraries is available only to members.

COSLA Directory (The Council of State Governments, 3560 Iron Works Pike, P.O. Box 11910, Lexington, KY 40578–1910; phones: 800/800–1910, 606/231–1939) $12.50 plus $3.75/shipping, 30 pages, 1992. Lists information on state library agencies, consultants and administrative staff. Includes INTERNET addresses, electronic mail letters and FAX numbers.

American Library Directory 1993–94 (R.R. Bowker; available through Reed Reference Publishing, P.O. Box 31, New Providence, NJ 07974; phone: 800/521–8110) $225 plus 7 percent shipping and handling, two volumes, published each June. Provides information on over 38,000 public, government, academic, and special libraries and library–related organizations in the U.S. and Canada. Also available on CD–ROM and by modem on DIALOG, file number 460, $78/per hour search time, plus nominal charge for display.

World Guide to Libraries (K.G. Saur; available through Reed Reference Publishing, P.O. Box 31, New Providence, NJ 07974; phone: 800/521–8110) $350, plus 7 percent shipping and handling, last published 1993, 1,100 pages. Provides information on over 40,000 libraries worldwide.

World Guide to Special Libraries (K.G. Saur; available through Reed Reference Publishing, P.O. Box 31, New Providence, NJ 07974; phone: 800/521–8110) $325, two–volume set, plus 7 percent shipping and handling, last published 1990. 1,200 pages. Provides information on over 32,000 libraries in 160 countries.

Libraries, Information Centers and Databases in Science and Technology (K.G. Saur; available from Reed Reference Publishing, P.O. Box 31, New Providence, NJ 07974; phone: 800/521–8110) $225 plus 7 percent shipping and handling, 696 pages, 1988 edition. Includes over 11,000 libraries, online databases, and documentation centers in all areas of pure and applied sciences. Independent specialized national libraries, technical college libraries, university and college libraries, and institute and seminar libraries are listed by country.

Who's Who in Special Libraries (Special Libraries Association, 1700 18th St., NW, Washington, DC 20009; 202/234–4700) $50/nonmembers, free/members, published each autumn. Includes alphabetical and geographical lists of special libraries.

Directory of Special Libraries and Information Centers (Gale Research, Inc., 835 Penobscot Bldg., Detroit, MI 48226; phone: 800/233–4253) $415, 2,230 pages, 1992. Provides comprehensive information on 20,850 information centers, archives, and special and research libraries in the U.S., Canada, and elsewhere. It's a good source for identifying libraries at which you might like to work and for learning about them.

New Special Libraries (Gale Research, Inc., 835 Penobscot Bldg., Detroit, MI 48226; phone: 800/233–4253) $360, 150 pages, 1993. Furnishes comprehensive information on new special libraries in the U.S., Canada, and elsewhere.

Subject Directory of Special Libraries (Gale Research, Inc., 835 Penobscot Bldg., Detroit, MI 48226; phone: 800/233–4253) $675/three volumes, 1992. These volumes contain the same material as the Directory of Special Libraries and Information Centers, which is described immediately above, but rearranged into 14 subject areas in three volumes, available individually: Business, Government, and Law Libraries, $265; Computers, Engineering, and Science Libraries, $265; Health Sciences Libraries, $265.

Directory of Federal Libraries (Oryx Press, 4041 N. Central, Phoenix, AZ 85012–3397; phone: 800/279–6799) $97.50, 1993, 383 pages. Includes close to 3,000 special and general libraries, presidential and national libraries, as well as federal libraries in technical centers, hospitals, and penal institutions. Includes each library's administrator and selected staff.

Directory of the Medical Library Association (MLA, 6 N. Michigan Ave., Suite 300, Chicago, IL 60602; phone: 312/419–9094) $150/nonmembers, free/members, published each September.

Salary surveys

MLA Salary Survey (Medical Library Association, 6 N. Michigan Ave., Suite 300, Chicago, IL 60602; phone: 312/419–9094) $52/nonmembers, $26/members. Triennial, last published April 1992. Association members: medical librarians/health information professionals in medical libraries in hospitals, medical schools, and other institutions. These are cross referenced by region, type of institution, position, gender, and number of people supervised.

State Library Agencies Financial Survey (The Council of State Governments, 3560 Iron Works Pike, P.O. Box 11910, Lexington, KY 40578–1910; phones: 800/800–1910, 606/231–1939) $12.50 plus $3.75 shipping and handling, 1992, 25 pages. Includes tables on salaries, federal and state expenditures, and appropriations.

Regional job sources

Job ads in print

MPLA Newsletter (Mountain Plains Library Association, I.D. Weeks Library, University of South Dakota, Vermillion, SD 57069; phone: 605/677–6082) bimonthly, $20/nonmember annual subscription (U.S.), $26/foreign, free/members. States covered: Arizona, Colorado, Kansas, Montana, Nebraska, Nevada, North Dakota, Oklahoma, South Dakota, Utah, and Wyoming. Jobs listed under "Joblist." Three or four job ads per issue.

Job services

Drexel University College of Information Studies Jobline (c/o Placement Office Assistant, College of Information Studies, Drexel University, Philadelphia, PA 19104; phone: 215/895–2478). Call 215/895–1672 for a recording of job openings. States include: Delaware, New Jersey, and Pennsylvania. Call 215/895–1048 for job openings in the information and computer systems field.

Jobline (Mountain Plains Library Association, I.D. Weeks Library, University of South Dakota, Vermillion, SD 57069; phone: 605/677–6082). This is a 24–hour tape recording of open public and private library positions in Arizona, Colorado, Kansas, Montana, Nebraska, Nevada, North Dakota, Oklahoma, South Dakota, Utah, and Wyoming. Updated each Friday. Job hotline numbers are in operation Monday through Thursday 5 p.m. to 8 a.m. and runs through the weekend from Friday at 5 p.m. to 8 a.m. Monday morning. Call: 605/677–5757, 800/356–7820 (from only within states listed).

New England Library Jobline (GSLIS, New England Library Jobline, Simmons College, 300 The Fenway, Boston, MA 02115). Call 617/738–3148 to hear a 24–hour tape recording of library and information science positions requiring an MLS degree. Updated each Wednesday.

Pacific Northwest Library Association Jobline (PNLA Jobline, c/o Graduate School of Library and Information Sciences, FM–30, University of Washington, Seattle, WA 98195). Call 206/543–2890 for a recording of available positions.

New York Chapter Special Libraries Association Hotline (c/o David Jank, The New York Public Library, 4th Floor, 20 W. 53rd St., New York, NY 10019). Call 212/740–2007 for a recording with job vacancies in New York, New Jersey, and Connecticut.

State job sources

Job services and newsletters

Many state library associations publish newsletters with job announcements in them or operate 24–hour job hotlines with tape recorded job announcements. American Libraries, the first periodical listed under "Library Services," frequently publishes a list of all the state library association job hotlines (if a job hotline has been disconnected, contact the American Library Association to get the new phone number or address). The following state library associations operate a job hotline or publish a periodical with job ads or announcements:

Arizona Library Jobline (Research Division, Room 300, Arizona Department of Library, Archives, and Public Records, 1700 W. Washington, Phoenix, AZ 85007). Call 602/275–2325 for taped job announcements.

British Columbia Library Association Jobline (BCLA, #110—6545 Bonsor Ave., Buraby, British Columbia V5H 1H3, Canada; phone: 604/430–9633). Call 604/430–6411 for a recording of positions in British Columbia.

California Library Association Jobline (CLA, Suite 300, 717 K St., Sacramento, CA 95814–3477; phone: 916/447–8541). Call 916/443–1222 or 818/797–4602 for tape recording of job openings.

California Media and Library Educators Association Job Hotline (CMLEA, Suite 142, 1499 Old Bayshore Highway, Burlingame, CA 94010; phone: 415/692–2350). Call 415/697–8832 for taped job announcements.

San Andreas–San Francisco Bay Special Libraries Association Job Hotline For a tape recording of job openings call 415/856–2140, or use these electronic mail services: Dialmail or Ontyme.

Southern California Chapter, Special Libraries Association Job Hotline (c/o Paul Morton, Southern California Edison, 2244 Walnut Grove Blvd., Mail Stop G–55, G.O. 1, Rosemead, CA 91770; phone: 818/302–8966). Call 818/795–2145 for a tape recording of job openings.

Colorado State Library Jobline (Jobline, 201 E. Colfax, Denver, CO 80203; phone: 303/866–6732). Call 303/866–6741 for job openings. Updated weekly.

Connecticut Library Association Jobline (CLA Jobline, Connecticut State Library, 638 Prospect Ave., Hartford, CT 06105). Call 203/645–8090 for a 24–hour recording updated weekly.

Metropolitan Washington (D.C.) Library Jobline. Nobody, and we mean nobody, can identify for us who actually operates this job hotline, but it still is in operation. Call 202/962–3712 to hear the Jobline recording.

Bound & Gagged reprinted by permission of Tribune Media Services.
Copyright 1993. All rights reserved.

Delaware Library Association Jobline. Call 302/739–4748 extension 69 (800/282–8696 only within Delaware) for job openings. Delaware positions are also listed on the New Jersey, Pennsylvania, and Maryland joblines.

Florida Jobline (State Library of Florida, R.A. Gray Building, Tallahassee, FL 32301; phone: 904/487–2651). Call 904/488–5232 for job openings.

Illinois Library Hotline (Illinois Library Association, Suite 301, 33 W. Grand Ave., Chicago, IL 60610; phone: 312/644–1896). Call 312/828–0930 for a recording of job openings for professional staff. Call 312/828–9198 for a recording of job openings for support staff. Includes positions with special libraries.

Indiana Statewide Library Jobline (1100 W. 42nd St., Indianapolis, IN 46208; phone: 317/926–6561). Call or write for printout of job openings. Direct access to the *Jobline* is available through the RBBS Computer Bulletin Board, 317/924–9584.

Iowa Library Joblist (Doris Collette, Editor, State Library of Iowa, Historical Building, Des Moines, IA 50319; phone: 515/281–6788) monthly. Contact for rates.

Maryland Library Association Jobline (MLA, 400 Cathedral St., Baltimore, MD 21201; phone: 410/685–5760, Call 410/685–5760 for job listings 24–hours, 7 days a week.

Michigan Library Association (1000 Long Blvd., Lansing, MI 48911; phone: 517/694–6615). This 24–hour Job Hotline recording is changed on Monday afternoons. Call 517/694–7440.

Missouri Library Association Jobline (1306 Business 63 South, Columbia, MO 65201). Job Hotline recording changed every other Friday: 314/442–6590

Nebraska Job Hotline (Nebraska Library Commission, The Atrium, 1200 N St., Suite 120, Lincoln, NE 68508–2023). Call 402/471–2045 for a recording of job vacancies. In Nebraska only, call 800/742–7691.

New Jersey Library Association Job Hotline (P.O. Box 1534, Trenton, NJ 08607). $10/nonmembers, free/members. Call 609/695–2121 for 24–hour recording of job openings. Updated each Tuesday.

New York Library Association Jobline (252 Hudson Ave., Albany, NY 12210) biweekly, $40/nonmember six–month subscription, $25/nonmember three–month subscription, $25/member six–month subscription, $15/member three–month subscription. Anywhere from 8 to 20 job ads for library positions in New York and surrounding areas.

New York Chapter Special Libraries Association Hotline (c/o David Jank, The New York Public Library, 4th Floor, 20 W. 53rd St., New York, NY 10019). Call 212/740–2007 for recording of jobs in New York, New Jersey, and Connecticut.

North Carolina Jobline (North Carolina Information Network, State Library of North Carolina, 109 E. Jones St., Suite 208, Raleigh, NC 27601–2807; phone: 919/733–2570) Call 919/733–6410 for recording or use Western Union's EASYLINK, NCJOBS for computer viewing of job openings.

Jobline (Cleveland Area Metropolitan Library System, 3645 Warrenville Center Rd., Suite 116, Shaker Heights, OH 44122). For jobs only in northeast Ohio, call 216/921–4702 24–hours a day.

Oklahoma Department of Libraries Jobline (Department phone: 405/521–2502). Call 405/521–4202 for recording of 5 to 10 jobs 8 a.m. to 5 p.m. on weekdays, and all day on weekends. Updated on fifteenth and last day of month.

Oregon Library/Media Jobline (Oregon State Library, State Library Bldg., Salem, OR 97310; phone: 503/378–4243). Call 503/585–2232 for job recording.

Pennsylvania Cooperative Job Hotline (Agency phone: 717/233–3113). Call 717/234–4646 for job openings.

RILA Bulletin (Rhode Island Library Association, R. Stoddard, Government Publications Office, University Library, University of Rhode Island, Kingstown, RI 02881) nine issues/year. For copies, send self–addressed, stamped envelopes. Jobs listed under "Jobline."

University of South Carolina College of Library and Information Science Jobline (Admissions and Placement Coordinator, CLIS, University of South Carolina, Columbia, SC 29208). Call 803/777–8443 for job openings.

Texas State Library Jobline (Sarah Woelfel, Texas State Library, P.O. Box 12927 Capital Station, Austin, TX 78711; phone: 512/463–5447). Call 512/463–5470 for a 24–hour recording of job openings, which is changed weekly.

VLA Jobline (Virginia Library Association, 669 South Washington St., Alexandria, VA 22314). Call 703/519–8027 for an average of five to 10 job recordings. Updated on the 1st and 15th of every month.

West Virginia. Call 717/234–4646 for job openings.

Media and the arts

For an extensive list of job sources for the media and the arts that include some government jobs as well as private and non–profit sector positions, also see the ***Professional's Private Sector Job Finder*** *and the* ***Non–Profits' Job Finder****.*

Job ads in print

Job Information Letter (National Association of Government Communicators, 669 S. Washington St., Alexandria, VA 22314; phone: 703/519–3902) biweekly, $50/nonmember annual subscription plus send 26 self-addressed stamped #10 envelopes (two ounce postage) for NAGC to mail the issues to you; free/members. Typical issue lists about 30 to 35 federal government positions plus photocopies of 50 or more classified ads for editorial and art positions for several metropolitan areas. Also identifies over a dozen job hotlines and referral services.

Monthly Mailer (Women in Government Relations, 1029 Vermont, NW, Suite 510, Washington, DC 20005; phone: 202/347–5432) monthly, $150/annual subscription. Around 35 job ads appear for government relations positions in the public and private sector.

PR Marcom Jobs West – Southern California (Rachel P.R. Services, 513 Wilshire Blvd., Suite 238, Santa Monica, CA 90401; phones: 800/874–8577, within California call 310/326–2661) biweekly, $35/three–month subscription (first class mail), $45/three–month subscription (sent to you via fax). Ten to 20 percent of the 50 job announcements, virtually all for positions in Southern California, are for positions in government or for government relations positions with private companies.

PR Marcom Jobs West – Northern California (Rachel P.R. Services, 298 Fourth Avenue, Suite 344, San Francisco, CA 94118; phones: 800/874–8577, within California call 415/666–0481) biweekly, $35/three–month subscription (first class mail), $45/three–month subscription (sent to you via fax). Ten to 20 percent of the 50 job announcements, virtually all for positions in Northern California and the Pacific Northwest, are for positions in government or for government relations positions with private companies.

PR Marcom Jobs East (Rachel P.R. Services, 208 E. 51st St., Suite 1600, New York, NY 10022; phone: 212/962–9100) biweekly, $35/three–month subscription (first class mail), $45/three–month subscription (sent to you via fax). Ten to 20 percent of the 50 job openings for positions in New York, New Jersey, Boston, Washington DC, and surrounding states, are for positions in government or for government relations positions with private companies.

PR Marcom Jobs Mid–America (Rachel P.R. Services, 513 Wilshire Blvd., Suite 238, Santa Monica, CA 90401; phones: 800/874–8577, within California call 310/326–2661) biweekly, $35/three–month subscription (first class mail), $45/three–month subscription (sent to you via fax). Of the approximately 50 job openings for positions in the Midwest, Southeast, South, and Rocky Mountain regions, ten to 20 percent are for positions in government or for government relations positions with private companies.

WESTAF's Artjob (236 Montezume Ave., Santa Fe, NM 87501; phone: 505/988–1166) biweekly, U.S.: $36/annual subscription, $24/six–month subscription; foreign: $45/annual, $27/six–month. Generally a number of government positions are included in the 100+ job vacancies in arts administration, performance, production/technical, and academia.

Government and Military Video (PSN Publications, 2 Park Ave., Suite 1920, New York, NY 10016; phone: 212/779–1919) monthly, free to qualified professionals. The "Classifieds" section usually has three or four positions in broadcast engineering.

Documentary Editing (Association for Documentary Editing, c/o Department of History, University of South Carolina, Columbia, SC 29208; phone: 803/777–6526) quarterly, available only to members, free. Four or five jobs for documentary editors appear under "Positions Available."

See also ***APCO Bulletin*** listed under "Public safety."

Job Services

Jobphone (Editorial Freelance Association, P.O. Box 2050, Madison Square Station, New York, NY 10159; phone: 212/677–3357). Anybody can call the "Jobphone," 212/929–5411, to hear a recording that briefly describes about 40 freelance writing, editing, proofreading, and translating opportunities. Listings are updated Tuesday and Thursday. Only EFA members who subscribe to this service can call another phone number to get details (such as pay and whom to contact) on the listed jobs. Members can subscribe to "Jobphone" for $20/year. Write for membership rates (they're too complicated to explain here).

CU Career Connection (University of Colorado, Campus Box 133, Boulder, CO 80309–0133; phone: 303/492–4127) $30/two–month fee entitles you to a "passcode" which unlocks this job hotline. You need a touch–tone phone to call and request the field in which you are interested in hearing job openings. The hotline is turned off Monday through Friday, 2 to 4 p.m. for daily updating.

The Agency Connection (Rachel P.R. Services, 513 Wilshire Blvd., Suite 238, Santa Monica, CA 90401; phones: 800/874–8577, within California call 310/326–2661) monthly, $15/includes your ad for one month, $25/two consecutive months. This is a newsletter of available talent sent to the general managers of over 250 top public relations agencies, some of which seek government relations professionals for private companies. Call or send for an application which you submit with a 30 to 50 word ad describing your work experience, salary range, job sought, contact information, and whatever else you can fit in. If you wish, the Agency Connection will write your ad for you at no extra charge. You may also request a blind ad at no extra charge. Specify whether you want to be included in the East or West edition.

Directories

Locations (Association of Film Commissioners International, c/o Utah Film Commission, 324 South State, Suite 500, Salt Lake City, UT 84114; phone: 801/538–0540) semiannual, free. Includes names, addresses, and phone numbers for municipal and state film commissioners as well as film commissioners abroad.

Madison Avenue Handbook: The Image Makers Source (Peter Glenn Publications, 42 West 38th St., Suite 802, New York, NY 10018; phones: 800/223–1254, 212/869–2020) $45, published every April. Includes directory of state and local film commissions for the U.S. and possessions as well as for Canada and other foreign countries.

The Source (Rachel P.R. Services, 513 Wilshire Blvd., Suite 238, Santa Monica, CA 90401; phones: 310/326–2661 inside California; 800/874–8577 elsewhere in the U.S.) $45, 30 pages, published annually with quarterly updates included. Provides details on hundreds of job sources in public relations, journalism, advertising, and marketing: job banks, trade publications, job hotlines, free–lance cooperatives, executive recruiters, employment agencies, and associations. Subscribing to this directory makes you a lifelong member of their *Job Bank Gratis* resume referral service. Contact Rachel P.R. Services for further details.

The New Careers Directory: Internships and Professional Opportunities in Technology and Social Change (Student Pugwash USA, 1638 R St., NW, Suite 32, Washington, DC 20009; phone: 202/328–6555) $18, $10/students (add $3 shipping), last published in 1993. Offers full details on where and how to apply for internships and entry–level jobs in communications with socially responsible organizations.

Mental health

*Also see listings under "Public administration," "Public health and health care," and "Social services." Also see the **Professional's Private Sector Job Finder** and the **Non-Profits' Job Finder.***

Job ads in print

The APA Monitor (American Psychological Association, 750 First St., NE, Washington, DC 20002–4242; phone: 202/336–5500) $25/nonmember annual subscription (U.S.), $37/foreign, free/members. Jobs listed under "Position Openings." From 400 to 800 job ads for psychologists and support staff grace the pages of a typical issue.

Psychiatric News (American Psychiatric Association, 1400 K St., NW, Washington, DC 20005; phone: 202/682–6000) bimonthly, $40/nonmember annual subscription (U.S.), $60/foreign, included in membership package. Jobs listed under "Classified Notices." Between 300 and 350 job ads in the typical issue.

Archives of General Psychiatry (American Medical Association, Circulation Dept., 515 N. State St., Chicago, IL 60610; phones: 800/621–8335, 312/464–5000) monthly, $90/annual subscription, $125/foreign, call about special rates for residents and medical students. About 20 positions, including Veterans Administration, are listed under "Classified Advertising."

National Council News (National Council of Community Mental Health Centers, Suite 320, 12300 Twinbrook Pkwy, Rockville, MD 20852; phone: 301/984–6200) 11 issues/year, $25/nonmember annual subscription, included in dues. Jobs listed under "JOBank." Typical issue features 20 to 30 job ads for social workers and counselors, psychiatrists, psychologists, clinical workers, and administrative positions.

AMHA Newsletter (Association of Mental Health Administrators, 60 Revere Drive, Suite 500, Northbrook, IL 60062; phone: 708/480–9626) semimonthly, $46/six month nonmember subscription, free/members. 4 or 5 job ads appear under "Executive Classified Service" for administrative positions in behavioral health facilities.

AMHCA Advocate (American Mental Health Counselors' Association, 5999 Stevenson Ave., Alexandria, VA 22304; phones: 800/326–2642, 703/823–9800) ten issues/year, $25/nonmember annual subscription, included in membership package. Jobs listed under "Classifieds." About four job ads in the usual issue.

Job service

Psychiatric Placement Service (American Psychiatric Association, 1400 K St., NW, Washington, DC 20005; phone: 202/682–6000) free. Obtain an application form and submit it with your resume. After being matched with a vacancy, both the job seeker and the potential employer are notified. Resumes are kept on file indefinitely.

Directories

Mental Health Directory (Superintendent of Documents, Government Printing Office, P.O. Box 371954, Pittsburgh, PA 15250; phone: 301/443–2792) $23. Stock number: 017–024–01419–2. Prepared by the National Institute of Mental Health, this directory includes hospitals, group homes, and halfway houses by city and state.

APA Membership Register (American Psychological Association, 750 First St., NE, Washington, DC 20002–4242; phone: 202/336–5500) $35/nonmembers, $22.50/members, published every year. Most recent edition, 1992. Provides names and phone numbers of APA members.

APA Membership Directory (American Psychological Association, 750 First St., NE, Washington, DC 20002–4242; phone: 202/336–5500) $70/nonmembers, $50/members, published every four years. Most recent edition, July 1993. Provides names, phone numbers, and educational backgrounds of APA members.

National Registry of Community Mental Health Services (National Council of Community Mental Health Centers, Suite 320, 12300 Twinbrook Pkwy., Rockville, MD 20852; phone: 301/317–8912) $59/nonmembers,

$29/members, December 1991. This directory contains information on over 1,900 agencies in the U.S. and possessions.

AMHA Membership Directory (Association of Mental Health Administrators, 60 Revere, Suite 500, Northbrook, IL 60062; phone: 708/480–9626) contact them for price. This directory of mental health administrators was first published in August 1991.

Association of State and Provincial Psychology Boards Membership Roster (Association of State & Provencial Psychology Boards, P.O. Box 4389, Montgomery, AL 36103; phone: 205/832–4580) $4, prepaid. Lists addresses and phone numbers of state and provincial psychology licensing boards in the U.S. and Canada.

Salary survey

Survey of Salary Benefits and Staffing Patterns of Community Mental Health Providers (National Council of Community Mental Health Centers, Suite 320, 12300 Twinbrook Pkwy, Rockville, MD 20852; phone: 301/317–8912) $69/nonmembers, $49/members, published in December 1991. Based on a sample of over 500 community mental health providers, this survey gives salary and fringe benefit figures by region, service area type, and nationally.

Parks and recreation

Also see listings under "Environment" and "Forestry and horticulture."

Job ads in print

Park and Recreation Opportunities Job Bulletin (National Recreation and Park Association, 2775 South Quincy St., Suite 300, Arlington, VA 22206; phone: 703/820–4940) 22 issues/year, individual copies available to nonmembers and members for $5 prepaid; annual subscription available only to members, $30. Typical issue includes 40 to 60 jobs by geographic area in the U.S. and foreign positions.

Opportunities (Natural Science for Youth Foundation, 130 Azalea Dr., Roswell, GA 30075; phones: 800/992–6793, 404/594–9367) bimonthly, $35/annual subscription, $10/single issue, free/ members. "Positions available " lists details on 45 to 70 jobs for naturalists, curators, raptor rehabilitators, and administrative positions, largely at nature centers.

Workamper News (201 Hiram Rd., Heber Springs, AR 72543; phone: 800/446–5627) bimonthly, contact for current subscription rates. Lists over 300 different employers who are actively seeking employees for public parks

and campgrounds as well as commercially–operated parks, resorts, campgrounds with positions available at all levels, from housekeeping and grounds maintenance to upper management.

Parks and Grounds Management (P.O. Box 1936, Appleton, WI 54913; phone: 414/733–2301) monthly, $20/annual subscription (U.S.), $25/Canada, $33/elsewhere. Two or three ads for administrators of large outdoor grounds such as parks, golf courses, and campuses appear under "Classifieds."

Golf Course Management (Golf Course Superintendents Association of America, 1421 Research Park Dr., Lawrence, KS 66049–3859; phones: 800/422–6383, 913/832–4466) monthly; $30/annual nonmember subscription, free/members. Jobs listed under "Classifieds." About eight ads including municipal golf courses, appear in a typical issue.

Employment Referral Service (Golf Course Superintendents Association of America, 1421 Research Park Dr., Lawrence, KS 66049–3859; phones: 800/422–6383, 913/832–4466) Available only to members for $10/six months. Typical issue lists ten job openings in golf course management and landscape architecture.

Marine Technology Society Currents (Marine Technology Society, 1828 K St., NW, Suite 906, Washington, DC 20036; phone: 202/775–5966) bimonthly, included in dues ($55). Two or three ads for various marine type positions appear near the back of the newsletter.

Job service

NRPA/SCHOLE Network (National Recreation and Park Association, 2775 South Quincy St., Suite 300, Arlington ,VA 22206; phone: 703/820–4940) $75/annual nonmember individual's subscription, $225/nonmember agencies, $50/member individuals, $150/member agencies, updated biweekly. This computer information and communications network includes the job vacancies advertised in the NRPA's Park and Recreation Opportunities Job Bulletin described above under "Job ads in print."

Directories

The National Association of State Park Directors recommends that job applicants contact the state park agency for the state in which they are interested. For a list of state park directors, write to the National Association of State Park Directors (c/o Ney Landrum, Executive Director, 126 Mill Branch Rd., Tallahassee, FL 32312) or see The National Directory of State Agencies, State Administrative Officials Classified by Function described in Chapter 3.

Special Recreation Inc., [for people with disabilities] (Special Recreation, Inc., 362 Koser Ave., Iowa City, IA 52246–3038; phone: 319/337–7578 $49.95/nonmembers, free/members, 1992 edition. Lists organizations that deal with recreation for people who have disabilities.

Directory of Natural Science Centers (Natural Science for Youth Foundation, 130 Azalea Dr., Roswell, GA 30075; phones: 800/992–6793, 404/594–9367) $78.50/nonmembers, $58.50/members, published in 1990 and every four years thereafter. This 600 page tome gives details on over 1,350 nature centers.

Society of Municipal Arborists Membership List (Society of Municipal Arborists, c/o Office of the City Forester, 6801 Delmar Blvd., University City, MO 63130; phone: 314/862–1711) available only to members, included in $40 annual dues, published every March.

Who's Who in Golf Course Management (Golf Course Superintendents Association of America, 1421 Research Park Dr., Lawrence, KS 66049–3859; phones: 800/422–6383, 913/832–4466) free/members only, published each March.

Summer Jobs '94 (Peterson's Guides; available from Planning/Communications' catalog at the end of this book) $15.95, 344 pages, annual. Describes over 20,000 summer job openings in the United States and Canada with camps, national parks, environmental programs, resorts, amusement parks, expeditions, theaters, and government. Each detailed employer description includes salary and benefits, employer background, profile of employees, and whom to contact to apply. Includes category, employer, and job title indexes.

Personnel/human resources

Also see listings under "Public Administration."

Job ads in print

HR News (Society for Human Resource Management, 606 N. Washington St., Alexandria, VA 22314; phone: 703/548–3440) monthly, $39/nonmember subscription, included in membership package. Jobs listed under " HR News Employment Service." Contains 30 to 35 job ads in a typical issue.

Personnel Journal (A. C. Croft, Inc., Suite B–2, 245 Fischer Ave., Costa Mesa, CA 92626; phone: 714/751–1883) monthly; $55/annual subscription. Jobs listed under "Classified." Typical issue features five to 12 jobs ads, mostly in the private sector.

IPMA News (International Personnel Management Association, 1617 Duke St., Alexandria, VA 22314; phone: 703/549–7100) monthly, $21/nonmember annual subscription, free/members. Jobs listed under "Recruiter Service." Typical issue carries about 4 job ads for personnel and public administration.

National Public Employer Labor Relations Newsletter (National Public Employer Labor Relations Association, 1620 I St. NW, Washington, DC 20006; phone: 202/296–2230) monthly, free/members only; membership limited to labor–manager and personnel professionals in local, state, and federal government. Just a few jobs are listed under "Positions Available."

Job service

CU Career Connection (University of Colorado, Campus Box 133, Boulder, CO 80309–0133; phone: 303/492–4127) $30/two–month fee entitles you to a "passcode" which unlocks this job hotline. You need a touch–tone phone to call and request the field in which you are interested in hearing job openings. The hotline is turned off Monday through Friday, 2 to 4 p.m. for daily updating.

Directories

Who's Who in Human Resources (Society for Human Resource Management, 606 N. Washington St., Alexandria, VA 22314; phone: 703/548–3440) free/members only, published annually.

IPMA Membership Directory (International Personnel Management Association, 1617 Duke St., Alexandria, VA 22314; phone: 703/549–7100) $150/nonmembers, free/members, published annually.

State Personnel Offices: Roles and Functions (The Council of State Governments, 3560 Iron Works Pike, P.O. Box 11910, Lexington, KY 40578–1910; phone: 800/800–1910) $35 plus $3.75/shipping, 110 pages, 1991; new edition expected in 1994. Includes roster of state personnel officials.

NPELRA Membership Directory (National Public Employer Labor Relations Association, 1620 I St., NW, Washington, DC 20006; phone: 202/296–2230) Available only as part of membership package. Membership limited to labor–manager and personnel professionals in local and state government.

Planning

Also see listings under "Community and economic development," "Housing," and "Public administration."

Job ads in print

JobMart (American Planning Association, 1313 E. 60th St., Chicago, IL 60637; phone: 312/955–9100) 22 issues/year, $75/annual nonmember subscription; $30/first class mail member annual subscription (U.S.), $40/Canada, $70/elsewhere; $20/bulk rate member annual subscription (U.S. only); write for salary–based dues schedule. Spring issues include job ads for summer internships. With over 800 public agency and consulting firm jobs listed annually, the typical issue features from 20 to 50 ads itemized by state.

Planning (American Planning Association, 1313 E. 60th St., Chicago, IL 60637; phone: 312/955–9100) monthly, $40/annual subscription (U.S.), $50/elsewhere, free/members. Write for salary–based dues schedule. Generally you'll find three to eight display ads, generally for job higher–level positions with public agencies.

Most of APA's state chapters publish newsletters that include timely job announcements. Many of these chapters allow nonmember subscriptions or chapter–only membership which includes the chapter newsletter. Many chapters also publish inexpensive rosters of planners within their state. Contact APA for names, addresses, and phone numbers of the hard–working presidents of the state chapters you wish to reach.

Regional Reporter (National Association of Regional Councils, Suite 1300, 1700 K St., NW, Washington, DC 20006; phone: 202/457–0710) monthly, available only to members. Jobs listed under "Job Opportunities." Four job ads in typical issue.

Historic Preservation News (National Trust for Historic Preservation, 1785 Massachusetts Ave., NW, Washington, DC 20036; phone: 202/673–4075) free/members only; membership is $15/year. Five job ads for positions in the historic preservation field are listed under "Marketplace."

URISA and AM/FM Marketplace (Urban and Regional Information Systems Association, 900 Second St., NE, Suite 304, Washington, DC 20002; phone: 202/289–1685) monthly, free/members only. Typical issue includes about 20 to 25 positions, largely in geographic information system management, operation, and design.

GIS World (155 E. Boardwalk Drive, Suite 250, Fort Collins, CO 80525; phone: 303/223–4848) monthly, $72/annual U.S. subscription, $89/Canada, $108/elsewhere. Under "Classified Ads—Positions Available" appear five to ten job vacancies for geographic information system operators, managers, programmers, and engineers.

ACSM Bulletin (American Congress on Surveying and Mapping, 5410 Grosvenor Ln., Bethesda, MD 20814; phone: 301/493–0200) bimonthly, $75/annual nonmember subscription (U.S.), $85/foreign, free to members. About six openings for land surveyors, cartographers, and geographic information system specialists appear under "Professional Directory." The November/December issue is a directory that lists companies who are sustaining members of ACSM, see description below under "Directories."

Photogrammetric Engineering & Remote Sensing (American Society for Photogrammetry & Remote Sensing, 5410 Grosvenor Ln., Suite 210, Bethesda, MD 20814–2160; phone: 301/493–0290) monthly, $120/annual nonmember subscription, $65/members. Job openings for GIS/LIS specialists, computer specialists, and engineers and scientists in the surveying and mapping sciences appear under "Classified."

AAG Newsletter (Association of American Geographers, 1710 16th St., NW, Washington, DC 20009; phone: 202/234–1450) monthly, free/members only. From 25 to 50 positions, primarily academic, are listed under "Jobs in Geography."

Bulletin (Society of Government Economists, 9333 Creekview Drive, Laurel, MD 20708; phone: 202/254–6639) 11 issues/year, free/members only; $25/annual dues. Jobs listed under "Job Announcements." About half of the five or six job announcements are for federal positions.

Job Openings for Economists (American Economic Association, 2014 Broadway, Suite 305, Nashville, TN 37203; phone: 615/322–2595) bimonthly, $25/annual nonmember subscription (U.S.), $32.50/foreign, $15/AEA regular members, $7.50/AEA junior members. Among the 150+ jobs in a typical issue are just four or five government positions, primarily federal.

Job Placement Bulletin (National Economics Association, School of Business, University of Michigan, Ann Arbor, MI 48109–1234; phone: 313/763–0121) available only to members. About eight jobs for economists appear in typical issue.

Practicing Anthropology (Society for Applied Anthropology, P.O. Box 24083, Oklahoma City, OK 73124; phone: 405/843–5113) quarterly, $20/nonmember annual subscription (U.S.), $40/foreign, free/members. Two or three display ads for anthropologists and sociologists including planning positions are in the typical issue.

Bulletin of the SAA (Society for American Archaeology, The Railway Express Building, 900 2nd Street, NE Suite 12, Washington, DC 20006; phone: 202/789–8200) five issues/year, $15/annual nonmember subscription, included in dues. About six ads for archaeologists and anthropologists are listed under "Positions Open."

Job service

National Registry for Economists (c/o Illinois Department of Employment Security, 401 S. State St., Chicago, IL 60605; phone: 312/793–4904; operated in conjunction with the Allied Social Science Association) free. Request application form. Completed forms kept on file for one year. The Registry submits forms of qualified registrants to employers seeking economists. Employers then contact registrants directly.

Directories

American Planning Association Membership Directory (American Planning Association, 1313 E. 60th St., Chicago, IL 60637; phone: 312/955–9100) $36.95 plus $4.95/shipping, published in even–numbered years, although at this time it is unknown if APA will publish it again after 1992. Alphabetical listing of 26,000 professional planners and planning commissioners plus geographical and specialty indexes.

AICP Roster (American Institute of Certified Planners, c/o American Planning Association, 1776 Massachusetts Ave., NW, Washington, DC 20036; phone: 202/872–0611) $30/nonmember, $20/APA member, free/AICP members, issued in even–numbered years. AICP is an institute within the American Planning Association. This directory lists the 7,000+ AICP members alphabetically and by city within states. Although AICP membership is achieved by passing a very difficult test, it does not indicate that AICP members are better qualified nor more competent than other professional planners. It does mean, however, that they are dedicated to their profession and abide by a pretty demanding code of ethics. Since titles are listed, this is a good source to identify directors of municipal and county planning departments and related departments.

MPO Directory (National Association of Regional Councils, Suite 1300, 1700 K St., NW, Washington, DC 20006; phone: 202/457–0710) $35/nonmembers, $25/members, 1992. Lists metropolitan planning agencies and organizations.

Directory of Regional Councils (National Association of Regional Councils, Suite 1300, 1700 K St., NW, Washington, DC 20006; phone: 202/457–0710) $100/nonmembers, first copy free/members.

Directory, National Association of County Planners (c/o National Association of Counties, 440 First St., NW, Washington, DC 20001; phone: 202/393–6226) free/members, 25¢ per name/nonmembers. Lists about 200 county planners around the country.

Directory of Black Economists (National Economic Association, School of Business, University of Michigan, Ann Arbor, MI 48109–1234; phone: 313/763–0121) $25/nonmembers, free/members, published in even–numbered years.

ACSM November/December Bulletin (American Congress on Surveying and Mapping, 5410 Grosvenor Ln., Bethesda, MD 20814; phone: 301/493–0200) $13. This listing of companies that are ACSM members gives addresses, phone numbers, descriptions for each company, and the products and services they supply.

ASPRS Directory of Mapping Sciences (American Society for Photogrammetry & Remote Sensing, 5410 Grosvenor Ln., Suite 210, Bethesda, MD 20814–2160; phone: 301/493–0290) $30/nonmembers, free/members, published each May.

Salary surveys

Planners' Salaries and Employment Trends (American Planning Association, 1313 E. 60th St., Chicago, IL 60637; phone: 312/955–9100) $20/general public and APA members, $10/subscribers to APA's Planning Advisory Service, 1992. Next edition expected in 1995.

NARC Salary Survey (National Association of Regional Councils, Suite 1300, 1700 K St., NW, Washington, DC 20006; phone: 202/457–0710) $10/nonmembers, free/members, published every two years in February. Covers top salaries and benefits of high ranking positions with regional councils.

Cartography and Geographic Information Systems: A Career Guide (American Congress on Surveying and Mapping, 5410 Grosvenor Ln., Bethesda, MD 20814; phone: 301/493–0200) free, published in odd–numbered years. Includes a one–page summary of estimated salary ranges.

Political industry

Note: Jobs in political campaigns and with campaign consultants usually are found via word of mouth. The magazines and job service listed here represent nascent attempts to move beyond networking. This is one field in which directories are an extremely valuable job–quest aid.

Job ads in print

Roll Call (Levitt Communications, 900 Second St., NE, Washington, DC 20002; phone: 202/289–4900) twice weekly, $195/annual subscription. Among the 15+ job ads under "Roll Call Classifieds—Employment," are positions with political campaigns (during the campaign season) and jobs with non–profit organizations, political organizations, and private industry that require a knowledge of politics and Capitol Hill: lobbyists, government affairs/relations directors, legislative assistants, press directors, etc. The "Hill Climbers" column announces when legislative staff leave their jobs. It's a good source to learn about pending vacancies.

Campaigns and Elections Magazine (1511 K St., NW, Suite 1020, Washington, DC 20005; phone: 800/888–5767) bimonthly, $29.95 annual subscription. The Political Jobline ad appears monthly along with personalized ads of job seekers. The February issue includes the "Political Pages," a thorough directory of all facets of the political industry.

Walnut Cover reprinted by special permission of King Features Syndicate. Copyright 1993.

Job services

Campaigns and Elections Magazine Political Jobline (1511 K St., NW, Suite 1020, Washington, DC 20005; phone: 800/888–5767) $95/annually. Submit a copy of your resume along with this service's resume form and through a database you are matched to job openings sent in by employers. When a match is made the employer is responsible for contacting the job seeker. Resumes are kept in the database for up to one year.

Democratic Job Bank and Talent Pool (Democratic National Committee, 430 S. Capitol St., SE, Washington, DC 20003; phone: 202/863–8115) free. Submit completed application form to DNC. This service matches job candidates with Democratic Senate and Congressional campaigns around the country. There is no comparable service for any other political party.

Internships for College Students Interested in Law, Medicine and Politics (Graduate Group, 86 Norwood Rd., West Hartford, CT 06117; phones: 203/232–3100, 203/236–5570) $27.50, published annually. Includes information on hundreds of actual internship opportunities with government agencies and in politics.

Directories

Political Resource Directory (Political Resources, Inc., P.O. Box 4278, Burlington, VT 05406; phone: 800/423–2677) $95 plus $3.50 postage if not prepaid. Published each January, this 400–page book is the official directory of the American Association of Political Consultants on this $2 billion industry. Over 4,100 individuals and 2,800 organizations are listed with party affiliation and a description of services. Entries are listed alphabetically with a specialization index and principals index. Also listed are federal and state boards of election and state Republican and Democratic party offices which are also potential employers.

Political Resource Directory (Gale Research, Inc., 835 Penobscot Bldg., Detroit, MI 48226; phones: 800/877-4253, 313/961-2242) $95, 1991; out of print, but may be available at libraries. Includes 2,400 companies and 3,400 key executives including all members of the American Association of Political Consultants. Also listed are federal and state boards of election and state Republican and Democratic party offices which are also potential employers. This is a good source for identifying political consultants.

Election Results Directory 1993 (National Conference of State Legislatures, Book Order Department, 1560 Broadway, Suite 700, Denver, CO 80202; phone: 303/830-2054) $36, 1993. Complete listing of state and federal legislative and executive branch officials as well as general information on each state such as: legislative information and bill status phone numbers, current data on the legislative process, a legislative calendar, party control charts, legislative rules, and more. The directory is also available in computerized formats and on mailing labels. For more information call 303/830-2200.

American Lobbyists Directory (Gale Research, Inc., 835 Penobscot Bldg., Detroit, MI 48226; phones: 800/877-4253, 313/961-2242) $175, 1,158 pages, 1989. Includes about 4,000 federal lobbyists representing 8,000 organizations, the 57,000 lobbyists who represent 26,000 organizations at the state level, and a list of state and federal agencies that regulate lobbyists. Although this is getting a bit long in the tooth, it may still help you locate lobbying firms.

Port management

Job ads in print

The Advisory (American Association of Port Authorities, 1010 Duke St., Alexandria, VA 22315; phone: 703/684-5700) weekly, available only to members (membership fee: $600/year). Jobs listed under "Help Wanted." Few jobs ads; job ads not in every issue.

Directories

Traffic Management Buyers Guide Issue (Cahners Publishing, 44 Cook St., Denver, CO 80206-5800; phone: 800/622-7776) monthly, $69.95/annual subscription (U.S.), $101.60/Canada and Mexico, $95/elsewhere (surface), $129.95/air mail. Buyers Guide published as the March issue; available for $25/U.S., $35/foreign. Includes directory of major North American port authorities, shippers associations, and agents.

Mini–Directory to U.S. Port Authorities (American Association of Port Authorities, 1010 Duke St., Alexandria, VA 22314; phone: 703/684–5700) free, 11 pages, updated frequently.

Public administration

Also see listings under "Library services" and "Planning."

Job ads in print

ICMA Newsletter (International City/County Management Association, 777 N. Capitol St., NE, Washington, DC 20002; phone: 202/289–4262) biweekly, $115/nonmember annual subscription, free/members. Jobs listed under "Placement and Support Services." The typical issue features about 25 to 40 job listings in all phases of local government, particularly public administration.

J.O.B. The Job Opportunities Bulletin for Minorities and Women in Local Government (International City/County Management Association, 777 N. Capitol St., NE, Washington, DC 20002; phone: 202/289–4262) biweekly, $12/nonmember annual subscription, free/members. Thirty to 50 ads for all phases of local and regional government, mostly in public administration, appear throughout this newsletter.

Public Administration Times (American Society for Public Administration, Suite 700, 1120 G St., NW, Washington, DC 20005; phone: 202/393–7878) 12 issues/year, $40/nonmember annual subscription for first class mail (U.S.), $25/nonmember annual subscription for third class mail (U.S.), $70/foreign air mail, $35/foreign surface mail, free/members. Jobs listed under "The Recruiter." Typical issue features about 20 to 25 ads for government jobs plus additional ads for university positions.

News Digest (International Institute of Municipal Clerks, 1206 N. San Dimas Canyon Rd., San Dimas, CA 91773; phone: 818/795–6153) monthly, $15/nonmember annual subscription, included in membership package. Jobs listed under "Positions Available." About four job ads for municipal clerk and assistant clerk positions appear in the typical issue, but it has gone two or three consecutive issues without any job ads at all.

Job services

Job Opportunities Notices (International Institute of Municipal Clerks, 1206 N. San Dimas Canyon Rd., San Dimas, CA 91773; phone: 818/795–6153) free. Sends notices of job vacancies for municipal clerks and assistant clerks to individuals who request to be sent them.

CU Career Connection (University of Colorado, Campus Box 133, Boulder, CO 80309–0133; phone: 303/492–4127) $30/two–month fee entitles you to a "passcode" which unlocks this job hotline. You need a touch–tone phone to call and request the field in which you are interested in hearing job openings. The hotline is turned off Monday through Friday, 2 to 4 p.m. for daily updating.

Directories

The Municipal Yearbook (International City/County Management Association, 777 N. Capitol St., NE, Washington, DC 20002; phones: 800/745–8780, 202/289–4262) $79.95 plus $5 shipping if not prepaid, 416 pages, published each May.

Includes the following directories: officials in U.S. municipalities which features the form of government, manager/administrator, city clerk, finance officer, fire chief, police chief, and public works director; county officials in U.S. counties which lists county board chairperson, county executive or appointed administrator, clerk, chief financial officer, personnel director, and chief law enforcement officer; state municipal leagues, state agencies for community affairs; state, provincial (Canadian), and international municipal management associations; state associations of counties; provincial (Canadian) and territorial associations; provincial and territorial agencies for local affairs in Canada; directors of councils of governments recognized by ICMA; local government chief administrators in other countries; and professional, special assistance, and educational organizations serving local and state governments.

Who's Who in Local Government Management (International City/County Management Association, 777 N. Capitol St., NE, Washington, DC 20002; phones: 800/745–8780, 202/289–4262) free/members only. Annual directory of ICMA members and ICMA–recognized governments.

Salary survey

Compensation 94: An Annual Report on Local Government Executive Salaries and Fringe Benefits (International City/County Management Association, 777 N. Capitol St., NE, Washington, DC 20002; phone: 202/289–4262) $180/nonmembers, $125/members (add $5/ shipping and handling if not prepaid), 300 pages, published annually. Presents salary and fringe benefit information on city and county managers, councils of governments directors, assistant managers, police and fire chiefs, finance directors, parks and recreation directors, and public works directors. Includes average salaries by state, region, and jurisdiction size.

Public health and health care

*Also see listings under "Public administration," "Public safety," and "Social services." For 60 pages of job sources in health care, see the **Professional's Private Sector Job Finder**.*

Job ads in print

The Nation's Health (American Public Health Association, 1015 15th St., NW, Washington, DC 20005; phone: 202/789–5600) 11 issues/year, $15/annual subscription (U.S.), $18/foreign. Jobs listed under "Job Openings" in the "Classified Advertising" section. Typical issue announces about 50 job openings.

BioScience (American Institute of Biological Sciences, 703 11th St., NW, Washington, DC 20001–4521; phone: 202/628–1500) 11 issues/year, $49.50/annual subscription. "Professional Opportunities" features about three ads for biologists.

American Journal of Public Health (American Public Health Association, 1015 15th St., NW, Washington, DC 20005; phone: 202/789–5600) monthly, $100/annual subscription (U.S.), $140/foreign. Jobs listed under "Job Opportunities." The typical issue features about 40 job ads.

Emergency Medical Services (Summer Communications, Inc., 7626 Densmore Ave., Van Nuys, CA 91406–2088) monthly, $18.95/annual subscription (U.S.), $29/foreign. About four positions for paramedics and emergency physicians appear under "Employment Opportunities."

Journal of the American Dietetic Association (ADA, 216 W. Jackson Blvd., Chicago, IL 60606; phone: 312/899–0040) monthly, $98/nonmember annual subscription, free/members. About 40 ads for dietitians appear under "Classified Advertising" each issue.

Nationwide Jobs in Dietetics (P.O. Box 3537, Santa Monica, CA 90408–3537; phone: 310/453–5375) monthly, with mid–month updates, $84/annual subscription, $36/two–month subscription, $24/one–month subscription. California residents add 8.25 percent sales tax. Around 10 percent of the 400 dietitian and nutritionist jobs in a typical issue fall under the moniker "Public Health & Community Nutrition." Your first issue will include a sheet that names additional sources of government and private sector positions.

Journal of Perentology (Mosby Yearbook, 11830 Westline Industrial Drive, St. Louis, MO 63146; phone: 314/453–4406) quarterly, $50/annual subscription (U.S.), $62.50/foreign. The "Classified" section has around ten positions for nutritionists, perentologists (prenatal), and nurses.

California Jobs in Dietetics (P.O. Box 3537, Santa Monica, CA 90408–3537; phone: 310/453–5375) biweekly, $48/six–issue subscription. California residents add 8.25 percent sales tax. Almost 10 percent of the 230 dietitian and nutritionist jobs in a typical issue are listed under "Public Health & Community Nutrition." Your first issue will include a sheet that names additional sources of government and private sector positions in California and nationally.

Indian Health Service (Chief, Nutrition and Dietetics Section, Indian Health Service, 5600 Fishers Ln., Rockville, MD 20857; phone: 301/443–1114) free. Contact for a list of openings available nationally to work in the Indian community as a dietitian ad an employee of a tribe, Civil Service, or the U.S. Public Health Service.

U.S. Public Health Service (Maternal & Child Health Bureau, HRSA/HHS, Room 1805, Rockville, MD 20857; phone: 301/443–2370). Contact the Chief Nutritionist for information on available dietitian positions with the U.S. Public Health Service.

U.S. Army Reserve (AMEDD Personnel Counselor/AMSC, Captain Andrea Eigel, U.S. Army Medical Department, 8610 N. New Braunsels, Suite 419, San Antonio, TX 78217–6358; phones: 210/826–3044) Write or call for information on clinical and administrative dietitian positions in the army reserve medical units throughout the world.

Paid Internship Opportunities—U.S. Army Reserve (AMEDD Personnel Counselor/AMSC, Captain Andrea Eigel, U.S. Army Medical Department, 8610 N. New Braunsels, Suite 419, San Antonio, TX 78217–6358; phones: 210/826–3044) Write or call for information on paid dietitian internships in the U.S. army and reserves.

Journal of Nuclear Medicine (Society of Nuclear Medicine, 136 Madison Ave., New York, NY 10016; phone: 212/889–0717) monthly, $120/annual nonmember subscription, $130/Canada, $160/elsewhere; free/members. Among the 20 to 25 positions for physicians, technologists, and radiologists are a number of positions in Veterans Administration hospitals. This group plans to move its offices to Reston, VA in October of 1994 – they ask that you call, not write, after this date.

SOT Newsletter (Society of Toxicology, 1101 14th St., NW, Suite 1100, Washington, DC 20005; phone: 202/371–1393) five issues/year, free, available only to members. "Placement Service" typically has about eight job ads for toxicologists.

NACHO News (National Association of County Health Officials, 440 First St., NW, Washington, DC 20001; phone: 202/783–5550) bimonthly, $55/annual subscription. Seven or more job ads appear under "Job Opportunities" for positions in health, mostly health director or officer jobs.

Local Health Officers News (U.S. Conference of Local Health Officers, 1620 I St., NW, Washington, DC 20006; phone: 202/293–7330) bimonthly, $35/nonmember annual subscription, free/members. When job ads appear—which is not every issue—they are listed under "Employment Opportunities.

Journal of Environmental Health (National Environmental Health Association, Suite 970, South Tower, 720 S. Colorado Blvd., Denver, CO 80222; phone: 303/756–9090) bimonthly, $75/nonmember annual subscription, included in dues ($60/year, $15/students). Jobs listed under "Opportunities." Five to ten job ads appear in the typical issue for sanitarians, toxicologists, health planners, and related positions.

Career Mart (American College of Healthcare Executives, 840 N. Lake Shore Dr., Chicago, IL 60611; phone: 312/943–0544) monthly, available only to members, $35/member six–month subscription. Typical issue includes more than 70 upper–level health care management positions listed under "Career Mart."

Healthcare Forum Journal (The Healthcare Forum, 830 Market St., San Francisco, CA 94102; phone: 415/421–8810) bimonthly, $45/annual subscription (U.S.), $60/Canada and Mexico, $90/elsewhere. Jobs listed under "Classified." Two or three job ads per issue.

Modern Healthcare (Crain Communications, 740 N. Rush St., Chicago, IL 60611; phone: 312/649–5350) weekly, $110/year. About 20 jobs listed under "People/Career Opportunities and Professional Exchange."

Rural Health Care (National Rural Health Care Association, 301 E. Armour Blvd., Kansas City, MO 64111; phone: 816/756–3140) bimonthly, available only to members, included in dues. About 25 physician and nursing positions appear under "Classified."

New England Journal of Medicine (Massachusetts Medical Society, 10 Shattuck St., Boston, MA 02115–6094; phone: 617/893–3800) weekly, $96/annual subscription. From 300 to 500 physician positions are advertised in the "Classifieds" section and in display ads throughout the magazine. A handful of government positions are included.

Annals of Internal Medicine (American College of Physicians, Independence Mall West, 6th St. at Race, Philadelphia, PA 19106; phone: 800/523–1546) $84/annual nonmember subscription (U.S.), $134.82 (includes GST)/Canada, $142/elsewhere; $59.25/nonmember physicians, $42/nonmember medical students, free/member. From 100 to 150 vacancies for physicians in internal medicine appear under "Classified." A handful of government positions are included.

JAMA: The Journal of the American Medical Association (American Medical Association, Subscription Dept., 515 N. State St., Chicago, IL 60610; phones: 800/621–8335, 312/464–5000) weekly, $115/annual nonmember subscription, $190/nonmember foreign (air mail), included in membership package. "Classified Advertising" offers openings for 275 to 325 physicians of all types. A handful of government positions are included.

The New Careers Directory: Internships and Professional Opportunities in Technology and Social Change (Student Pugwash USA, 1638 R St., NW, Suite 32, Washington, DC 20009; phone: 202/328–6555) $18, $10/students (add $3 shipping), last published in 1993. Offers full details on where and how to apply for internships and entry–level jobs in health care and related fields.

Internships for College Students Interested in Law, Medicine and Politics (Graduate Group, 86 Norwood Rd., West Hartford, CT 06117; phones: 203/232–3100, 203/236–5570) $27.50, published annually. Includes information on hundreds of actual internship opportunities with government agencies.

See also ***NELS*** *under "Law enforcement."*

See also ***The Jobank*** and ***Water Environment Today*** *under "Water/wastewater operations."*

Job services

CU Career Connection (University of Colorado, Campus Box 133, Boulder, CO 80309–0133; phone: 303/492–4127) $30/two–month fee entitles you to a "passcode" which unlocks this job hotline. You need a touch–tone phone to call and request the field in which you are interested in hearing job openings. The hotline is turned off Monday through Friday, 2 to 4 p.m. for daily updating.

National Registry for Pharmaceutical Scientists (c/o American Association of Pharmaceutical Scientists, 1650 King St., Alexandria, VA 22314; phone: 703/548–3000) free. Operated in conjunction with the AAPS, this service keeps your resume application form on file for one year. Obtain the application form by calling the AAPS. The Registry submits a copy of the forms of qualified applicants to employers who are seeking pharmaceutical scientists. Employers then contact them directly for an interview.

National Physicians Register (8 Park Plaza, Suite 422J, Boston, MA 02116; phone: 800/342–1007) free. A physician submits a copy of her resume and gives her geographic preference and type of position sought. NPR creates a synopsis of the resume and assigns a code number to it. These synopses are published with code numbers rather than the physician's name in a bulletin sent bimonthly to 9,300 hospitals, clinics, group practices, and health maintenance organizations. The potential employer tells NPR which doctors interest it and NPR sends the contact information to the employer. Then, the employer can ask for the resume. (Employers usually ask for 20 to 50 persons per week at this service.) However, if the physician tells NPR that he doesn't want his name given out, NPR sends the job seeker a letter telling him a particular facility is interested in him and that he should contact the potential employer directly. Between 300 and 1,000 physicians are registered at any one time, although that number is growing. Serves both M.D. and osteopathic physicians.

BioTron (American Institute of Biological Sciences, 703 11th St., NW, Washington, DC 20001–4521; phone: 202/628–1500) free. Using your computer modem, call 202/628–2427 anytime to access job vacancies. The communications configuration is 300, 1200, or 2400 baud, 8 data bits, 1 stop bit, no parity, full duplex, Xon/Xoff active, carriage return (ASCII 13) at end of lines. Received text may be stopped and started by pressing CTRL S/Q.

SOT Placement Service (Society of Toxicology, 1101 14th St., NW, Suite 1100, Washington, DC 20005; phone: 202/371–1393) $10/full–associate member, free/post–doctoral member, free/full–time student member, $25/full–associate eligible nonmember, $20/post–doctoral nonmember, $15/full–time student nonmember. Complete this services narrative resume form and computer form to be a part of SOT's annual meeting placement service. This is a service that matches job seekers to employers through networking by attending their annual meeting. At the meeting, job listings are posted in a separate room and contact between candidates and employers are made through a message board and interviews. Although it may be helpful for a candidate to attend the meeting to make personal contact with employers it is not necessary. Even if you are not registered for the meeting, jobs posted at the meeting may be obtained by calling SOT. Meetings held annually, usually towards the beginning of the year. The 1994 meeting will be held March 13 to 17. Call for registration cut–off date. You are able to register late but fee triples if you do.

Toll–Free Instant RSVP Nursing Career Directory (Springhouse Corp., 1111 Bethlehem Pike, Springhouse, PA 19477; phone: 215/646–8700) free. Published each January, this directory lists over 600 hospitals and health centers that are looking for nursing professionals. Job openings are listed under "Nurse Recruitment." You can be put directly in touch with a facility's nurse recruiter by calling 800/633–2648 (in Pennsylvania, call 800/633–2649) and giving your qualifications and specialty interests or sending in the reader service card from the directory. The RSVP line calls the nurse recruiter at the facilities of your choice. The nurse recruiter sends you an application form.

Jobs for Dietitians Job Advice Hotline (P.O. Box 3537, Santa Monica, CA 90408–3537; phone: 310/453–5375) available only to subscribers to either the national or California edition of *Jobs for Dietitians* described above under "Job ads in print." Hotline number is given in the newsletter.

New England Technologists Section Job Hotline (Society of Nuclear Medicine, 136 Madison Ave., New York, NY 10016; phone: 212/889–0717) free. Medical technologists can call 800/562–6387 to register. They are sent a list of vacancies from Tom Starno who operates this service which is funded by the Tech Physicians of New England. To reach Tom Starno for more information, call 207/945–7186. Vacancies are kept on the list for three months.

Directories

1993 Directory of Key Health Legislators and Legislative Staff (National Conference of State Legislatures, Book Order Department, 1560 Broadway, Suite 700, Denver, CO 80202; phone: 303/830–2054) $15, 82 pages. Compiled by the NCSL Health and Human Services Department staff this lists state legislatures and staff involved or interested in health programs, policies, and funding. This includes those who sit on state legislative committees, subcommittees, joint committees, interim committees, and special committees that address specific health issues.

Hospital Phone Book (U.S. Directory Service, 121 Chanlon Rd., New Providence, NJ 07074; phone: 908/464–6800) $69.95 plus $4.75 shipping. Information on over 7,940 government and private hospitals in the U.S. Most recent edition, 1993.

National Directory of Local Health Departments (National Association of County Health Officials, 440 First St., Suite 500, NW, Washington, DC 20001; phone: 202/783–5550) biannual, $20.

Society of Toxicology Membership Directory (SOT, 1101 14th St., NW, Suite 1100, Washington, DC 20005; phone: 202/371–1393) free, available only to members, issued each June.

American College of Healthcare Executives Directory (American Association of Healthcare Executives, 840 N. Lake Shore Dr., Chicago, IL 60611; phone: 312/943–0544) $100/nonmembers, $75/members, published in the spring of even–numbered years. Lists over 16,000 health care executives in public and private sectors.

Nationwide Jobs in Dietetics (P.O. Box 3537, Santa Monica, CA 90408–3537; phone: 213/453–5375) monthly, with mid–month updates, $84/annual subscription, $36/two–month subscription, $24/one–month subscription. California residents add 8.25 percent sales tax. The first issue includes an insert with a list of the directors of state departments of health, public health nutrition or the WIC program—agencies that employ dietitians.

Membership Directory for the Society of Nuclear Medicine (Society of Nuclear Medicine, 136 Madison Ave., New York, NY 10016; phone: 212/889–0717) $50/nonmembers, free/members, issued in odd–numbered years.

Salary surveys

Hospital Salary & Benefits Report (Hospital Compensation Service, John R. Zabka Associates, 69 Minnehaha Blvd., Oakland, NJ 07436; phone: 201/405–0075) $250, annual. Covers dozens of administration, nursing, rehabilitation and mental health, radiology, laboratory, medical records and library, dietary, pharmacy, and technical positions at both governmental and nongovernmental hospitals.

Physician Salary Survey Report (Hospital Compensation Service, John R. Zabka Associates, 69 Minnehaha Blvd., Oakland, NJ 07436; phone: 201/405–0075) $250. For physicians employed by hospitals, group practice, and health maintenance organizations. Reports on salaries and benefits in governmental and nongovernmental medical facilities for staff physicians, department heads, medical directors, residents, and interns.

Public safety

Also see listings under "Engineering," "Fire protection," "Law enforcement," "Public administration," and "Public health."

Job ads in print

JobLine Bulletin (American Society of Safety Engineers, 1800 E. Oakton St., Des Plaines, IL 60018–2187; phone: 708/692–4121, ext. 33) monthly, $90/nonmember six–month subscription, $35/members, free/unemployed members. Special issues are published occasionally upon employer request. About 30 safety and health job openings in government, construction, communications, insurance, manufacturing, utilities, and transportation appear throughout the typical issue.

Professional Safety (American Society of Safety Engineers, 1800 E. Oakton St., Des Plaines, IL 60018–2187; phone: 708/692–4121, ext. 13) monthly, $43/nonmember annual subscription (U.S., Canada, and Mexico), $50/elsewhere surface mail, $102/elsewhere by air mail; included in membership package. About 25 safety and health job openings in government, construction, communications, insurance, manufacturing, utilities, transportation, and petrochemical industries as well as university faculty opportunities are listed under "Personnel Center."

Applied Occupational and Environmental Hygiene (American Conference of Governmental Industrial Hygienists, 6500 Glenway Ave., Bldg. D-7, Cincinnati, OH 45211; phone: 513/661–7881) monthly, $85/nonmember annual subscription, $45/members. About five positions for occupational safety and health inspectors and industrial hygienists appear in "Classified Advertising."

Safety & Health (National Safety Council, 1121 Spring Lake Drive, Itasca, IL 60143–3201; phone: 708/775–2277) monthly, $56/annual nonmember subscription, $45/members. Only a few job ads for industrial hygienists appear under "Classifieds."

APCO Bulletin (Associated Public–Safety Communications Officers, Inc., 2040 S. Ridgewood Ave., South Daytona, FL 32119–2257; phone: 904/322–2500) $50/annual nonmember subscription (U.S.), $100/Canada, $20/members. Jobs listed under "Public Safety Job Opportunities."

Job Service

ACFE Job Bank (Association of Certified Fraud Examiners, 716 West Avenue, Austin, TX 78701; phone: 800/245–3321) free/members only ($75/membership fee). Send two copies of your resume along with a cover letter stating salary requirements and place(s) where you would be willing to relocate if possible. Copies of your resume will be sent to federal government offices and/or private sector companies where they are looking to fill positions. Sometime in mid–1994 they will be switching this service over to a computerized database where you will be required to fill out an application along with sending your resume. To be on the safe side you may want to call before sending anything to them.

Directory

ACFE Membership Directory (Association of Certified Fraud Examiners, 716 West Avenue, Austin, TX 78701; phone: 800/245–3321) $75, annual. Includes companies along with locations for some 10,000 members.

Salary survey

Comparative Retirement Benefits for General State Employees and Public Safety Personnel (National Conference of State Legislatures, Book Order Department, 1560 Broadway, Suite 700, Denver, CO 80202; phone: 303/830–2054) $5, 14 pages, 1991 edition. 50 state comparison of general state and public safety personnel retirement benefits, including benefit formulas and age and service for regular retirement.

Public works

See also listings under "Engineering," "Public administration," "Sanitation/solid waste management," "Utilities management," and "Water/wastewater operations."

Job ads in print

APWA Reporter (American Public Works Association, 106 W. 11th, Suite 1800, Kansas City, MO 64105; phone: 816/472–6100) monthly, free/members only. Annual membership: $70/professionals and libraries, $10/full–time students. Sometime in early 1994 APWA will move to 816 Broadway, Kansas City, MO 64105. Seventeen or so jobs are listed under "Positions."

Public Works (Public Works Journal Corp., 200 S. Broad St., Ridgewood, NJ 07451; phone: 201/445–5800) monthly, $45/annual subscription (U.S.), $75/elsewhere. Jobs listed under "Classified Advertisements/Public Works Careers." Typical issue features 25 to 30 job ads. April issue includes a buyer's guide.

American City & County (Argus Business, 6151 Powers Ferry Rd., NW Atlanta, GA 30339; phone: 404/955–2500) monthly, $50/annual subscription (U.S.), $78/foreign (surface mail), $118/foreign (air mail). Jobs listed under "Job Search & Classified." Ads are mostly for engineers, public works, and public administration.

See also ***APCO Bulletin*** under "Public safety."

Directory

American Public Works Association Directory (American Public Works Association, 106 W. 11th, Suite 1800, Kansas City, MO 64105; phone: 816/472–6100) available to members only, contact for price. annual, last published January 1994. Phone numbers and addresses of APWA chapter officers. Sometime in early 1994, APWA will move to 816 Broadway, Kansas City, MO 64105.

Purchasing

Also see listings under "Public administration."

Job ads in print

Employment Opportunity Listing (National Association of Purchasing Management, c/o Dave Kosteva, P.O. Box 160, Northville, MI 48167; phone: 313/348–8040) monthly, distributed to NARMS 172 affiliate offices. Twelve to 20 purchasing and materials management positions are in the usual issue.

Contract Management (National Contract Managers Association, 1912 Woodford Rd., Vienna, VA 22182; phones: 800/344–8096, 703/448–9231) monthly, $72/nonmember annual subscription, included in dues. Typical issue has about 14 ads for contract managers, procurement, materials management, contractor negotiators, administrators, buyers, attorneys, and certified public accountants listed under "Job Watch" and in display ads in the "CM Final Edition" supplement. The vast majority of positions are private sector.

NIGP Technical Bulletin (National Institute of Governmental Purchasing, Suite 1050, 11800 Sunrise Valley Drive, Reston, VA 22091; phone: 703/715–9400) bimonthly, $30/nonmember annual subscription, free/members. The two or three jobs that are advertised are either listed under "Employment Opportunities."

Government Procurement (National Institute of Governmental Purchasing, 11800 Sunrise Valley Drive, Suite 1050, Reston, VA 22091; phone: 703/715–9400) quarterly, $20/annual nonmember subscription, free/members. Just one or two job ads for purchasing positions per issue appear under "Classifieds."

Job services

NAPM Services, Inc.—Employment Services (National Association of Purchasing Management, c/o Dave Kosteva, P.O. Box 160, Northville, MI 48167; phone: 313/348–8040) free/ members only. The job seeker submits a copy of her resume along with an enrollment form. When a match is found, the Employment Service contacts the job seeker to confirm her interest in the position and then sends the job seeker's resume to the employer who is responsible for contacting the potential employee for an interview.

Job Matching Service (American Purchasing Society, 11910 Oak Trail Way, Port Richey, FL 34668; phone: 813/862–7998) free. Send your resume to APS with a request that it be kept on file for job openings. When an employer submits a request for job candidates, APS sends a copy of the resume of qualified persons to the employer who is responsible for contacting candidates for interviews. APS also sends a letter to each candidate when her resume has been sent to an employer to tell her the employer's name and address, and suggest that she contact the employer for more information about the job. Resumes are kept on file for three years.

NCMA's Job Referral Service (National Contract Managers Association, 1912 Woodford Rd., Vienna, VA 22182; phones: 800/344–8096, 703/448–9231) $70/nonmembers, free/members. Complete the service's resume form and submit it with ten copies of your resume. The service forwards the resumes of qualified applicants to employers who are responsible for contacting the job hopeful. Resumes are kept on file for six months. The vast majority of positions are private sector.

Employment Opportunities Register (National Institute of Governmental Purchasing, 11800 Sunrise Valley Drive, Suite 1050, Reston, VA 22091; phone: 703/715–9400). In this very informal service, NIGP keeps resumes of members on file and sends job notices to them which include the jobs advertised in the NIGP Technical Bulletin described above under "Job ads in print."

Directory

Membership Directory (National Institute of Governmental Purchasing, 11800 Sunrise Valley Drive, Suite 1050, Reston, VA 22091; phone: 703/715–9400) free/members only, 325 pages, annual. Gives names, phones, and addresses of government purchasing agents who belong to NIGP.

Salary Survey

NIGP Procurement Survey (National Institute of Governmental Purchasing, 11800 Sunrise Valley Drive, Suite 1050, Reston, VA 22091; phone: 703/715–9400) free/members, contact for price to nonmembers, published every March in even–numbered years. Breaks down salaries for government purchasing agents by type of employer, size of employer, budget, etc.

Property appraisal & tax assessment

Job ads in print

Appraiser News (Appraisal Institute, 875 N. Michigan Ave., Suite 2400, Chicago, IL 60611; phone: 312/335–4100) monthly, $20/annual nonmember subscription, free/members. The "Job Search" section features 20 to 30 positions including a number of local and state government positions.

Real Estate Appraisal Newsletter (National Association of Real Estate Appraisers, 8383 E. Evans Rd., Scottsdale, AZ 85260–3614; phone: 602/948–8000) quarterly, free/members only. Jobs listed under "Appraiser Job Mart." Four to ten positions in typical issue.

IAAO Update (International Association of Assessing Officers, 130 East Randolph, Suite 850, Chicago, IL 60601; phone: 312/819–6100) monthly, free/members, nonmembers can receive free sample issues. Write for information. Lists jobs under "Opportunities." Two to seven job ads per issue.

Appraiser–Gram (National Association of Independent Fee Appraisers, 7501 Murdoch, St. Louis, MO 63119; phone: 314/781–6688) monthly, $20/annual nonmember subscription, free/members. Jobs listed under "Career Opportunities." Few job ads.

FMRA News (American Society of Farm Managers and Rural Appraisers, Inc., Suite 508, 950 S. Cherry St., Denver, CO 80222; phone: 303/758–3513) bimonthly, $15/annual subscription, free/members. Jobs listed under "Career Corner." Usually two to four job ads per issue, but some issues have no ads.

Tax Administrators News (Federation of Tax Administrators, 444 North Capitol St., NW, Washington, DC 20001; phone: 202/624–5890) monthly; $30/annual subscription. Jobs listed under "Positions Open." Very few job ads. Most issues have no ads.

Job services

NAREA Job Referral Service (National Association of Real Estate Appraisers, 8383 E. Evans Rd., Scottsdale, AZ 85260–3614; phone: 602/948–8000) free/members only. This is a very informal member service where the NAREA puts job candidates in touch with potential employers.

NAMA Member Referral Program (National Association of Master Appraisers, 303 W. Cypress, San Antonio, TX 78212; phones: 800/531–5333, 512/225–2897) free/members only. Your resume is placed on file. Employers request resumes of qualified candidates contact candidates directly.

NAMA Internship Program (National Association of Master Appraisers, 303 W. Cypress, San Antonio, TX 78212; phones: 800/531–5333, 512/225–2897) free/members only. New appraisers can request free list of agencies and firms that offer internships. Candidate is responsible for contacting possible internship employers.

If you haven't found all the job sources for your specialty...

Yo, dude! You probably skipped Chapter 1, the chapter that tells you how to use this book most effectively—and the chapter nobody ever wants to read. Please read it! It's a most excellent chapter that explains how to use this chapter and the Index to find job sources in your field, whether it's professional, trades, office support, labor, or technical.

Directories

Appraisal Institute Directory of Members (Appraisal Institute, 875 N. Michigan Ave., Suite 2400, Chicago, IL 60611; phone: 312/335–4100) free, published each spring. Contains business information on 13,000 members.

NAMA Membership Directory (National Association of Master Appraisers, 303 W. Cypress, San Antonio, TX 78212; phones: 800/531–5333, 512/225–2897) free, published each February.

IAAO Membership Directory (International Association of Assessing Officers, 130 East Randolph, Suite 850, Chicago, IL 60601; phone: 312/819–6100) $150/nonmembers, free/members, published annually. Lists member real estate assessors and appraisers.

Accredited and General Membership Directory (American Society of Farm Managers and Rural Appraisers, Inc., 950 S. Cherry Street, Suite 508, Denver, CO 80222; phone: 303/758–3513) free, published each February.

Real estate/property management

Also see listings under "Housing" and "Public administration." A more extensive set of job sources appears in the "Real estate and construction " chapter of the ***Professional's Private Sector Job Finder***.

Job ads in print

FMRA News (American Society of Farm Managers and Rural Appraisers, Inc., Suite 500, 950 Cherry, Denver, CO 80222; phone: 303/758–3513) bimonthly, available only as part of membership package. Jobs listed under "Job Mart." Usually two to four job ads per issue, but some issues have no ads.

See also ***Economic Developments*** *under "Community and economic development."*

Directory

Accredited and General Membership Directory (American Society of Farm Managers and Rural Appraisers, Inc., Suite 500, 950 Cherry, Denver, CO 80222; phone: 303/758–3513). Write for price.

Records management and archives

Job ads in print

Archival Outlook (Society of American Archivists, Suite 504, 600 S. Federal, Chicago, IL 60605; phone: 312/922–0140) published in alternating months with SAA Employment Bulletin, free/members only. Jobs listed under "Employment Opportunities." About 20 job ads per issue.

SAA Employment Bulletin (Society of American Archivists, Suite 504, 600 S. Federal, Chicago, IL 60605; phone: 312/922–0140) published in alternating months with Archival Outlook, available to members for $24/year; nonmembers can purchase individual issues for $6. Lists only jobs. About 20 jobs ads per issue.

AIC Newsletter (American Institute for Conservation of Historic and Artistic Works,, Suite 340, 1400 16th St., NW, Washington, DC 20036; phone: 202/232–6636) bimonthly, available to members only. Jobs listed under "Positions Available." Around 20 job ads per issue, largely for conservators.

OAH Newsletter (Organization of American Historians, 112 N. Bryan St., Bloomington, IN 47408; phone: 812/855–7311) quarterly, free/members only. About 12 positions for government, public, and U.S. historians; archivists; and university faculty appear under "Professional Opportunities." OAH also runs a job registry at its annual national meeting.

See also ***FEDfacts*** *listed under "Data processing and computers."*

Job service

Association of Records Managers and Administrators Job Hotline (4200 Somerset Dr., Suite 215, Prairie Village, KS 66208; phone: 913/341–3808) Call 913/752–4030 (24 hours.) to hear a recording of 8 to 10 job vacancies for records management in the U.S. and nationwide. Updated weekly. Send your resume to employer directly.

Directories

AIC Directory (American Institute for Conservation of Historic and Artistic Works, Suite 340, 1400 16th St., NW, Washington, DC 20036; phone: 202/232–6636) $53/nonmembers, free/members, published each August. Members listed alphabetically, geographically, and by specialty.

NAGARA Directory (National Association of Government Archives and Records Administrators, 48 Howard St., Albany, NY 12207; phone: 518/463–8644) $10, 55 pages, published every summer. Lists state government record management and archival programs.

Risk Management/Insurance

Also see listings under "Public administration" and "Public safety."

Job ads in print

Business Insurance (Crain Communications, 965 E. Jefferson Ave., Detroit, MI 48207; phone: 800/678–9595) weekly, $80/annual subscription (U.S.), $118/Canada (surface mail), $185/Canada (air mail), $200/elsewhere (surface mail). About 20 job ads appear in the typical issue, including municipal and state positions.

PARMAFacts (Public Agency Risk Managers Association, c/o Conference Connection, P.O. Box 6810, San Jose, CA 95150; phone: 408/865–0196) semimonthly, free/members only, $50/annual dues. Lists about 5 or 6 positions in each issue, mostly in California.

RiskWatch (Public Risk and Insurance Management Association, 1117 N. 19th St., Suite 900, Arlington, VA 22209; phone: 703/528–7701) monthly, $125/nonmember annual subscription, free/members. Jobs listed under "Job Descriptions." Four to seven job ads are in a typical issue.

Sanitation/solid waste management

Also see listings under "Engineering," "Public administration," and "Public works."

Job ads in print

Solid Waste & Power (HCI Publications, 410 Archibald St., Kansas City, MO 64111; phone: 816/931–1311) bimonthly, $49/annual subscription (U.S.), $67/foreign. About five job vacancies in all aspects of solid waste management are listed under "Job Mart."

Biocycle (419 State Ave., Emmaus, PA 18049; phone: 215/967–4135) monthly, $58/annual subscription (U.S.), $80/Canada, $85/foreign. About ten job ads are in the typical issue, generally focusing on recycling and composting.

Recycling Times (1730 Rhode Island Ave., NW, Suite 1000, Washington, DC 20036; phone: 202/861–0708) semiweekly, $95/annual subscription (26 issues). Five job ads appear for recycling and solid waste positions.

Recycling Today, Municipal Market Edition (4012 Bridge Ave., Cleveland, OH 44113; phone: 216/961–4130) monthly, $32/annual subscription. About three vacancies for recycling coordinators, operations handlers, and directors of solid waste operations appear under "Classifieds."

Resource Recycling (P.O. Box 10540, Portland, OR 97210; phone: 503/227–1319) monthly, $42/annual subscription. About two recycling and solid waste management positions are listed under "Positions Available."

World Wastes (Argus Business, 6151 Powers Ferry Rd., NW, Atlanta, GA 30339; phone: 404/955–2500) monthly; $40/annual subscription (U.S.), $60/Canada. Five to ten jobs are listed under "The Job Mart."

Waste Age (Suite 1000, 1730 Rhode Island Ave., NW, Washington, DC 20036; phone: 202/861–0708) monthly, $45/annual subscription (U.S. and Canada), free to professionals in the industry (U.S. and Canada only), $125/elsewhere. About 20 jobs listed under "Classifieds" for solid and hazardous waste professionals, collection specialists, and operation managers.

Municipal Solid Waste News (Solid Waste Association of North America, P.O. Box 7219, Silver Spring, MD 20907–7219; phone: 301/585–2898) monthly, free/members only ($100/year membership fee for public institution, $250 private institution, $35/students). Jobs listed under "Jobs." About four job ads per issue.

Pollution Engineering (Cahners Publishing Company, 44 Cook St., Denver, CO 80206; phone: 303/388–4511) 21 issues/year, $69.95/annual subscription (U.S.), $101.60/Canada and Mexico, $129.95/elsewhere (surface mail); free to qualified professionals. Among the 15 to 20 positions in the "Classified" section are a few government jobs.

Hazardous Materials Control (Hazardous Materials Control Resources Institute, 7237A Hanover Pkwy., Greenbelt, MD 20070–3602; phone: 301/982–9500) bimonthly, $18/annual subscription (U.S.), $25/Canada, $25/elsewhere (surface mail), $50/elsewhere (air mail). Jobs listed under "Focus." Few job ads.

Directories

Solid Waste Management Officials Membership Directory (Association of State Solid Waste Management Officials, 444 N. Capitol St., NW, Suite 388, Washington, DC 20001; phone: 202/624–5828) $40/nonmembers, free/members, 1991. This directory catalogues the state government officials in this field.

Solid Waste Association of North America Membership Directory (Solid Waste Association of North America, P.O. Box 7219, Silver Spring, MD 20907–7219; phone: 301/585–2898) $500.

Hazardous Materials Control Directory (Hazardous Materials Control Resources Institute, 7237A Hanover Pkwy., Greenbelt, MD 20070–3602; phone: 301/982–9500) $65/nonmembers, free/members, published each November.

Careers in Hazardous Waste Management: A Job Hunters Guide to the Hazardous Waste Management Field (Environmental Employment Clearinghouse, 3304 Marcus Ave., Newport Beach, CA 92663; phone: 714/675–

8278) $12.95 plus $3.50/shipping, 1989, new edition expected in 1994 or 1995. We've generally excluded these sorts of books, but this one is different. Even though it's getting pretty old, it includes a good list of job hunting resources (periodicals and directories) and a thorough directory of government job contacts in this specialty.

Salary survey

Police, Fire, and Refuse Collection Personnel and Expenditures (International City/County Management Association, 777 N. Capitol St., NE, Washington, DC 20002; phone: 202/289–4262) $16.50 (add $2.50 shipping and handling if not prepaid), 1992. A comparative study depicting trends in salary and expenditures data from police, fire, and refuse collection and disposal services.

Social services

Also see listings under "Mental health," "Public administration," and "Public health." Also see the ***Non–Profits' Job Finder.***

Job ads in print

NASW News (National Association of Social Workers, 750 First St., Suite 700, NE, Washington, DC 20002; phone: 800/638–8799) ten issues/year, $25/nonmember subscription, free/members. Jobs listed under "The Classifieds." The typical issue is filled to the brim with over 200 job ads in the arenas of social work, human services, mental health, public health, and social services.

Social Service Jobs (Employment Listings for Social Services, 10 Angelica Dr., Framingham, MA 01701; phone: 508/626–8644) biweekly, $42/six–issue subscription, $62/twelve issues, $118/twenty–four issues. Typical issue features 140+ positions listed by geographic region.

Job Exchange (Association for Education and Rehabilitation of the Blind, 206 N. Washington St., Suite 320, Alexandria, VA 22314; phone: 703/836–6060) monthly, available only to members: first six months free, $10/year thereafter. From 40 to 60 vacancies for administrators and practitioners (orientation and mobility specialists, teachers of persons with visual impairments, etc.) grace a typical issue.

Occupational Therapist Weekly (164 Rollins Ave., Suite 301, Rockville, MD 20852; phone: 301/881–2490) weekly, free to qualified professionals. About 200 positions fill the pages of this magazine.

Guidepost (American Rehabilitation Counseling Association, 5999 Stevenson Ave., Alexandria, VA 22304–3300; phone: 703/823–9800, ext. 244) 12 issues/year, $30/annual subscription. "Employment Classifieds" describe around 35 vacancies for psychologists and counselors in private practice, agencies, and universities.

Hospital and Community Psychiatry (American Psychiatric Association, 1400 K St., NW, Washington, DC 20005; phone: 202/682–6228) monthly, $40/annual subscription (U.S.), $60/foreign. Jobs listed under "Classified Advertising." Typical issue runs around 75 job ads including Veterans Administration positions.

in COMMON BULLETIN–Career Opportunities Working with Deaf People (Parkhill Press, P.O. Box 60, New Market, MD 21774; phone: 301/865–1701) biweekly, $25/three–month subscription, $40/six–months, $60/annual subscription. Each issue features 100 to 120 positions in human services, sign–language interpreting, social work, counseling, psychology, school administration, teaching, and other areas of working with people who are deaf or hard of hearing.

Special Recreation Digest (Special Recreation, Inc., 362 Koser Ave., Iowa City, IA 52246–3038; phone: 319/337–7578) quarterly, $39.95/annual subscription. Fifteen activity or recreation positions such as therapists, coordinators, and administrators appear under "Recreation."

The Counselor (National Association of Alcoholism and Drug Abuse Counselors, 3717 Columbia Pike, Suite 300, Arlington, VA 22204; phone: 703/920–4644) bimonthly, $36/nonmember annual subscription, included in membership package. Jobs listed under "Employment Classifieds." Typical issue features over ten job ads, usually for upper level counselors with medical facilities; has carried openings in the federal prison system.

Professional Report (National Rehabilitation Counseling Association, 1910 Association Drive, Suite 206, Reston, VA 22091; phone: 703/620–4404) bimonthly, available to members only. Jobs listed under "Job Openings." Some issues have no jobs listed. Few job ads.

AAMR News & Notes (American Association on Mental Retardation, 1719 Kalorama Rd. NW, Washington, DC 20009; phones: 800/424–3688, 202/387–1968) six issues/year, $35/nonmember annual subscription (U.S.), $50/elsewhere, included in dues. Jobs listed under "Classifieds." Five to 20 ads appear in the typical issue.

Mental Retardation (American Association on Mental Retardation, 1719 Kalorama Rd. NW, Washington, DC 20009; phones: 800/424–3688, 202/387–1968) bimonthly, $75/nonmember annual subscription (U.S.), $81/Canada, $90/elsewhere. Jobs listed under "The Exchange." Five to ten ads an issue.

TASH Newsletter (The Association for Persons with Severe Handicaps, 11201 Greenwood Ave., North, Seattle, WA 98133; phones: 206/361–8870, TDD: 206/361–0113) monthly, free/members only. Jobs listed under "Positions Open." About ten positions advertised in the typical issue.

*See also **NELS** listed under "Law enforcement."*

Job services

CU Career Connection (University of Colorado, Campus Box 133, Boulder, CO 80309–0133; phone: 303/492–4127) $30/two–month fee entitles you to a "passcode" which unlocks this job hotline. You need a touch–tone phone to call and request the field in which you are interested in hearing job openings. The hotline is turned off Monday through Friday, 2 to 4 p.m. for daily updating.

Career Guidance and Placement Service (Special Recreation, Inc., John Nesbitt, 362 Koser Ave., Iowa City, IA 52246–3038; phone: 319/337–7578) free. Call the SRI career advisement hotline for career planning and tracking suggestions, recommendations, and referrals. This informal service requests that you be familiar with the book What Color is Your Parachute? by Richard Bolles before calling (it's available from Planning Communications' catalog at the end of this book). After calling, you may submit your resume and this service will match you with appropriate activity or recreation coordinator, specialist, or therapy positions.

The Job Bank (Occupational Therapist Weekly, 164 Rollins Ave., Suite 301, Rockville, MD 20852; phone: 301/881–2490). This is an on–line databank that computers can access to learn about 650 jobs in occupational therapy. Contact for details.

Directories

Public Welfare Directory (American Public Welfare Association, 810 First St., NE, Suite 500, Washington, DC 20002; phone: 202/682–0100) $70/nonmembers, $65/members, plus $5 shipping if not prepaid, published every August. Lists federal social service agencies, state and local social service agencies by state, Canadian provincial, and federal agencies.

National Staff Development and Training Association Directory (NSDTA, 810 First St., NE, Suite 500, Washington, DC 20002; phone: 202/682–0100) $70/nonmembers, $65/members, published each August. In–depth directory of public welfare program and agencies by state.

Directory of Experiential Therapy and Adventure Based Counseling Programs (Association for Experiential Education, CU 249, Boulder, CO 80309; phone: 303/492–1547) $15/nonmembers, $12.50/members; add $3.50

shipping. This is a state–by–state listing of adventure and experiential alternative programs for people with special needs which use adventure programming as part of their therapeutic process.

Experience Based Training and Development: International and Domestic Programs (Association for Experiential Education, 2885 Aurora Ave., Suite 28, Boulder, CO 80303–2252; phone: 303/440–8844) $15/nonmembers, $12.50/members; add $3.50 shipping. Descriptions of training and development programs in the U.S. and abroad.

National Association of Area Agencies on Aging Membership Directory (National Association of Area Agencies on Aging, 1112 16th St., NW, Suite 100, Washington, DC 20036; phone: 202/296–8130) $40/nonmembers, $30/members, annual. Lists state and area agencies on aging as well as providers of services to elderly persons.

Senior Citizen Services (Gale Research, Inc., 835 Penobscot Bldg., Detroit, MI 48226; phone: 800/877–4253) $90/set of four volumes: Northeast, Southeast, Midwest, West; $29.95/each volume individually; 1993. Features information on 21,000 local government and private agencies and organizations that furnish services for America's older citizens including adult day care, case management, respite care, and home delivered meals. A good source for identifying potential employers and learning about them.

The National Housing Directory for People with Disabilities (Gale Research, Inc., 835 Penobscot Bldg., Detroit, MI 48226; phone: 800/877–4253) $180, 1993. You'll find descriptions of 900 state and federal agencies that provide or regulate housing for individuals who have disabilities, as well as 6,500 referral agencies, 3,700 large institutional and intensive care facilities, 7,500 group homes, and 3,200 independent living centers and facilities.

Trades and labor

Also see advice in Chapter 1 on how to use this book to find trades, labor, technical, and office support positions. Also see the Index.

Job ads in print

Women in the Trades (W.I.T.) Newsletter (Northern New England Tradeswomen, 1 Prospect Ave., St. Johnsbury, VT 05819; phone: 802/748–3308) quarterly, first issue free. Two or three job vacancies are advertised under "Jobs."

Trade Trax Newsletter (Tradeswomen, Inc., P.O. Box 40664B, San Francisco, CA 94140; phone: 415/821–7334) bimonthly, $15/annual nonmember subscription, $20/Canada, $25/elsewhere, free/members. Twenty skilled trade jobs and apprenticeships, primarily in the San Francisco Bay Area, appear under "Employment." For an extra $20 if you are employed, or an extra $5 if you are unemployed you can receive Tradeswomen Magazine. This quarterly magazine has more than 44 resources and job networking sources for women in the trades and all aspects of blue–collar work.

Job service

Tradeswomen's Job–Matching Service (Northern New England Tradeswomen, 1 Prospect Ave., St. Johnsbury, VT 05819; phone: 802/748–3308) free. Service seeks to match skilled and unskilled tradeswomen with trades job openings.

Traffic engineering and parking

Also see the listings under "Transit management."

Job ads in print

ITE Journal (Institute of Transportation Engineers, Suite 410, 525 School St., SW, Washington, DC 20024–2797; phone: 202/554–8050) monthly; $50/annual subscription (U.S., Canada, and Mexico), $65/elsewhere. Jobs listed under "Positions." Usually ten to 30 ads appear each issue.

Traffic World (Knight–Ritter, 741 National Press Building, Washington, DC 20045; phone: 202/383–6140) weekly; $159/annual subscription, write for student rates. Jobs listed under "Classified."

Roads & Bridges (Scranton Gillette Communications, Inc., 380 Northwest Highway, Des Plaines, IL 60016; phone: 708/298–6622) monthly, $15/annual subscription (U.S.), $22.50/foreign. Jobs listed under "Classified." Seven to ten job ads in typical issue.

Better Roads (P.O. Box 558, Park Ridge, IL 60068; phone: 312/693–7710) monthly, $20/annual subscription (U.S. and Canada), $90/elsewhere, free/qualified professionals. Two to five jobs with highway departments appear under "Help Wanted."

The Parking Professional (Institutional and Municipal Parking Congress, 901 Kenmore Ave., Fredericksburg, VA 22401; phone: 703/371–7535) monthly, $60/annual subscription (U.S. and Canada), $72/elsewhere. One or two ads for parking administrators or directors appear in a typical issue.

See also ***APCO Bulletin*** *listed under "Public safety."*

Mister Boffo reprinted by permission of Tribune Media Services.

Job service

The Professional Register (Institutional and Municipal Parking Congress, 701 Kenmore Ave., Fredericksburg, VA 22401; phone: 703/371–7535) free. Contact Colleen Williamson for the new brochure with the new fee structure. Obtain a registration form which will serve as your resume. When a job match is made, information about you is given to the employer which is then responsible for contacting you for more information or an interview.

Directory

Transportation Officials and Engineers Directory (American Road and Transportation Builders Association, 501 School St., SW, Washington, DC 20024; phone: 202/488–2722) $35/nonmembers, $32/members, published each May, 196 pages. This directory features a state–by–state listing of over 4,000 transportation decision makers and engineers at the local, state, and federal levels.

Transit management

Job ads in print

Passenger Transport (American Public Transit Association, 1201 New York Ave., NW, Suite 400, Washington, DC 20005; phone: 202/898–4119) weekly, $65/annual subscription (U.S. and Canada, $77/elsewhere. "Help Wanted" features six to 15 vacancies for transit and transportation managers and planners, transportation engineers, marketing directors, and administrators.

Community Transportation Reporter (Community Transportation Association of America, 1440 New York Ave., Suite 440, NW, Washington, DC 20008; phones: 800/527–8279, 202/628–1480) ten issues/year, $35/an-

nual subscription (U.S.), $47/foreign, free/members. Jobs listed under "Employment—Help Wanted." About four ads for transit managers and operators per issue.

METRO Magazine (Bobit Publishing Co., 2512 Artesia Blvd., Redondo Beach, CA 90278; phone: 310/376–8788) bimonthly, $25/annual subscription (U.S.), $30/Canada, $38/elsewhere. Jobs listed under "Classified Ads." Few job ads.

Railway Age (Simmons–Boardman Publishing, 1809 Capitol Ave., Omaha, NE 68102; phones: 800/228–9670, 402/346–4740) monthly, $45/annual subscription, free/qualified professionals. Three to five jobs in all aspects of railroad management and operations appear under "Classified."

Directories

APTA Membership Directory (American Public Transport Association, 1201 New York Ave., NW, Washington, DC 20005; phone: 202/898–4119) available only to members, published each January.

Community Transportation Resource Guide (Community Transportation Association of America, 1440 New York Ave., Suite 440, NW, Washington, DC 20008; phones: 800/527–8279, 202/628–1480) $10, published every January. Includes transportation/transit industry.

Transportation planning

Also see listings under "Planning" and "Transit management."

Directory

AASHTO Reference Book (American Association of State Highway and Transportation Officials, Suite 249, 444 N. Capitol St., Washington, DC 20001; phone: 202/624–8500) published annually, $35.50/nonmembers, $29.29/members. Extensive listing of key personnel in the highway and/or transportation departments of each state and U.S. possession; the U.S. Department of Transportation, U.S. Coast Guard, Federal Aviation Administration, Federal Highway Administration, Federal Railroad Administration, National Highway Traffic Safety Administration, U.S. Mass Transportation Administration, St. Lawrence Seaway Development Corporation, and Maritime Administration; and Canadian provincial transportation departments.

Utilities management

Also see listings under "Engineering," "Public administration," and "Public works."

Job ads in print

Public Power (American Public Power Association, 2301 M. St., NW, Washington, DC 20037;phone: 202/467–2970) bimonthly, $50/nonmember annual subscription, included in dues. Jobs listed under "Classified. Four or five job ads in a typical issue.

Power (McGraw–Hill, 11 W. 19th St., New York, NY 10011; phone: 609/426–7233) monthly, $55/annual subscription (U.S.), $60/Canada, $150/elsewhere, free to qualified executives, engineering, and supervisory personnel in electric utilities and process industries. About ten ads for electric utility supervisors, management, engineers, and instrument technicians appear under "Employment Opportunities."

Public Utilities Fortnightly (Public Utilities Reports, Inc., Suite 200, 2111 Wilson Blvd., Arlington, VA 22201; phone: 703/243–7000) bimonthly, $97/annual subscription. Few job ads.

Journal of Petroleum Marketing (Petroleum Marketers Association of America, 1901 N. Fort Meyer Drive, Suite 1200, Arlington, VA 22209–1604; phone: 703/351–8000) monthly, free to qualified professionals. A few ads in utilities management appear under "Help Wanted."

Journal of Petroleum Technology (Society of Petroleum Engineers, P.O. Box 833836, Richardson, TX 75083–3836; phone: 214/952–9393) monthly, $40/annual nonmember subscription, $15/members. A number of government positions are among the 7 or so jobs for all aspects of the energy industry.

AEE Energy Insight (Association of Energy Engineers, 4025 Pleasantdale Rd., Suite 420, Atlanta, GA 30340; phone: 404/447–5083) three issues/year, free/members only. Two or three ads for energy engineers appear under "AEE Referral Service."

APGA Newsletter (American Public Gas Association, 11094–D Lee Highway, Suite 102, Fairfax, VA 22033; phone: 703/352–3890) biweekly, available only to members, included in dues. Jobs listed under "Position Available." Few job ads; job ads not in every issue.

Directories

Public Power Directory (American Public Power Association, 2301 M St., NW, Washington, DC 20037; phone: 202/467–2970) $90/nonmembers, free/members. Published in the January–February issue of *Public Power* described above under "Job ads in print."

Publicly Owned Natural Gas System Directory (American Public Gas Association, 11094D Lee Highway, Suite 102, Fairfax, VA 22030; phone: 703/352–3890) $17/nonmembers, free/members, published annually.

Nuclear Power Plants Worldwide (Gale Research, Inc., 835 Penobscot Bldg., Detroit, MI 48226–4094; phone: 800/877–4253) $129, 550 pages, 1993. You'll find nontechnical profiles of 741 commercial nuclear power plants in the U.S. and elsewhere that are currently operating, planners, or inactive. Learn the number of employees, reactor type, contact data, plant programs, start–up dates, and more. This is a good source for identifying potential employers and for preparing for an interview.

Annual Membership Issue of the Journal of Petroleum Technology (Society of Petroleum Engineers, P.O. Box 833836, Richardson, TX 75083–3836; phone: 214/952–9393) $150/nonmembers, $50/members. This is the May issue. It's obviously less expensive to just subscribe as described above under "Job ads in print."

The Geophysical Directory (The Geophysical Directory, Inc., P.O. Box 130508, Houston, TX 77219; phone: 713/529–8789) $50/U.S. (Texas residents add 8.25 percent sales tax), $65/foreign (via air mail). Lists domestic and foreign geophysical contractors and suppliers, oil and gas companies, and mining companies using geophysics. Includes government agencies that utilize geophysics.

Brown's Directory of North American and International Gas Companies (Advanstar Communications, 131 W. First St., Duluth, MN 55806; phone: 218/723–9200) $255/U.S. and Canada, $275/elsewhere, annual in November. Includes listings of U.S., federal, state, and Canadian regulatory agencies.

Water/wastewater operations

Also see listings under "Engineering," "Environment," and "Public works."

Job ads in print

The Jobank (Water Pollution Control Federation, 601 Wythe St., Alexandria, VA 22314; phone: 703/684–2400) bimonthly, contact for current rates. About 16 positions in pollution control and wastewater operations are in the typical issue.

Water Environment Technology (Water Pollution Control Federation, 601 Wythe St., Alexandria, VA 22314; phone: 703/684–2400) monthly, contact for current rates. Jobs listed under "Classifieds." About 10 to 15 job ads are in the typical issue.

Water Well Journal (National Ground Water Association, 6375 Riverside Dr., Dublin, OH 43017; phone: 614/761–3222) monthly, $12/annual subscription, free/members. About eight vacancies for drillers, hydrogeologists, and hydrologists are listed under "Opportunities."

Water Engineering & Management (Scranton Gillette Communications, 380 East Northwest Highway, Des Plaines, IL 60016; phone: 708/298–6622) monthly, $25/annual subscription. Six to 12 jobs listed under "Classified" for design engineers, sanitation engineers, and water system engineers.

Journal AWWA (American Water Works Association, 6666 W. Quincy, Denver, CO 80235; phone: 303/794–7711) monthly, $85/nonmember annual subscription (North America), $110/elsewhere; included in annual dues ($72/U.S., $115/foreign). Jobs listed under "Classified." Five to 20 job ads grace each issue.

Groundwater (Association of Groundwater Scientists, 6375 Riverside Dr., Dublin, OH 43017; phones: 800/423–7748 [outside Ohio], 614/761–1711) bimonthly, $90/annual subscription. A handful of government vacancies are among the 40 to 50 ads for geologists, hydrogeologists, environmental engineers, and hazardous waste engineers presented under "Ground-Water Employment Opportunities."

Mainstream (American Water Works Association, 6666 W. Quincy, Denver, CO 80235; phone: 303/794–7711) monthly, $13/nonmember annual subscription (U.S.), $18.50/foreign, free/members (annual dues: $65/U.S., $93/foreign). Jobs listed under "Employment." About 15 job ads appear in the typical issue.

Directories

AWWA Membership Roster (American Water Works Association, 6666 W. Quincy, Denver, CO 80235; phone: 303/794–7711) free/members only, published in 1988–89 and a new one will come out in 1995.

California Water Resources Directory: A Guide to Organizations and Information Resources (California Institute of Public Affairs, P.O. Box 189040, Sacramento, CA 95818; phone: 916/442–2472) $25, 120 pages, 1991. Includes nearly 1,000 governmental and non–governmental organizations that deal with water policy, development, supply, and conservation as well as related health, environmental quality, energy, and economic aspects.

Chapter 3

Local sources for local and state government jobs

This chapter is divided into several sections. First up are several publications that carry ads for all types of local government jobs within a specific region of the country. These are followed by national directories of local governments and officials. A second set of directories identifies state officials and agencies for each of the 50 states, and in many cases, U.S. possessions and territories as well. Several direct sources of job vacancies are also presented.

Each of the directories listed in these two sections furnishes the names, addresses, and phone numbers of department and agency heads plus the other officials listed in the description of the directory. These directories will help you identify the proper person or agency to contact to learn of job openings in local or state government.

The bulk of this chapter consists of sources for job vacancies in local, state, and the federal government that focus on each individual state or U.S. possession. These include periodicals, job–matching services, job hotlines, and state directories of local governments and officials. The scope of most of these job sources is broad: they cover everything in local, state, or federal government rather than a single occupation. Please note, however, that Chapter 2 does contain an extensive listing of job sources for librarians that cover a single state "Library services."

Specific information on how to find state jobs is also provided for each state. In addition, you are guided to information on state–operated Job Service Centers which often operate computer–based job–matching services for professional and office support, trades, labor, and technical positions in local and state government. You are also directed to the appropriate Federal Job Information Centers for each state.

Be sure to read the discussion at the beginning of the section entitled "Job sources: State–by–state."

Job sources for multi–state regions

Only a few periodicals provide job information for multi–state regions in the U.S. These are among the best sources of job vacancies for some states.

Job ads in print

Rocky Mountain Employment Newsletter (Intermountain Publishing, 703 S. Broadway, Suite 311–B0, 14th Street, Glenwood Springs, CO 81601–3949; phone: 303/945–8991) 18 issues/year, $21/three–month subscription to one edition, $26/any two editions, $31/three editions. Two and one month subscriptions also available. Published in four editions: Colorado–Wyoming, Arizona–New Mexico, Idaho–Montana, and Washington–Oregon. Combined, the four editions include over 500 positions, about 20 to 25 percent of them in government. The positions tend to orient toward the outdoors, with quite a few in natural resources, environment, and wildlife.

The Job Finder: A Checklist of Openings for Administrative and Governmental Research Employment in the West (Western Governmental Research Association, 10900 Los Alamitos Blvd., Suite 201, Los Alamitos, CA 90720; phone: 310/795–6694) semimonthly; $20/annual, $15/student for membership in Western Governmental Research Association which includes subscription. Typical issue features about 20 to 30 job openings in planning and public administration. Serves: 14 western states.

Western Planner (Western Planning Resources, Inc., c/o Steve Kurtz, 632 S. David St., Casper, WY 82601; phone: 307/266–2524) eight issues/year; $24/annual subscription, $15/annual subscription for members of the American Planning Association, $15/annual student subscription. Serves: Alaska,

Arizona, Colorado, Idaho, Montana, Nebraska, Nevada, New Mexico, North and South Dakota, Utah, Washington, and Wyoming. Two or three planning and related positions are listed under "Jobs Wanted."

National sources for local jobs

Directories

The Municipal Yearbook (International City/County Management Association, 777 N. Capitol St., NE, Washington, DC 20002; phones: 800/745–8780, 202/289–4262) $79.90 plus $5 shipping if not prepaid, published each May.

Includes the following directories: officials in U.S. municipalities which features the form of government, manager/administrator, city clerk, finance officer, fire chief, police chief, and public works director; county officials in U.S. counties which lists county board chairperson, county executive or appointed administrator, clerk, chief financial officer, personnel director, and chief law enforcement officer; state municipal leagues, state agencies for community affairs; state, provincial (Canadian), and international municipal management associations; state associations of counties; provincial (Canadian) and territorial associations; provincial and territorial agencies for local affairs in Canada; directors of councils of governments recognized by ICMA; local government chief administrators in other countries; and professional, special assistance, and educational organizations serving local and state governments.

Braddock's Federal–State–Local Government Directory (Braddock Communications, 909 N. Washington St., Suite 310, Alexandria, VA 22314; phone: 703/549–6500) $20 plus $3.50 shipping, 1990. Lists names, addresses, and phone numbers of over 10,000 elected officials and key personnel at all levels of government.

Election Results Directory (National Conference of State Legislatures, Book Order Department, 1560 Broadway, Suite 700, Denver, CO 80202; phone: 303/830–2054) $35 plus $4 shipping, 282 pages, annual. Lists names, addresses, and phone numbers for all state legislators, members of congress, and state and federal executive branch officials. Summaries of party composition and demographic information for each state is also included.

Directory of Legislative Leaders (National Conference of State Legislatures, Book Order Department, 1560 Broadway, Suite 700, Denver, CO 80202; phone: 303/830–2054) $15 plus $3 shipping, 112 pages, published each April. Includes state presiding officers, majority and minority leaders, and key staff members by both capitol and direct addresses, telephone numbers, and interim home or business telephone numbers.

State Legislative Staff Directory 1993 (National Conference of State Legislatures, Book Order Department, 1560 Broadway, Suite 700, Denver, CO 80202; phone: 303/830–2054) $35 plus $3 shipping, 162 pages, published each May. Identifies legislative policy analysts in 19 issue areas including education, health care, agriculture, energy, fiscal, labor, criminal justice, and more. Listings provide: subject area, state, key staff names and addresses, phone numbers, and area of specialty.

Municipal Yellow Book (Monitor Publishing, Co., 104 Fifth Ave., 2nd Floor, New York, NY 10011; phone: 212/627–4140) semiannual, $165/annual subscription. In over 700 pages, this directory supplies the names, addresses, and phone numbers of nearly 20,000 key elected and administrative officials of leading cities, counties, and regional jurisdictions as well as a complete breakdown of municipal and county departments, agencies, and subdivisions.

Municipal Executive Directory (Carroll Publishing Co., 1058 Thomas Jefferson St., NW, Washington, DC 20077–0007; phone: 202/333–8620) $130/annual subscription, updated and published in full twice a year, 500+ pages. Over 65,000 entries covering all U.S. municipalities. Lists 32,000 elected, appointed, and career officials and provides information about each municipality over 15,000 in population.

Directory of City Policy Officials (National League of Cities, 1301 Pennsylvania Ave., NW, Washington, DC 20004; phone: 202/626–3000) $35/nonmembers, $15/members; published annually, 155 pages. List 16,500 chief elected officials, administrative officers, and members of governing bodies in the 1,750 NLC member cities plus other municipalities over 30,000 population.

County Executive Directory (Carroll Publishing Co., 1058 Thomas Jefferson St., NW, Washington, DC 20077–0007; phone: 202/333–8620) $130/annual subscription, updated and published in full twice a year, 375 pages. Over 60,000 entries covering all U.S. counties or equivalent listed by state. Provides information about each county over 25,000 in population. Covers 27,150 officials in more than 3,100 county governments. Organizational listing includes managers of government functions.

Municipal/County Executive Directory (Carroll Publishing Co., 1058 Thomas Jefferson St., NW, Washington, DC 20077–0007; phone: 202/333–8620) $127. Published annually, it guides you to more than 32,000 elected and appointed municipal and county officials throughout the country. Details are given about every municipality of 15,000 or more and every county of 25,000, including a locator phone number and the names and numbers of key personnel.

State Municipal League Directory (National League of Cities, 1301 Pennsylvania Ave., NW, Washington, DC 20004; phone: 202/626–3000) $10/nonmembers, $5/members; published annually, 60 pages. Lists profiles of 49 state municipal leagues, personnel policies, programs, facilities, and publications.

State and Regional Associations (Columbia Books, 1212 New York Ave., NW, Suite 300, Washington, DC 20005; phone: 202/898–0662) $50, published annually. This volume guides you to thousands of associations at the state and regional levels including those in government. As discussed under "Job sources: State–by–state," many of these localized groups offer job services. For purely practical reasons, the *Government Job Finder* does not generally report on these because there are just so many of them that they could fill a book this size on their own.

Salary surveys

Compensation 94: An Annual Report on Local Government Executive Salaries and Fringe Benefits (International City/County Management Association, 777 N. Capitol St., NE, Washington, DC 20002; phones: 800/745–8780, 202/289–4262) $180/nonmembers, $125 members (add $5 shipping and handling if not prepaid), published annually. Presents salary and fringe benefit information on city and county managers, councils of governments directors, assistant managers, police and fire chiefs, finance directors, parks and recreation directors, and public works directors. Includes average salaries by state, region, and jurisdiction size.

Comparative Retirement Benefits for General State Employees and Public Safety Personnel (National Conference of State Legislatures, Book Order Department, 1560 Broadway, Suite 700, Denver, CO 80202; phone: 303/830–2054) $5, 14 pages, 1991 edition. 50 state comparison of general state and public safety personnel retirement benefits, including benefit formulas and age and service for regular retirement.

National sources for state jobs

Job ads in print

State Legislatures (National Conference of State Legislatures, 1560 Broadway, Suite 700, Denver, CO 80202; phone: 303/830–2054) monthly, $49/annual subscription (U.S.), $51.50/Canada. A small munchkin's handful of positions with legislatures and organizations that lobby legislators appear under "Classified Advertising."

Internships in State Government (Graduate Group, 86 Norwood Rd., West Hartford, CT 06117; phones: 203/232–3100, 203/236–5570) $27.50, published annually. Includes information on hundreds of internships with state government.

Directories

State Administrative Officials Classified by Function 1993–94 (The Council of State Governments, Iron Works Pike, P.O. Box 11910, Lexington, KY 40578; phones: 800/800–1910, 606/231–1939) $30 plus $3.75 postage, published in November of odd–numbered years. Lists names, addresses, and phone numbers of directors of state agencies in over 150 categories along with definitions of each function.

State Legislative Staff Directory (National Conference of State Legislatures, Book Order Department, 1560 Broadway, Suite 700, Denver, CO 80202; phone: 303/830–2054) $35 plus $4 shipping, 172 pages, published each April. Lists legislative staff by state and 19 subject areas.

State Yellow Book (Monitor Publishing, Co., 104 Fifth Ave., 2nd Floor, New York, NY 10011; phone: 212/627–4140) quarterly, $215/annual subscription. Over 1,000 pages furnish detailed information on the executive and legislative branches of every states' government (and the District of Columbia and the four insular U.S. territories) as well as information on the counties in each state.

State Executive Directory (Carroll Publishing Co., 1058 Thomas Jefferson St., NW, Washington, DC 20077–0007; phone: 202/333–8620) $160/annual subscription, updated and published in full three times a year, 500+ pages. Over 92,000 entries listing officers, committee heads, legislators, mangers of boards and authorities, and department heads.

State Directors of Administration and General Services–1992 Directory (The Council of State Governments, 3560 Iron Works Pike, P.O. Box 11910, Lexington, KY 40578–1910; phones: 800/800–1910, 606/231–1939) $22.50 plus $3.75 shipping and handling, 30 pages.

State Legislative Leadership, Committees and Staff 1993–94 (The Council of State Governments, 3560 Iron Works Pike, P.O. Box 11910, Lexington, KY 40578–1910; phones: 800/800–1910, 606/231–1939) $30 plus $3.75 postage, 279 names, addresses, and phone numbers of state legislative leaders, committee and chairpersons, principal legislative staff officers, and staff members, plus organizational patterns.

State Elective Officials and the Legislatures 1993–94 (The Council of State Governments, 3560 Iron Works Pike, P.O. Box 11910, Lexington, KY 40578–1910; phones: 800/800–1910, 606/231–1939) $35 plus $3.75

postage. Lists names, addresses, and phone numbers of members of state legislative bodies and elected officials with statewide jurisdiction.

50 State Legislative Directory (California Journal, 2101 K Street, Sacramento, CA 95816; phone: 916/444-2840) $95 plus 7.75 percent sales tax and $2.75 shipping. In over 400 pages, this directory provides the names, district and capitol addresses for all state legislators, plus all committees and frequently called phone numbers.

50 State Roster on Diskette (California Journal, 2101 K Street, Sacramento, CA 95816; phone: 916/444-2840) $495. For each state legislator, includes party, district, house and state, district address, capitol address, committees, and committee assignments. Available for every state legislature in the country. Available in 5.25–inch and 3.5–inch MS–DOS diskettes in ASCII, comma–delimited fields; in dBase; or WordPerfect.

Organizations of State Government Officials Directory (The Council of State Governments, 3560 Iron Works Pike, P.O. Box 11910, Lexington, KY 40578–1910; phones: 800/800–1910, 606/231–1939) $25 plus $3.75 postage, 85 pages, 1992. Lists more than 140 organizations associated with state government. Includes addresses, phone numbers, membership requirements, programs, publications, and organizational structures.

BNA's Directory of State and Federal Courts, Judges, and Clerks (Bureau of National Affairs Books, P.O. Box 6036, Rockville, MD 20850–9914; phone: 800/372–1033) $85 plus $3/shipping, 513 pages, last published in July 1992. Gives name, address, phone number, court number, district, and geographical area served, for over 15,900 state judges and court clerks in more than 2,100 state courts in the U.S. and possessions.

List of State Departments of Community Affairs (Council of State Community Development Agencies, Suite 224, 444 North Capitol St., NW, Washington, DC 20001; phone: 202/393–6435) free, four pages. Lists directors of State Departments of Community Affairs.

Secretaries of State Handbook (The Council of State Governments, 3560 Iron Works Pike, P.O. Box 11910, Lexington, KY 40578–1910; phones: 800/800–1910, 606/231–1939) $35 plus $3.75 postage, published in odd–numbered years. Lists the services each state's secretary of state (or lieutenant governor who functions as secretary of state) furnishes.

Interstate Conference of Employment Security Agencies State Agencies, Inc. (ICESA, 444 N. Capitol St., NW, Suite 142, Washington, DC 20001; phone: 202/628–5588) free, published each January. Lists the name, address, phone, and fax number of the director of each state or U.S. possession's employment security agency, such as a department of labor, employment security, or department of employment and training.

National Association of State Alcohol and Drug Abuse Membership Directory (NASADA, 444 N. Capitol St., NW, Suite 642, Washington, DC 20001; phone: 202/783–6868) $5. Updated monthly.

National Assembly of State Arts Agencies Membership Directory (NASAA, 1010 Vermont Ave., NW, Suite 920, Washington, DC 20005; phone: 202/347–6352) $10, revised monthly. This is simply a list of the names, addresses, and phone numbers of state arts agencies.

National Association of State Budget Officers Membership Directory (NASBO, 400 N. Capitol St., NW, Suite 299, Washington, DC 20001; phone: 202/624–5382) free/members only, published semiannually.

National Association of State Departments of Agriculture Membership Directory (NASDA, 1156 15th St., Suite 1020, Washington, DC 20005; phone: 202/296–9680) free, published each May.

National Association of State Units on Aging Membership Directory (NASUA, 1225 I St., NW, Suite 725, Washington, DC 20005; phone: 202/898–2578) free/members only, updated as necessary.

American Association of Motor Vehicle Administrators Membership Directory (AAMVA, Suite 1100, 4200 Wilson Blvd., Arlington, VA 22203; phone: 703/522–4200) $100. It is what it says it is.

State Employment Opportunities for Anthropologists (American Anthropological Association, Suite 640, 4350 N. Fairfax Dr., Arlington, VA 22203) $5/nonmembers, $3.50/members. This is a useful guide for anthropologists seeking work in state government. Learn how to move strategically toward an anthropology relevant state career, where to apply, whom to see, and what to say.

Encyclopedia of Associations: Regional, State, and Local Organizations (Gale Research, Inc., 835 Penobscot Bldg., Detroit, MI 48226; phone: 800/877–4253) $469/five–volume set, $99 for each regional volume individually, 3,716 pages total, 1992. Describes over 50,000 non–profit organizations with interstate, state, city, or local scope and interest, including professional associations for just about every specialty within government. Also available on CD–ROM and online via DIALOG as File 114 (DIALOG Information Services, 3460 Hillview Ave., Palo Alto, CA 94304; phones: 800/334–2564).

See also the listing for the ***Federal/State Executive Directory*** *in Chapter 4.*

Job sources: State–by–state

The entries that comprise the rest of this chapter provide job sources for both local and state government positions, as well as information on the Federal Job Information Center or Centers for each state.

State Operated Job Services. Most states offer employment services that include career counseling and a job–matching service of some kind. The listings in this chapter for each state include information to help you locate each state's employment services, including Job Service Offices. Some states were very forthcoming about their job services and gave us lots of information which we've included in this chapter. Others acted as if the location of their Job Service Offices was top secret information and told us very little. You may have to contact them directly for more details if what we've given you here is not enough for your needs.

Many of these state employment services periodically publish a listing of available job openings with locations and starting salaries. Some states offer a job hotline. Only a few states publish directories of state officials. The national directories of state officials described earlier in this chapter are usually your best source for information on specific state agencies and departments.

In addition, these state operated Job Service Offices provide information on local, state, and federal government job vacancies. Job Service Offices participate in the Interstate Job Bank Service which the U.S. Department of Labor's Employment and Training Administration developed. Jobs in other states are on microfiche which can be viewed at your local Job Service office. In some states you can view these job openings on a computer, including computer terminals you can use yourself. Any Job Service Office can also call the Interstate Job Bank on its toll–free number to get further information on out–of–state positions. You can learn about government job vacancies in other states through this job bank which should be accessible from most Job Service Centers that have a personal computer. But be aware that some employees at some Job Service Offices just don't offer this information to you. You may have to be a bit assertive to get it.

These job–matching services furnished by Job Service Offices really amount to a free employment service for government professionals and technical, labor, and clerical workers. However, habitually–employed individuals rarely take advantage of these services. Perhaps they are turned off by the generic moniker for these offices: the "unemployment office." Don't let misconceptions steer you away from a state's Job Service Offices no matter how high in the government hierarchy you wish to work. They are usually an effective source of government job openings.

These job–matching services furnished by Job Service Offices really amount to a free employment service for government professionals and technical, labor, and clerical workers. However, habitually–employed individuals rarely take advantage of these services. Perhaps they are turned off by the generic moniker for these offices: the "unemployment office." Don't let misconceptions steer you away from a state's Job Service Offices no matter how high in the government hierarchy you wish to work. They are usually an effective source of government job openings.

State jobs. The state–by–state listings include specific information on locating state government positions. Some states offer easily accessible and extensive listings of state government jobs. Others pretty much let job seekers twist slowly in the wind. Some are so patronage–laden that you're usually wasting your time if you try to get a state job without a political sponsor. Generally, a state's Job Service Offices carry listings of jobs with that state's government.

Chapter newsletters of speciality organizations. The newsletters produced by the state chapters of many professional organizations frequently carry job advertisements. Usually, these newsletters are available only to chapter members. Some chapters, however, allow nonmembers to subscribe or join only the chapter. Because officers of state chapters change so frequently, you should contact the national headquarters of the appropriate professional organization to obtain the address of any chapter president you wish to contact.

Local Newspapers. As mentioned earlier, the classified section of local newspapers is sometimes the best source of local and, occasionally, state government job ads.

Many municipal and county governments advertise job vacancies only in local papers because the lead time for ads is much shorter than for magazines and newsletters. Local ads also help to minimize the number of applicants. Some local governments limit their advertising to local papers in the hope of keeping the jobs in the family, so to speak. In a handful of states, local newspaper advertisements are just about the only decent source of ads for local government positions.

Municipal League Publications. The listings in the remainder of this chapter often include both a periodical and directory published by the state's municipal league.

Types of job sources listed

For each state, the following types of job sources are identified:

Periodicals. Periodicals are listed if they carry ads for local and/or state government jobs within that state. We'll tell you about the rare instances where a local newspaper is the best source for government job ads.

Job–matching services and job hotlines. Job–matching services and job hotlines that handle local and/or state government positions are described.

Directories. Directories of local governments and/or officials are included to get you to the right official concerning local or state government jobs. These include names, addresses, and phone numbers. Each listing identifies the types of officials that the directory includes if it's not clear from the directory's title.

State Jobs. Periodicals, job banks, and job hotlines that service only state government jobs are identified under this heading. Many of these also carry announcements of local and federal government positions in the state.

Job Service Offices. Information is provided to help you find the locations of Job Service Offices (also known in some states as Employment Security Offices) throughout each state. This information is usually listed under the "State Jobs" heading for each state.

State Agency Locator. By calling this phone number, you can track down the phone and address of any state department, agency, or employee. When you find that the phone number of a state agency listed in the *Government Job Finder* has been changed, disconnected, or the agency has moved without leaving a forwarding address, call the state agency locator to quickly obtain the new phone number or address and please use the *Reader Feedback Form* on page 311 to let us know of the change so we can include it in the free *Update Sheet* (see page 313) and our next edition.

FJIC. The addresses and telephone numbers of the Federal Job Information Centers that list federal positions for each state are provided in this chapter. When a state is split between several FJICs, the *Government Job Finder* tells you which parts of a state are assigned to which FJIC. If a FJIC answers its phone only during certain hours, those hours are cited. Centers are open only on weekdays. Whenever possible, we've included the hours when staff are present and identified which centers are self–service. The addresses and phone numbers were accurate as of December 1993. To receive a more up–to–date list of FJICs, contact the Office of Personnel Management at 202/606–2700 (press 000 after the recorded prompts to talk with a job counselor). Federal positions are also announced on a number of **TDD** job hotlines and by modem using the *Federal Job Information Center Electronic Bulletin Board Service* which includes a national electronic bulletin board and several regional ones. These are all reported in Chapter 4 where you'll find an in–depth discussion of using FJICs.

State job sources

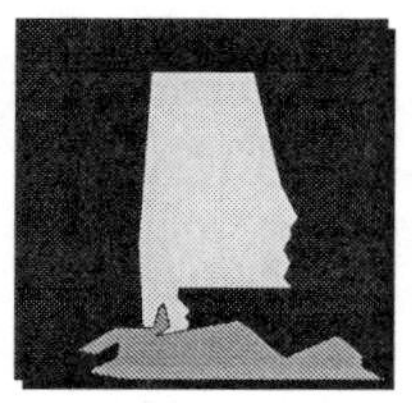

Alabama

Alabama Municipal Journal (Alabama League of Municipalities, 535 Adams Ave., Montgomery, AL 36104; phone: 205/263–1042) monthly; $12/annual subscription. Few job ads.

Directory (Alabama League of Municipalities, 535 Adams Ave., Montgomery, AL 36104; phone: 205/263–1042) published annually; $20/nonmembers, first copy free to members; extra copies $20/each. Lists elected officials and city managers.

Local job hotlines

Huntsville: 205/535–4942

Montgomery: 205/241–2217

State Jobs

Contact the State Personnel Department (64 N. Union St., Montgomery, AL 36130; phone: 205/242–3389).

To locate **Job Service Offices**, contact the Employment Services Division (Department of Industrial Relations, 649 Monroe St., Montgomery, AL 36131; director's phone: 205/242–8003).

Alabama State Agency locator: 205/261–2500

FJIC: Suite 341, Building 600, 3322 Memorial Parkway South, Huntsville, AL 35801–5311; phone: 205/544–5803, self service 7 a.m. to 4 p.m.

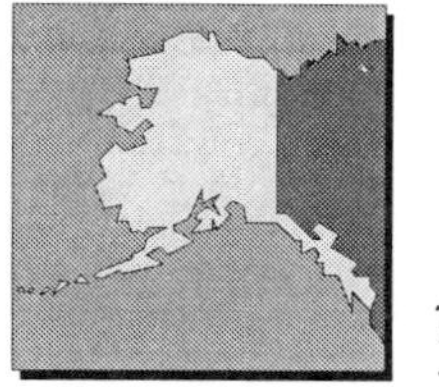

Alaska

The Touchstone (Alaska Municipal League, Suite 200, 217 Second St., Juneau, AK 99801; phone: 907/586–1325; FAX: 907/463–5480) bimonthly, $20/annual nonmember subscription, free/members. Two to four jobs are listed under "Job Opportunities."

AML Legislative Bulletin (Alaska Municipal League, Suite 200, 217 Second St., Juneau, AK 99801; phone: 907/586–1325; FAX: 907/463–5480) weekly when state legislature is in session, free/members, $150/annual nonmember subscription. Two or three jobs are listed under "Job Opportunities."

Alaska Municipal Officials Directory (Alaska Municipal League, Suite 200, 217 Second St., Juneau, AK 99801; phone: 907/586–1325; FAX: 907/463–5480) $50, published annually, 160 pages.

Municipal Salary Survey (Alaska Municipal League, Suite 200, 217 Second St., Juneau, AK 99801; phone: 907/586–1325; FAX: 907/463–5480) $50, published each September.

Local job hotlines

Several of the Alaska Employment Service Offices offer a daily recorded job hotline message which includes the following information about government as well as private sector and non–profit job openings:

Anchorage (907/269–4740), professional, technical, and clerical positions: requirements, salary for new and hard–to–fill positions
Dillingham (907/842–5575): titles of all job vacancies
Eagle River (907/694–6999): titles of rush and hard–to–fill jobs
Fairbanks (907/451–2875): titles and salary of all job openings, descriptions of some jobs
Homer (907/235–7200): titles of all job vacancies
Juneau (907/790–4571): titles of new job openings
Kenai (907/283–4606): qualifications of all job openings, no salary information
Kodiak (907/486–6838): titles and salary of all job vacancies, descriptions of some positions
MatSu (907/376–8860): titles and salary of new job openings, titles only for previously listed positions
Seward (907/224–5274): titles of all job vacancies

State jobs

The state uses a pre–qualification system for most positions. Generally, you can learn about the different job classifications, their requirements, and how to apply by contacting the Department of Administration, Division of Personnel (P.O. Box C, Juneau, AK 99811–0201; phone: 907/465–4430). Job seekers found eligible are placed on a list from which agencies hire when actual vacancies occur. When there are not enough qualified candidates on the list for a position, a vacancy announcement is issued at this office.

About 95 percent of the state government positions are available only to Alaska residents. There are, however, about 20 classifications at any one time which are open non–residents. To learn which these are, contact the Division of Personnel and ask for a copy of the *Current Out–of–State Recruitment List*. Also ask for an application form (they do accept photocopies).

When the state has difficulty filling a vacancy, it may also advertise in newspapers in the vicinity of the job's location.

Find **Job Service Offices** by contacting the Alaska Employment Service (Department of Labor, suite 208, 111 W. Eighth St., P.O. Box 25509, Juneau, AK 99802–5509; phone: 907/465–4531).

Alaska State Agency locator: 907/465–4648

FJIC: 222 W. 7th Ave., P.O. Box 22, Anchorage, AK 99513; phone: 907/271–5821, staff present Tuesday through Thursday, 11 a.m. to 1 p.m.

Arizona

Also see the listings under "Job sources for multi–state regions" at the beginning of this chapter.

Local Government Directory (League of Arizona Cities and Towns, 1820 W. Washington St., Phoenix, AZ 85007; phone: 602/258–5786) published each January and July, $15. Lists all elected officials, managers, and department heads for cities and towns, counties, councils of governments, and selected state offices.

Local job hotlines

Chandler: 602/786–2294

Glendale: 602/435–4402

Mesa: 602/644–2759

Phoenix: 602/252–5627

Pima County: 602/740–3530

Tempe: 602/350–8217

Tucson: 602/791–5068

State jobs

Job Hotline (State Personnel Division, Department of Administration, 1831 W. Jefferson, Phoenix, AZ 85007; phone: 602/542–5216). For a recording of state jobs that are currently open (usually for only a week), call the 24–hour hotline 602/542–4966. Updated weekly.

Open Continuous Job Listing (State Personnel Division, Department of Administration, 1831 W. Jefferson, Phoenix, AZ 85007; phone: 602/542–5216) monthly, free. This lists jobs for which the state is continuously recruiting. It is also available at all state Job Service Offices. The State Personnel Division will mail it to out–of–staters and to state residents who live outside Maricopa and Pima counties.

To locate **Job Service Offices**, contact the Employment and Rehabilitation Services Division (Department of Economic Security, P.O. Box 6123–010A, Phoenix, AZ 85005; director's phone: 602/542–4016).

Arizona State Agency locator: 602/542–4900

FJIC: Room 1415, 3225 N. Central Ave., Phoenix, AZ 85012; phone: 602/640–4800.

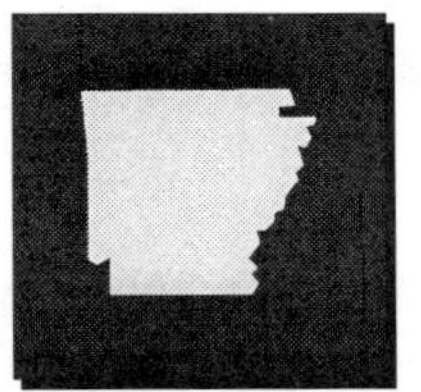

Arkansas

City & Town (Arkansas Municipal League, P.O. Box 38, North Little Rock, AR 72115; phone: 501/374–3484) monthly, $15/annual subscription. Jobs listed under "Municipal Mart."

Directory of Arkansas Municipal Officials (Arkansas Municipal League, P.O. Box 38, North Little Rock, AR 72115; phone: 501/374–3484) $10, published annually.

Arkansas Employment Security Department Job–Matching Service (Employment Security Department, Capitol Mall, Little Rock, AR 72201; director's phone: 501/682–2121; available at any of the 33 local Employment Security Department offices) free. A job seeker completes the service's resume form and is then matched with jobs. The service contacts matched applicants to arrange job interviews with employers. Applications are kept active for 60 days.

Local job hotline

Little Rock: 501/371–4505

State jobs

Each state agency does its own hiring. They generally advertise in the local newspapers and at the Job Service Offices. Eventually every job applicant will go through the Employment Security Department (Room 506, ESD Building, P.O. Box 2981, Little Rock, AR 72203; phone: 501/682–2121).

For information on the location of the 34 **Job Service Offices** (known in Arkansas as local Employment Security Department offices), contact the Employment Security Department, (Room 506, ESD Building, P.O. Box 2981, Little Rock, AR 72203; phone: 501/682–2121).

Arkansas State Agency locator: 501/682–3000

FJIC: 8610 Broadway, Room 305, San Antonio, TX 78217; phones: 210/229–6611, 210/229–6600. For forms call 210/229–6618; staff present 7:30 a.m. to 4:30 p.m.

California

*Also see **Jobs Available** listed under "Government jobs in general" in Chapter 2.*

Western City (League of California Cities, 1400 K St., Sacramento, CA 95814; phone: 916/444–8960) monthly; $24/annual U.S. subscription, $32/annual foreign subscription, $15/annual student subscription (U.S.). Jobs listed under "Job Opportunities." About 50 job ads in typical issue.

Job vacancies are listed in the monthly membership newsletters of the following three municipal management assistant groups. Addresses are particularly subject to change, but as of this writing you can contact the following management assistant groups for information on how to join and receive the membership newsletter:

> ***MMANC Newsletter*** (Municipal Management Assistants of Northern California, c/o Connie Sandberg, City of Mountain View, P.O. Box 7540, Mountain View, CA 94039; phone: 415/903–6382) $25/annual nonmember subscription, free/members. About three or four "Job Announcements" for all types of professional positions in municipal management are in a typical issue. The contact person changes each November. Ms. Sandberg should be able to give you the new contact for 1995.

MMANC Roster (Municipal Management Assistants of Northern California, c/o Connie Sandberg, City of Mountain View, P.O. Box 7540, Mountain View, CA 94039; phone: 415/903–6382) $10/nonmembers, free/members, published each February. The contact person changes each November. Ms. Sandberg should be able to give you the new contact for 1995.

PMACC News (Public Management Assistants of Central California, c/o Robert Groeber, City of Visalia, 707 W. Acequia Ave., Visalia, CA 93291; phone: 209/738–3423) monthly, free/members. You can ask to be placed on their mailing list which will get you the newsletter free for a while, but why not join since the dues are only $20 a year and as a member you'll make some valuable networking contacts? Each issue has announcements of three or four municipal vacancies in central California.

The Outlook (Municipal Management Assistants of Southern California, c/o Graduate School for Public Policy, 1250 Bellflower Blvd., Long Beach, CA 90840; phone: 310/985–4039) quarterly, free/members only, $40/annual dues, $20/students. From two to ten job openings appear under "Jobs Available."

MMASC Update (Municipal Management Assistants of Southern California, c/o Graduate School for Public Policy, 1250 Bellflower Blvd., Long Beach, CA 90840; phone: 310/985–4039) eight issues/year (in months *The Outlook* is not published), free/members only, $40/annual dues, $20/students. From two to five job vacancies appear under "Jobs Available."

MMASC Membership Roster (Municipal Management Assistants of Southern California, c/o Graduate School for Public Policy, 1250 Bellflower Blvd., Long Beach, CA 90840; phone: 310/985–4039) free/members only, $40/annual dues, $20/students, published each summer.

PiES Job Alert! (Public Interest Clearinghouse, 200 McAllister St., San Francisco, CA 94102–4978; phone: 415/255–1714) semimonthly, three–month subscriptions: $30/employed nonmembers, $15/unemployed nonmembers, students, or members; annual subscription: $125/schools and institutions. Over 50 professional and support positions are described per issue for work with legal aid offices, progressive law firms, and other kinds of law/advocacy–related public interest organizations largely in the San Francisco Bay area. They're getting an increasingly large number of job openings from elsewhere in California and from other western states.

The Advocate (Public Interest Clearinghouse, 200 McAllister St., San Francisco, CA 94102–4978; phone: 415/255–1714) eight issues/year, $75/annual subscription, $50 if also subscribing to *PiES Job Alert* described immediately above. Describes several dozen jobs, largely in California, of interest to law

Travels with Farley reprinted by permission of Phil Frank.

students such as internships, clerkships, and work–study positions with legal services and governments.

Directory of Bay Area Public Interest Organizations (Public Interest Clearinghouse, 200 McAllister St., San Francisco, CA 94102–4978; phone: 415/255–1714) $27/nonmembers, $22/members. Features 600 organizations working for social change in the nine–county San Francisco Bay Area. Indexed by subject and county. Includes a chapter on finding paid public interest jobs in the Bay Area that tells you about over 40 local job resources including local periodicals with job ads and job services. The most recent edition was published in 1991.

Public Interest, Private Practice: A Directory of Public Interest Law Firms in Northern California (Public Interest Clearinghouse, 200 McAllister St., San Francisco, CA 94102–4978; phone: 415/255–1714) $11/nonmembers, $8/members, last published in 1991, updated slightly in 1993. Lists over 200 for–profit law firms that devote a substantial portion of their legal work to the public interest.

Public Interest Employment Service Resource Center Clipboards (Public Interest Clearinghouse, 200 McAllister St., San Francisco, CA 94102–4978; phone: 415/255–1714) free to members and subscribers to the Public Interest Clearinghouse's publications, $1 donation for nonmembers. You can drop in between 9 a.m. and 5 p.m. Monday through Friday (open until 7 p.m. on Wednesdays) to examine the five *Job Clipboards* (attorneys, paralegals, more non–attorneys, law students, and other public interest jobs) which are updated daily with new job openings. These vacancies later appear in the next issue of the *PiES Job Alert!* described above. Also available for examination are other job newsletters and resource files on potential employers.

The California Directories (California Journal, 2101 K Street, Sacramento, CA 95816; phone: 916/444-2840) ***Volume. 1: State Government*** provides names, district and capitol addresses, phone, and staff of the legislature; description of state departments and top staff. 171 pages; updated quarterly.

$95 plus 7.75 percent sales tax and $2.75 shipping. ***Volume 2: Lobbyists/PACs*** gives the name, address, and phone number of nearly 1,000 lobbyists in California and the more than 2,000 firms that employ them. 230 pages. $40 plus 7.75 percent sales tax and $2.75 shipping. ***Volume 3: Local Government*** gives the address and phone for top elected and appointed officials in every California city and county. Price: $60 plus 7.75 percent sales tax and $2.75 shipping. Get all three directories for $195 plus 7.75 percent tax and $2.75 shipping.

California Roster on Diskette (California Journal, 2101 K Street, Sacramento, CA 95816; phone: 916/444-2840) $79. Includes party, district, house and state, district address, capitol address, committees, committee assignments, executive branch departments, and executive directors. Available in 5.25–inch and 3.5–inch MS–DOS diskettes in ASCII, comma–delimited fields; in dBase; or WordPerfect.

Who's Who in the California Legislature (Capitol Enquiry Inc., Suite 10, 1228 N St., Sacramento, CA 95814; phone: 916/442–1434) $69.95 plus $4/shipping and 7.75 percent sales tax for California residents, 280 pages, specify hardbound or three–ring binder format, published in late spring of odd–numbered years; supplement added in January of even–numbered years. If you want to work on the staff of a California legislator, this book will tell you all about her with its concise, nonpartisan personal and political biographies. Also offers information about each district, election results, demographic data, and maps.

California City Hall Address Book (League of California Cities, 1400 K St., Sacramento, CA 95814; phone: 916/444–5790) $24.

California Roster (California Roster, c/o Secretary of State, Suite 209, 1230 J St., Sacramento, CA 95814; phone: 916/445–3085, recording only) $14 includes shipping, prepaid only, mail order only, published irregularly, make check payable to: "California Secretary of State". Lists names, addresses, and phones for city, county, state, and federal officials in California.

The California Planner's 1994 Book of Lists (Department of General Services, ATTEN: Publications, P.O. Box 1015, North Highlands, CA 95660; phone: 916/973–3700) $9 includes shipping, prepaid only, mail order only, published each January [Stock No. 7540–931–1005–0; be sure to specify stock number and make check payable to: "State of California"]. Includes directories of city and county planning agencies, councils of governments, and local agency formation commissions. Usually sold out by September.

Local job hotlines

Alameda: 510/748–4635
Anaheim: 714/254–5197
Berkeley: 510/644–6122
Concord: 510/671–3151
Davis: 916/757–5645
Fairfield: 707/428–7396
Fresno: 209/498–1573
Hayward: 510/293–5313
Huntington Beach: 714/374–1570
Irvine: 714/724–6096
Long Beach: 310/590–6201
Los Angeles: 213/485–2441
Modesto: 209/577–5498
Monterey: 408/646–3751
Napa: 707/257–9542
Oakland: 510/238–3111
Oxnad: 805/385–7580
Palo Alto: 415/329–2222
Sacramento (city): 919/443–9990
Sacramento (county): 916/440–6771
San Diego: 619/450–6210
San Jose: 408/277–5627
Santa Ana: 714/953–9675
Santa Clara: 408/984–3150
Santa Monica: 310/458–8697
Stockton: 209/944–8523
Torrance: 310/618–2969
Ventura: 805/658–4777
Walnut Creek: 510/943–5817
West Sacramento: 916/371–5669
Yuba City: 916/741–4766

State jobs

Capitol Weekly (1930 9th St., Suite 200, Sacramento, CA 95814; phone: 916/444–7665) weekly, $59/annual subscription, $39/six–month subscription. This is the closest thing to a central listing of state job vacancies. Hundreds of vacancies are listed under "State Jobs." Each issue also includes information about 100 exams for state positions listed under "The Exam Section."

Although there is no official central listing of state jobs in California, many are listed at the state's 135 **Job Service Centers**. An exam is required to obtain a job with the State of California. Contact the State Personnel Board (801 Capitol Mall, Sacramento, CA 94244; phone: 916/653–1705, **TDD:** 916/323–7490) for a copy of the pamphlet *How to Get a Job with the State of California* and a copy of the three–page list of Testing Offices. All open job examinations are announced on the 24–hour job hotlines operated by the State Personnel Board and are updated at 5 p.m. every Friday.

California Journal Roster and Government Guide (California Journal, 2101 K Street, Sacramento, CA 95816; phone: 916/444–2840) $2.95 plus 7.75 percent sales tax for California residents plus $2.75 shipping, published every February. Lists state agencies and boards, legislators, and legislative committees.

This roster is also available on 5.25–inch and 3.5–inch MS-DOS compatible computer disks in ASCII comma delimited format, dBase, or WordPerfect — actually they can convert the database into nearly any IBM–compatible format, just specify the format you want — ($79 plus 7.75 percent sales tax for California residents plus $2.75 shipping; monthly updates available for $10).

California Political Almanac (California Journal, 2101 K Street, Sacramento, CA 95816; phone: 916/444–2840) $34.95 plus 7.75 percent sales tax for California residents plus $2.75 shipping, published every April. Includes biographies of state legislators, their district and capitol addresses and phones, their voting records, party affiliation, and term limits.

Hotlines for California State Jobs

Type of Job	Sacramento	San Francisco	Los Angeles
Information staff	916/653–1705	—	—
Legal, professional, technical	916/653–1365	†415/557–9357	†213/897–4409 *†619/292–7334
Law enforcement and social services	916/653–1835	†415/557–9358	†213/897–3154 *†619/236–9238
Health and related	916/653–1367	†415/557–9359	†213/897–3161 *†619/236–9239
Trades and labor	916/653–1837	†415/557–9350	†213/897–3168 *†619/695–8891
Office services	916/653–1369	†415/557–0310	†213/897–3168 *†619/695–8891
Promotions only (general)	916/653–1847	—	†213/897–3152
Promotions only (career executive assignments)	916/653–1391	—	—
TDD hotline	916/653–1511	—	—

* Indicates the number of the Los Angeles office to call toll–free from the San Diego area

† You'll get a recording, not a live person, at these numbers.

The job hotlines in the table above are recordings which can be reached 24–hours a day, seven days–a–week. The information staff (real live people) can be reached only during normal business hours.

To locate **Job Service Offices**, contact the Employment Development Department (P.O. Box 826880, MIC 62, Sacramento, CA 94280–0001; phone: 916/653–0707).

California State Agency locator: 916/322–9900

FJIC: Los Angeles area: 9650 Flair Dr., Suite 100A, El Monte, CA 91731, phone: 818/575–6510, staff present 9 a.m. to 3 p.m.; **Sacramento area:** 1029 J St., Second Floor, Sacramento, 95814, phone: 916/551–1464, staff present 9 a.m. to noon; **San Francisco area:** Room 235, 211 Main St., San Francisco, phone: 415/744–5627, staff present 9 am. to noon.

Colorado

Also see the listings under "Job sources for multi–state regions" at the beginning of this chapter.

Colorado Job Finder (Colorado Municipal League, 1660 Lincoln, Suite 2100, Denver, CO 80264; phone: 303/831–6411; fax: 303/860–8175) biweekly, $38 annual/subscription, $20/six–month subscription, plus sales tax for Colorado residents. Typical issue features about 25 to 30 ads for all types and levels of municipal work. Each issue also carries an updated list of job hotlines operated by Colorado municipalities and counties.

Directory of Municipal and County Officials (Colorado Municipal League, 1660 Lincoln, Suite 2100, Denver, CO 80264; phone: 303/831–6411; fax: 303/860–8175) $35/nonmembers, $25/Colorado state agencies, $17.50/members and associate members, plus sales tax for Colorado residents and 10 percent for shipping and handling, published annually in September. Lists elected officials and major department heads plus Councils of Governments, Regional Planning Commissions, selected state and federal offices, selected state associations.

Salaries and Fringe Benefits: Management Compensation Report for Colorado Cities (Colorado Municipal League, 1660 Lincoln, Suite 2100, Denver, CO 80264; phone: 303/831–6411; fax: 303/860–8175) $30/nonmembers, $15/members, plus sales tax for Colorado residents and 10 percent for shipping and handling, 192 pages, published annually in June. Reports on salaries, fringe benefits, and job characteristics for 24 types of municipal executive and administrative positions. Also includes general municipal information and supplemental information.

Salaries and Fringe Benefits: Benchmark Employee Compensation Report (Colorado Municipal League, 1660 Lincoln, Suite 2100, Denver, CO 80264; phone: 303/831–6411; fax: 303/860–8175) $76/nonmembers, $38/members, plus sales tax for Colorado resident, and 10 percent for shipping and handling, 224 pages, published each April. Covers 46 job classifications for municipalities over 3,000 population. Includes data on salary, fringe benefits, and fringe benefit policies.

Salaries and Fringe Benefits in Colorado Cities and Towns under 3,000 Population (Colorado Municipal League, 1660 Lincoln, Suite 2100, Denver, CO 80264; phone: 303/831–6411; fax: 303/860–8175) $30/nonmembers, $15/members, plus sales tax for Colorado residents and 10 percent for shipping and handling, 76 pages, published every July. Reports salaries, fringe benefits, and municipal data.

Local job hotlines in Colorado

Municipalities

Arvada (24 hour): 303/431–3008, select message 453

Aurora (24 hour): 303/695–7222

Boulder (24 hour): 303/441–3434

Brighton: 303/659–4050, extension 294

Commerce City (24 hour): 303/289–3618

Denver: 303/640–1234

Englewood (24 hour): 303/762–2304

Fort Collins (24 hour): 303/221–6586

Golden (24 hour): 303/279–3331, ext. 223

Grand Junction: 303/244–1449

Lakewood: 303/987–7777

Littleton (24 hour): 303/795–3858

Longmont (24 hour): 303/651–8710

Louisville: 303/666–6565, ext. 413

Loveland: 303/667–6130, extension 374 (8 a.m..—5 p. m..), 303/667–0145 (recording: 5 p. m..—8 a.m..)

Northglenn (24 hour): 303/450–8789

Thornton (24 hour): 303/538–7240

Vail (24 hour): 303/479–2343

Westminster (24 hour): 303/650–0115

Wheat Ridge (24 hour): 303/234–5927

Counties

Adams County: 303/654–6075 (weekdays, 8 a.m..—4:45 p. m..)

Arapahoe County (24 hour): 303/795–4480

Boulder (24 hour): 303/441–3434

Douglas County: 303/660–7420 (weekdays, 8 a.m..—4:30 p. m..)

Eagle County (24 hour): 303/328–8891

Jefferson County (24 hour): 303/271–8401

Larimer County (24 hour): 303/498–7379

Weld County: 303/352–1993

State jobs

For details on how to apply for a state job, contact the Department of Personnel (1313 Sherman, Denver, CO 80203; phone: 303/866–4230).

To locate **Job Service Offices**, contact the Department of Labor and Employment (600 Grant St., Denver, CO 80203–3528; phone: 303/837–3819).

Colorado State Agency locator: 303/866–5000

FJIC: 12345 W. Alameda Parkway, Lakewood, CO; 303/969–7050; send mail to: P.O. Box 25167, Lakewood, CO 80225; for forms and local supplements, call 303/969–7065; staff present noon to 3:45 p.m.; self service 9 a.m. to noon.

Connecticut

Connecticut Town and City (Connecticut Conference of Municipalities, 900 Chapel St., New Haven, CT 06510; phone: 203/498–3000) six issues/year, $18/annual nonmember subscription. Jobs listed under "Classified." Four to seven job ads appear in the usual issue.

Connecticut Municipal Directory (Connecticut Conference of Municipalities, 900 Chapel St., New Haven, CT 06510; phone: 203/498–3000) $85/nonmembers, $50/members, published annually. Lists demographic information about each city, elected officials and major department heads, Regional Planning Agencies, Regional Councils of Government, and organizations of Connecticut municipal officials.

Local job hotline

New Haven: 203/787–8265

State jobs

Examinations for state jobs are announced on alternate Sundays in the display and classified advertising sections of the following Connecticut newspapers: *Bridgeport Post, Danbury New–Times, Hartford Courant, Meriden Record–Journal, New Haven Register, New London Day, Norwalk Hour* [Monday edition], *Norwich Bulletin, Register Citizen* (Torrington) [Monday edition], *Stamford Advocate, Waterbury American,* and *Willimantic Chronicle* [Monday edition].

For an explanation of the hiring process, ask the State Recruitment and Testing Center (Suite 101A, 1 Hartford Square West, Hartford, CT 06105; phone: 203/566–2501) to send you a copy of the brochure "Working for the State of Connecticut" which explains the difference between competitive and non–competitive positions. The best way to find out about the non–competitive positions which do not require a merit system examination, is to call the individual agency and ask.

To locate the state **Job Service Offices** (called "Job Centers" in Connecticut) in Ansonia, Bridgeport, Bristol, Danbury, Danielson, Enfield, Hamden, Hartford, Manchester, Meriden, Middletown, New Britain, New London, Norwich, Stamford, Torrington, Waterbury, and Willimantic, see the state government section (the blue pages) of the local white pages telephone directory or contact the Connecticut Department of Labor (200 Folly Brook Blvd., Wethersfield, CT 06109; phone: 203/566–5031) for a list of Job Center Offices.

Connecticut State Agency locator: 203/566–2211

FJIC: Thomas P. O'Neill Federal Building, 10 Causeway St., Boston, MA 02222–1031; phone: 617/565–5900; staff present weekdays 9 a.m. to 2 p.m.

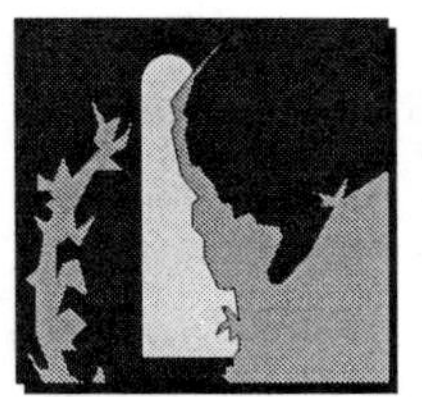

Delaware

League Directory (Delaware League of Local Governments, P.O. Box 484, Dover, DE 19901; phone: 302/678–0991) published annually, $30/nonmembers, free/members. Lists elected officials for each municipality.

Local job hotline

Wilmington: 302/571–4666

State jobs

Weekly Recruitment Listings (State Personnel Office, Townsend Bldg., Dover, DE 19903; phone: 302/739–4195 and Carvel State Office Bldg., 820 N. French St., Wilmington, DE 19801; phone: 302/577–3950) weekly, free. Call or write to get on mailing list. Issued each Monday, this list consists of jobs that are being filled at the time and for which you can apply right away.

Continuous Job Listings (State Personnel Office, Townsend Bldg., Dover, DE 19901; phone: 302/739–5458 and Carvel State Office Bldg., 820 N. French St., Wilmington, DE 19801; phone: 302/577–3950) monthly, available for viewing at either of these personnel offices. This is a listing of state jobs for which applications are taken continuously. When a position opens, hiring is done from the list of people who have applied instead of announcing the job opening and taking new applications. These jobs do not appear in the *Weekly Recruitment Listings*.

You can obtain actual job announcements from Applicant Services in either personnel office. Also, be sure to ask for a copy of the brochure *Steps to State Employment*.

To locate **Job Service Offices**, contact the Division of Employment and Training (Delaware Department of Labor, The Hudson State Service Center, 501 Ogletown Rd., Newark, DE 19711; phone: 302/368–6825).

Delaware State Agency locator: 302/739–4000

FJIC: Room 1416, William Green, Jr. Federal Building, 600 Arch St., Philadelphia, PA 19106, phone: 215/597–7440, staff present 10:30 a.m. to 2:30 p.m., also self–service 8:30 a.m. to 3:30 p.m.

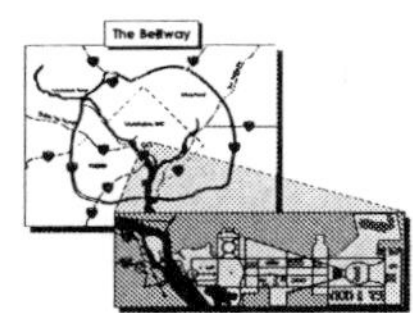

District of Columbia

Also see the nationwide job sources enumerated in Chapter 2 and the federal job sources noted in Chapter 4.

Opportunities in Public Affairs (Brubach Publishing Company, P.O. Box 15629, Chevy Chase, MD 20825; phone: 301/986–0658) $29/two–month subscription, $49/four months, $69/six months, $129/annual, $7.95/single issue. You'll find announcements of over 200 positions with local, state, and federal government agencies; non–profits; and private companies in government affairs, public relations, broadcasting, and publishing. In addition to job announcements, this periodical also reports on unadvertised jobs its editors have uncovered. Most job openings are in the District of Columbia area. It includes a good number of positions with Congress.

Jobs in Washington, DC: 1001 Great Opportunities for College Graduates (available from Planning/Communications' at the end of this book) $11.95, 217 pages, 1992. Includes over 1,000 names, addresses, and phone numbers of many government agencies (particularly federal), organizations and associations for government professionals, and international development groups located in the District.

The 1993 Washington Job Source (MetCom, Inc. 1708 Surrey Lane, NW, Washington, DC 20007) $14.95 plus $3/shipping. Briefly describes 2,100 federal agencies, Congressional, non–profits, and corporations with the name, address, and phone number of the hiring contact.

Reprinted by permission from *What Niche?* by John Shingleton, illustrated by Phil Frank. Copyright 1989. All rights reserved.

1994 Internships (Peterson's Guides; available from Planning/Communications' catalog at the end of this book) $29.95, published every October. This 422–page book provides detailed descriptions and application instructions for paid and unpaid internships with over 1,700 organizations and companies, including hundreds with government agencies in the District and surrounding area, mostly with the federal government. It includes geographic and alphabetical indexes, and details on regional and national internship clearinghouses.

Internships in Congress (Graduate Group, 86 Norwood Rd., West Hartford, CT 06117; phones: 203/232–3100, 203/236–5570) $27.50, published annually. Includes in–depth information on internships with Congress.

Internships + Job Opportunities in New York City and Washington, DC (Graduate Group, 86 Norwood Rd., West Hartford, CT 06117; phones: 203/232–3100, 203/236–5570) $27.50, published annually. Describes internship and job opportunities for a wide variety of fields.

Washington 93 (Columbia Books, 1212 New York Ave., NW, Suite 330, Washington, DC 20005; phone: 202/898–0662) $75, published annually each June. Nearly 600 pages of addresses, phone numbers, and information including one chapter on local government in the District and surrounding counties and towns with populations over 5,000, and regional authorities.

The Capitol Source: The Who's Who, What, Where in Washington (National Journal, Inc., 1730 M St., NW, Washington, DC 20036; phones: 800/424–2921, 202/862–0644) $24.95. Published in April and October, this directory includes names, addresses, and phone numbers for the District of Columbia. Also included are corporations, interest groups, think tanks, labor unions, real estate, financial institutions, trade and professional organizations, law firms, political consultants, advertising and public relations firms, private clubs, and the media. All entries are also available on computer diskette. Call 202/857–1449 for information.

District Government Jobs

The Job Opportunities Bulletin (District of Columbia Office of Personnel, Suite 301, 613 G St., NW, Washington, DC 20001; phone: 202/727–6099) biweekly, posted on bulletin boards at all District personnel offices and city agencies, obtain actual detailed vacancy announcements at personnel offices, see the next paragraph for details. Lists titles, closing dates, and job announcement numbers of job vacancies for all District government offices and independent agencies. Each issue tells you how to obtain full individual position vacancy announcements (including a **TDD** phone number) and gives advice on how to apply (the District currently uses the same SF 171 form the federal government requires, but is developing its own, more manageable application form), how to obtain a detailed vacancy announcement, and how rankings are determined. If you ask, the able folks at the District's personnel offices will provide you with a printout of the job descriptions that interest you. Note that D.C. residency is required within six months of starting the job. The typical issue lists about 300 positions. Relatively few entry level positions.

The District operates four Servicing Personnel Offices where this bulletin is available and full job descriptions can be obtained. They are open on weekdays from 8:15 a.m. to 4:45 p.m. For information on jobs with the departments of Human Services and Recreation, call 202/727–0803 (801 N. Capitol St., NE); with the departments of Consumer and Regulatory Affairs, Public Works, Administrative Services, and the D.C. Energy Office, call 202/939–8700 (2000 14th St., NW); for information on vacancies with the police and fire departments and the Department of Corrections and Board of Parole, call 202/727–4272 (300 Indiana Ave., NW); and for the remaining District agencies, call 202/525–1050 (Room 326, 1133 North Capital St., NE).

To locate **Job Service Offices**, contact the District's Department of Employment Services (500 C St., NW, Washington, DC 20001; phone: 202/724–7100).

District of Columbia Agency Locator: 202/727–1000

FJIC: Room 1416, 1900 E St., NW, Washington, DC 20415; phone: 202/606–2700; staff present 8 a.m. to 4 p.m.; includes federal jobs for D.C. metropolitan area.

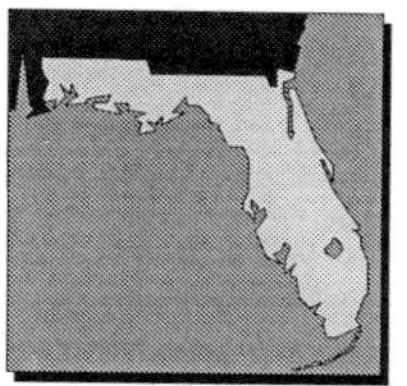

Florida

Quality Cities (Florida League of Cities, P.O. Box 1757, 201 W. Park Ave., Tallahassee, FL 32302–1757; phone: 904/222–9684) 11 issues/year; $20/annual nonmember subscription, $6/members, $15/government agencies. Jobs listed under "Report from City Hall."

Officials of Florida Municipalities (Florida League of Cities, P.O. Box 1757, 201 W. Park Ave., Tallahassee, FL 32302–1757; phone: 904/222–9684) $50/nonmembers, free/members, published each May. Lists all local officials.

County Reporter (Florida Association of Counties, P.O. Box 549, Tallahassee, FL 32302; phone: 904/224–3148) monthly; $30/annual subscription. Jobs listed under "JobLine."

Membership Directory (Florida Association of Counties, P.O. Box 549, Tallahassee, FL 32302; phone: 904/224–3148) $45.80, published annually. Lists county elected officials and major department heads.

Directory of Planning Officials (Florida Department of Community Affairs, Division of Resource Planning and Management, Bureau of Local Planning, 2740 Centerview Dr., Tallahassee, FL 32399–2100) write for price; published annually. Lists state, regional, and local planning officials.

Local job hotlines

Altamonte Springs: 407/830–0363
Boca Raton: 407/393–7981
Broward County: 305/357–6450
Dade County: 305/375–1871
Daytona Beach: 904/258–3167
Delray Beach: 407/243–7085
Fort Lauderdale: 305/761–5317
Fort Meyers: 813/334–1251
Hialeah: 305/883–8057
Hollywood: 305/921–3292
Jacksonville: 904/630–1144
Miami: 305/579–2400
North Miami: 305/895–8095
Oakland Park: 305/561–6255
Orange County: 407/836–5674
Orlando: 407/246–2178
Plantation: 305/797–2298
St. Petersburg: 813/893–7033
Tallahassee: 904/891–8219
Tamarac: 305/726–8980
Tampa: 813/223–8115

State jobs

Job Hotline (Florida Department of Management Resource, 435 Carlton Building, Tallahassee, FL 32399–0950; phone: 904/487–1749). Call 800/848–8477 (from within Florida only) or 904/487–2851 to hear a recording of available state positions of all types. But before you call, obtain the free Employment Information Packet which contains application instructions and the job classifications and classification codes needed to use the job hotline. You need a touch–tone phone to call the hotline because you'll have to punch in the classification code to indicate each job for which you want vacancy information as well as to indicate the county in which you wish to work, and whether you are interested in career service (Florida's civil service) or management positions.

Vacancy Listings (Florida Department of Management Services, 435 Carlton Building, Tallahassee, FL 32399–0950; phone: 904/487–1749). This periodic bulletin contains a description of every available position with the State of Florida. It is not available to individuals by mail. However, it is available for your perusal at all Job Service Offices through the Job Information System (JIS), at the personnel office of all state agencies, and at the Applicant Information Center (4th Floor, Carlton Building, Tallahassee, FL).

To locate **Job Service Offices**, contact the Department of Labor and Employment Security (2012 Capital Cr., SE, Tallahassee, FL 32399–2154; phone: 904/488–4398).

Florida State Agency locator: 904/488–1234

FJIC: Suite 125, 3444 McCrory Pl., Orlando, FL 32803; phone: 407/648–6148, staff present Monday, Wednesday, and Friday 9 a.m. to 3 p.m.; self service Tuesday and Thursday 8 a.m. to 4 p.m.

Georgia's Cities (Georgia Municipal Association, 201 Pryor St., SW, Atlanta, GA 30303; phone: 404/688–0472) monthly, $30/annual subscription. Jobs listed under "City Exchange." Few job ads.

Directory (Georgia Municipal Association, 201 Pryor St., SW, Atlanta, GA 30303; phone: 404/688–0472) published annually, $40/nonmembers, free/members.

Local job hotlines

Atlanta: 404/330–6456
Chatham County: 912/652–7931
Clayton County: 404/473–5800
Cobb County: 404/528–2555
DeKalb County: 404/371–2331
Douglas County: 404/920–7363
Macom: 912/751–2733
Marietta: 404/528–0593
Rockdale County: 404/929–4157

State, local, and federal jobs

Job Information Service (Georgia Department of Labor, 148 International Blvd., NE, Atlanta, GA 30303). Descriptions of non–profit sector vacancies throughout the state, and nation, are available on a computerized statewide database which can be viewed at any of the department's 35 field offices throughout the state. Two **Job Service** offices are in Atlanta (North Metro, 2943 N. Druid Hills Rd., Atlanta, GA 30329; phone: 404/679–5200; and South Metro, 2636–14 Martin Luther King, Jr. Dr., Atlanta, GA 30311; phone: 404/699–6900). Contact the department for a list of all field offices of this Job Service or check the local phone book.

State Merit System Public Announcement also lists state government jobs. Contact the Georgia Department of Labor for further information.

Georgia State Agency locator: 404/656–2000

FJIC: Richard B. Russell Federal Building, Room 940A, 75 Spring St., SW, Atlanta, GA 30303; phone: 404/331–4315; staff present 9 a.m. to 4 p.m.

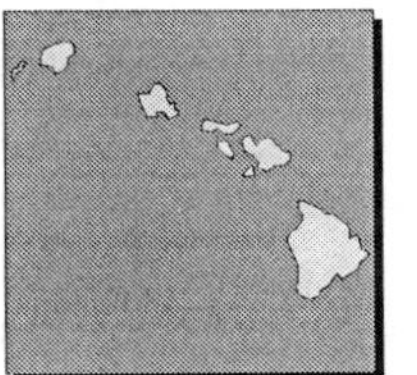

Hawaii

The Honolulu Advertiser (605 Kapiolani Blvd., Honolulu, HI 96813; phone: 808/525–8000) published weekly on Sunday. Write for subscription prices. Government jobs are usually listed under "300 – General Help Wanted." Local and state jobs ads.

Star–Bulletin (605 Kapiolani Blvd., Honolulu, HI 96813; phone: 808/525–8000) published Monday through Sunday. Write for subscription prices. Government jobs are usually listed under "300 – General Help Wanted." Local and state jobs ads.

Contact each county directly for the list of available government jobs it maintains:

County of Hawaii: Department of Civil Service (101 Aupuni St., Suite 133, Hilo, HI 96720; phone: 808/961–8361)

County of Kauai: Department of Personnel Services (4280 Rice St., Lihue, HI 96766; phone: 808/241–6595)

City and County of Honolulu: Department of Personnel (550 S. King St., Honolulu, HI 96813; phone: 808/523–4301; ***24–hour Job Hotline:*** 808/523–4303) Job listings updated weekly and posted at this address and at Satellite City Halls. Job applicants must be legal residents of Hawaii at the time they apply for a government job with this city or county.

County of Maui: Department of Personnel Services (County Building, 200 S. High St., Wailuku, Maui, HI 96793; phone: 808/243–7850).

Directory of State, County, and Federal Officials (Legislative Reference Bureau, ATTEN: LRB Library, 1177 Alakea St., Honolulu, HI 96813; phone: 808/587–0690) $4 (add $2.90 for air mail), 165 pages, issued every March.

State jobs

For all but a few positions, the State of Hawaii requires prior residency to even apply for a state job. See the discussion immediately below.

State Recruiting Office (Hawaii Department of Personnel Services, 830 Punchbowl St., Honolulu, HI 96813; phone: 808/587–0977). At any one time, 300 to 400 state jobs are open, but remember, you must be a resident of Hawaii just to apply. However, in the absence of qualified and interested resident applicants, the residency requirement may be waived. These are usually health or education positions. Usually about 25 positions with the residency requirement waived are available. Job descriptions and minimum qualification requirements are available at this office and also at the state's Job Service Offices. You can obtain a State Civil Service Employment Application by writing or calling the Hawaii Department of Personnel Services (phones: 808/587–0974, 587–0975, or 587–0976), or obtain one at any Job Service office. Be sure to follow the application instructions exactly.

JOBLink (Hawaii State Recruiting Office, 830 Punchbowl St., Honolulu, HI 96813; phone: 808/587–0942) free, updated weekly. Call 808/587–0977 to hear descriptions of about 200 vacant jobs in state government. Operates 24–hours every day.

For information on **Job Service Offices**, contact the Department of Labor and Industrial Relations (830 Punchbowl St., Honolulu, HI 96813; phone: 808/586–8812).

Hawaii State Agency locator: 808/586–2211

FJIC: Federal Building, Room 5316, 300 Ala Moana Blvd., Honolulu, HI 96850; phone: 808/541–2791; call 808/541–2784 for federal jobs overseas; staff present 9 a.m. to noon.

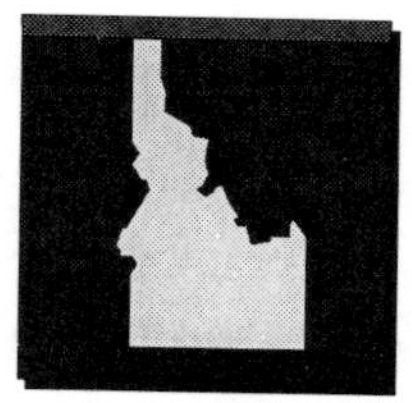

Idaho

Also see the listings under "Job sources for multi–state regions" at the beginning of this chapter and listings under "Montana."

Idaho Cities (Association of Idaho Cities, 3314 Grace St., Boise, ID 83703; phone: 208/344–8594) monthly, $18/annual subscription. Jobs listed under "Employment." Job ads are rare.

Directory of Idaho Government Officials (Association of Idaho Cities) published annually, $20. Lists city, county, and state elected officials and department heads as well as highway district officials, area–wide planning organizations and state legislators.

Local job hotline

Boise: 208/384–3855

State jobs

Idaho Personnel Commission (700 W. State St., Boise, ID 83720; phone: 208/334–2263). Contact for information and procedures. Job announcements for state, as well as local government positions, are available at Job Service Offices throughout the state. Call the ***Job hotline*** recording for current listings: 208/334–2568.

For the addresses and phones of **Job Service Offices**, contact the Department of Employment (317 Main St., Boise, ID 83735; phone: 208/334–6100).

Idaho State Agency locator: 208/334–2411

FJIC: Federal Building, Room 110, 915 Second Ave., Seattle, WA 98174; phone: 206/220–6400; staff present noon to 3:30 p. m.; self service 8 a.m. to noon.

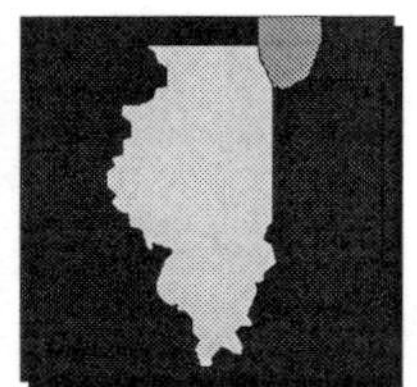

Illinois

Illinois Municipal Review (Illinois Municipal League, 500 E. Capitol, Springfield, IL 62701; phone: 217/525–1220) monthly; $5/annual subscription. Jobs listed under "Municipal Exchange Service." About 15 ads per issue.

Illinois Municipal Directory (Illinois Municipal League, 500 E. Capitol, Springfield, IL 62701; phone: 217/525–1220) $25, published in late autumn of odd–numbered years. Lists elected officials and department heads.

Local job hotlines

Chicago: 312/744–1369

DuPage County: 708/665–8828

Springfield: 217/789–2440

State jobs

Roster of State Government Officials (Illinois Issues, Building A, Room 8, Sangamon State University, Springfield, IL 62794–9243; phone: 217/786–6084 $3.95 plus $2 shipping; make checks payable to "Bursar, Sangamon State University," published each April. Contains the names, addresses, and phone numbers of the state's constitutional officers, legislators, agency directors, board and commission members, etc.

The hiring situation in Illinois state government continues to be less than promising. With over 100,000 applications on file, the state hires only about 5,000 employees a year, generally to replace retiring workers. Despite the U.S. Supreme Court's ruling in *Ruttan v. Illinois Republican Party* that prohibits considering party affiliation when hiring, promoting, or transferring most state employees, patronage's grip on state jobs is stronger than ever under the current Republican governor. Combine that with severe budget difficulties, and finding a job with the State of Illinois, outside of law enforcement, can be a nightmare.

To Apply: For any state position, obtain a state job application from the Bureau of Personnel (Department of Central Management Services, 500 Stratton Bldg., Springfield, IL 62706; phone: 217/524–1321). Complete the application and return it to the bureau. Some jobs, like clerical positions, also require a written test. Individuals for different job categories are ranked according to application, and where applicable, test scores. All state agencies and departments are supposed to hire from the ranked lists.

To Identify State Job Openings: There is no easily accessible single source of state job vacancies. To find available positions, contact the personnel division of each agency or department for which you wish to work. You can get their phone numbers from the State Agency Locator, any of the directories of state agencies enumerated at the beginning of this chapter, or the Springfield, Illinois, telephone directory.

Employee Information System Computer. Many, but not all, state departments and agencies voluntarily list job openings on this user–friendly computer which operates via artificial intelligence. You can easily print lists of available state jobs by type of position, location, and department. These computers are located in the State of Illinois Center in Chicago (100 W. Randolph) and in Springfield, the state capitol, at the Stratton Office Building (basement), Willard Ice Building, Transportation Building, Harris Public Aid Building, and Centennial Building.

Illinois Department of Employment Security Offices (Office Manager, Employment Security Consolidated Office South, 1300 S. 9th St., Springfield, IL 62705; phone: 217/524–7838; and 401 S. State St., Chicago, IL 60605; 312/793–5700). Sixty–three of these Job Service Offices across the state offer computer–based job searches that include some state, local, and federal government jobs. For a list of **Job Service Offices**, contact one of these offices or see the state government section of your local white pages telephone directory.

The IDES has started what sounds like an incredible system to help job seekers find job openings. It's developing an "Unemployment Office of the Future" based on a self–service, multilingual computer system dubbed "**Touch Illinois**." It's currently operating as a pilot program only at the IDES office in Arlington Heights (723 W. Algonquin Rd.; phone: 708/981–7400). As of this writing, the decision on when to expand to other Job Service offices has yet to be made.

Touch Illinois enables even the most computer–illiterate person to find job vacancies anywhere in the state and across the country. Here's how it works. At the Arlington Heights Job Service office, you seat yourself at one of the 25 Touch Illinois kiosks. You don't need to use a computer keyboard. To tell the computer what to do, you simply touch different parts of the computer's screen. The computer will ask you a few questions about yourself. Then you tell the computer what zip code you want to find jobs in or within how many miles of a certain zip code you want to find jobs in. Next you can tell the computer your level of education or training. Finally, you can specify the job categories for which you are qualified. The computer then searches the Job Service's database (it's the same one to which all Illinois Job Service offices are connected), compiles the open jobs that meet your criteria, and puts them into an electronic file, access to which may be gained only with your social security number. If you wish, you will be issued a magnetic card which you put in a special slot on the kiosk and it will log you onto the computer automatically.

Next you'll meet with a Job Service staffer who will look at your electronic file and review with you the jobs your search turned up to make sure you are qualified for them. You'll be given a printed referral slip to give to each employer where you wish to apply for a job. Eventually, the system will also be able to give you a printout of each job description in your file, and enable you to write a resume on it. This system is hooked into the national job database which means that you could specify a zip code in another state and find job government openings for that state.

Eventually, Touch Illinois kiosks will sprout up throughout the state in public libraries, malls, and universities. The timetable has not yet been set. But first the IDES prudently wants to get everything running smoothly at its Arlington Heights office before trying it elsewhere.

Illinois State Agency locator: 217/782–2000

FJIC: Room 530, 175 W. Jackson, Chicago, IL 60604; phone: 312/353–6192 (only from 9 a.m. to noon); self–service only 7 a.m. to 4:45 p. m.. Madison and St. Clair Counties, East St. Louis area: Room 400, 815 Olive St., St. Louis, MO 63101; 314/539–2285; self service only 8 a.m. to 4 p. m.. You can also learn about current federal job openings in Illinois by calling the Chicago Service Center's Complete Answering Machine at 312/353–6192 any time except between 1 p. m.. and 4 p. m.. on Fridays when it is updated. You'll need a touch–tone telephone. You'll have a series of choices which you dial with a two–digit number followed by the pound (#) sign: 33# gets you descriptions of jobs available through this office (updated the first Monday of every month); 35# describes current vacancies, including the job title and the closing date; 6# gives you starting salary rates; and 7# explains how to apply for a federal job.

Indiana

Actionlines (Indiana Association of Cities and Towns, Suite 728, 150 W. Market St., Indianapolis, IN 46204–2882; phone: 317/237–6200) monthly, $30/annual subscription. Very few job ads.

Roster of Indiana City and Town Officials (Indiana Association of Cities and Towns, Suite 728, 150 W. Market St., Indianapolis, IN 46204–2882; phone: 317/237–6200) $30/nonmembers, free/members, published in U.S.

Presidential election years. Updated periodically. Lists elected officials and major department heads along with addresses and phone numbers.

Informal Job Registry The Executive Director of the Indiana Association of Cities and Towns (Suite 728, 150 W. Market St., Indianapolis, IN 46204–2882; phone: 317/237–6200) maintains a very informal job registry. Send your resume to him and he will keep it on file. Upon request, he sends the resumes of qualified individuals to municipalities to fill positions.

IACT Salaries, Wages & Benefits Surveys (Indiana Association of Cities and Towns, Suite 728, 150 W. Market St., Indianapolis, IN 46204–2882; phone: 317/237–6200). $25, published in April of odd–numbered years.

Local job hotline

Fort Wayne: 219/427–1186

State jobs

Indiana Department of Employment and Training Service (IDETS) (10 N. Senate Ave., Indianapolis, IN 46204; phone: 317/232–3270) has personnel who specialize in matching applicants with government jobs through the statewide automated **Job Service** Matching System. This service is available only by an in–person visit to a IDETS office. Write for a list of offices or consult the state government section in local telephone directories. All these services are free.

For information on specific positions and residency requirements, contact the Indiana Department of Employment and Training Services, (10 N. Senate Ave., Indianapolis, IN 46204; phone: 317/232–3270).

Indiana State Agency Locator: 317/232–3140

FJIC: Minton–Capehart Federal Building, 575 N. Pennsylvania Ave., Indianapolis, IN 46204; phone: 317/226–7161; for information on federal jobs in Clark, Dearborn, and Floyd counties: Federal Building, Room 506, 200 W. Second St., Dayton, OH 45402; phone: 513/225–2720.

Iowa Municipalities and ***Iowa Interlink*** (League of Iowa Municipalities, 317 6th Ave., Suite 1400, Des Moines, IA 50309; phone: 515/244–7282) both bimonthly, $18/annual subscription for both for Iowa residents, $20/outside Iowa for both. Jobs listed under "Classifieds."

Directory (League of Iowa Municipalities, 317 6th Ave., Suite 1400, Des Moines, IA 50309; phone: 515/244–7282) $30/nonmembers, free/member municipalities, published in even–numbered years. Lists elected officials, department heads, and local government offices.

Local job hotline

Des Moines: 515/283–4115

Local and state jobs

For information on available local and state government jobs contact the Department of Employment Services (1000 East Grand, Des Moines, IA 50319; phone: 515/281–5365) or the Department of Personnel (Grimes State Office Building, E. 14th and Grand, Des Moines, IA 50319–0150; phone: 515/281–3087).

State jobs

Job Class Opening Announcement (Department of Personnel, Grimes State Office Building, E. 14th and Grand, Des Moines, IA 50319–0150; phone: 515/281–3087, **TDD**: 515/281–7825) weekly, available for inspection at the department's Job Information Center. Local and federal jobs are also listed at the center. Contact this department for a copy of the brochure *Working for the State of Iowa: Getting on Board.*

JOBLINE is a recording that lists state job openings: 800/247–6002 from within Iowa, except Des Moines; from out of state and Des Moines, call 515/281–5820.

Iowa State Agency Locator: 515/281–5011

FJIC: Federal Building, Room 134, 601 E. 12th St., Kansas City, MO 64106; phone: 816/426–5702; self service only 8 a.m. to 4 p. m.. For information on federal jobs in Scott County: Room 530, 175 W. Jackson, Chicago, IL 60604; phone: 312/353–6192 (9 a.m. until noon) self–service only; for information on federal jobs in Pottawattamie County: Room 101, 120 S. Market St., Wichita, KS 67202; phone: 316/269–6794.

Kansas

Kansas Government Journal (League of Kansas Municipalities, 112 SW 7th, Topeka, KS 66603; phone: 913/354–9565) monthly, $24/annual subscription. Jobs listed under "Want Ads."

Local job hotlines

Kansas City: 913/573–5688

Wichita: 316/268–44537

State jobs

Contact the Department of Recruitment and Employment Information, Division of Personnel Services, Room 951–South, Landon State Office Building, 900 SW Jackson St., Topeka, KS 66612–1251; phones: 913/296–5390, **TDD**: 913/296–4798)

Jobline (Kansas Department of Administration, Personnel Services, Room 105–S, 900 SW Jackson Topeka, KS 66612; phone: 913/296–4278). Call 913/296–2208 for a recording that lists state vacancies. Updated every Friday at 4 p. m.., this 24–hour service gives you the name and phone of the person to contact about a vacancy. It also tells you which openings are limited to current state employees.

To find **Job Service Offices**, contact the Department of Human Resources (Pat Pritchard, 401 SW Topeka Blvd., Topeka, KS 66603; phone: 913/296–7474) for a copy of the "DHR Office Directory" which lists 36 Department of Human Resources offices that offer job services.

Kansas State Agency Locator: 913/296–0111

FJIC: Room 101, 120 S. Market St., Wichita, KS 67202; phone: 316/269–6764; self service only 8 a.m. to 4 p. m.. Residents of Johnson, Leavenworth, and Wyandotte counties: Federal Building, Room 134, 601 E. 12th St., Kansas City, MO 64106; phone: 816/426–5702.

Kentucky

The Kentucky City (Kentucky League of Cities, Suite 100, 2201 Regency Rd., Lexington, KY 40503; phone: 606/277–2886) monthly, $11/annual subscription. Jobs listed under "Career Opportunities." Few job ads.

Directory (Kentucky League of Cities, Suite 100, 2201 Regency Rd., Lexington, KY 40503; phone: 606/277–2886) $30/nonmembers, $10/members, published every two years.

Local job hotline

Louisville: 502/625–3355

State jobs

There is no central listing of state job vacancies. The closest you'll come to a central listing is the general list of job vacancies at Job Service offices. However, to obtain a job application and calendar of state tests, you should contact the Department of Personnel (Room 249, Capitol Annex, Frankfort, KY 40601; phone: 502/564–8030). You should know that this department will move in February, 1994, but as of this writing doesn't have its new address or phone number. If you can't reach them, call the state locator number, given below, to track them down.

To locate the state's 28 **Job Service Offices**, contact the Field Services Division (Department for Employment Services, Suite 2W, 275 E. Main St., Frankfort, KY 40621; phone: 502/564–7456) and ask for a copy of the ***Professional Placement Network*** (PNN) brochure. This brochure will also tell you how to participate in the PNN's computer job–matching service which matches your resume with job vacancies on file with the Department of Employment Services. This free service keeps your resume on file for one year. When you are matched with an employer, your resume is forwarded to the employer who is then responsible for contacting you for an interview. You submit a one–page typewritten resume, a six–line mini–resume summary, and complete and sign an Applicant Profile Form which you obtain from the department. Call 800/562–6397 to obtain the Applicant Profile Form and instructions, or contact your local Department of Employment Services office.

Kentucky State Agency Locator: 502/564–2500

FJIC: Federal Building, Room 506, 200 W. Second St., Dayton, OH 45402; phone: 513/225–2720; self service only 7 a.m. to 6 p. m.. For information on federal jobs in Henderson County: 575 N. Pennsylvania Ave., Indianapolis, IN 46204; phone: 317/269–7161.

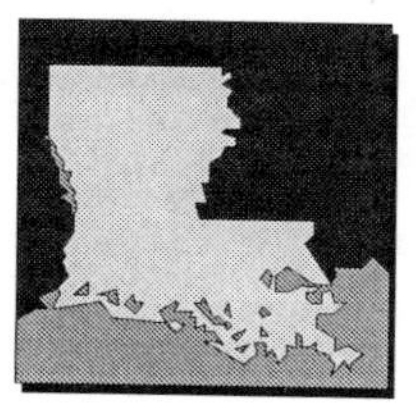

Louisiana

Louisiana Municipal Review (Louisiana Municipal Association, 700 N. 10th St., P.O. Box 4327, Baton Rouge, LA 70821; phone: 504/344–5001) monthly; $12.84/annual subscription. Few job ads.

LMA News (Louisiana Municipal Association, 700 N. 10th St., P.O. Box 4327, Baton Rouge, LA 70821; phone: 504/344–5001) monthly, free/members only. Occasionally sports a job announcement or two.

Directory of Louisiana Municipal Officials (Louisiana Municipal Association, 700 N. 10th St., P.O. Box 4327, Baton Rouge, LA 70821; phone: 504/344–5001) $26, published in January of odd–numbered years. Lists elected officials and major department heads.

State jobs

Information Hotline (State Department of Civil Service, Information and Recruiting Office, 5825 Florida Blvd., Baton Rouge, LA 70806; phone: 504/925–1911). If you call this number between 2:30 p. m.. and 4:30 p. m.., Monday through Friday, you'll get a live person. Call between 8 a.m. and 2:30 p. m.. and you'll get a recording that will tell you the following: You need to complete a job application form for each state job that interests you. You can obtain these forms at this Information and Recruiting Office or any Louisiana Job Service Office. The Job Service Offices have the titles and descriptions of state jobs. You must submit a separate application for each job, but you may submit photocopies. Within four weeks of applying, you'll be notified if your application was accepted and you will be told when the civil service exam, if required, will be held. You'll get your grade about two weeks after taking the test. Passing candidates are then placed on a list from which each agency selects people to interview when a job opens.

For information on the location of **Job Service Offices**, contact the Department of Labor (1001 N. 23rd Street, Baton Rouge, LA 70804; phone: 504/342–3111).

Louisiana State Agency Locator: 504/342–6600

FJIC: Suite 608, 1515 Poydras, New Orleans, LA 70112; phone: 504/589–2764; self service only, 9 a.m. to 4 p. m..

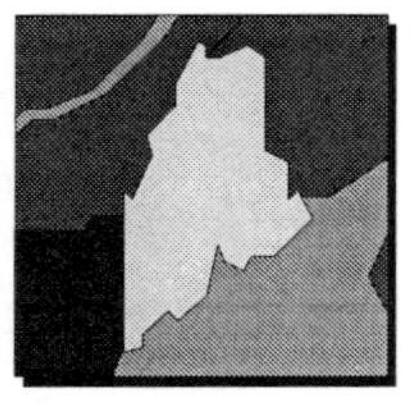

Maine

Maine Sunday Telegram and ***Portland Press Herald*** (P.O. Box 1460, Portland, ME 04104; phone: 207/780–9000) are the state's best sources of job ads for government positions.

Maine Townsman (Maine Municipal Association, Local Government Center, 37 Community Drive, Augusta, ME 04330; phone: 207/623–8428) monthly, $13/annual subscription. Jobs listed under "Classifieds." Few job ads.

Municipal Directory (Maine Municipal Association, Local Government Center, 37 Community Drive, Augusta, ME 04330; phone: 207/623–8428) $25/nonmembers, $15/members, published annually.

State jobs

Contact the Bureau of Human Resources, Department of Administration (State House Station #4, Augusta, ME 04333; phone: 207/287–3761).

To locate **Job Service Offices**, contact the Department of Labor (State House Station #54, Augusta, ME 04333; director's phone: 207/287–3431).

Maine State Agency Locator: 207/287–1110

FJIC: Thomas P. O'Neill Federal Building, 10 Causeway St., Boston, MA 02222–1031; phone: 617/565–5900; staff present 9 a.m. to 2 p. m..

Maryland

Maryland Municipal League Information Bulletin (Maryland Municipal League, 1212 West St., Annapolis, MD 21401; phone: 410/268–5514) biweekly, $50/annual nonmember subscription, $25/members. Four or five positions in all aspects of local government appear under "Jobs and Equipment."

Municipal Maryland (Maryland Municipal League, 1212 West St., Annapolis, MD 21401; phone: 410/268–5514) ten issues/year, $21/annual subscription. Jobs listed under "Market Place." Few job ads.

Maryland Municipal League Personnel Exchange Program (Maryland Municipal League, 1212 West St., Annapolis, MD 21401; phone: 410/268–5514) $5/six months. Job seeker submits copy of resume which is kept on file for six months. When this program matches a job seeker's resume with an available local government job, it sends a copy of the job announcement to the job hunter who is then responsible for contacting the potential employer.

1993–94 Directory of Maryland Municipal Officials (Maryland Municipal League, 1212 West St., Annapolis, MD 21401; phone: 410/268–5514) $20/nonprofit/governments, $30/commercial, $10/members, published annually. Lists city and town officials.

Opportunities in Public Affairs (Brubach Publishing Company, P.O. Box 15629, Chevy Chase, MD 20825; phone:301/986–0658) $29/two–month subscription, $49/four months, $69/six months, $129/annual, $7.95/single issue. You'll find announcements of over 200 positions with local, state, and federal government agencies; non–profits; and private companies in government affairs, public relations, broadcasting, and publishing. In addition to job announcements, this periodical also reports on unadvertised jobs its editors have uncovered. Most job openings are in the District of Columbia metropolitan area. It includes a good number of positions with Congress.

The 1993 Washington Job Source (MetCom, Inc. 1708 Surrey Lane, NW, Washington, DC 20007) $14.95 plus $3/shipping. Briefly describes 2,100 federal agencies, Congressional, non–profits, and corporations with the name, address, and phone number of the hiring contact.

Washington 93 (Columbia Books, 1212 New York Ave., NW, Suite 330, Washington, DC 20005; phone: 202/898–0662) $75, published annually each June. Nearly 600 pages of addresses, phone numbers, and information including one chapter on local government in the District and surrounding counties and towns with populations over 5,000, and regional authorities.

State jobs

Contact the Department of Personnel (Room 609, 301 W. Preston St., Baltimore, MD 21201; phone: 410/225–4715).

To pinpoint **Job Service Offices**, contact the Job Training and Placement Administration (Department of Economic and Employee Development, Room 700, 1100 N. Eutaw St., Baltimore, MD 21201; director's phone: 410/333–5070).

Job–Matching Service (Job Training and Placement Administration, Department of Economic and Employment Development, 1100 N. Eutaw St., Baltimore, MD 21201; director's phone: 410/333–5353) free. Matches your skills to job vacancies in the government, private, and non–profit sectors.

Maryland is among the first states to use ALEX, the Automated Labor EXchange computer service that enables job seekers to look up job vacancies in Maryland and nationwide, themselves. ALEX terminals are available at Job Service Offices and in shopping malls, libraries, and schools. Note that many of the ALEX terminals in Maryland give you access only to jobs within the state and are not part of the national hookup.

Maryland State Agency Locator: 410/974–3901

FJIC: Room 101, 300 W. Pratt St., Baltimore, MD 21201; phone: 410/962–3822; staff present 1 p. m.. to 3 p. m..; self service 9 a.m. to 4 p. m..

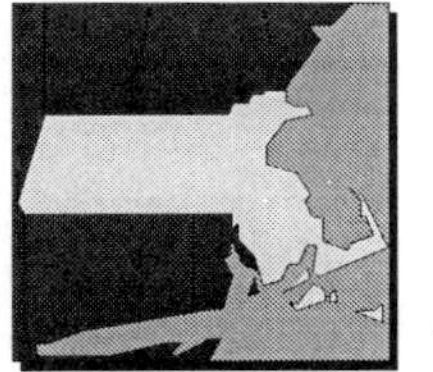

Massachusetts

The Beacon (Massachusetts Municipal Association, 60 Temple Place, Boston, MA 02111; phones: 800/882–1498, 617/426–7272) 11 issues/year, $36/nonmember annual subscription, $18/members. Jobs listed under "Employment Opportunities." Typical issue carries 10 to 20 job ads.

Municipal Directory (Massachusetts Municipal Association, 60 Temple Place, Boston, MA 02111; phones: 800/882–1498, 617/426–7272) $30/non-members, $15/members, published annually in early winter. Lists all elected local officials and department heads, planning agencies, statewide municipal associations.

State jobs

Notices for civil service exams for all job openings are posted by all local municipal clerks. Within the Department of Personnel Administration's Examination Administration Group (1 Ashburton Place, Room 205, Boston, MA 02108), the Public Information Unit (Room 201; general phone: 617/727–8370) provides information on job exam entrance requirements (800/392–6178, **TDD** 617/727–8370) and a recording of upcoming civil service exams (617/727–9244). The exam for each job area is given every other year. Write or call to receive an exam schedule from the Public Information Unit. The next schedule is released in mid–January 1994.

To locate **Job Service Offices**, contact the Department of Employment and Training (19 Staniford St., Boston, MA 02114; phone: 617/727–6529). *Massachusetts State Agency Locator: 617/727–2121*

FJIC: Thomas P. O'Neill Federal Building, 10 Causeway St., Boston 02222–1031; phone: 617/565–5900; staff present 9 a.m. to 2 p. m..

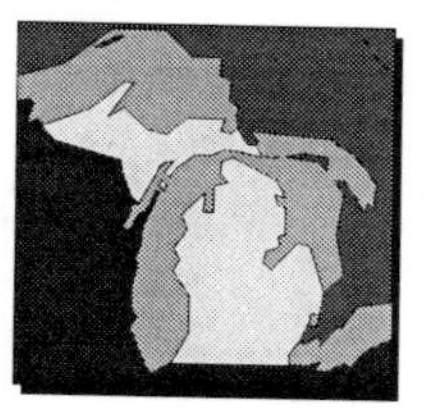

Michigan

Michigan Municipal Review (Michigan Municipal League, 1675 Green Rd., P.O. Box 1487, Ann Arbor, MI 48106; phone: 313/662–3246) ten issues/year, $15/annual subscription. Jobs listed under "Municipal Want Ads." About 20 ads per issue.

Directory of Michigan Municipal Officials (Michigan Municipal League, 1675 Green Rd., P.O. Box 1487, Ann Arbor, MI 48106; phone: 313/662–3246) published each January and July, $30/nonmembers, free/members. Lists elected officials and department heads.

Resume Referral Service (Michigan Municipal League, 1675 Green Rd., P.O. Box 1487, Ann Arbor, MI 48106; phone: 313/662–3246). Contact for information on this service which is actually operated by the Michigan City Management Association.

Planning & Zoning News (Planning and Zoning Center, Inc., 302 S. Waverly Rd., Lansing, MI 48917; phone: 517/886–0555) monthly, $150/annual subscription. Two to five jobs are advertised under "Jobs Available."

Local job hotline

Detroit: 313/224–6928

State jobs

Each state agency does its own hiring. To learn of current vacancies, you must contact the individual agency's placement office. For a list of state agencies, see the directories of state agencies near the beginning of this chapter.

To learn the requirements for state jobs, contact the Recruitment Office (Michigan Department of Civil Service, 400 S. Pine St., Lansing, MI 48933; phone: 517/373–3030). This office can tell you the qualifications for each job and whether a civil service exam is required. Civil service exam dates are posted here, at the service's other two offices, and at the state's Job

Service Offices. Educational institutions are eligible to be sent notices of civil service exams.

To find **Job Service Offices**, contact the Employment Security Commission (7310 Woodward Ave., Detroit, MI 48202; phone: 313/876–5000).

Michigan State Agency Locator: 517/373–1837

FJIC: Room 565, 477 Michigan Ave., Detroit, MI 48226; phone: 313/226–6950; self service only, 8 a.m. to 4:30 p. m..

Minnesota

Cities Bulletin (League of Minnesota Cities, 183 University Ave., East, St. Paul, MN 55101; phone: 612/227–5600) weekly during legislative session, semimonthly during rest of the year, $50/annual nonmember subscription, $35/members. Lists five or more local government jobs, primarily professional.

Directory for Minnesota Municipal Officials (League of Minnesota Cities, 183 University Ave., East, St. Paul, MN 55101; phone: 612/227–5600) $20 plus sales tax for Minnesota residents, plus $1/shipping, issued each January.

Local job hotlines

Minneapolis: 612/673–2666

Ramsey County: 612/266–2666

St. Paul: 612/298–4942

State jobs

Minnesota Career Opportunities (Department of Employee Relations, 658 Cedar St., St. Paul, MN 55155; phone: 612/296–6700) biweekly, first issue free, $30/annual subscription, $24/six–month subscription; send subscription requests and a check payable to the "State of Minnesota" to: Minnesota Book Store, 117 University Ave, St. Paul, MN 55155; phones: 800/657–9747, 612/297–3000. Copies are available at all state Job Service Offices. Includes information on filling out job applications, examination procedures, and training classes. Fifteen to 30 job vacancies are described in each issue.

Job Hotline (Minnesota Department of Employee Relations, 658 Cedar St., St. Paul, MN 55155; phone: 612/296–6700). Call 612/296–2616 for a 24–hour recording of available state government jobs. Updated every two weeks. For assistance from a real person, call 612/296–2616 between 9 a.m. and 4 p. m.. Monday through Friday.

For information on the location of **Job Service Offices**, contact J.S. and U.I. Operations (Department of Jobs and Training, 390 N. Robert St., St. Paul, MN 55101; phone: 612/296–3644).

Minnesota State Agency Locator: 612/296–6013

FJIC: Bishop Henry Whipple Federal Bldg., Room 501, 1 Federal Dr., Ft. Snelling, MN 55111; phone: 612/725–3430; self service, 7:30 a.m. to 4:30 p. m..

Mississippi

Mississippi Municipalities (Mississippi Municipal Association, 600 E. Amite, Jackson, MS 39201; phone: 601/353–5854) 11 issues/year, $10/annual subscription. Jobs listed under "MMA Employment Service."

Mississippi Municipal Directory (Mississippi Municipal Association, 600 E. Amite, Jackson, MS 39201; phone: 601/353–5854) $50, published every four years, most recent edition is 1989, one planned for 1993–1997. Lists all municipal elected officials and department heads.

Local job hotline

Jackson: 601/960–1003

State jobs

Job vacancies are announced through a computer network connected to the State Employment Service (Job Service) offices. Job descriptions can be viewed at these offices. County positions are sometimes also listed on this system. These state job vacancies are also available for review at the State Personnel Board (301 N. Lamar St., Jackson, MS 39201; phone: 601/359–1406). Although the State Personnel Board does not mail out job notices, you can find out what Mississippi state jobs are available through the Interstate Job Bank in which your local Job Service Office almost certainly participates.

For a list of **Job Service Offices**, contact the Mississippi State Employment Service (1520 W. Capitol St., Jackson, MS 39203; phone : 601/354–8711) for a copy of the Directory of Employment Service Offices.

Mississippi State Agency Locator: 601/359–1000

FJIC: Suite 341, Building 600, 3322 Memorial Parkway South, Huntsville, AL 35801–5311; phone: 205/544–5803; self service only, 7 a.m. to 4 p. m..

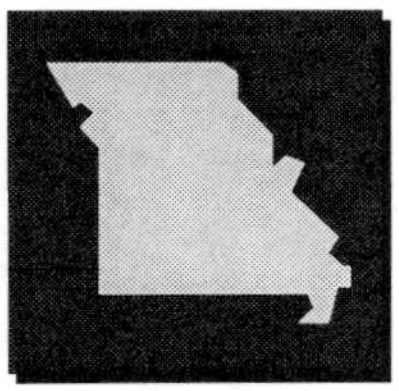

Missouri

Missouri Municipal Review (Missouri Municipal League, 1727 Southridge Drive, Jefferson City, MO 65109; phone: 314/635–9134) 10 issues/year, $18/annual subscription. Jobs listed under "Municipal Hunting Ground." About ten job ads per issue.

Missouri Municipal Officials Directory (Missouri Municipal League, 1727 Southridge Drive, Jefferson City, MO 65109; phone: 314/635–9134) published annually each July, $30/nonmembers (prepaid), free/members. Lists municipal elected officials and department heads.

Missouri Wage Surveys and ***Employment Projections*** (Division of Employment Security, Research and Analysis Section, 421 E. Dunklin, Box 59, Jefferson City, MO 65105; phone: 314/751–3591).

Local job hotline

Kansas City: 816/274–11127

State jobs

Job Opportunity Announcements from the Division of Personnel, Office of Administration (P.O. Box 388, Jefferson City, MO 65102; phone: 314/751–4162) are sent periodically to Job Service offices throughout the state. These announcements describe the positions available on the merit system.

To locate **Job Service Offices**, contact the Division of Employment Security (Labor and Industrial Relations Department, 421 E. Dunklin, Box 59, Jefferson City, MO 65104; director's phone: 314/751–3215).

Missouri State Agency Locator: 314/751–2000

FJIC: For federal jobs west of and including Mercer, Grundy, Livingston, Carroll, Saline, Pettis, Benton, Hickory, Dallas, Webster, Doublas, and Ozark counties: Room 134, 601 E. 12th St., Kansas City, MO 64106; phone: 816/426–5702; self service only, 8 a.m. to 4 p. m.. For all other counties:

Federal Building, Room 134, 815 Olive St., St. Louis, MO 63101; phone: 314/539-2285.

Montana

Also see the listings under "Job sources for multi-state regions" at the beginning of this chapter.

Montana League of Cities and Towns Newsletter (Montana League of Cities and Towns, Suite 201, 208 N. Montana Ave., P.O. Box 1704, Helena, MT 59624; phone: 406/442-8768) two issues/annually, free. Ads are rare, but when they do appear they cover Montana, Idaho, and Oregon.

Directory of Montana Municipal Officials (Montana League of Cities and Towns, Suite 201, 208 N. Montana Ave., P.O. Box 1704, Helena, MT 59624; phone: 406/442-8768) published in even-numbered years; $12.50. Lists elected officials and department heads of incorporated municipalities.

Montana Planners Directory (Montana Department of Commerce, Local Government Assistance Division, 1424 9th Ave., Helena, MT 59620; phone: 406/444-3757) $3.75, except free to Montana local government planners, last published in 1989. The State Library (1515 E. Sixth Ave., Helena, MT 59620; phone: 406/444-3004) has copies available for inter-library loan. Lists all planners in the state and planning agencies, Councils of Governments, and related federal departments.

Local job hotline

Billings: 406/657-8441

State and local jobs

Most state agencies use the Job Service for recruitment.

Directory of Job Service Offices (Job Service Division, Department of Labor and Industry, P.O. Box 1728, Helena, MT 59624; phone: 406/444-4100). Lists detailed information on the state's 24 Job Service Offices. Competition for government jobs is intense. For information on available local and state government positions, inquire at the Job Service Office in the area in which you wish to live.

Montana State Agency Locator: 406/444-2511

FJIC: P.O. Box 25167, 12345 W. Alameda Parkway, Lakewood, CO 80225; 303/969-7050; for forms and local supplements, call 303/969-7055; staff present noon to 3:45 p. m..; self service, 9 a.m. to noon.

Nebraska

Nebraska Municipal Review (League of Nebraska Municipalities, 1335 L St., Lincoln, NE 68508; phone: 402/476–2829) monthly; $25/annual subscription. Jobs listed under "Classifieds."

Nebraska Directory of Municipal Officials (League of Nebraska Municipalities 1335 L St., Lincoln, NE 68508; phone: 402/476–2829) $40, published annually.

Local job hotlines

Lincoln: 402/441–7736

Omaha: 402/444–5302

State jobs

State Job Listings (Department of Personnel, 301 Centennial Mall South, P.O. Box 94905, Lincoln, NE 68509–4905; phone: 402/471–2075) free. Complete the application form and attach your resume and recommendation letters. Check the job listings each week and call or write to activate your file when you find jobs that interest you.

Job Hotline (Department of Personnel, 301 Centennial Mall South, P.O. Box 94905, Lincoln, NE 68509–4905; phone: 402/471–2075). Call 402/471–2200 for the latest vacancies in state government.

To locate **Job Service Offices**, contact the Job Service Division (Department of Labor, 550 S. 16th St., Lincoln, NE 68509; phone: 402/471–9828).

Nebraska State Agency Locator: 402/471–2311

FJIC: Room 101, 120 S. Market St., Wichita, KS 67202; phone: 316/269–6774.

Nevada

Information Exchange (Nevada League of Cities, Box 2307, Carson City, NV 89701; phone: 702/882–2121) monthly, free. Job ads appear occasionally.

Nevada League of Cities Directory (Nevada League of Cities, Box 2307, Carson City, NV 89701; phone: 702/882–2121) $7.50/nonmembers, free/members, published annually.

Nevada Association of Counties Directory (Nevada Association of Counties, Suite 205, 308 N. Curry St., Carson City, NV 89703; phone: 702/883–7863) $20, published annually in February. Lists elected county officials and department heads, state and federal officials.

Local job hotlines

Las Vegas: 702/229–3968 (police department positions only)

Reno: 702/344–2287

State jobs

Job Recording Line (Department of Personnel, 209 E. Musser St., Carson City, NV 89710; phone: 702/687–4050). Call 702/687–4160 for a 24–hour recording of available jobs (titles, department, location). To receive a full job description and application form, contact the Department of Personnel.

Job Announcements (Department of Personnel, 209 E. Musser St., Carson City, NV 89710; phone: 702/687–4050) weekly. Distributed to state agencies, including Job Service Offices and universities. Call for individual listings to be sent to you. Lists state government positions.

To obtain a list of **Job Service Centers**, contact the Employment Security Department (500 E. Third St., Carson City, NV 89713; phone: 702/687–4630).

Nevada State Agency Locator: 702/885–5000

FJIC: Los Angeles area: 9650 Flair Dr., Suite 100A, El Monte, CA 91731; phone: 818/575–6510, staff present 9 a.m. to 3 p. m..; **Sacramento area:** 1029 J St., Second Floor, Sacramento, 95814, phone: 916/551–1464, staff present 9 a.m. to noon.

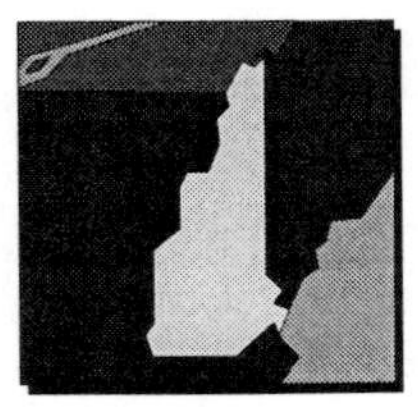

New Hampshire

Local government job openings are advertised in local newspapers and the ***New Hampshire Sunday News*** (100 William Loeb Dr., Manchester, NH 03109; phone: 603/668–4321), ***Maine Sunday Telegram*** (P.O. Box 1460, Portland, ME 04104; phone: 207/775–

5811), and ***Boston Globe*** (135 Morrissey Blvd., Boston, MA 02125; phone: 617/929–2000).

New Hampshire Town and City (New Hampshire Municipal Association, 25 Triangle Park Dr., P.O. Box 617, Concord, NH 03302; phone: 603/224–7447) ten issues/year; $10/annual subscription. Jobs listed under "Municipal Want Ads." Few job ads.

Directory of New Hampshire Municipal Officials (New Hampshire Municipal Association, P.O. Box 617, Concord, NH 03302; phone: 603/224–7447) $35/nonmembers, $25/members, published every July. Lists elected officials and major department heads.

County Directory of New Hampshire (New Hampshire Association of Counties, 16 Centre St., Concord, NH 03301; phone: 603/224–9222) $5, published in March of odd–numbered years. Lists elected and appointed officials.

State jobs

Opportunities in New Hampshire State Government (Division of Personnel, State House Annex, Room 1, School Street, Concord, NH 03301; phone: 603/271–3261). Write for details on how to receive this job vacancy notice and to receive the published list of state job vacancies.

To locate **Job Service Offices**, contact the Bureau of Employment Services (Department of Employment Security, 32 S. Main St., Concord, NH 03301; phone: 603/224–3311).

New Hampshire State Agency Locator: 603/271–1110

FJIC: Thomas P. O'Neill Federal Building, 10 Causeway St., Boston, MA 02222–1031; phone: 617/565–5900; staff present 9 a.m. to 2 p. m..

New Jersey

New Jersey Municipalities (New Jersey State League of Municipalities, 407 W. State St., Trenton, NJ 08618; phone: 609/695–3481) nine issues/year, $9/nonmember annual subscription, $6/members, $10/foreign. Jobs listed under "Municipal Job Line." About 10 job ads per issue.

Municipal Directory (New Jersey State League of Municipalities, 407 W. State St., Trenton, NJ 08618; phone: 609/695–3481) $22/nonmembers, $12/municipal members, published each February. Lists elected officials and major department heads.

Revised Statutes, Administrative Rules and Regulations, Roster (New Jersey Board of Professional Planners, P.O. Box 45016, Newark, NJ 07101; phone: 201/504–6465). $10, published each July.

State jobs

Job Opportunities Bulletin (Department of Personnel, 44 S. Clinton Plaza, Trenton, NJ 08625, phone: 609/292–7467) issued the first of each month; available only at local libraries, New Jersey Employment Service Offices (see immediately below), and the Department of Personnel's offices in Camden, Newark, New Brunswick, and Trenton; copies are not mailed out to anybody. Each issue includes instructions on applying for state jobs and a state job application you can photocopy to submit. A typical issue features announcements of examinations for about 175 available state jobs. Each job description includes residency requirements, salary range, duties, and experience and education requirements. There is a five dollar processing fee for each job application you file. Job applications are generally due by the fourteenth of each month, so you'd be wise to see this bulletin as early as possible each month.

Job Service Offices (Division of Programs, Department of Labor, John Fitch Plaza, Trenton, NJ 08625; phone: 609/984–7480). Request a list of the 23 full–service offices and 16 satellite offices. Many state, local, and federal jobs can be found in their computers.

New Jersey State Agency Locator: 609/292–2121

FJIC: For Bergan, Essex, Hudson, Hunterdon, Middlesex, Morris, Passaic, Somerset, Sussex, Union, and Warren Counties, you have to go to New York City: Jacob B. Javits Federal Building, Room 120 (second floor), 26 Federal Plaza, New York, NY 10278, phone: 212/264–0422/0423, staff present 10 a.m. to 2 p. m..

For all other counties, you'll have to go to Philadelphia: Room 1416, William Green, Jr. Federal Building, 600 Arch St., Philadelphia, PA 19106, phone: 215/597–7440, staff present 10:30 a.m. to 2:30 p. m.., also self service 8:30 a.m. to 3:30 p. m..

New Mexico

Also see the listings under "Job sources for multi–state regions" at the beginning of this chapter.

Albuquerque Journal (7777 Jefferson, NE, Albuquerque, NM 87109; phone: 505/823–4400). The Sunday edition is the best source of ads for local government positions in three–fourths of the state. For the southern and southeast portions of the state, see the Sunday ***El Paso Times*** (300 N. Campbell, El Paso, TX 79901; phone: 915/546–6260). For jobs in the extreme southern section, beginning with Clovis and going south, the Sunday editions of the local newspapers from nearby Texas are the best sources in which to find ads for local government job vacancies.

The Municipal Reporter (New Mexico Municipal League, 1229 Paseo de Peralta, Santa Fe, NM 87501; phone: 505/982–5573) monthly, $20/annual subscription. Jobs listed under "Positions Available." When there are ads, there will be two or three.

Directory of New Mexico Municipal Officials (New Mexico Municipal League, 1229 Paseo de Peralta, Santa Fe, NM 87501; phone: 505/982–5573) $28, published each May. Lists municipal elected officials and department heads, councils of governments, and relevant state officials and agencies.

Directory of New Mexico County Officials (New Mexico Association of Counties, 1215 Paseo de Peralta, Santa Fe, NM 87501; phone: 505/983–2101) $25. Published in January of odd–numbered years. Lists elected county officials, managers, attorneys, and extension agents.

State jobs

Contact the State Personnel Office (810 W. San Mateo, Santa Fe, NM 87503; phone: 505/827–8190).

To locate **Job Service Offices**, contact the Department of Labor (401 Broadway, NE, Albuquerque, NM 87102; phone: 505/841–8609).

New Mexico State Agency Locator: 505/872–4011

FJIC: Federal Building, Suite 910, 505 Marquette Ave., Albuquerque, NM 87102; phone: 505/766–2906; staff present Monday through Thursday, 8 a.m. to 4 p. m..

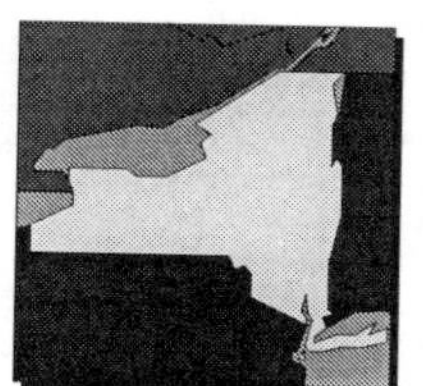

New York

The Chief–Civil Service Leader (150 Nassau St., New York, NY 10038; phone: 212/962–2690) weekly, $20/annual subscription. Includes ads and announcements of civil service exams for hundreds of professional, trades, labor, technical, and clerical jobs in city, state, and the federal government.

The New York State Municipal Bulletin (New York Conference of Mayors, 119 Washington Ave., Albany, NY 12210; phone: 518/463–1185) bimonthly, $25/nonmember annual subscription. Job ads printed at the rear. Few job ads.

Directory for City and Village Officials (New York State Conference of Mayors, 119 Washington Ave., Albany, NY 12210; phone: 518/463–1185) $50/nonmembers, $20/members, published each January. Lists elected officials and major department heads of cities and villages. The state's 932 towns, which range in population from 40 to over 700,000 are not included. The nationwide directories of local officials described at the beginning of this chapter include New York towns.

NYSAC News (New York State Association of Counties, 150 State St., Albany, NY 12207; phone: 518/465–1473) $24/annual nonmember subscription, free/members. A handful of jobs in county government of all types appear under "Municipal Want Ads."

NYSAC County Directory (New York State Association of Counties, 150 State St., Albany, NY 12207; phone: 518/465–1473) $20/nonmembers, free/members, published each March.

NYSAC Salary Survey of Executive, Legislative, and Administrative Positions in New York State Counties (New York State Association of Counties, 150 State St., Albany, NY 12207; phone: 518/465–1473) free, published each April. For each position and county, includes base salary plus actual salary for each of the last two years, whether the position is full–time or part–time, additional compensation, department budget and size, and comments. Positions covered include department heads and elected officials.

Regional and County Planning Directors (New York Department of State, Office of Local Government Services, 162 Washington Ave., Albany, NY 12231; phone: 518/473–3355) free. Revised frequently. Lists county and regional planning directors with addresses and phone numbers.

Directory, New York Metropolitan Chapter American Planning Association (c/o Peter Hart, Buckhurst Fish Hutton Katz Inc., 72 Fifth Ave., New York, NY 10011; phone: 212/620–0050; if no longer at that address, obtain the new address from APA's Director of Chapter Services [1776 Massachusetts Ave., NW, Washington, DC 20036; phone: 202/872–0611]); $6 prepaid, make check payable to "New York APA Metro Chapter". Published in even–numbered years. Lists public planning agencies in New York City and surrounding region, consulting firms, and the 800+ members of APA's New York Metropolitan Chapter.

Internships + Job Opportunities in New York City and Washington, DC (Graduate Group, 86 Norwood Rd., West Hartford, CT 06117; phones: 203/232–3100, 203/236–5570) $27.50, published annually. Describes internship and job opportunities for a wide variety of fields.

Town jobs

Many of the state's 932 "towns" advertise positions in national specialty publications and local newspapers. However, half of these towns have populations of 5,000 or less. Local officials make oral vacancy announcements at town board meetings. Newspaper coverage and word of mouth seem to suffice for filling these jobs.

Those jobs covered by civil service require civil service examinations. Use the government section of the local telephone directory to locate a civil service office (often only at the county level) to contact for information on which local jobs are subject to civil service and how to apply.

State jobs

Guide to Career Opportunities in New York State Government (New York State Department of Labor, Publications Unit, Room 401, State Office Campus Building #12, Albany, NY 12240; phone: 518/457–3801) $50, free/first annual update, $25/subsequent annual updates, most recent edition 1991. This extremely detailed, but lively, book is the authoritative guide to 178 civil service occupations in 26 state agencies, occupations which either offer a large number of employment opportunities or for which the state has historically had difficulty finding qualified applicants. It specifies detailed job duties, salary schedule, qualifications, testing requirements, job and office locations, state agency functions, the job environment, promotion opportunities and career ladders, total positions and annual hiring by job title, and an outline of the civil service law. Comes in a two–volume loose–leaf binder. This guide is expected to also be available on computer disk. Contact for details.

For information on specific job openings and exams, contact the New York State Department of Civil Services' General Exam Information Office (State Office Campus Building #1, Albany, NY 12239; phone: 518/457–6216).

The New York State Directory (Walker's Western Research, 1650 Borel Pl., Suite 130, San Mateo, CA 94402; phone: 800/258–5737) $112, published annually in the summer, 500 pages. Lists executive and legislative state offices in 25 major policy areas; senior officials in all counties; senior government officials in Albany, Binghamton, Buffalo, New York City, Rochester, Syracuse, and Yonkers; public school administrators; judges; chambers of commerce; statewide and county political party chairpersons; registered lobbyists and political action committees.

To find **Job Service Offices**, called Community Service Centers in New York, contact the Department of Labor (Room 590, State Campus Building #12, Albany, NY 12240; phone: 518/457–7030).

New York State Agency Locator: 518/474–2121

FJIC: New York City area: Jacob B. Javits Federal Building, Room 120 (second floor), 26 Federal Plaza, New York, NY 10278, phone: 212/264–0422/0423, staff present 10 a.m. to 2 p. m..; **Syracuse area:** James M. Hanley Federal Building, 100 S. Clinton St., Syracuse, NY 13260; phone: 315/423–5660, self service 9 a.m. to 3 p. m..

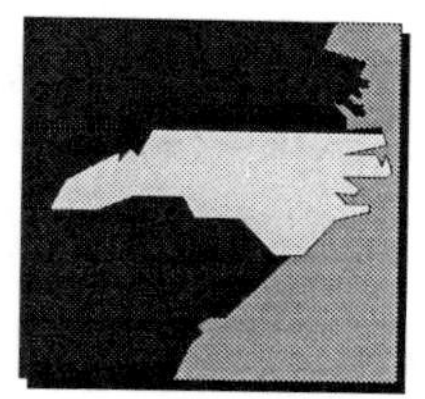

North Carolina

Southern City (North Carolina League of Municipalities, 215 N. Dawson St., P.O. Box 3069, Raleigh, NC 27602; phone: 919/834–1311) monthly, $6/annual subscription. Jobs listed under "Career Opportunities."

Directory of North Carolina Municipal Officials (North Carolina League of Municipalities, 215 N. Dawson St., P.O. Box 3069, Raleigh, NC 27602; phone: 919/834–1311) $30 plus sales tax for North Carolina residents, published each March. Lists only municipal elected officials and department heads.

County Lines (North Carolina Association of County Commissioners, 215 N. Dawson, P.O. Box 1488, Raleigh, NC 27602; phone: 919/832–2893) biweekly, $20/annual subscription. Jobs listed under "Classifieds." About ten to 15 job ads per issue.

Directory of North Carolina County Officials (North Carolina Association of County Commissioners, 215 N. Dawson, P.O. Box 1488, Raleigh, NC 27602; phone: 919/832–2893) $22 plus sales tax for North Carolina residents, published in odd–numbered years. Lists elected officials and department heads.

Local job hotlines

Cary: 919/460–4905
Charlotte: 704/336–3968
Greensboro: 910/373–2080
Raleigh: 919/890–3305
Wake County: 919/856–6115

State jobs

State hiring is decentralized. To learn about job vacancies, go to a state Job Service Office. Obtain an application form there and send it to the agency to which you are applying. For a list of agencies, see the various directories of state agencies at the beginning of this chapter.

To locate **Job Service Offices**, contact the Employment Security Commission (P.O. Box 25903, Raleigh, NC 27611; phone: 919/733–7546).

North Carolina State Agency Locator: 919/733–1110

FJIC: Suite 202, 4407 Bland Rd., Raleigh, NC 27609–6296; phone: 919/790–2822; self service 8 a.m. to 4:30 p. m..

North Dakota

North Dakota League of Cities Bulletin (North Dakota League of Cities, 1731 N. 13th St., Box 2235, Bismarck, ND 58502; phone: 701/223–3518) ten issues/year, $15/annual subscription. Very few job ads. Jobs listed under "Jobs Available."

Directory of North Dakota Officials (North Dakota League of Cities, 1731 N. 13th St., Box 2235, Bismarck, ND 58502; phone: 701/223–3518) $12/nonmembers, free/members, published in even–numbered years. Lists elected city officials and selected department heads.

North Dakota Wage & Benefit Survey (Job Service North Dakota, P.O. Box 1537, Bismarck, ND 58502; phone: 701/224–2868) free, 51 pages, published each January. For each occupation in government and private sector, gives the average salary and the average starting and average high salaries, plus fringe benefits.

State jobs

Job Service North Dakota (1000 E. Divide Ave., P.O. Box 1537, Bismarck, ND 58502; phone: 701/224–2825). State and many other government job announcements can be viewed at any local Job Service Office. Ask for the brochure entitled "Your Step–by–Step Guide to Using Job Services."

North Dakota State Agency Locator: 701/224–2000

FJIC: Bishop Henry Whipple Federal Building, Room 501, 1 Federal Dr., Ft. Snelling, MN 55111; phone: 612/725–3430; self service 7:30 a.m. to 4:30 p. m..

Ohio

Cities & Villages (Ohio Municipal League, Suite 510, 175 S. Third St., Columbus, OH 43215; phone: 614/221–4349) monthly, $10/annual subscription. Five to ten jobs are listed under "Classified Ads."

County Information and Data Service (County Commissioners Association of Ohio, Suite 500, 175 S. Third St., Columbus, OH 43215; phone: 614/221–5627) $150/annual nonmember subscription, free/members. Only one or two job ads make it into the "Classifieds."

Local job hotline

Cincinnati: 513/352–2489

State jobs

Each state agency does its own hiring. There is no civil service exam. To get a list of the personnel offices of state agencies, contact the Division of Personnel, Department of Administrative Services (28th Floor, 30 E. Broad St., Columbus, OH 43266; phone: 614/466–3455). Also see the various directories that include state agencies near the beginning of this chapter to identify state government agencies in Ohio.

The state operates a **Job Information Center** (30 E. Broad St., B1 Level, Columbus, OH 43266–0405; phone: 614/466–4026).

To obtain a list of the state's 76 **Job Service Offices**, contact the Public Information Office (Bureau of Employment Services, 145 S. Front St., P.O. Box 1618, Columbus, OH 43216; phone: 614/466–3859). Ask for the "Programs and Services Brochure."

Ohio State Agency Locator: 614/466–2000

FJIC: Room 506, 200 W. Second St., Dayton, OH 45402; phone: 513/225–2720. Residents of the counties north of and including Van Wert, Auglaize, Hardin, Marion, Crawford, Richland, Ashland, Wayne, Stark, Carroll, and Columbiana: Room 565, 477 Michigan Ave., Detroit, MI 48226; phone: 313/226–6950; self service only.

Oklahoma

Oklahoma Cities & Towns (Oklahoma Municipal League, 201 N.E. 23rd St., Oklahoma City, OK 73105; phone: 405/528–7515) biweekly, $18/annual subscription for nonmembers, $12/annual subscription for member cities and towns. A pretty extensive listing of government job vacancies appears under "Employment Opportunities."

Directory of Oklahoma City and Town Officials (Oklahoma Municipal League, 201 N.E. 23rd St., Oklahoma City, OK 73105; phone: 405/528–7515) $29.34, published annually.

Local job hotline

Oklahoma City: 405/297–2419

Tulsa: 918/596–7444

State jobs

Contact the Office of Personnel Management (2101 N. Lincoln Blvd., Oklahoma City, OK 73105; phone: 405/521–2177).

To pinpoint **Job Service Offices**, contact the Employment Security Commission (2401 N. Lincoln Blvd., Oklahoma City, OK 73105; phone: 405/557–7105).

Oklahoma State Agency Locator: 405/521–2011

FJIC: 8610 Broadway, Room 305, San Antonio, TX 78217; phones: 210/229–6611, 210/229–6600. For forms call 210/229–6618; staff present 7:30 a.m. to 4:30 p. m..

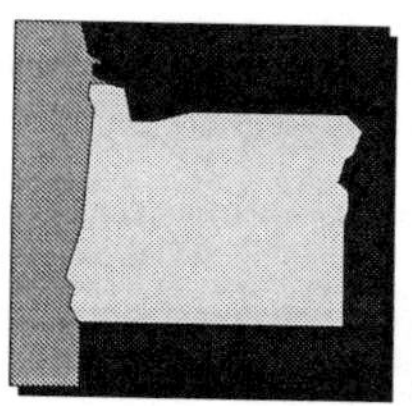

Oregon

Newsletter (League of Oregon Cities, P.O. Box 928, Salem, OR 97308; phone: 503/588–6550) monthly, $60/annual subscription. Jobs listed under "Career Opportunities."

Local job hotlines

Beaverton: 503/526–2299
Corvallis: 503/757–6955
Eugene: 503/687–5060
Portland: 503/823–4573
Salem: 503/588–6103

State and local jobs

Job Hotline (Executive Department, Attention: Announcement Clerk, 155 Cottage St., NE, Salem, OR 97310; phones: 503/378–3006, **TDD**: 503/373–1660). Updated daily, this 24–hour hotline gives detailed information on currently available state jobs and how to apply for them. Out–of–state job seekers can request up to three recruitment announcements of specific jobs at a time. You must send a self–addressed, stamped #10 business envelope with your request. These job vacancies are also listed on the computers at the state's Employment Division field offices where you can print out as many job descriptions as you like. You can also request a free copy of the brochure, *Job Hunter's Guide to Oregon State Service,* which takes you through the hiring process.

Announcement Bulletin (Executive Department, Attention: Announcement Clerk, 155 Cottage St., NE, Salem, OR 97310; phone: 503/378–3006) semimonthly, $25/month. This bulletin, affectionately known to staff as the "OC Bulletin," contains brief descriptions of all state and local government jobs currently open. Once you've received this bulletin, an out–of–state job seeker can request up to three recruitment announcements of specific jobs at a time. You must send a self–addressed, stamped #10 business envelope with your request. You can also request a free copy of the brochure, *Job Hunter's Guide to Oregon State Service* which takes you through the hiring process.

Local Office Directory (Employment Division, Department of Human Resources, 875 Union St., NE, Salem, OR 97301; phones: 503/378–3211, 800/237–3710 within Oregon only). Contact these folks for this list of 33 local **Job Service** offices from which listings of local and state government jobs are available.

Oregon State Agency Locator: 503/378–3131

FJIC: Federal Building, Room 376, 1220 SW Third St., Portland, OR 97204; phone: 503/221–4141; staff present noon to 3 p. m..; self service 8 a.m. to noon.

Pennsylvania

Pennsylvanian (Local Pennsylvanian, Room 207, 2941 N. Front St., Harrisburg, PA 17110; phone: 717/236–9526) monthly, $17/annual subscription. Six to ten jobs are listed under "Classifieds."

Pennsylvania State Association of Township Supervisors Magazine (PSATS, 3001 Gettysburg Rd., Camp Hill, PA 17011; phone: 717/763–0930) monthly, $25/annual subscription. Few job ads for township positions.

Pennsylvania League of Cities Directory (Pennsylvania League of Cities and Municipalities, 414 N. Second St., Harrisburg, PA 17101; phone: 717/236–9469) $50/nonmembers, $20/members, published in February of even-numbered years. Lists elected officials and major department heads.

Directory of City Officials (Distribution Services Unit, P.O. Box 2028, Harrisburg, PA 17105; phone: 717/787–6746) $2; when ordering, give publication number 137, published each May by the Pennsylvania Department of Transportation, Local Government Services (717/787–2183). Lists elected officials and major department heads.

Directory of County Commissioners (Distribution Services Unit, P.O. Box 2028, Harrisburg, PA 17105; phone: 717/787–6746) $2; when ordering, give publication number 136, published each May by the Pennsylvania Department of Transportation, Local Government Services (717/787–2183). Lists elected officials and major department heads.

Directory of Borough Officials (Distribution Services Unit, P.O. Box 2028, Harrisburg, PA 17105; phone: 717/787–6746) $7; when ordering, give publication number 138, published each May by the Pennsylvania Department of Transportation, Local Government Services (717/787–2183). Lists elected officials and major department heads.

Pennsylvania Municipal Yearbook (Pennsylvania State Association of Boroughs, 2941 Front St., Harrisburg, PA 17110; phone: 717/236–9526) $100/nonmember, $30/member, published each summer. Lists many top elected and administrative officials for each of the state's 970 boroughs.

State Association of Township Commissioners Directory (Pennsylvania League of Cities, 414 N. Second St., Harrisburg, PA 17101; phone: 717/236–9469) $50/nonmember, $20/member, published in February of even–numbered years. Lists elected officials and major department heads for townships and member boroughs.

Directory of First Class Township Officials (Distribution Services Unit, P.O. Box 2028, Harrisburg, PA 17105; phone: 717/787–6746) $2; when ordering, give publication number 139, published each May by the Pennsylvania Department of Transportation, Local Government Services (717/787–2183). Lists elected officials and major department heads.

Directory of Second Class Township Officials (Distribution Services Unit, P.O. Box 2028, Harrisburg, PA 17105; phone: 717/787–6746) $11; when ordering, give publication number 140, published each May by the Pennsylvania Department of Transportation, Local Government Services (717/787–2183). Lists elected officials and major department heads.

Local job hotline

Pittsburgh: 412/255–2388

State jobs

Civil service positions: To determine your eligibility, contact the Pennsylvania Civil Service Commission (P.O. Box 569, Harrisburg, PA 17108–0569; phone: 703/783–7811) or Job Service Offices. Obtain locations of **Job Service Offices** (called "Job Centers") from the Office of Employment Services and Training (Department of Labor and Industry, Room 1115, Seventh and Forster Streets, Harrisburg, PA 17121; phone: 717/787–4811).

Positions exempt from civil service: For trades, labor, technical, and office support positions with all state agencies, submit your application and resume to the Division of State Employment (Room 110, Finance Building, Harrisburg, PA 17120; phone: 717/787–5703). Applications are kept on file for one year. State agency personnel officials examine the applications and contact qualified applicants for an interview when a vacancy occurs.

Pennsylvania State Agency Locator: 717/787–2121

FJIC: Harrisburg area: Room 168, Federal Building, P.O. Box 761, Harrisburg, PA 17108, phone: 717/782–4494, staff present weekdays except Wednesday, 8 a.m. to noon; **Philadelphia area:** Room 1416, William Green, Jr. Federal Building, 600 Arch St., Philadelphia, PA 19106, phone:

215/597–7440, staff present 10:30 a.m. to 2:30 p. m.., also self service 8:30 a.m. to 3:30 p. m..; **Pittsburgh:** Room 119, Federal Building, 1000 Liberty Ave., Pittsburgh, PA 15222; phone: 412/644–2755 gets you a recording, open from 9 a.m. to 4 p. m.., self service only, to reach a live person call the Philadelphia office.

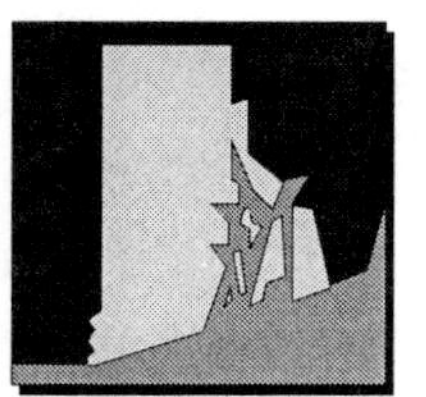

Rhode Island

There is no central source for local government job openings in Rhode Island. See the classified advertising sections of the Sunday editions of local Rhode Island newspapers for local government job ads.

Also contact the personnel offices of the cities in which you might be interested in working. The Rhode Island League of Cities and Towns (Suite 502, 1 State St., Providence, RI 02903; phone: 401/272–3434) is willing, on an informal basis, to help job seekers from out–of–state find job vacancies. The league will, upon request, informally check to see if there are any local government positions available.

Directory of City–Town Officials (Rhode Island Dept. of Administration, Office of Municipal Affairs, 1 Capitol Hill, Providence, RI 02908; phone: 401/277–2867) $5, published each March. Lists all state department heads and division chiefs as well as municipal elected officials, department heads, and state associations of local government officials.

State jobs

Contact the Department of Administration, Office of Personnel (1 Capitol Hill, Providence, RI 02908; phone: 401/277–2160).

Find the ten **Job Service Offices**, by contacting the Department of Employment and Training (101 Friendship St., Providence, RI 02903; phone: 401/277–3722) or see your telephone directory. Job Service staff will match job seekers with positions and refer them to potential employers.

Rhode Island State Agency Locator: 401/277–2000 (8 a.m. to 4 p. m.. only)

FJIC: Thomas P. O'Neill Federal Building, 10 Causeway St., Boston 02222–1031; phone: 617/565–5900; staff present 9 a.m. to 2 p. m..

South Carolina

Uptown (Municipal Association of South Carolina, P.O.. Box 12109, Columbia, SC 29211; phones: 800/658–3633, 803/799–9574) 11 issues/year, $10/annual nonmember subscription, free/members. Two or three jobs in municipal government appear under "Job Market."

South Carolina Municipal Officials Directory (Municipal Association of South Carolina, P.O. Box 12109, Columbia, SC 29211; phones: 800/658–3633, 803/799–9574) $15/nonmembers, free/members, published annually. Lists municipal elected officials and department heads.

Local job hotlines

Charleston: 803/720–3907

Columbia: 803/733–8478

Lexington County: 803/359–8562

State jobs

Career Lines (Department of Human Resources Management, Job Information Center, 2221 Devine, Columbia, SC 29205; phone: 803/734–9080). For a 24–hour recording of professional positions with the State of South Carolina, call 803/734–9333; for clerical, technical, and skilled labor positions, call 803/734–9334.

While many state jobs are listed on the Career Lines, many others are posted on the bulletin board at the Job Information Center. All should be available at Job Service Offices. Each state agency does its own hiring. See the directories of state agencies at the beginning of this chapter.

To locate **Job Service Offices**, contact the Employment Security Commission (1550 Gadsden St., Columbia, SC 29202; phone: 803/737–2400).

South Carolina State Agency Locator: 803/734–1000

FJIC: Suite 202, 4407 Bland Rd., Raleigh, NC 27609–6296; phone: 919/790–2822; self service only 8 a.m. to 4:30 p. m..

South Dakota

South Dakota Municipalities (South Dakota Municipal League, 214 E. Capitol, Pierre, SD 57501; phone: 605/224–8654) monthly, $20/annual subscription. Jobs listed under "Classified Ads." Few job ads.

Directory of South Dakota Municipal Officials (South Dakota Municipal League, 214 E. Capitol, Pierre, SD 57501; phone: 605/224–8654) $15, published each July. Lists elected officials and major department heads.

South Dakota Counties: County Comment (South Dakota Association of Counties Commissioners, 207 E. Capitol, Pierre, SD 57501; phone: 605/224–4554) monthly, $12/nonmember annual subscription, free/members. Few job ads.

South Dakota Directory of County Officials (South Dakota Association of Counties Commissioners, 207 E. Capitol, Pierre, SD 57501; phone: 605/224–4554) $10/nonmembers, included in membership package, published in January of odd–numbered years. Lists elected county officials and some department heads.

South Dakota Directory of Local Development Corporations (Governor's Office of Economic Development, 711 E. Wells Ave., Pierre, SD 57501–3369; phone: 605/773–5032) free, published each summer. Lists local development corporations, planning districts, etc.

South Dakota Counties: Salary Survey (South Dakota Association of Counties Commissioners, 207 E. Capitol, Pierre, SD 57501; phone: 605/224–4554) free, published every June. Gives salary ranges and fringe benefits for all county offices.

State, local, and federal jobs

Job openings in the private sector can be found by contacting a local **Job Service** office. You can obtain a list of these offices by contacting the South Dakota Department of Labor (P.O. Box 4730, Aberdeen, SD 57402–4730; phones: 800/592–1882, 605/622–2302). The offices are computerized, so you can obtain up–to–the–minute information on job vacancies in South Dakota and nationally.

State Job Hotline (South Dakota Bureau of Personnel) For a 24–hour a day recording of available state government jobs (including agency, title, salary, qualifications, and closing date), call 605/773–3326.

South Dakota State Agency Locator: 605/773–3011

FJIC: Bishop Henry Whipple Federal Bldg., Room 501, 1 Federal Dr., Ft. Snelling, MN 55111; phone: 612/725–3430; self service, 7:30 a.m. to 4:30 p. m..

Tennessee

Tennessee Town and City (Tennessee Municipal League, 226 Capitol Blvd., Nashville, TN 37219; phone: 615/255–6416) 23 issues/year, $10/nonmember annual subscription, $6/members. Jobs listed under "Classified Ads." Few job ads. Local newspapers are the best source of job ads.

Directory of Tennessee Municipal Officials (University of Tennessee, Municipal Technical Advisory Service, 600 Henley, Knoxville, TN 37996–4105; phone: 615/974–0411) $50 (bound version), $100 (looseleaf, updated monthly), free to Tennessee municipal government officials, bound version published each January. Lists municipal elected officials and department heads plus state and regional government agencies.

Directory of Tennessee County Officials (University of Tennessee, County Technical Assistance Service, Suite 400, 226 Capitol Boulevard Bldg., Nashville, TN 37219–1804; phone: 615/242–0358) $35 plus postage, first copy free to Tennessee county government officials, published every October. Lists elected county officials and department heads.

Local job hotlines

Knoxville: 615/521–2562

Memphis: 901/576–6548

Nashville: 615/862–6660

State jobs

Contact individual state agencies directly to learn of job vacancies. For a list of state agency phone numbers and addresses, contact the Tennessee Department of Personnel, 2nd Floor, James K. Polk Building, 505 Deaderick St., Nashville, TN 37243–0635; phone: 615/741–7973).

To obtain a list of **Job Service Offices**, contact the Department of Employment Security (500 James Robertson Parkway, 12th Floor, Volunteer Plaza, Nashville, TN 37245–0001; phone: 615/741–2131).

Tennessee State Agency Locator: 615/741–3011

FJIC: Suite 1312, 200 Jefferson Ave., Memphis, TN 38103–2335; self service only 8 a.m. to 4 p. m.. Send mail or call the Alabama office, Suite 641, 3322 Memorial Pkwy., Huntsville, AL 35801–5311; phone: 205/544–5803.

Texas

JOBTRAC (6856 Arboreal Dr., Dallas, TX 75231; modem phone only: 214/349–0527) free. Run by volunteers, this online computerized job database offers mostly job opportunities within Texas at all levels of government, including federal. Dial up the modem number (they won't publicize their voice number) and download job descriptions that interest you. You can also send your resume by modem directly to the employers in this database.

TML Texas Town & City (Texas Municipal League, 211 E. 7th, Austin, TX 78701–3283; phone: 512/478–6601) monthly; $20/annual subscription. Jobs listed under "Classifieds." With about 40 job ads per issue, this is one of the most comprehensive sources for local government employment.

Prospects (Texas Municipal League, 211 E. 7th, Austin, TX 78701–3283; phone: 512/478–6601) bimonthly, $25/nonmember annual subscription, free/members. This job announcement newsletter describes 15 to 20 municipal and county government positions each issue.

Directory of Texas City Officials (Texas Municipal League) $60/nonmembers, $30/members, published each August. Lists elected city officials and major department heads, Regional Planning Agencies, councils of governments, etc.

Local job hotlines

Addison: 214/450–2815
Arlington: 817/265–7938
Austin:
  Clerical: 512/499–3203
  Hospital/Health: 512/499–3205
  Professional: 512/499–3202
  Technical: 512/499–3204
  Maintenance: 512/499–3204
Dallas: 214/670–5908
Denton: 817/566–8347
El Paso: 915/541–4094
Fort Worth: 817/871–7760
Garland: 214/205–2349
Grand Prairie: 214/660–8190
Harris County: 713/755–5044
Houston:
  Clerical: 713/658–3798
  Professional: 713/658–3799
Irving: 214/721–2351
Mesquite: 214/216–6484
San Antonio: 210/299–7280

State jobs

Each state agency hires its own staff. See the various directories that include state agencies near the beginning of this chapter to identify state government agencies in Texas. Many state job openings, however, are listed on the Texas Employment Commission's statewide, computer–assisted job matching system. Request a list of the more than 100 local Texas Employment Commission (**Job Service Offices**) offices throughout the state from the TEC State Office (101 E. 15th St., Austin, TX 78778–0001; phone: 512/463–2222) or see the state government section of the local telephone directory.

Texas State Agency Locator: 512/463–4630

FJIC: Dallas area: Room 6B10, 1100 Commerce St., Dallas, TX 75242; phone: 214/767–8035; Corpus Christi, Houston, and San Antonio areas: 8610 Broadway, Room 305, San Antonio, TX 78217; phones: 210/229–6611, 210/229–6600. For forms call 210/229–6618; staff present 7:30 a.m. to 4:30 p. m..

Directory of Local Government Officials (Utah League of Cities and Towns, 50 South 600 East, Salt Lake City, UT 84102; phone: 801/328–1601) $20.

Local and state jobs

Job listings are available by in–person application from the Utah **Job Service**, 720 South 200 East, Salt Lake City, UT 84111 (phone: 801/536–7000) or 5735 S. Redwood Rd., Salt Lake City, UT 84107 (phone: 801/269–4700).

Local job hotline

Salt Lake City: 801/535–6625

State jobs

State of Utah Job Opportunities Bulletin (Room 2120, State Office Building, Salt Lake City, UT 84114; phone: 801/538–3025) weekly, $20/six–month subscription.

To locate **Job Service Offices**, contact the Utah Department of Employment Security (P.O. Box 11249, Salt Lake City, UT 84147; phone: 801/536–7401).

Utah State Agency Locator: 801/538–3000

FJIC: 12345 W. Alameda Parkway, Lakewood, CO; 303/969–7050; staff present noon to 3:45 p. m..; self service 9 a.m. to noon. For forms and local supplements, call 303/969–7065.

Vermont

Vermont Job Service (Vermont Department of Employment and Training, P.O. Box 308, Montpelier, VT 05601–0308; phone: 802/828–3860) free. Provides job matching services including municipal and state government positions. Resumes are kept on file up to three years.

VLCT Newsletter (Vermont League of Cities and Towns, 12 1/2 Main St., Montpelier, VT 05602; phone: 802/229–9111) monthly, $60/nonmember annual subscription, free/members. Jobs listed under "Classified." Few job ads, primarily in planning and community development. City manager ads are very rare.

List of Mayors and Managers (Vermont League of Cities and Towns, 12 1/2 Main St., Montpelier, VT 05602; phone: 802/229–9111) available as mailing labels. Contact for prices.

Local job hotline

Burlington: 802/865–7147

State jobs

Open Competitive Recruitment Announcements (Vermont Department of Personnel, 110 State St., Montpelier, VT 05602; phone 802/828–3483) bimonthly, free. Lists open state job positions, location, and starting salary.

24 Hour JOBLINE (Vermont Department of Personnel). Call 802/828–3484 for frequently updated tape recording of state job vacancies.

To locate **Job Service Offices**, contact the Department of Employment and Training (P.O. Box 488, Montpelier, VT 05601–0488; phone: 802/828–4000).

Vermont Jobs Line (Vermont Department of Employment and Training, Office of Policy and Information, P.O. Box 488, Montpelier, VT 05601; phone: 802/828–4153) free. From within Vermont, call 800/464–4473; from outside the state dial 802/828–3939. This 24–hour job hotline can be called with a touch–tone or rotary telephone. The only difference is that rotary users must clearly enunciate their choices (and pronounce the number 0 as "zero" and say each digit separately such as one two for the number 12. First you get to select one of the 12 regions within the state. The you get to select if you want to hear the job listings received only during the last 24 hours, or all the job listings. Finally, you select which of nine general occupation categories for which you want to hear job information. At any time you can press "1" to skip to the next job listing or the asterisk to hear a job listing again (you don't get either of these options if you use a rotary phone). When you find a job that is right for you, be sure to write down its job order number given at the end of its description. Then call or visit any Employment and Training office to discuss the job and get full details on how to apply. The department does have a brochure on this service which is yours for the asking.

DET Board (Vermont Department of Employment and Training, Office of Policy and Information, P.O. Box 488, Montpelier, VT 05601; phone: 802/828–4153) free, updated daily. Anyone with a personal computer and modem can access this 24–hour a day electronic bulletin board which features job opening bulletins, which is a condensed version of the job openings available at local Job Service offices. If you find a job opening in your occupation, you should contact the local Job Service office for more information and procedures on how to contact the employer. Only the job title, wage, town, and job order number are shown. Within Vermont, call 800/924–4443 if you're using a 1,200 or 2,400 baud modem (the system cannot handle anything faster). From out of state, call 802/828–4108 or 802/828–4322. Set communication parameters at 8–N–1; duplex full. At the new user sign on, type "new" as your USER–ID. To see job vacancies, choose I to learn how to use the system. You can download information. The department has a short brochure that explains how to use the system. Ask for the DET Board PC Access to Labor Market Information brochure. If you have questions about the system, call Michael Griffen at 802/828–4153 (voice).

Vermont State Agency Locator: 802/828–1110

FJIC: Thomas P. O'Neill Federal Building, 10 Causeway St., Boston, MA 02222–1031; phone: 617/565–5900; staff present 9 a.m.. to 2 p. m..

Virginia

Virginia Town and City (Virginia Municipal League, 13 E. Franklin St., P.O. Box 12164, Richmond, VA 23241; phone: 804/649–8471) monthly; $8/annual nonmember subscription, $4/members. Jobs listed under "Market Place."

Virginia Municipal League Letter (Virginia Municipal League, 13 E. Franklin St., P.O. Box 12164, Richmond, VA 23241; phone: 804/649–8471) bi-weekly, $25/annual subscription. Jobs listed under "Available Positions."

Virginia Review (Review Publications, Inc., P.O. Box 860, Chester, VA 23831; phones: 800/827–3843, 804/748–6351) bimonthly, $14/annual subscription. A small number of government positions, if any, are advertised in here.

Virginia Review Directory of State and Local Government Officials (Review Publications, Inc., P.O. Box 860, Chester, VA 23831; phones: 800/827–3843, 804/748–6351) $29.95 plus sales tax for Virginia residents, published each spring, 280 pages. One of the most thorough state and local government directories in the country. Includes the names, addresses, telephone numbers, and fax numbers for key local and state government and association officials.

Virginia Directory of State and Local Government Officials (Virginia Municipal League, 13 E. Franklin St., P.O. Box 12164, Richmond, VA 23241; phone: 804/649–8471) $35, published in odd–numbered years. Lists elected officials and department heads for all municipalities and counties, planning district commissions and their directors, regional planning agencies, some state and federal offices, and statewide government professional organizations.

Opportunities in Public Affairs (Brubach Publishing Company, P.O. Box 15629, Chevy Chase, MD 20825; phone: 301/986–0658) $29/two–month subscription, $49/four months, $69/six months, $129/annual, $7.95/single issue. You'll find announcements of over 200 positions with local, state, and federal government agencies; non–profits; and private companies in government affairs, public relations, broadcasting, and publishing. In addition to job announcements, this periodical also reports on unadvertised jobs its editors have uncovered. Most job openings are in the District of Columbia area. It includes a good number of positions with Congress.

The 1993 Washington Job Source (MetCom, Inc. 1708 Surrey Lane, NW, Washington, DC 20007) $14.95 plus $3/shipping. Briefly describes 2,100 federal agencies, Congressional posts, non–profits, and corporations with the name, address, and phone number of the hiring contact.

Washington 93 (Columbia Books, 1212 New York Ave., NW, Suite 330, Washington, DC 20005; phone: 202/898–0662) $75, published annually each June. Nearly 600 pages of addresses, phone numbers, and information including one chapter on local government in the District of Columbia and surrounding counties and towns with populations over 5,000, and regional authorities.

Directory of Local Planning in Virginia (Dept. of Housing and Community Development, Division of Community Development, The Jackson Center, 501 N. Second St., Richmond, VA 23219–1321; 804/371–7000) free, published in even–numbered years, last issued February of 1994. Lists all county, city and town planning directors, zoning and subdivision administrators, and planning district commission executive directors as well as the status of various planning activities.

Local job hotlines

Alexandria: 703/838–4422

Arlington County: 703/538–3363

Norfolk: 804/627–8768

Richmond: 804/780–5888

State jobs

Locate a local State Employment Service Office (Job Service) through a local telephone directory's state government section or obtain a list of the 42 local **Job Service Offices** from the Virginia Employment Commission (703 E. Main St., Richmond, VA 23219; phone: 804/786–7097). Announcements of local, state, and federal job openings are available for examination at each job service office.

Virginia is one of the first states to use ALEX, the Automated Labor EXchange computer service that enables job seekers to look up job vacancies in Virginia, and nationwide, themselves. ALEX terminals are available at Job Service Offices and in shopping malls, libraries, and schools.

Virginia State Agency Locator: 804/786–0000 (that's not a typographical error, honest)

FJIC: Federal Building, Room 220, 200 Granby St., Norfolk, VA 23510–1886; phone: 804/441–3355; self service only 9 a.m.. to 4 p. m.. Also Norfolk VEC Job Service Office, 5145 E. Virginia Beach Blvd., Norfolk, VA 23502; staff present 8:15 a.m.. to 4:30 p. m..

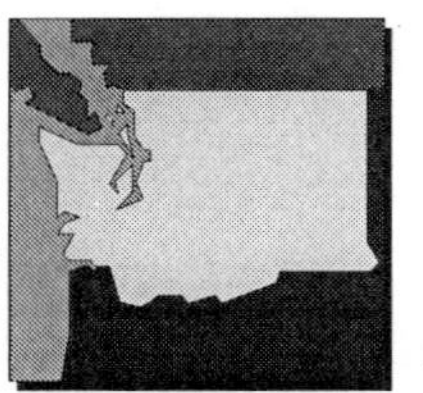

Washington

AWC Job–Net (Association of Washington Cities, 1076 Franklin St., SE, Olympia, WA 98501; phone: 206/753–4137) monthly, $15/annual subscription. Lists managerial, administrative, and professional government job vacancies.

Officials of Washington Cities (Municipal Research and Services Center of Washington, 10517 NE 38th Pl., Kirkland, WA 98033–7926; phone: 206/827–4334) $12/prepaid only, published in even–numbered years. Lists elected city officials and major department heads.

Directory of County Officials in Washington State (Washington State Association of Counties, 206 10th Ave., SE, Olympia, WA 98501; phone: 206/753–1886) $7.50, published every January. Lists county elected officials and major department heads, members of state boards and committees, and members of the following Washington state associations: County Administrative, County Engineers, Local Public Health Officials, County Human Services, County/Park Recreation Boards and Departments, County and Regional Planning Directors.

The Directory of Planning and Community Development Agencies (Washington State Department of Community Development, Growth Management Division, 906 Columbia St., NW, P.O. Box 48300, Olympia, WA 98504–8300; phone: 206/753–2222) free, 139 pages. Lists all city, county, and regional planning agencies; major state departments and agencies; federal agencies; housing authorities and state housing contacts; community action agencies; economic development organizations; social service agencies; government–related professional associations and organizations; hearing examiners; boundary review boards; Indian tribes; university and college planning departments; county extension offices.

Local job hotlines

Everett: 206/259–8768
Redmond: 206/556–2121
Seattle: 206/684–7999
Spokane: 509/625–6161
Tacoma: 206/591–5795

State jobs

Washington State Department of Personnel (521 Capitol Way, South, P.O. Box 47500, Olympia, WA 98504–7500; phone: 206/753–5368) mails job announcements on a weekly basis with semimonthly summaries on the first and third Wednesday of each month. To receive this list, send a stamped, self–addressed #10 envelope for each issue you wish to receive. (Can send up to three envelopes at a time.) This list, as well as announcements of jobs at other levels of government are posted at each of the state's 33 Job Service Centers.

Joblines (P.O. Box 1789, Olympia, WA 98507–1789; phone: 206/753–5368). Call any of these numbers for a recorded announcement of new state job openings available each week: 206/586–0545 (Olympia), 206/464–7378 (Seattle), and 509/456–2889 (Spokane).

To locate **Job Service Offices**, contact the Employment and Training Division (Employment Security Department, 212 Maple Park, Olympia, WA 98504; phone: 206/438–4804).

The state also offers biennial area wage surveys that supply occupational wage and salary rates for clerical, managerial, professional, technical, and general occupations: average wage rates with high and low ranges, average hours worked, and occupational descriptions. There's a separate Area Wage Survey report for each of the following regions: Chelan–Douglas–Okanogan, Clallam–Jefferson, Cowlitz, Grays Harbor–Pacific, Kitsap, Lewis, Moses Lake, Pierce, Seattle PMSA (Small firms), Skagit–Island–San Juan, Spokane, Thurston–Mason, Tri–Cities, Vancouver, Walla Walla, Whatcom, and Yakima. Each report costs $1 (add $2.50 shipping and handling for your entire order; Washington state residents must add 7.9 percent sales tax). Send your check or money order to: Washington State Employment Security Department, Labor Market and Economic Analysis – Wage, P.O. Box 9046, Olympia, WA 98507–9046.

Washington State Agency Locator: 206/753–5000

FJIC: Federal Building, Room 110, 915 Second Ave, Seattle, WA 98174; phone: 206/220–6400; staff present noon to 3:30 p. m..; self service 8 a.m. to noon.

West Virginia

West Virginia Municipal League Directory (West Virginia Municipal League, 1620 Kanawha Blvd., East, Suite 1B, Charleston, WV 25311; phone: 304/342–5564) $25. Updated regularly. Lists elected municipal officials, city managers, clerk/recorders.

State jobs

Contact Personnel, Civil Service System (B–456, 1900 Washington St., E, Charleston, WV 25305; phone: 304/558–3950).

To locate **Job Service Offices**, contact the Bureau of Employment Programs (112 California Ave., Charleston, WV 25305–0112; phone: 304/558–2660).

West Virginia State Agency Locator: 304/558–3456

FJIC: Federal Building, Room 506, 200 W. Second St., Dayton, OH 45402; phone: 513/225–2720; self service only 7 a.m.. to 6 p. m..

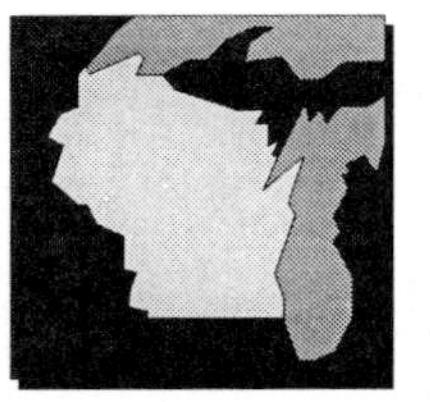

Wisconsin

The Municipality (League of Wisconsin Municipalities, 122 W. Washington Ave., Madison, WI 53703–2757; phone: 608/267–2380) monthly, $18/annual subscription. Very extensive listing of jobs under "Municipal Want Ads."

Wisconsin State Current Employment Opportunities Bulletin (State Division of Merit Recruitment, Department of Employment Relations, 137 E. Wilson St., P.O.. Box 7855, Madison, WI 5307–7855; phone: TDD/VOICE: 608/266–1731) 34 issues/year, $25/annual subscription, $13/six–month subscription. To subscribe, send check or money order to State Document Sales, 202 S. Thornton, P.O.. Box 7840, Madison, WI 53707–7840. Each issue is also posted at state Job Service offices, colleges, and all state offices. Includes all state and many local government positions.

Wisconsin Counties (Wisconsin Counties Association, 802 W. Broadway, Suite 308, Madison, WI 53713; phone: 608/266–6480) monthly, $21/annual subscription. One or two positions appear under "County Classified."

League of Wisconsin Municipalities Directory (League of Wisconsin Municipalities, 122 W. Washington Ave., Madison, WI 53703–2757; phone: 608/267–2380) $30/nonmembers, $15/members, published annually. Lists elected officials and department heads.

Local job hotlines

Madison: 608/266–6500

Milwaukee: 414/278–5555

State jobs

See the ***Wisconsin State Current Employment Opportunities Bulletin*** described just above. All state civil service jobs are included in that publication.

To locate **Job Service Offices,** contact the Job Service Division (Department of Industry, Labor, and Human Relations, P.O.. Box 7972, Madison, WI 53707; phone: 608/266–8212).

Wisconsin State Agency Locator: 608/266–2211

FJIC: Bishop Henry Whipple Federal Building, Room 501, 1 Federal Dr., Ft. Snelling, MN 55111; phone: 612/725–3430; self service only 7:30 a.m.. to 4:30 p. m.. For federal job information in Dane, Grant, Green, Iowa, Jefferson, Kenosha, Milwaukee, Racine, Rock, Walworth, Waukesha counties: Room 530, 175 W. Jackson, Chicago, IL 60604; phone: 312/353–6189; self service only 7 a.m. to 4:45 p. m.. You can also learn about current federal job vacancies in Wisconsin by calling the Chicago Service Center's *Complete Answering Machine* at 312/353–6189 any time except between 1 p. m.. and 4 p. m.. on Fridays when it is updated. You'll need a touch–tone telephone. You'll have a series of choices which you dial with a two–digit number followed by the pound (#) sign: 33# gets you descriptions of jobs available through this office (updated the first Monday of every month); 35# describes current vacancies, including the job title and the closing date; 6# gives you starting salary rates; and 7# explains how to apply for a federal job.

Wyoming

Also see the listings under "Job sources for multi–state regions" at the beginning of this chapter.

The WAM News (Wyoming Association of Municipalities, P.O.. Box 3110, Cheyenne, WY 82003–3110; phone: 307/632–0398) monthly, $25/annual subscription. Jobs listed under "Job Opportunities." Few jobs ads.

Official Municipal Roster (Association of Municipalities, P.O.. Box 3110, Cheyenne, WY 82003–3110; phone: 307/632–0398) $10/nonmembers, free to members, published each February.

State, local, and federal jobs

Job Service of Wyoming (Department of Employment, P.O.. Box 2760, Casper, WY 82602; phone: 307/235–3200). Local, state and federal government job openings are kept at 16 Job Service Centers throughout the state. No publication is available. Write or call for the addresses of local Job Service Centers.

Wyoming State Agency Locator: 307/777–7220

FJIC: 12345 W. Alameda Parkway, Lakewood, CO 80225; phone: 303/969–7050; staff present noon to 3:45 p. m..; self service 9 a.m.. to noon. For forms and local supplements, call 303/969–7065.

U.S. possessions and territories

American Samoa

Contact Department of Manpower Resources (Pago Pago, AS 96799; phone: 684/633–4485).

American Samoa government main switchboard: 684/633–4155.

Guam

Guam government main switchboard: 671/472–8931.

Federal Employment Information Hotline (U.S. Office of Personnel Management, 300 Ala Moana Blvd., Room 5316, Box 50028, Honolulu, HI 96850) Call 808/541–2784 for a recording of U.S. federal jobs in Guam and neighboring islands.

FJIC: Room 902, Pacific Daily News Building, Agana, Guam 96910; phone: 671/472–7451

Northern Mariana Islands

Contact Personnel Management Office (Civil Service Commission, Personnel Management Office, Office of the Governor, P.O.. Box 5150, Saipan, CHRB MP 96950; phones: 670/234–6958, 670/234–6925).

Puerto Rico

Contact the Bureau of Employment Security (Labor and Human Resources Department, 505 Munoz Rivera Ave., Hato Rey, PR 00918; phone: 809/754–5375) for information on state jobs as well as locations of Job Service Offices.

Puerto Rico main government switchboard: 809/721–6040.

FJIC: U.S. Federal Bldg., Room 340, 150 Carlos Chardon Ave., Hato Rey, PR 00918–1710; phone: 809/766–5242; staff present 7:30 a.m.. to noon.

Virgin Islands

Territorial government jobs

Virgin Islands main government switchboard: 809/774–8588.

To locate **Job Service Offices,** contact the Department of Labor (2131 Hospital St., Christenstead, St. Croix, VI 00820–0094; phone: 809/773–1994).

FJIC: U.S. Federal Bldg., Room 340, 150 Carlos Chardon Ave., Hato Rey, PR 00918–1710; phones: 809/774–8790 (local), 809/766–5242; staff present 7:30 a.m. to noon.

Chapter 4

Finding federal government jobs

Even during this recession–plagued decade, federal agencies still hire an average of 437,000 trained government professionals and technical, trades and labor, and office support staff every year. Federal jobs offer good pay, excellent benefits, and a high level of job security. In addition, federal employees generally enjoy greater prestige than many state and local officials, as well as a greater opportunity to travel.

With the Clinton-Gore administration, however, comes a great deal of uncertainty about future hiring processes (the dread SF 171 form used by most federal departments may be history in a few years) and the number of jobs that will be available. The administration hopes to cut the number of federal job by 252,000 during the next five years (a good trick if he's not re-elected), eight percent of its civilian workforce. Most cuts will be achieved through attrition. If Congress approves the administration's *Reinventing Government* plan, the number of supervisors, headquarters staff, personnel specialists, accountants, and auditors will decline. The Clinton-Gore proposals match the private sector's effort to cut out unnecessary layers of management and other nonessential staff. Just as the private sector discovered, the Clinton-Gore administration has realized that the federal government must learn to do more with less. However, departing government executives do not receive the excessively generous "golden parachute" hush money so many major private sector companies shower upon their exiting executives.

But even with this decline in federal positions, several hundred thousand federal jobs must still be filled each year thanks to retirement, career changes, and firings. Afterall, the feds employ 3 million people, 2.5 percent of the nation's total workforce. One-third of these work in defense; another 25 percent work for the United States Postal Service and Postal Rate Commission. Eight percent work for the Veterans Administration, five percent for the Treasury Department, and four percent for the Department of Health and Human Services. The remaining 25 percent are spread out among the rest of the executive branch, legislative branch, and judicial branch.

Federal government hiring process

Office of Personnel Management

For now, federal hiring procedures remain the same as they have for the last few years. Any changes will take a few years to implement. Rather than speculate about the changes, I'll restrict myself to giving the current hiring picture.

A federal government position can fall under one of two different hiring procedures. Most federal positions are Competitive Service jobs which are filled through the Office of Personnel Management (OPM), manager of the Civil Service System. The OPM acts as the recruiting agency for these positions and establishes job qualifications, distributes job announcements, and manages hiring procedures.

While each agency has its own personnel office, the Office of Personnel Management (OPM), an independent executive agency, stands at the apex of the federal personnel system. Until the mid–1980s, OPM played a central role in directly recruiting and screening applicants for many types of positions and for certain agencies. This agency was responsible for testing applicants, examining SF 171s, giving ratings, and maintaining registers of qualified applicants. When agencies had a personnel need, OPM would forward lists of qualified candidates to the agency for consideration. The agency, in turn, interviewed candidates and made the final selection decisions. Overall, the process was a mixture of centralized and decentralized hiring functions. Applicants understood that one had to first stop at OPM to get information on job vacancies, take any required tests, submit their SF 171 for evaluation, receive a rating, and wait on the register to be called for an interview. Such hiring procedures were very time consuming. Consequently, the employment process in the federal government rightfully deserved a reputation for being centralized, complicated, and lengthy. If you wanted to find a job quickly, the federal government was the last place to stop. Finding a federal job required a major investment of time and patience while this centralized bureaucracy tried to cope with thousands of applications that eventually had to be acted upon at the lowest level in the bureaucracy—the operating units.

However, the role of OPM in the hiring process has undergone major needed changes during the past five years. Unfortunately, few job applicants—including many federal employees—know about these changes. As a result, many people approach the federal hiring process as if it still operates according to the procedures of the 1960s, 1970s, and early 1980s. For example, they first approach OPM in search of a "rating" and then wonder how they can get on a "register" — the two most frequently asked questions that are inappropriate for today's new hiring procedures. In fact, if you want to demonstrate your ignorance of the federal hiring process, just ask these questions at your local Federal Job Information Center (FJIC). Indeed, personnel at the FJICs have learned to be very patient in answering what appears to be many of the same old questions over and over again. Applicants even go so far as to argue with OPM personnel about these procedures. After all, their friend the expert, who just happens to work in the federal government, told them this is what they had to do to get a federal job! Well, so much for advice from well–meaning friends.

Key personnel functions, such as issuing vacancy announcements, rating applicants, and training, has been increasingly decentralized to individual agencies since the mid–1980s. Today, OPM plays a more supportive role in helping agencies meet their personnel needs. While OPM is still the government's central personnel agency, it delegates hiring authority to other agencies and maintains oversight responsibilities at the same time. The degree to which it delegates this authority will depend on the capabilities of individual agencies to conduct their own hiring. In general, however, OPM is responsible for issuing government–wide personnel regulations; providing support services to agencies; managing some applications, testing, and screening processes; disseminating job vacancy information; providing limited training services; assisting agencies in meeting their personnel needs; and extending benefits to employees and government retirees. This agency still remains important to the federal government hiring process, but it is not a central personnel office that conducts hiring for individual agencies — a common misunderstanding of job applicants who continue to pester OPM with inappropriate questions when they should be addressing these questions to individual agencies.

Many federal agencies, however, hire their employees through their own personnel departments. These are called "exempted" or "excepted" service positions and their employees are not subject to the OPM's application procedures or job qualifications. Job candidates apply directly to these agencies rather than through the OPM.

Competitive service

The federal government does not have a single, unified personnel system. Its over 3 million employees are classified into different services and positions. The federal civil service, for example, classifies positions into competitive or exempted services. The majority of federal government positions (80 percent) are in the ***competitive service.*** These positions fall under the civil service regulations, codified in the Civil Service Reform Act of 1978, which are administered by the Office of Personnel Management. Such positions are made public through Job Vacancy Announcements and must adhere to the "merit principles" of openness, fairness, and nondiscrimination. These positions come under Presidential authority, are subject to periodic reductions–in–force regulations and hiring freezes, and follow internal seniority rules.

Exempted or excepted service

At the same time, Congress, the judiciary, and several agency positions are exempted from these regulations. These positions lie outside the authority of OPM and are subject to individual agency personnel regulations. Individuals in these positions do not accumulate civil service seniority which would apply to other positions in the competitive service. Executive agencies in the ***exempted or excepted services*** include:

- Central Intelligence Agency
- Defense Intelligence Agency
- Executive Protective Service (Secret Service—Uniformed Branch)
- Federal Bureau of Investigation
- Federal Reserve System, Board of Governors
- General Accounting Office
- U.S. Agency for International Development
- National Science Foundation (only scientific, engineering, and a few high–level managerial positions are exempted)
- National Security Agency
- Nuclear Regulatory Commission
- Postal Rate Commission

- U.S. Postal Service
- U.S. Department of State (skilled specialists and experienced secretaries only; all others take the foreign service exam)
- Tennessee Valley Authority
- U.S. Mission to the United Nations
- Judicial branch of the federal government (except the Administrative Office of the U.S. Customs Court)
- Legislative branch of the federal government (except the Government Printing Office)

These agencies have their own set of personnel procedures for hiring and managing personnel. For information on their particular application procedures, contact these agencies directly. The directories listed in this chapter will help you find the right person to contact. Also the personnel office numbers and job hotlines of many of these agencies are listed later in this chapter.

Exempted or excepted positions

The federal government also excludes certain positions (rather than whole agencies) from civil service regulations. These positions are not subject to OPM standards. Such positions are excepted because they are difficult to fill through normal recruitment channels. These positions include:

- Teachers in Department of Defense overseas schools
- Attorneys, doctors, dentists, and nurses with the Department of Veterans Affairs
- Scientists and engineers with the National Science Foundation
- Chaplains in Departments of Veterans Affairs and Justice
- Drug enforcement agents
- Professional and Administrative Careers (PAC)—GS–5 through GS–7. About one–third of the federal government's professional jobs fall into this PAC classification. When inquiring about a professional position, be sure to ask if it is a PAC or Excepted job.

  A significant proportion of the jobs at the following agencies are PAC jobs: Department of Agriculture (11 percent), Air Force (19 percent), Army (24 percent), Department of Commerce (19 percent), General Services Administration (6 percent), Department of Health and Human Services (13 percent), Department of the Interior (20 percent), International Communication Agency (74 percent), Navy (12 percent), Department of State (85 percent), Department of Transportation (4 percent),

Treasury Department (8 percent), and Veteran's Administration (31 percent).

The federal government operates a number of special hiring programs for persons with disabilities, veterans, women, and Hispanics, as well as a high school and college student program and a summer employment program. Information on these programs is available from each Federal Job Information Center and from any personnel office of the Office of Personnel Management. Descriptions and contact information on them is also presented in the *Federal Personnel Office Directory* which is described later in this chapter.

Classifications and compensation

The total federal workforce is divided into two major classification systems. White–collar professional, administrative, scientific, clerical, and technical employees are paid according to the ***General Schedule (GS)***, which is graded from GS–1 to GS–16 and uniformly applied throughout the federal government.

These salary rates encompass most white–collar positions in the competitive service. Under the 1990 Federal Employees Pay Comparability Act, the President can issue special raises of up to eight percent to federal employees who live in cities with a particularly high cost of living. The act seeks to bring federal salaries in line with those of local industries on an area–by–area basis. As of this writing, higher salary rates have been approved for clerical workers in Washington, San Francisco, New York, and Boston as well as for some engineering positions.

Trade, labor, and other blue–collar workers—70 percent of whom are employed by the Departments of Army, Navy, and Air Force—are paid on the ***Federal Wage System (WG)***. Grades range from WG–1 to WG–15 and the pay in each grade varies for each of 137 geographical areas. Altogether over 600,000 employees are classified as WG.

Other pay systems operate for the Senior Executive Service, management and executive positions at the former GS–16 to GS–18 levels, Senior Level, Scientific and Professional positions, the U.S. Postal Service, and a few other positions.

The following table gives the probable GS federal salary rates by grade and step for 1994. You can obtain the latest federal salary tables via modem by calling the national or regional *Federal Job Information Center Electronic Bulletin Board Service* office nearest you. This service is described later in this chapter under "Job services."

Federal salary rates by grade
General Schedule (GS) for 1994

Grade Levels	One	Two	Three	Four	Five	Six	Seven	Eight	Nine	Ten
GS-1	11,903	12,300	12,695	13,090	13,487	13,720	14,109	14,503	14,521	14,891
GS-2	13,382	13,701	14,145	14,521	14,783	15,115	15,547	15,979	16,411	16,843
GS-3	14,603	15,090	15,577	16,064	16,551	17,038	17,525	18,012	18,499	18,986
GS-4	16,393	16,939	17,485	18,031	18,577	19,123	19,869	20,215	20,761	21,307
GS-5	18,340	18,951	19,562	20,173	20,784	21,395	22,006	22,617	23,228	23,839
GS-6	20,443	21,124	21,805	22,486	23,167	23,848	24,529	25,210	25,891	26,572
GS-7	22,717	23,474	24,231	24,988	25,745	26,502	27,259	28,016	28,773	29,530
GS-8	25,159	25,998	26,837	27,676	28,515	29,354	30,193	31,032	31,871	32,710
GS-9	27,789	28,715	29,641	30,567	31,493	32,419	33,345	34,271	35,197	36,123
GS-10	30,603	31,623	32,643	33,663	34,683	35,703	36,723	37,743	38,763	39,783
GS-11	33,623	34,744	35,865	36,986	38,107	39,228	40,349	41,470	42,591	43,712
GS-12	40,298	41,641	42,964	44,327	45,670	47,013	48,356	49,699	51,042	52,385
GS-13	47,920	49,517	51,114	52,711	54,308	55,905	57,502	59,099	60,696	62,293
GS-14	56,627	58,515	60,403	62,291	64,179	66,067	67,955	69,843	71,731	73,619
GS-15	66,609	68,829	71,049	73,269	75,489	77,709	79,929	82,149	84,239	86,589
Sch. 4	*Senior Executive Service* positions' salaries range from $92,900 to $115,700									
Sch. 5	*Executive Service* positions' salaries range from $108,200 to $148,400									

Job types and alternatives

The federal government hires individuals in five categories of jobs. These consist of:

Professional occupations: These require knowledge of science or specialized education and training at a level equal to a bachelor's degree or higher. Examples include engineers, accountants, biologists, and chemists. Engineers (105,000) and nurses (40,000) are the largest professional groups with the Federal government.

Administrative occupations: These require increasingly responsible experience or a general college level education. Examples include personnel specialists and administrative officers.

Technical occupations: These are associated with a professional or administrative field, but they are not routine in nature. Examples include computer technician and electronic technician.

Clerical occupations: These involve work which supports office, business, or fiscal operations. Examples include clerk–typist, mail and file clerk.

Other occupations: All other occupations not classified as professional, administrative, technical, or clerical. Includes many blue–collar and trade occupations, such as painters, carpenters, and laborers.

The federal government has as many different types of positions as the private sector. A complete list of positions would take up the remainder of this book. There are other books described at the end of this chapter that go into detail about each of the federal classifications. Here, we'll identify just the major classifications.

The Office of Personnel Management, using a numerical code, classifies all General Schedule positions into 22 occupational groups and families. These include:

Classification of GS positions

GS–0000	Miscellaneous Occupational Group
GS–0100	Social Science, Psychology, and Welfare Group
GS–0200	Personnel Management and Industrial Relations Group
GS–0300	General Administrative, Clerical, and Office Services Group
GS–0400	Biological Sciences Group
GS–0500	Accounting and Budget Group
GS–0600	Medical, Hospital, Dental, and Public Health Group
GS–0700	Veterinary Medical Science Group
GS–0800	Engineering and Architecture Group
GS–0900	Legal and Kindred Group
GS–1000	Information and Arts Group
GS–1100	Business and Industry Group
GS–1200	Copyright, Patent, and Trademark Group
GS–1300	Physical Sciences Group
GS–1400	Library and Archives Group
GS–1500	Mathematics and Statistics Group
GS–1600	Equipment, Facilities, and Services Group

GS–1700	Education Group
GS–1800	Investigation Group
GS–1900	Quality Assurance, Inspection, and Grading Group
GS–2000	Supply Group
GS–2100	Transportation Group

Each classification is further subdivided into additional classifications. For example, here are the 23 categories of the Investigation Group of occupations (GS–1800):

GS–1801	General Inspection, Investigation, and Compliance
GS–1802	Compliance Inspection and Support
GS–1810	General Investigating
GS–1811	Criminal Investigating
GS–1812	Game Law Enforcement
GS–1815	Air Safety Investigating
GS–1816	Immigration Inspection
GS–1822	Mine Safety and Health
GS–1825	Aviation Safety
GS–1831	Securities Compliance Examining
GS–1850	Agricultural Commodity Warehouse Examining
GS–1854	Alcohol, Tobacco, and Firearms Inspection
GS–1862	Consumer Safety Inspection
GS–1863	Food Inspection
GS–1864	Public Health Quarantine Inspection
GS–1884	Customs Patrol Officer
GS–1889	Import Specialist
GS–1890	Customs Inspection
GS–1894	Customs Entry and Liquidating
GS–1895	Customs Warehouse Officer
GS–1896	Border Patrol Agent
GS–1897	Customs Aid
GS–1898	Ad measurement

TRAVELS WITH FARLEY

Classification of WG positions

Wage System occupations are also classified into groups and families. These consist of 36 WG categories as follows.

WG–2500	Wire Communications Equipment Installation and Maintenance Family
WG–2600	Electronic Equipment Installation and Maintenance Family
WG–2800	Electrical Installation and Maintenance Family
WG–3100	Fabric and Leather Work Family
WG–3300	Instrument Work Family
WG–3400	Machine Tool Work Family
WG–3500	General Services and Support Work Family
WG–3600	Structural and Finishing Work Family
WG–3700	Metal Processing Family
WG–3800	Metal Work Family
WG–3900	Motion Picture, Radio, Television, and Sound Equipment Operation Family
WG–4000	Lens and Crystal Work Family
WG–4100	Painting and Paperhanging Family
WG–4200	Plumbing and Pipefitting Family
WG–4300	Pliable Materials Work Family
WG–4400	Printing Family
WG–4600	Woodwork Family
WG–4700	General Maintenance Operations Work Family

WG–4800	General Equipment Maintenance Family
WG–5000	Plant and Animal Work Family
WG–5200	Miscellaneous Occupations Family
WG–5300	Industrial Equipment Maintenance Family
WG–5400	Industrial Equipment Operation Family
WG–5700	Transportation/Mobile Equipment Maintenance Family
WG–6500	Ammunition, Explosives, and Toxic Materials Work Family
WG–6600	Armament Work Family
WG–6900	Warehousing and Stock Handling Family
WG–7000	Packing and Processing Family
WG–7300	Laundry, Dry Cleaning, and Pressing Family
WG–7400	Food Preparation and Serving Family
WG–7600	Personal Services Family
WG–8200	Fluid Systems Maintenance Family
WG–8600	Engine Overhaul Family
WG–9000	Film Processing Family

The white–collar GS positions that employ the largest number of individuals include the following:

- Accountants and auditors (GS–510)
- Administrative assistants and officers (GS–341)
- Air traffic control specialists (GS–2152)
- Budget analysts or officers (GS–560)
- Civil rights analysts (GS–160)
- Computer specialists (GS–334)
- Contract representatives (GS–962)
- Contract and procurement specialists (GS–1102)
- Criminal investigators (GS–1810 and GS–1811)
- Economists (GS–110)
- Engineers (GS–800 series)
- Equipment specialists (GS–1670)
- Financial institution examiners (GS–570)
- Foresters (GS–460)

- Internal revenue officers (GS–1169)
- Lawyers (GS–905)
- Loan specialists (GS–1165)
- Management analysts (GS–343)
- Nurses (GS–610)
- Personnel management specialists (GS–201)
- Physicians (GS–602)
- Physicists (GS–1310)
- Production controllers (GS–1152)
- Program analysts (GS–345)
- Quality assurance specialists (GS–1910)
- Social insurance representatives and administrators (GS–105)
- Social insurance claims examiners (GS–993)
- Supply management specialists (GS–2003) and inventory management specialists (GS–2010)
- Teachers (GS–1710)
- Training instructors (GS–1712)

The blue–collar occupations, both under the GS and WG systems, which employ the largest number of individuals include the following.

- Accounting technicians (GS–525)
- Aircraft mechanics (WG–8852)
- Claims clerks (GS–998)
- Clerks (GS–300 and GS–500 series)
- Clerk–typists (GS–322)
- Computer operators (GS–332)
- Data transcribers (GS–356)
- Electricians (WG–2805)
- Electronics mechanics (WG–2604)
- Engineering aids and technicians (GS–802)
- Financial administration workers (GS–503)
- Firefighters and other fire protection workers (GS–081)
- Food service workers (GS–7408)
- Forestry technicians and smoke jumpers (GS–462)

- Heavy mobile equipment mechanics (WG–5803)
- Janitors or porters (GS–3566)
- Laborers (WG–3502)
- Machinists (WG–3414)
- Mail and file clerks (GS–305)
- Maintenance mechanics (WG–4749)
- Medical technicians (GS–600)
- Nursing assistants (GS–621)
- Personnel clerks and assistants (GS–203)
- Pipefitters (WG–4205)
- Reporting stenographers, shorthand reporters, clerk stenographers (GS–312)
- Secretaries (GS–318)
- Sheet metal mechanics (WG–3806)
- Supply clerks and technicians (GS–2005)
- Tax accountants and examiners (GS–592)

If you are interested in detailed information on each of these occupational groups, including the minimum qualifications as well as the typical duties and responsibilities for each position, you should examine copies of the federal government's standard personnel reference books: *Handbook X–118: Qualification Standards for Positions Under the General Schedule*, and *Position–Classification Standards*. Both books are available through the Federal Job Information Centers (FJICs) identified in Chapter 3, federal personnel offices, and federal agency libraries. Any serious federal job seeker should review these documents before completing a SF 171. These documents give the details, including the proper language for communicating qualifications, of positions that agency personnel must adhere to when evaluating SF 171s.

For example, the "KSAPs" (job elements consisting of knowledge, skills, abilities, and personal characteristics) you include on your SF 171 in reference to a specific vacancy announcement are critical in the evaluation process. Since the language of KSAPs is found in the *Handbook X–118*, you should consult this book before presenting your qualifications on the SF 171 in reference to the KSAPs. Consequently, the closer you can bring your SF

171 in line with the requirements of positions and the language of evaluators, the better should be your position in the federal hiring process.

The Department of Labor's *The Dictionary of Occupational Titles* and *The Occupational Outlook Handbook* (both are available from Planning/Communications by special order; phone: 800/829-5220) and publications and handouts issued by the Office of Personnel Management and personnel offices of individual agencies also include information on these positions.

Applications and special occupational categories

Because the federal hiring process is in transition, you should contact OPM, a Federal Job Information Center, or the agency for details concerning whether or not tests are required for a particular position and to whom you should send your application—directly to OPM or to the agency.

The application process will differ for different categories of positions, and especially for recent college graduates seeking entry–level positions with the federal government. Five categories of positions have special application procedures.

Administrative Careers With America (ACWA)

The Administrative Careers With America program covers nearly 100 different entry–level administrative and professional occupations which are filled through one of two applications methods—a written examination or an application based on scholastic achievement as reflected by an applicant's grade point average. This program is especially appropriate for recent college graduates and other qualified entry–level job seekers. Positions in this category start at the GS–5 and GS–7 levels. Individuals can apply for jobs under this program within nine months of graduation, or upon completion of qualifying academic courses or three years' work experience.

Written examinations under the ACWA program are given in six different occupational groups:

- Group I: Health, Safety, and Environmental
- Group II: Writing and Public Information
- Group III: Business, Finance, and Management
- Group IV: Personnel, Administration, and Computers
- Group V: Benefits Review, Tax, and Legal
- Group VI: Law Enforcement and Investigation

The largest number of job opportunities are in Groups III, IV, V, and VI.

Individuals can also apply for entry–level administrative or professional positions based on their scholastic record rather than take an exam. The scholastic record must demonstrate a GPA of 3.5 or higher on a 4.0 scale, or the individual must have graduated in the upper 10 percent of their class.

The Administrative Careers With America program also includes 16 entry–level positions which do not require a written test. However, they do require special college course work. These positions include:

- Archaeology
- Archival work
- Community planning
- Economics
- Educational programming
- Foreign affairs
- General anthropology
- General education/training
- Geography
- History
- International relations
- Manpower research/analysis
- Museum management
- Psychology
- Social science
- Sociology

Applications for these positions can be submitted to a local OPM Area Office only after the Area Office announces vacancies which are limited in number. Applications are then reviewed and rated based upon an evaluation of education and work experience or meeting GPA/scholastic requirements.

For information on entry–level opportunities available under the Administrative Careers With America program, contact one of OPM's Area Offices, a Federal Job Information Center listed in Chapter 3, or call the Career America Connection at 912/757–3000 (in Alaska, dial 912/471-3755) which is the federal government's official employment hotline (40¢ per minute).

Senior Executive Service

About 8,000 federal employees are part of this high–level service. While they do face the risk of transfer to a position far from home, they can earn outstanding salaries if their work is superior. These officials focus on broader responsibilities like long–range planning, general oversight, agency–wide issues, and more contact with high–level officials in the private sector.

Agencies fill SES positions in accord with guidelines issued by the Office of Personnel Management. An agency would nominate a candidate for SES whose qualifications are then certified by a review board. To be certified for SES, you must meet at least one of three criteria:

- Demonstrated executive experience;
- Participated successfully in a developmental program approved by the Office of Personnel Management; or
- Possess special or unique qualities that suggest success as an executive.

To learn more about SES, contact the personnel office for an agency for which you wish to work or the Office of Personnel Management. Ask to see a copy of *A Guide to Executive Qualifications* published by the Office of Personnel Management.

Specialized occupations

Entry into certain specialized occupations at the GS–5 and GS–7 levels only requires completion of certain college–level courses and a written application. These occupations include:

- Accountant/Auditor
- Biologist
- Engineer
- Forester
- Mathematical Science
- Physical Science

For application information relevant to these specialized occupations, call the Career America Connection at 1–912/757-3000, in Alaska call: 912/471-3755; 40¢ per minute.

Public safety occupations

Requirements for entry–level (GS–5 and GS–7) public safety occupations include a bachelor's degree or equivalent experience as well as a written test. Occupations included in this category are:

- Air Traffic Controller (employed with the Federal Aviation Administration)
- Deputy U.S. Marshal (employed with the U.S. Marshals Service, Department of Justice)
- Treasury Enforcement Agent (employed with the Internal Revenue Service, Customs Service, and the Bureau of Alcohol, Tobacco, and Firearms in the Department of Treasury)
- U.S. Park Police Officer (employed with the National Capital Region, National Park Service, Department of the Interior)

Technical occupations

Positions in this category provide support and technical assistance to professionals. Entry requirements include practical knowledge of specialized subjects and two years of technical experience, or a combination of two years of work experience and education above high school, or a two–year degree. A written test may be required. Most of these jobs start at the GS–4 grade level. For information on these positions, contact one of OPM's Area Offices or a Federal Job Information Center listed in Chapter 3, or the agency itself.

Clerical and administrative support positions

The single largest group of government employees are those who serve in clerical and administrative support positions which start at the GS–2 grade level. They usually require a high school diploma. Given the increased demand for these employees, the hiring process has been streamlined to the point where some individuals can be hired within 48 hours of taking a qualifying test and submitting their application for these positions. For information on positions in this category, contact one of OPM's Area Offices or a Federal Job Information Center listed in Chapter 3.

Job search strategies

Successful federal job applicants know how to cut through this somewhat confusing and frustrating hiring process. What separates them from unsuccessful candidates is their:

- Knowledge of the details of individual agencies, personnel procedures, and job vacancies. This knowledge enables them to quickly cut through what may appear to others to be a confusing and frustrating process.

- Skill in developing and marketing a good application (SF 171 and other documents) that clearly communicates their experience, qualifications, and strengths to agencies and hiring officials.
- Patience, persistence, and drive in seeing the process through to the end.
- Knowing where to find the job vacancies—a skill the remainder of this chapter will help you develop.

You should begin your job search with a thorough understanding of both the formal and informal hiring processes in the federal government. While you can get a job only by following the formal system of responding to vacancy announcements, taking tests, and completing application forms, your odds will improve considerably if you also pursue jobs in the informal system of prospecting, networking, informational interviews, and referrals—as well as finding job vacancies with the tools described in this chapter. The last portion of this chapter describes a number of books that will help you with even more with the federal hiring process.

Sources of federal jobs

There are several ways to find available federal professional and non–professional positions. The first two, consulting periodicals and directly contacting a federal agency's personnel office, are the most productive and are discussed in detail later in this chapter. The others are treated immediately below in their entirety.

- **Periodicals.** There are a number of periodicals that carry listings of federal government job openings. These may include both Competitive Service Jobs and Excepted Service and PAC positions.
- **Federal Agency's Personnel Office**. Contacting a federal agency's personnel office directly or using its job hotline to learn of job openings is the most sure–fire way to learn of all current openings with a department including Excepted and PAC positions.
- **Newspaper Advertisements**. The advertisements for federal jobs that appear in local newspapers are generally for professional positions in the geographic area the paper serves. They usually appear in the business section. National newspapers like ***The New York Times*** (229 W. 43rd St., New York, NY 10036; phone: 212/556–1234), ***Washington Post*** (1150 15th St. NW, Washington, DC 20071; phone: 202/334–6000), ***The Wall Street Journal*** (420 Lexington Ave., New York, NY 10170; phone: 212/808–6700), and ***U.S.A. Today*** (1000 Wilson Blvd.,

Arlington, VA 22209; phone: 703/276–5200) are often good sources of federal job ads.

- **College Career Planning and Placement Offices**. If you are in college, check with your school's placement office to see if it posts vacancy notices from any federal agencies and if federal recruiters interview on campus. Other campus offices worth checking for specialized information on federal jobs include: Minority, Veteran, and Handicapped Affairs; Cooperative Education, Internship, and Student Employment offices; the Financial Aid Office; and the Counseling Center.

  The OPM's regional offices distribute to colleges and universities a publication called *Career America News* which furnishes information about new federal hiring procedures and "hot" career opportunities in the federal government.

- **Office of Personnel Management**. The OPM's central office is aware of virtually all openings at the different federal agencies. In addition, local OPM offices should have listings of all available federal positions. You can locate offices of the OPM in the federal government section of local telephone directories or in some of the federal government directories identified later in this chapter.

- **Federal Job Information Centers (FJIC)**. These centers function as the regional and subregional offices of the U.S. Office of Personnel Management. They post the current weekly Federal Job Opportunity List which includes both Competitive Service positions and Excepted jobs. Contact the nearest center to see job titles of available federal jobs in your area and to obtain full job announcements and required application forms.

  Unfortunately, many FJICs are "self–service" centers where you'll never see nor speak to a government employee, living or dead. Announcements of federal job openings are posted on the wall. Applicants complete an address label and note the job number for which they'd like to apply. Slip the label through the mail slot and you'll receive a job application and full job description by mail within a few days. Although every FJIC has a telephone number, some answer it only during limited hours. The addresses and telephone numbers for FJICs are provided in the state–by–state listings in Chapter 3.

  A growing number of FJIC offices offer the *Federal Job Information Touchscreen Computer System* where you can easily find federal vacancies that interest you and print them out. You can search for jobs by state or nationally, and request application forms and materials to be sent to you. Job listings are updated daily. This is a relatively new service currently available at only a handful of FJICs.

The FJIC in Washington, DC,operates a self–service telephone system, the ***Federal Job Information Center Hotline*** (202/606–2700), which you can call any time to learn the status of your application or test results (code: 550), order forms or announcements (code: 280), learn about part–time and job sharing positions (code: 410), and much more. When you call, you'll get a lengthy announcement which will walk you through the system. You can skip this message by dialing 1, waiting a second or two and dialing 1 again. Then dial 000 to speak to a live "information specialist" to answer your questions on weekdays between 8 a.m. and 4 p.m. Washington time. Alternatively, if you don't want to speak to a live person, but would prefer to first hear a recorded message, dial the code for one of the messages that follow (be aware that these codes can change): 101–How Jobs are Filled; 102–Competitive Service; 103–Excepted Service; 105–How to Apply; 106–How Applications are Rated; 107–The Rule of Three; 108–Chances for Employment; 109–Temporary Employment; 110–Overseas Employment; 111–Employment of People with Disabilities; 112–How to Extend/Update Your Notice of Rating/Results; 113–Physical Requirements; 114–Age; 115–Citizenship; 116–Equal Employment Opportunity; 280–To Order Forms or Vacancy Announcements; 301–Clerical Examination; 401–Termination of the PAC–B; 402–Administrative Careers with America; 403–Other Registers/Written Tests; 404–Standing Registers; 405–Financial/Administrative/Social Science Jobs; 406–Job Vacancy Lists; 407–General Notice Listings; 408–Senior Executive Service Positions; 409–Upcoming Job Fairs; 410–Part Time/Job Sharing Programs; 550–To Check on Applications or Test Results; 601–Veterans' Preference; 602–Special Appointment Authority; 603–Retired Military Hiring Information; 701–Transfer; 702–Reinstatement; 703–Restoration. To repeat a message, press the # key.

People who have disabilities can make special arrangements to take any required federal government job test by calling 202/606-2528.

❑ **State Job Service Offices**. Serious job seekers should visit state–operated Job Service Centers which are supposed to carry all the job listings available at the nearest FJIC plus state and often local government jobs — and you'll usually get to talk to a live employee behind the counter. Job Service Centers are discussed in Chapter 3 and identified in the state–by–state listings.

The remainder of this chapter describes the privately–published periodicals that list available federal positions and a privately–operated service that tells you which federal jobs you are qualified for. It also guides you to the personnel offices of federal departments to learn of job openings, and presents a detailed review of several books that help you weave your way through the complex and often confusing federal job application process.

Sources of federal government vacancies

The federal government does not publish any lists of all available federal jobs. However, several private concerns publish magazines and newspapers which are the most timely inter–agency collections of federal openings for professional and technical, trades, labor, and support staff.

Reprinted with permission from *Which Niche?* by Jack Shingleton, illustrated by Phil Frank. Copyright 1989. All rights reserved.

Remember that many of the periodicals and job services presented in Chapter 2 also include federal positions, primarily professional. See this book's Index for listings under "Federal jobs." The Job Service Offices and Federal Job Information Centers noted in the state–by–state listings in Chapter 3 also carry federal government jobs. However, their lists of federal vacancies are rarely as complete as those offered by the publications described below or as the information you will receive directly from a federal agency's personnel office.

Job ads in print

Federal Career Opportunities Report (Federal Research Service, P.O. Box 1059–GJF, Vienna, VA 22183–1059; phones: 800/822–5627 [from outside D.C. area], 703/281–0200) biweekly, $38/three–month subscription, $75/six–months, $160/annual, $7.50/single issue. Each issue provides information on about 4,000 federal job vacancies from GS–5 to Senior Executive levels. All positions are open at the time they are listed in here.

Federal Times (6883 Commercial Dr., Springfield, VA 22159; phone: 800/368-5718) weekly, $48/annual subscription, $24/six–month subscription. Typical issue lists very brief descriptions of several hundred federal positions including the military. Jobs listed under "Jobs." Lists vacancies at GS–7 and above.

Federal Jobs Digest (Breakthrough Publications, P.O. Box 594, Millwood, NY 10546; phones: 800/824–5000, 914/762–5111) semiweekly, $29/three–month subscription, $54/six–month subscription, $110/annual subscription

(U.S.), $129/Canada, $160/elsewhere. Copies are available for inspection at the many public libraries and community colleges that subscribe. You'll actually find listings of as many as 20,000 federal positions by hiring agency under these general headings: National Office of Personnel Management (OPM) Announcements, Regional OPM Announcements, Overseas Job Vacancies, Veterans Administration Jobs, Federal Job Vacancies Nationwide, Senior Executive Service, and schedules for U.S. Postal Exams. Also listed are the addresses for the personnel offices of all Veterans Administration Hospitals. For each of the federal jobs located in the nation's capital and throughout the nation that are listed in each issue, *Federal Jobs Digest* gives the job title, grade, closing date, job announcement number, and application address. A number of more detailed display ads also appear in each issue. Includes Wage Grade (WG) and General Schedule (GS) jobs.

Federal Research Report (Business Publishers, Inc., 951 Pershing Dr., Silver Spring, MD 20910-4464; phone: 301/587–6300) weekly, $160.50/annual subscription. All eight pages of this newsletter feature information on federal grants and contracts for research and development.

Spotlight (College Placement Council, 62 Highland Ave., Bethlehem, PA 18042; phones: 800/544–5272, 215/868–1421) 21 issues/year, $72/annual nonmember subscription, free/members. Under "Jobwire" there are usually five to ten positions including positions for personnel directors and career counselors in the federal government.

VA Practitioner (Cahners Publishing Company, 44 Cook St., Denver, CO 80206–5191; phone: 303/388–4511) 13 issues/year, $44.95/annual subscription (U.S.), $95.95/Canada and Mexico, $89.95/elsewhere (surface mail), $140/air mail. From five to ten ads for physician and nurse positions at Veterans Administration hospitals appear under "Classifieds."

The Federal Network (American Sociological Association, 1722 N St., NW, Washington, DC 20036; phone: 202/833-3410) weekly, $75/nonmember six-month subscription, $60/members, $35/students and low-income ASA members ($15,000 or less annual income); $100/annual subscription for institutions — you can extend your subscription for another six months for these rates less $10. Each issue features announcements of new federal vacancies for which sociologists are qualified. These include permanent positions, temporary research opportunities, and paid student internships. As part of your subscription you'll receive a copy of the ASA's 84-page guide, *Accessing the Federal Network: A Manual for Sociologists Seeking Employment with the United States Government* (available by itself for $25) which is an incredible, detailed guide to federal employment for sociologists.

Federal Employment Opportunities for Anthropologists (American Anthropological Association, Suite 640, 4350 N. Fairfax Dr., Arlington, VA 22203) $4/nonmembers, $2.50/members. This is a useful beginner's guide to formal and informal ways for anthropologists to find and apply for professional level positions with executive agencies, congressional bureaus, and on the "Hill." And you thought there were no jobs for anthropologists in the federal government?

Business and Industry Bulletin (Career Development and Placement Services, Campus Box 4041, Emporia State University, Emporia, KS 66801; phone: 316/341–5407) weekly, $57.19/annual subscription, $31.77/six–month subscription. This eight to ten page newsletter includes federal government positions.

Science Education News (Directorate for Education and Human Resources, American Association for the Advancement of Science, 1333 H St., NW, Washington, DC 20005; phone: 202/326–6620) eight issues/year, free. Under "Opportunities," this newsletter frequently reports about federal agencies that need teachers and researchers.

Summer Jobs '94 (Peterson's Guides; for your convenience, this book is available from Planning/Communications; see the catalog at the end of this book) $15.95, 344 pages, annual. Describes over 20,000 summer job openings in the United States and Canada with environmental programs, resorts, camps, amusement parks, expeditions, theaters, national parks, and government, particularly federal positions with regional offices of the Department of Labor, and in the nation's capital with the Environmental Protection Agency. Each detailed employer description includes salary and benefits, employer background, profile of employees, and whom to contact to apply. Includes category, employer, and job title indexes.

New Internships in the Federal Government (Graduate Group, 86 Norwood Rd., West Hartford, CT 06117; phones: 203/232–3100, 203/236–5570) $27.50, published annually. This directory includes internships and some permanent job openings.

Internships in Congress (Graduate Group, 86 Norwood Rd., West Hartford, CT 06117; phones: 203/232–3100, 203/236–5570) $27.50, published annually. Provides in-depth information on internships available with members of Congress.

Also see several of the periodicals that focus on federal positions listed under "Legal services and court administration" in Chapter 2. ***Also look under "Federal jobs" in the Index of this book.***

Job services

ACCESS: Federal Career Opportunities On–Line (Federal Research Service, P.O. Box 1059–GJF, Vienna, VA 22180; phones: 800/822–5627 [from outside D.C. area], 703/281–0200) $45/first hour + $25/initial hook–up fee, updated daily, available 24 hours a day. Over 4,000 federal vacancies are on this on-line database you can access with an IBM-compatible computer and modem. The jobs are the same as those listed in *Federal Career Opportunities Report* described on page 231 plus jobs with less than a three week window of opportunity; however, using this database will save you a lot of time.

You can purchase your first hour of time by telephone with a MasterCard or VISA. You will be sent computer disks that enable you to communicate by modem (you'll get the ProComm program, a password, and modem number to call). When you call, you can specify up to five search parameters (GS-series or federal occupation, GS-grade or salary, job location, applicant eligibility, and/or federal agency). A typical search takes eight minutes. You can either download your results to your computer or print them on your printer. You have one year to use your hour of time.

kiNexus (Information Kinetics, Inc., Suite 560, 640 N. LaSalle St., Chicago, IL 60610; phones: 800/828-0422, 312/642-7560) $30/annual fee, $50/confidential listing (so your present employer can't learn that you are looking for a job), free if you are a student at one of the 1,500+ universities that subscribe to this service—check with your school's placement office. This is an online resume database service for college students and graduates with up to five years work experience. You complete their resume form and kiNexus puts your information into the computer. If you request the higher-cost "confidential" option, you'll be assigned a number. When a prospective employer wishes to interview you, you will be asked by kiNexus if you wish to be interviewed. Only after you agree to be interviewed will your name, address, and phone be given to the employer. Federal government agencies that subscribe to kiNexus, such as the Internal Revenue Service, can ask kiNexus to conduct searches to identify candidates for specific positions or can conduct their own searches since the database is online. The potential employer is responsible for contacting job candidates for an interview.

Federal Occupational and Career Information System (FOCIS) (National Technical Information Service; available from Planning/Communications' catalog at the end of this book) $55. Available only on high-density 3.5-inch disks for IBM-compatible computers, this dandy software enables you to access, via modem, the federal government's database of job openings and download them to your own computer. Using FOCIS, you can search through that database to find job openings appropriate for you. FOCIS also furnishes details on 600 federal occupations and 500 federal agencies.

Career America Connection (Office of Personnel Management) 40¢ per minute. Call 912/757-3000 (in Alaska, call 912/471-3755) to reach this 24-hour service of your federal government which includes an extensive job hotline. Be sure to have a pencil and paper handy when you call. You will need a touch-tone telephone.

Here's what will happen when you call. A friendly recorded voice will give you instructions on how to use the *Career America Connection,* including telling you that you can repeat a message by pressing 8 on your touch-tone phone, that you can hear the previous message by pressing 9, and that you can return to the beginning by pressing 0 (zero).

Press 1 to learn about federal job vacancies. Press 2 to obtain a job application form. Press 3 to learn about federal employment programs, including those for college students. If you choose the first selection for federal job vacancies, you'll get four choices: press 1 to hear announcements of current vacancies; press 2 to hear announcements of occupations for which the federal government accepts advance applications for future vacancies that *may* occur; press 3 to learn about positions filled directly by federal agencies due to an urgent need; press 4 to learn about positions for current or former federal employees. Once you've made your choice between these four options, you get to specify your education and experience level, the occupation that interests you, and the state for which you wish to hear job descriptions. You're able to leave a voice message to request that specific job announcements and application forms be mailed to you.

Federal Job Information for the Deaf (Office of Personnel Management; **TDD** phone: 202/606-0591). The federal government operates a number of regional telephone devices for the deaf (**TDD**) job hotlines: Washington, DC (202/606-0591); southeastern states (919/790-2739); northeastern states (617/565-8913); north central states (816/426-6022); Arizona (800/223-3131); New Mexico (505/766-8662); Dallas/Fort Worth area (214/767-8115); rest of Texas (210/229-4000); mountain states (303/969-7047); Louisiana (504/589-4614); Oklahoma (405/231-4614); California (800/735-2929); Nevada (800/326-6868); Hawaii (808/643-8833); Idaho (208/334-2100); Oregon (800/526-0661); Washington State (206/587-5500); and Alaska (800/770-8973).

Federal Job Information Center Electronic Bulletin Board Service (Office of Personnel Management, Staffing Service Center, 4685 Log Cabin Dr., Macon, GA 31298; modem phone: 912/757-3100) free, you pay only for the cost of a long distance phone call. Updated every Friday from noon to 3 p.m. Eastern time (don't call then), this electronic bulletin board features announcements for nearly all available federal job vacancies, nationwide. Modems with baud rates from 300 to 2400 can be used. Set your modem for 8 data bits, 0 parity, 1 stop bit (8-N-1) and call 912/757-3100.

The first time you connect, you'll need to answer a series of questions to log on and become a registered user. You'll be asked to designate your own password which you'll use to access the system on future calls to it. This BBS is a menu-driven system. Be sure to read the Newsletter and Bulletins which will give you helpful hints on how to use the system most effectively.

You can search for job openings by keying in job titles or using the job series numbering system, which you can see while in this system.

In addition, this service offers the latest federal salary tables as well as bulletins that guide you through the federal hiring maze.

If you are interested in federal job vacancies for a region rather than nationwide, you can call one of these regional bulletin boards using the same procedures described above: Washington, DC area and jobs overseas (modem: 202/606-1113); southeastern states (modem: 404/730-2370); northeastern states (modem: 215/580-2216); north central states (313/226-4423); mountain and southwestern states (214/767-0316); western states (modem: 818/575-6521).

Federal Job Matching Service (Breakthrough Publications, P.O. Box 594, Millwood, NY 10546; phones: 800/824–5000, 914/762–5111) $30 fee, $25 fee for subscribers to *Federal Jobs Digest* (submit address label with your order); fee refunded if applicant found unqualified for *any* federal job. This privately-operated service matches your education and experience to federal job requirements and gives you a list of the federal job titles (with official job description and list of qualifications) and grade levels that offer the best chance of getting a federal job. First obtain the very thorough "Federal Job Questionnaire" from this service. Return the completed form with your check to Breakthrough Publications. Include any of the following additional items which you feel may be pertinent to evaluating your background: resume, school transcript (if you received a degree within the last five years), professional licenses or certificates, and/or job narrative or history. Do not send any original material since this supplementary material will not be returned to you. Expect a response within three weeks. Note: This service identifies jobs for which, in its judgment, you are qualified. You must still consult the various sources of federal job listings to determine if there are any open positions.

Contacting federal personnel offices

One of the most productive sources of job openings is the main personnel office, in the District of Columbia, of the agencies for which you wish to work. Not only do they have the most up–to–date job openings, but they can also give you the appropriate application forms, full job announcements, and additional information about the department and job itself.

To help you contact these personnel offices, this chapter of the *Government Job Finder* includes a list of telephone numbers for the main personnel office of over 200 federal agencies. If an agency has more than one personnel office, the list includes the phone number for the director of personnel. Her staff will direct you to the proper personnel office.

Some agencies also maintain regional or district personnel offices around the country. To locate them, call the main personnel office in Washington, D.C. for a list or for the location of the one nearest you. Alternatively, you can find these numbers in many of the directories of federal departments and agencies described later in this chapter and in the blue pages of the local telephone directory of the city in which the office is located.

A number of agencies operate 24–hour job hotlines with tape recorded messages that list the latest job vacancies as well as eligibility status and instructions for submitting an application. In the following list, these job hotlines are indicated by a black dot (•), or "bullet" as the printing industry calls it. Nearly all the phone numbers in this list are for the central personnel office of the federal agency. In a few cases, the central switchboard number is given because no separate personnel office number was available. We've tried to be as accurate as possible. In fact, we called every one of these numbers late in 1993 to make sure they were still good. But these numbers do change frequently. So please use the Reader Feedback Form near the end of this book to let us know if any of these have changed.

Phone numbers for central personnel offices of selected federal government agencies

The area code is 202 unless otherwise noted

• indicates job hotline phone number

Agency	Telephone Number
ACTION	606-5263
	• 606-5000
Administrative Office of U.S. Courts	273-2777
	•273-2760
Agency for International Development	663-1401
Agency for Toxic Substances and Disease Registry	404/639–3615
Agriculture, Department of	720-5626
Agricultural Research Service	301/344–1518
	• 301/344–1124
	• 301/344–2288
Alcohol, Drug Abuse, and Mental Health	301/443-4826
	• 301/443-2282
	TDD: 301/443-5407

Animal and Plant Health Inspection Service	301/436-7799
Army Corps of Engineers	272–0720
Bureau of Alcohol, Tobacco, and Firearms	927-8610
Bureau of Engraving and Printing	824-2485
Bureau of Indian Affairs	208-7518
Bureau of Land Management	208-5717
Bureau of Mines	501-9649
Bureau of Public Debt	622-5000
Bureau of Prisons	307-1304
	• 514-6388
Bureau of Reclamation	303/236-3819
Bureau of the Census	301/763-7470
	• 301/763–6064
Center for Disease Control	404–639–3615
Central Intelligence Agency	703/874-4400
	• 703/351–2028
Commerce, Department of	377-3827
	• 377-5138
	• 377–4285
	TDD: 377-5246
	TDD: 377-3706
Commission on Civil Rights	376–8364
Commodity Futures Trading Commission	254–3275
Consumer Product Safety Commission	301/504-0100
Courts, Administrative Office of U.S.	273-2777
Defense, Department of	
Air Force	703/695-4389
	• 703/693-6550
Army (jobs in District of Columbia area)	703/325–8840
Navy	703/697-6181
	TDD: 703/697-6181
One Stop Job Information	703/780-4655
	• 703/780-4677
Walter Reed Medical Center	576-0546
Consolidated Personnel Center	433-5370
National Naval Medical Center	295-6800
Investigative Service	703/325-5344
Defense Communications Agency	703/683-7787
	• 703/746–1724
Defense Contract Audit Agency	703/274-2735
Defense Logistics Agency	703/274-7088

Defense Mapping Agency	703/285-9148
District of Columbia Government	727-6406
	• 727-9726
	TDD: 347-5509
Drug Enforcement Administration	307–4055
	TDD: 307–8903
Education, Department of (Jobs in District of Columbia area)	401-0559
	708-5939
Employment and Training Administration	219-8743
Energy, Department of	586–8563
	• 586–4333
Environmental Protection Agency	260-3144
	• 260–5055
Equal Employment Opportunity Commission	663–4264
	TDD: 800/800-3302
Export–Import Bank of the U.S.	566–8990
Farm Credit Administration	703/883-4000
Farmers Home Administration	245-5561
Federal Aviation Administration	267-3870
	• 267-3902
Federal Bureau of Investigation	324–4981
Federal Communications Commission	632–7000
	TDD: 632–6999
Federal Deposit Insurance Corporation	898–8890
Federal Election Commission	800/424–9530
Federal Emergency Management Agency	646–3970
	• 646–3244
Federal Energy Regulatory Commission	208-0200
	• 219-2791
	TDD: 219-2995
Federal Housing Finance Board	408–2532
	408–2517
Federal Labor Relations Authority	482–6690
Federal Maritime Commission	523–5773
Federal Mediation and Conciliation Service	653–5290
Federal Reserve System	800/448–4894
	• 452–3038
Federal Trade Commission	326-2022
	TDD: 326-2502
Financial Management Service	622-1470
	•622-1029

Food and Drug Administration	301/443–1970
	• 301/443–1969
	TDD: 301/463–1970
Food and Nutrition Service	703/756–3351
Foreign Agricultural Service	387–1587
Foreign Service	703/875-7490
	• 703/516-0025
Forest Service	703/235–8145
	• 703/235–2730
General Accounting Office	275–6092
(GS 13 & above)	• 275–6361
(GS 2–12)	• 275–6017
General Services Administration	501-0370
Government Printing Office	512-0000
Health and Human Services, Department of	619-2560
	TDD: 475-0099
Health, Office of Assistant. Secretary	690-7694
	• 301/443–7000
Health Care Financing Administration	410/966–5505
	TDD: 410/966-0723
Housing and Urban Development, Department of	707-0416
Immigration and Naturalization Service	514-2530
	• 514–4301
Indian Health Service	301/443–6520
Interior, Department of	208-3100
	208-5701
	• 800/336-4562
	TDD: 208-5817
Internal Revenue Service	622-6340
	• 622-6340
International Trade Administration	482-2000
(Jobs in U.S.)	• 482-1533
	TDD: 482-4670
International Trade Commission	205-2651
Interstate Commerce Commission	275–7288
Justice, Department of	514-6813
	• 514-6818
	TDD: 514-7972
Labor, Department of	219–6666
	• 219–6646
Library of Congress	707–5000

	• 707–4315
	TDD: 707-6200
Marine Corps	703/640-2048
Merit Systems Protection Board	653–5916
	TDD: 653–8892
Minerals Management Service	703/787-1414
	• 703/787–1402
National Aeronautics and Space Administration (NASA)	453–8478
	• 755-6299
NASA Goddard Space Center	301/286-7918
	• 301/286-5326
National Archives and Records Administration	501-6100
National Capital Planning Commission	724–0170
National Capitol Park Service	619-7256
	• 619–7111
	TDD: 619-7364
National Credit Union Administration	703/518-6510
National Endowment for the Arts	682–5405
	• 682-5799
National Endowment for the Humanities	786–0415
National Gallery of Art	842–6282
	• 842–6298
	TDD: 789-3021
National Institute of Health	301/496–2403
(Professional)	• 301/496–9541
(Clerical)	• 301/496–9452
National Institute of Standards and Technology	301/975-3007
	•301/763-4944
	TDD: 301/975-2039
National Labor Relations Board	254–9044
	TDD: 634–1669
National Library of Medicine	301/496-4943
(Professional)	• 301/496-9541
(Clerical)	• 301/496-9452
	TDD: 301/496-9452
National Oceanic and Atmospheric Administration	301/713-0677
National Park Service	619-7256
	• 301/619-7111
	• 301/619-7364
National Science Foundation	357–7602
	TDD: 357–7492

	• 357–7735
	• 800/628–1487
National Security Agency	800/255–8415
National Transportation Safety Board	382–6717
Naval Submarine Base (King Bay, GA)	912/673-4774
	• 800/544–1707
Naval Undersea Warfare Engineering Station	• 206–396–5111
Nuclear Regulatory Commission	301/492–8260
Occupational Safety and Health Administration	219-8013
	• 800/366-2753
Office of the Comptroller of the Currency	622-2000
Office of Inspector General	377-4948
	• 377-3476
	TDD: 377-5897
Office of Management and Budget (OMB)	395–3765
	TDD: 395–5892
Office of Personnel Management (OPM)	606-2424
	TDD: 606–2118
OPM Job Information Center	• 606-2700
Overseas Private Investment Corporation	836-8400
Office of U.S. Trade Representative	205-2651
Panama Canal Commission	634–6441
Patent and Trademark Office	703/305-8231
	• 703/305-8586
Peace Corps	606-3400
	• 606-3214
	• 800/424-8580
(Overseas volunteers)	800/424–8580, ext. 93
Pension Benefit Guaranty Corporation	778–8800
Postal Rate Commission	789–6800
Postal Service	268–3646
	• 268-3218
President, Executive Office of the	395-3000
Public Health Service (Civil Service positions)	301/443–1986
Railroad Retirement Board	312–751–4500
Securities and Exchange Commission	272–2550
Selective Service System	703/235-2555
Small Business Administration	653-6504
Smithsonian Institution	287-3100
	• 287–3102
Social Security Administration	410/965-4506

	TDD: 410/965-4404
Soil Conservation Service	720-4264
	•720-6365
State, Department of	647-7284
	• 647-7284
Foreign service (overseas)	• 703/875-7109
Tennessee Valley Authority	615/632–3341
Transportation, Department of	366–9394
	TDD: 366-9402
Treasury, Department of	377-9205
Treasury, U.S. Mint	• 415–744–9364
U.S. Arms Control and Disarmament Agency	647–2034
U.S. Coast Guard	267–2229
U.S. Customs Service	634–5270
	TDD: 634-2069
U.S. Fish and Wildlife	703/358-1743
	• 703/358-2120
U.S. Geological Survey	703/648–6131
	• 703/648–7676
	TDD: 703/648-7788
U.S. House of Representatives	226–6731
U.S. Information Agency	619-4659
	• 619–4539
Overseas positions	619-0909
U.S. International Development Cooperation Agency	647-1850
	• 663-2658
U.S. Marshals Service	307–9629
U.S. Mint	622-2000
U.S. Savings Bond Division	447-1775
U.S. Secret Service	395-2020
U.S. Senate	224–3121
Urban Mass Transportation Administration	366-2513
Veterans Employment and Training Administration	219-9110
Veterans' Affairs	233–3771
	TDD: 233–3225
(Department of Veteran's Benefits)	872-1151
Voice of America	619-3117

Directories of federal agencies

An extensive array of federal agency directories will also help you locate the personnel offices of any federal agency and, in most cases, give you very valuable background information before you apply for a specific federal job. They are well–worth consulting. Public libraries tend to have at least one of these directories on their reference shelves.

The single best source for addresses and phone numbers of federal personnel offices has been the ***Federal Personnel Office Directory*** (Federal Reports, Inc., Suite 408, 1010 Vermont Ave., NW, Washington, DC 20005; phone: 202/393–3311; 1990–1991 edition. Unfortunately, this is currently out of print but may be available at libraries.

An essential source when you don't know exactly what federal job you want to seek, is ***The Almanac of American Government Jobs and Careers*** by Ronald and Caryl Krannich ($14.95, 1991; available from Planning/Communications' catalog at the back of this book). Its 392 pages give detailed information about virtually every federal department, commission, and agency in all three branches, including occupational titles, college majors, and the address and phone of the personnel office official to contact. It's described in more detail on page 249.

Other sources of value include:

Federal Yellow Book (Monitor Publishing, Co., 104 Fifth Ave., 2nd Floor, New York, NY 10011; phone: 212/627–4140) quarterly, $215/annual subscription. Thanks to its frequency of publication, this is the most up–to–date of all the directories of federal departments and agencies. Its 900 pages give you details on over 35,000 top decision makers in the White House, Executive Office of the President, and all federal departments and agencies, including regional offices.

Federal Regional Yellow Book (Monitor Publishing, Co., 104 Fifth Ave., 2nd Floor, New York, NY 10011; phone: 212/627–4140) semiannual, $165/annual subscription. Learn how to get in contact with over 18,000 key decision makers in the regional offices of over 4,000 federal departments, independent agencies, courts (including librarians), military installations, and service academies — all outside Washington, D.C.

Washington Information Directory (Congressional Quarterly, Inc., 1414 22nd St., NW, Washington, DC 20037; phones: 800/673–2730, 202/887–8500) $89.95, 1,100 pages, June 1993-94 edition. Divides the federal government into 18 broad subject categories and furnishes detailed information on each federal department and agency. Also provides details on regional federal information sources, non–governmental organizations in the Washington area, and Congressional committees and subcommittees.

Federal Staff Directory (Staff Directories, Ltd., P.O. Box 62, Mt. Vernon, VA 22121; phone: 703/739–0900) $59 per volume, published every January (volume 1, hard cover) and August (volume 2, paperback) which updates volume one. Lists 30,000 key decision makers and staff for all federal departments and agencies, including the White House. Includes personnel departments. Also contains biographies of 2,400 key federal executives and senior staff. Keyword index.

Federal Executive Directory (Carroll Publishing Company, 1058 Thomas Jefferson St., NW, Washington, DC 20007; phone: 202/333–8620) updated and published in full six times a year, $180/annual subscription, 535 pages. Contains more than 86,000 entries in both the executive and legislative branches, including Cabinet departments, federal administrative agencies, Congressional committee members and staff, areas of responsibility for legal and administrative assistants. Features alphabetical, organizational for congress and executive branches, and keyword indexes.

Federal Executive Directory Annual (Carroll Publishing Company, 1058 Thomas Jefferson St., NW, Washington, DC 20007; phone: 202/333–8620) $127, published annually. This is essentially an annual edition of the *Federal Executive Directory* described immediately above.

Federal Regional Executive Directory (Carroll Publishing Company, 1058 Thomas Jefferson St., NW, Washington, DC 20007; phone: 202/333–8620) updated and published in full twice a year, $130/annual subscription, 390 pages. Over 65,000 entries of non–Washington based executive managers in Cabinet departments, Congress, the courts, and administrative agencies. Includes alphabetical, organizational, geographical (city within state), and keyword indexes.

Federal Organization Service (Carroll Publishing Company, 1058 Thomas Jefferson St., NW, Washington, DC 20007; phone: 202/333–8620) updated every six weeks, $500/annual subscription. Delineates the complex infrastructure of the civil branch of the federal government, with nearly 140 fold–out charts identifying who's who in over 1,600 departments and offices. The direct–dial phone numbers for more than 10,000 federal employees are given.

Federal Managers' Association Membership Directory (FMA, 1000 16th St., NW, Suite 701, Washington, DC 20036; phone: 202/778–1500) free/members only, $50/annual dues, published each month. This directory guides you to managers and supervisors who work for the federal government.

The Federal Statistical Source: Where to Find Agency Experts and Personnel (Oryx Press, 4041 N. Central, Phoenix, AZ 85012–3997; phone: 800/279–6799) $37.50, 176 pages, 1991. Lists 4,000 federal employees' addresses, phone, and fax numbers by department, agency, or organization.

These are all federal employees who assemble and disseminate statistical information.

Who Knows: A Guide to Washington Experts/Federal Fast Finder (Washington Researchers Publishing, 2612 P St., NW, Washington, DC 20007; phone: 202/333–3533) $155, 1994. This is a key word telephone directory to over 1,500 federal government departments, agencies, and electronic bulletin boards operated by the federal government. Direct numbers and addresses are given.

Congressional Staff Directory (Staff Directories, Ltd., P.O. Box 62, Mt. Vernon, VA 22121; phone: 703/739–0900) $59 per volume, published every April (volume 1, hard cover) and September (volume 2, paperback) which updates volume one. Complete listing of members of Congressional committees, subcommittees, and staffs and the 20,000 people who make Congress work. Includes biographies of 3,200 key staff. Keyword index.

Congressional Staff Directory on DISK (Staff Directories, Ltd., P.O. Box 62, Mt. Vernon, VA 22121; phone: 703/739–0900) $250, released in May. An effective tool to track a Congressman, her staff, and home district, this database and program include a zip code locator, print labels feature, user file for customized data, and the ability to export data in ASCII format for use with most word processors. Includes all 16,000 names and addresses as they appear in the *Congressional Staff Directory*.

Braddock's Congressional Directory (Braddock Communications, 909 N. Washington St., Suite 310, Alexandria, VA 22314; phone: 703/549-6500) $10.95 plus $2 shipping. This list of congressional members is published every two years.

Congressional Yellow Book (Monitor Publishing, Co., 104 Fifth Ave., 2nd Floor, New York, NY 10011; phone: 212/627–4140) quarterly, $215/annual subscription. Over 750 pages in each edition give you detailed information on Congressional staff positions, committees and subcommittees, top staff in Congressional support agencies like the Congressional Budget Office, General Accounting Office, and Library of Congress.

The Almanac of American Politics 1994 (National Journal, P.O. Box 46909, St. Louis, MO 63146-9719; phone: 800/356-4838) $48.95/softcover, 1993. This highly respected directory gives you the real low down on the members of Congress (as well as the nation's governors) and key members of the President's Cabinet. If you're looking for a member of Congress you can work for without selling your soul, this is a great place to start your search.

Washington 93 (Columbia Books, 1212 New York Ave., NW, Suite 300, Washington, DC 20005; phone: 202/898–0662) $75, published annually. Over 600 pages of addresses, phone numbers, and information including chapters on the federal government, international affairs, national issues, and community affairs. Also includes chapters on the media, business, national associations, labor unions, law firms, medicine and health, foundations and philanthropy, science and policy research, education, religion, cultural institutions, clubs, and community affairs.

The Capitol Source: The Who's Who, What, Where in Washington (National Journal, Inc., 1730 M St., NW, Washington, DC 20036; phones: 800/424–2921, 202/862–0644) $26.45. Published in April and November, this directory includes names, addresses, and phone numbers for the District of Columbia. Also included are corporations, interest groups, think tanks, labor unions, real estate, financial institutions, trade and professional organizations, law firms, political consultants, advertising and public relations firms, private clubs, and the media. All entries are also available on computer diskette. Call 202/857–1449 for information.

BNA's Directory of State and Federal Courts, Judges, and Clerks (Bureau of National Affairs Books Distribution Center, P.O. Box 6036, Rockville, MD 20850-9914; phone: 800/372-1033) $85 plus $3/shipping, 513 pages, last published in July 1992. Gives names of judges and court clerks, address, phone number, and geographical area served, for over 92 U.S. District Courts, 14 U.S. Courts of Appeals, the U.S. Tax Court, and the U.S. Supreme Court.

Judicial Staff Directory (Staff Directories Ltd., P.O. Box 62, Mt. Vernon, VA 22121; phone: 703/739–0900) $59, published every November. Complete listing of staff and judges in all of the federal courts. Keyword index.

Encyclopedia of Governmental Advisory Organizations 1994-95 (Gale Research, Inc., 835 Penobscot Bldg., Detroit, MI 48226; phones: 800/877–4253, 313/961–2242) $505, 1,450 pages, June 1993. Over 6,000 entries describe the activities and personnel of groups and committees that advise the President plus federal departments and bureaus.

New Governmental Advisory Organizations Supplement (Gale Research, Inc., 835 Penobscot Bldg., Detroit, MI 48226; phones: 800/877–4253, 313/961–2242) $345, June 1994. Updates the *Encyclopedia of Governmental Advisory Organizations* described immediately above.

Federal Regulatory Directory (Congressional Quarterly, Inc., 1414 22nd St., NW, Washington, DC 20037; phones: 800/673–2730, 202/887–8600) $110, most recent edition November 1990, 986 pages. Provides details on more than 100 federal regulatory agencies including each agency's functions, the laws they enforce, and the names, addresses, and phone numbers of key personnel in Washington and regional offices.

Government Research Directory, 1992-93 (Gale Research, Inc., 835 Penobscot Bldg., Detroit, MI 48226; phones: 800/877–4253, 313/961–2242) $405, 1,300 pages, 1992. Describes over 3,700 research facilities and programs of the United States government. Includes government agencies and bureaus that are research organizations and user–oriented facilities supported by the federal government.

Directory of Military Bases in the U.S. (Oryx Press, 4041 N. Central, Phoenix, AZ 85012–3997; phone: 800/279–6799) $95, 208 pages, 1991. Provides information on 700 bases and installations of the Army, Navy, Air Force, Marines, Coast Guard, National Guard, Reserve, and Joint Service Installations.

Directory of U.S. Military Bases Worldwide (Oryx Press, 4041 N. Central, Phoenix, AZ 85012–3997; phone: 800/279–6799) $95, 416 pages, June 1994. This new directory will include everything in the *Directory of Military Bases* in the U.S. described immediately above plus the same sort of information about bases outside the U.S.

International Military Community Executives Association Membership Directory (IMCEA, 1800 Diagonal Rd., Suite 285, Alexandria, VA 22314; phone: 703/548–0093) $200, published each May.

Defense Organization Service (Carroll Publishing Company, 1058 Thomas Jefferson St., NW, Washington, DC 20007; phone: 202/333–8620) updated every six weeks, $925/annual subscription plus $30 shipping. Provides direct–dial phone numbers for 11,500 key individuals in 1,500 military departments and offices.

Books on applying for a federal job

The federal government offers a fiercely competitive, complex, slow, and confusing hiring process for both non–professional and professional positions that is not uniform between agencies. Whole books have been written about the federal hiring process, and I'm not going to be so presumptuous to think I have any profound advice to add to them.

Instead, the *Government Job Finder* explains how to find job openings in the federal government and leads you to directories that describe the activities of federal agencies and provide phone numbers and addresses for the appropriate persons to contact about jobs within those agencies. These other books focus on helping a job seeker determine which types of federal positions to seek and how to apply for them. With one exception, these books concentrate on positions for college graduates.

Federal job overview

For an overview of federal job–seeking, see ***The Complete Guide to Public Employment*** (by Ronald and Caryl Krannich, Impact Publications, $19.95, 528 pages, 1994; available from the catalog at the end of this book). In the first of three detailed chapters on federal hiring, the Krannichs explain the federal government's structure, its competitive and exempted services, job classifications, pay systems, job types and alternatives, strategies, and useful resources, including guides to federal job examinations.

An entire chapter is devoted to writing an effective SF 171, the standard job application form which is to the federal "government what applications and resumes are to the rest of the work world." The chapter also refers readers to a number of publications and videotapes that explain how to complete the SF 171 form.

The third chapter on federal positions explains the types of employment available with the legislative branch (40,000 employees), on Capitol Hill, and with the federal judiciary (17,000 employees).

Dennis Damp's, ***The Book of U.S. Government Jobs*** (D-Amp Publications, $15.95, 224 pages, 1994; available in the catalog at the end of this book), also gives a good overview of the federal system and hiring processes. It includes chapters on the post office, civil service exams, veterans and military dependent hiring, overseas employment, work opportunities for people with disabilities, and brief descriptions of many federal agencies, and federal occupation lists.

For a more extensive introduction to federal government agencies, you should see Caryl and Ron Krannich's book, ***The Almanac of American Government Jobs and Careers*** (Impact Publications, $14.95, 392 pages, 1991; available from the catalog at the end of this book). Not only does it describe each federal agency, but it also tells you what college majors are required for the positions each one hires, occupational titles, and whom to contact for job information. It also includes a lengthy chapter on jobs with Congress where it gives you the addresses and phones for Washington and local offices for each member of Congress as well as a contact name for each Congressman (obviously some of this information is out of date — some of the other directories described in this chapter give you more timely information since they are published annually). The book also lists federal boards and commissions along with the number of employees for each.

Technical, trades, and labor positions

While a number of books address all federal jobs, the ***Guide to Federal Technical, Trades and Labor Jobs*** (Resource Directories, Suite 302, 3361 Executive Parkway, Toledo, OH 43606; phones: 800/274–8515, 419/536–5353) $69.95 plus $4 shipping, 1992. Appears to be the only one to focus exclusively on the 950,000 non–professional positions that do not require a college degree, plus the U.S. Postal Service.

This volume includes job descriptions for federal Wage Grade, U.S. Postal Service, Competitive Service, and General Schedule positions. It explains the skills, education, and/or experience required for these positions as well as whether a written exam is required. The major agencies to employ non–professionals are named.

This hefty book also walks job seekers through the application procedures with step–by–step application instructions and sample forms and vacancy notices.

Postal service

In his ***Book of $16,000–$60,000 Post Office Jobs*** ($14.95, 1989, 186 pages; available from Planning/Communications' catalog at the end of this book), author Veltisezar Bautista explains the duties and salaries of, and qualifications and examinations for, all U.S. Postal Service jobs including those open to the general public and those available only to current postal employees. Nearly 300 specific job classifications are covered. It also includes a nationwide directory of the more than 370 U.S. Postal Examination Centers.

Bound & Gagged reprinted by permission of Tribune Media Services. Copyright 1992. All rights reserved.

Bautista's ***Book of U.S. Postal Exams*** ($13.95, 1991, 264 pages, also available from Planning/Communications) explains dozens of tests the Postal Service uses, teaches techniques alleged to improve test performance, and includes realistic sample exams with answers. Also included is a national directory of the 370 plus U.S. Postal Examination Centers.

Professional positions

One of the more detailed books on obtaining professional positions with the federal government is the ***Guide to Federal Jobs*** (Resource Directories, Suite 302, 3361 Executive Parkway, Toledo, OH 43606; phones: 800/274–8515, 419/536–5353; $69.95 plus $4 shipping, 1992, 352 pages). This book contains profiles of federal agencies and departments with the names, addresses, and phone numbers of hiring contacts. Job descriptions, pay scales, and benefits are also identified.

For each of the 206 job descriptions of professional positions, the *Guide to Federal Jobs* presents current employment data on supervisory positions, average salary, and number of persons in each GS employment classification by sex. The locations of these jobs is also given, divided between overseas positions and domestic jobs outside D.C., and in D.C. The book also identifies the top agencies that employ people for the job described and the exact number employed by each.

Don't read more into these listings than there is. For example, the description of GS–5 Community Planners shows them employed by the Departments of Transportation, the Air Force, and the Army. However, community planners are also employed by other federal departments, particularly the Department of Housing and Urban Development, at GS–5 and other GS levels.

Detailed instructions on how to locate and apply for federal jobs are furnished as are instructions for completing the dread SF 171 form. The *Guide to Federal Jobs* explains how to use a vacancy notice to make your SF 171 job specific and examines the quality ranking factors the feds use to queue job applicants. The book concludes with employer job category indexes which enable you to relate specific jobs to specific agencies, and types of skills to specific jobs.

All federal positions

One of the most useful resources is ***How to Get a Federal Job*** (by David E. Waelde; seventh edition, 1989; $14.95; 186 pages; available from Planning/Communications' catalog at the end of this book). Fifteen chapters take readers step–by–step through each section of the SF 171 form; and offer advice on handling agency vacancy announcements, applying for a specific federal job, and surviving a reduction–in–force (RIF). This book closely examines the Office of Personnel Management's rules and regulations that govern the application and selection processes. The sample forms and examples are most helpful.

Another practical aid for the federal job seeker is the Krannich's ***Find a Federal Job Fast!*** ($9.95, 1992, 196 pages; available from Planning/Communications' catalog at the end of this book). While this book covers much of the same territory as Dave Waelde's volume, this one does more to debunk the myths of federal hiring and help you formulate your job search strategy. It includes a sample SF 171 form and solid advice on how to complete it most effectively.

Completing the SF 171 application form

As of this writing, the word out of Washington is that the SF 171 form may be phased out during the next few years as hiring authority is transferred to each individual federal agency. Until then, you're still going to have to complete it to get most federal jobs. You may very likely find the following books and software helpful if you need to complete the SF 171.

Dr. Russell Smith's new book, ***The Right SF 171 Writer*** (Impact Publications, 211 pages, 1994, $19.95; available from Planning/Communication's catalog at the end of this book) very effectively shows you how to write a successful SF 171 that will enhance your chances of getting hired by a federal agency. It outlines what federal employers look for in a SF 171, major writing principles, the best language to use (KASOs), how to customize your form, and many examples. It also explains all terms, lists general schedule and wage grade occupations,and gives position qualification standards. This may be the most thorough book written on completing the federal job application form.

Patricia Wood's ***The 171 Reference Book*** (Workbooks, Inc., $18.95, 1991, 120 pages; since this book is not available in bookstores, Planning/Communications carries it in the catalog at the end of this book) details how to successfully complete the SF 171 form. If you are having trouble figuring out what to write on your SF 171, this is the book for you. It teaches all the right buzzwords that get the attention of the often overworked personnel official who reviews your SF 171. If you have any doubt as to how to write an effective SF 171 form, these two books may be the best aids you'll ever find.

Computer programs for the SF 171

You can complete a SF 171 form on any MS–DOS (IBM compatible) computer with virtually any laser, desk jet, or dot matrix printer using ***Quick & Easy for the SF 171*** (DataTech, DOS or Windows version: $49.95/single user, $59.95/two users, $129.95/eight users, $399.95/unlimited number of users; available from Planning/Communications' catalog at the end of this book; the DOS version is available on 3.5–inch or 5.25–inch floppy disks while the Windows version comes only on 3.5–inch disks). Use this program to create customized versions of your SF 171 for different jobs without having to retype it each time. It includes a built-in word processor with spell checker. You can print on an existing SF 171 form or have the program print the form with your answers all at once. You will need an IBM–compatible computer with a hard disk drive.

Two other programs that you can use to complete the SF 171 are ***171 Laser*** ($39) and ***FedForm 171 Plus*** ($29), both available from Formtronix, Inc. (2516 McHenry Dr., Silver Spring, MD 20904–1623; phones: 800/237–6821, extension 576, 301/572-6902). The first program enables you to print a completed SF 171 on plain paper on your laser printer (as long as it's

Application for Federal Employment—SF 171
Read the instructions before you complete this application. ***Type or print clearly in dark ink.***

Form Approved: OMB No. 3206-0012

GENERAL INFORMATION

1 What kind of job are you applying for? *Give title and announcement no. (if any)*

2 Social Security Number

3 Sex ☐ Male ☐ Female

4 Birth date *(Month, Day, Year)*

5 Birthplace *(City and State or Country)*

6 Name *(Last, First, Middle)*

Mailing address *(include apartment number, if any)*

City State ZIP Code

7 Other names ever used *(e.g., maiden name, nickname, etc.)*

8 Home Phone — Area Code | Number

9 Work Phone — Area Code | Number | Extension

10 Were you ever employed as a civilian by the Federal Government? If "NO", go to Item 11. If "YES", mark each type of job you held with an "X".

☐ Temporary ☐ Career-Conditional ☐ Career ☐ Excepted

What is your highest grade, classification series and job title?

Dates at highest grade: FROM TO

DO NOT WRITE IN THIS AREA

FOR USE OF EXAMINING OFFICE ONLY

Date entered register | Form reviewed: Form approved:

Option	Grade	Earned Rating	Veteran Preference	Augmented Rating
			☐ No Preference Claimed	
			☐ 5 Points *(Tentative)*	
			☐ 10 Pts. *(30% Or More Comp. Dis.)*	
			☐ 10 Pts. *(Less Than 30% Comp. Dis.)*	
			☐ Other 10 Points	

Initials and Date ☐ Disallowed ☐ Being Investigated

FOR USE OF APPOINTING OFFICE ONLY

Preference has been verified through proof that the separation was under honorable conditions, and other proof as required.

☐ 5-Point ☐ 10-Point—30% or More Compensable Disability ☐ 10-Point—Less Than 30% Compensable Disability ☐ 10-Point—Other

Signature and Title

Agency | Date

AVAILABILITY

11 When can you start work? *(Month and Year)*

12 What is the lowest pay you will accept? *(You will not be considered for jobs which pay less than you indicate.)*

Pay $______ per______ OR Grade______

13 In what geographic area(s) are you willing to work?

14 Are you willing to work:	YES	NO
A. 40 hours per week *(full-time)*?		
B. 25-32 hours per week *(part-time)*?		
C. 17-24 hours per week *(part-time)*?		
D. 16 or fewer hours per week *(part-time)*?		
E. An intermittent job *(on-call/seasonal)*?		
F. Weekends, shifts, or rotating shifts?		
15 Are you willing to take a temporary job lasting:		
A. 5 to 12 months *(sometimes longer)*?		
B. 1 to 4 months?		
C. Less than 1 month?		
16 Are you willing to travel away from home for:		
A. 1 to 5 nights each month?		
B. 6 to 10 nights each month?		
C. 11 or more nights each month?		

MILITARY SERVICE AND VETERAN PREFERENCE

	YES	NO
17 Have you served in the United States Military Service? *If your only active duty was training in the Reserves or National Guard, answer "NO".* If "NO", go to Item 22.		
18 Did you or will you retire at or above the rank of major or lieutenant commander?		

THE FEDERAL GOVERNMENT IS AN EQUAL OPPORTUNITY EMPLOYER

PREVIOUS EDITION USABLE UNTIL 12-31-90

Page 1

MILITARY SERVICE AND VETERAN PREFERENCE *(Cont.)*

19 Were you discharged from the military service under honorable conditions? *(If your discharge was changed to "honorable" or "general" by a Discharge Review Board, answer "YES". If you received a clemency discharge, answer "NO".)* If "NO", provide below the date and type of discharge you received.	YES	NO

Discharge Date *(Month, Day, Year)*	Type of Discharge

20 List the dates *(Month, Day, Year)*, and branch for all active duty military service.

From	To	Branch of Service

21 If all your active military duty was after October 14, 1976, list the full names and dates of all campaign badges or expeditionary medals you received or were entitled to receive.

22 **Read the instructions that came with this form before completing this item.** When you have determined your eligibility for veteran preference from the instructions, place an "X" in the box next to your veteran preference claim.

☐ NO PREFERENCE

☐ 5-POINT PREFERENCE – You must show proof when you are hired.

10-POINT PREFERENCE – If you claim 10-point preference, place an "X" in the box below next to the basis for your claim. To receive 10-point preference you must also complete a Standard Form 15, Application for 10-Point Veteran Preference, which is available from any Federal Job Information Center. ATTACH THE COMPLETED SF 15 AND REQUESTED PROOF TO THIS APPLICATION.

☐ Non-compensably disabled or Purple Heart recipient.

☐ Compensably disabled, less than 30 percent.

☐ Spouse, widow(er), or mother of a deceased or disabled veteran.

☐ Compensably disabled, 30 percent or more.

NSN 7540-00-935-7150 171-109 Standard Form 171 (Rev. 6-88) U.S. Office of Personnel Management FPM Chapter 295

compatible with the Hewlett Packard LaserJet and has at least 1.5 megabytes of printer memory). The second program prints only your answers which must be placed under a transparency of the 171 form (included with the program) and photocopied (which is acceptable to the feds). Unlike the *Fedform 171 Laser* program, this one can be run from just a floppy disk and does not require a laser printer. Both programs are available on 3.5–inch or 5.25–inch floppy disks.

A windows program for completing the SF 171 is ***FormWorx for Windows*** ($69.95) which includes a SF 171 Template. This program allows you to use your computer to produce a completed SF 171 form on blank paper or print your answers onto a preprinted SF 171 form. The program occupies six megabytes on your hard drive and is available on 5.25–inch or 3.5–inch floppy disks from the PowerUp! Software Corporation (P.O. Box 7600, San Mateo, CA 94403; phones: 800/992–0085, 415/345-0551). Make certain you buy the Windows version of this program; the DOS version does *not* include a SF 171 template.

There are reportedly other computer programs for Macintosh and MS–DOS personal computers that help you complete the SF 171 form. Since we haven't tried them, we'd sure appreciate hearing about your experiences with them. You can usually buy these programs at major computer stores or from the major mail order software companies.

Chapter 5

Finding jobs in Canada and abroad

To avoid being labeled an "ugly American" when looking and applying for work in government outside the U.S., you will have to adapt your notions of job hunting to the cultures of the countries in which you wish to work as well as to any different hiring procedures or customs they may have.

In addition to introducing you to periodicals and directories that will facilitate your job search in Canada and overseas, this chapter presents information on a number of books that describe the different hiring procedures and customs you will encounter in other countries. If you wish to work overseas for the United States government, be sure to read Chapter 4, in addition to the job sources identified in this chapter. Also, be sure to look under "Foreign jobs" in the index of this book to identify sources of foreign positions noted in chapters 2 and 4.

Before you begin your search for government jobs outside the United States, you should first develop a pretty good idea where you would like to work. It may help your decision to know the political, social, and economic natures of the countries you are considering for your next home. In addition, if you wish to work for a national, state, or local government in another country, you will want to know something about these governments and to whom you should apply for work, *assuming foreigners are even eligible to work for the government in that country.*

A good place to start is at your local library with a copy of the ***Worldwide Government Directory*** (Belmont Publications, sold by Gale Research, Inc., 835 Penobscot Bldg., Detroit, MI 48226; phone: 800/877–4253; $325, published annually). This rather thorough tome proffers detailed information on the governments of over 195 countries: full names and addresses of heads of state, ministers, department directors, cabinet members, legislative, and military personnel; complete addresses, phones, and telex numbers for national capitals, government offices and departments; proper forms of address, so you don't violate protocol; and the directors of state agencies and commercial enterprises the government operates.

In addition, the *Worldwide Government Directory* includes complete listings of each country's embassies and consulates, including United Nation's missions; addresses, phones, and officers of central banks; and basic facts on each country such as the capital city, official and business languages, religious affiliations of the population, local currency and rate of exchange against the U.S. dollar, international telephone dialing code, national holidays, and the next scheduled presidential election and political parties, if any.

This directory also furnishes information on over 100 international organizations and the United Nations. You'll find its information on Canada to be very helpful for targeting your job search.

Another similar volume is ***Countries of the World and Their Leaders Yearbook 1993*** (Gale Research, Inc., 835 Penobscot Bldg., Detroit, MI 48226; phone: 800/877–4253; $160, 1,900 pages, published annually; *Supplement* published in June between annual editions costs $81) which includes the U.S. State Department's "Background Notes on the Countries of the World;" basic social, economic, and political data on 170 countries; current travel warnings from the State Department; and U.S. embassies and consulates and their personnel. The "Travel Notes" section describes the immigration and customs requirements of each country. This is a very useful source for determining which countries should be part of your overseas job search.

The ***Handbook of the Nations*** (Gale Research, Inc., 835 Penobscot Bldg., Detroit, MI 48226; phone: 800/877–4253; $105, 420 pages, 1993) contains timely information on the governments, politics, sociology, and economies of nearly 250 nations.

Specialty associations in foreign countries provide many of the same job services offered by associations of government professionals in the United States. Although it was practical for the Government Job Finder to identify only some of those associations in Canada, Great Britain, and New Zealand, you can identify professional associations outside the U.S. by using the ***Encyclopedia of Associations: International Organizations 1994*** (Gale Research, Inc., 835 Penobscot Bldg., Detroit, MI 48226; phone: 800/877–4253; $455, 3,000 pages; September 1993) which describes around 13,000 international and foreign national organizations in 180

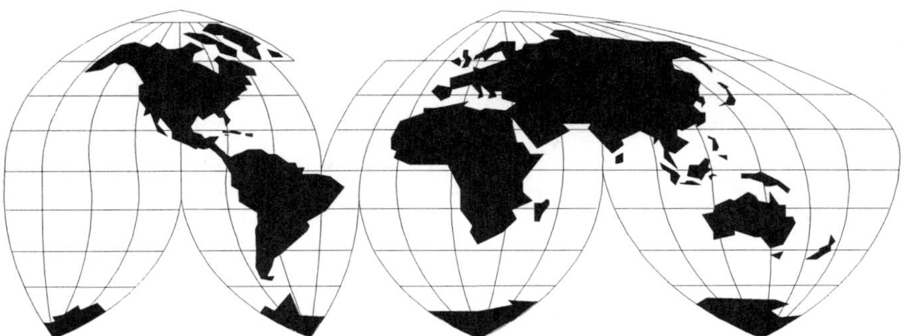

countries outside the U.S. in government, public administration, legal, social welfare, public affairs, and health/medical.

For more details on choosing work abroad. Six books, the first two by Caryl and Ronald Krannich are almost essential for starting your international job search. In ***The Complete Guide to International Jobs & Careers*** (Impact Publications, $13.95, 1992, 320 pages; available from Planning/Communications' catalog at the end of this book), the Krannichs present the most effective approaches for entering the international job market and describe, in excruciating detail, each of the different sectors of the international job market including government. The book is divided into three parts: understanding and action; effective job search skills and strategies; and finding your best work setting, which examines job opportunities with government, international organizations, contractors, consultants, non–profit organizations and volunteer opportunities, associations, foundations, educational organizations, and business and travel industry.

Moving beyond this introduction, the Krannichs get down to the nitty gritty in ***The Almanac of International Jobs & Careers*** (Impact Publications, $19.95, 1994, 348 pages; available from Planning/Communications' catalog at the end of this book), where they provide the names, addresses, and phone numbers of over 1,000 key international employers including a detailed examination of the U.S. government as well as international organizations, colleges and universities, non-profit corporations and foundations, private contractors and consultants, businesses, and education and teaching. The book goes into detail on work permit requirements, job listings, and relocation resources.

Also extremely valuable is the ***Guide to Careers in World Affairs*** by the editors of the Foreign Policy Association (Impact Publications, $14.95, 1993, 422 pages; available from Planning/Communications' catalog beginning on page 321). While most of this book is devoted to describing private and non–profit sector international employers, there's a whole chapter that describes job and internship opportunities overseas with the federal government and many state governments. For each potential government employer you'll learn about the types of positions they fill and how to apply.

Over 130,000 American civilians work for the federal government in posts outside the U.S. It would take a whole book of its own to describe these job opportunities. Fortunately, Will Cantrel and Francine Modderno have written such a book: ***How to Find an Overseas Job with the U.S. Government*** (WorldWise Books, $28.95, 1992, 421 pages; impossible to find in bookstores, it's available from the catalog at the end of this book). Agencies covered include the U.S. Department of State, U.S. Information Agency, U.S. Department of Commerce, U.S. Department of Agriculture, Agency for International Development, CIA, U.S. Department of Defense, National Security Agency, Peace Corps, Radio Free Europe/Radio Liberty, U.S. Customs Service, and more. For each type of position, you'll get a detailed job description, information on career progression, how to qualify, how to apply, testing procedures, forms to submit, and where to send your application. Positions cover the whole gamut, including secretarial, clerks, administrators, and everything else. There's a helpful occupational index that tells you which federal agencies hire which specialties.

If you're interested in internships outside the U.S., you should see Will Cantrell's and Francine Modderno's book, ***International Internships and Volunteer Programs: International Options for Students and Professionals*** (WorldWise Books, $18.95, 233 pages, 1992; impossible to find in bookstores, this book is available from Planning/Communication's catalog at the end of this book). The first chapter focuses on U.S. government and international organizations that offer internships. For each potential employer, the book tells you the types of internships offered, requirements, application procedures, and whom to contact. Internships covered are both U.S. based and assignments abroad.

Work permits

Restrictive work permit, visa, or immigration policies may interfere with your plans to work outside the U.S. of A. Most countries require workers from abroad to acquire a resident visa that includes a work permit. Usually, a foreigner must apply for the visa and work permit before entering the country, although a few nations allow you to apply after being in the country and obtaining a job. But generally, you've got to have an employment contract, visa, and work permit before arriving in the country.

Work permits are temporary and must be periodically renewed. The permit and visa may restrict the number of times you can enter and leave the country. Some countries invalidate the work permit if you leave the country even once. You may also be restricted as to how much local currency you can take out of the country. You must pay local taxes and special resident visa fees.

Your best bet is to always learn about the local restrictions on foreign nationals before seeking a job in a particular country. Foreign embassies and consulates in the U.S. are good sources for information on work permits and visas. These are listed in some of the directories identified at the beginning of this chapter and in *The Almanac of International Jobs & Careers* discussed above. Try to have your employer handle all the paperwork necessary for you to obtain a visa and work permit.

Don't try to enter a country on a tourist visa and then seek work. You'll be able to find only menial, low–paying jobs—certainly no jobs of any sort in government—and probably will not be eligible for any health benefits. So, be sure to arrange for your job, visa if needed, and work permit before you pack up for a foreign abode.

Canada

Although many of the periodicals described in Chapter 2 include government jobs in Canada, there are a number of Canada–based periodicals, directories, and job services that focus on jobs in Canada rather than on the "States." The most helpful of these are identified below. While some of them cover a broad area of government work, many sport a narrower focus. Unfortunately, only a few professional associations in Canada could be identified that include job listings in their periodicals or offer job services. Additional job–search aides are given for the Canadian provinces for which they could be found. Be sure to also check the index of this book under "Canadian jobs" for job sources listed elsewhere in the book that include a fair number of positions in Canada.

In this section, prices are given first in terms of the country from which the publication or service emanates. Major U.S. banks can write checks for you in the currency of nearly every foreign country. For purposes of this chapter, U.S. citizens are the foreigners.

Job ads in print

The Toronto Globe and Mail (444 Front St., West, Toronto, Ontario M5V 2S9; phone: 416/585–5000) See the classifieds section of the Saturday edition. This is probably the single best nationwide source of local and provincial government positions.

Municipal World (Municipal World Ltd., Box 399, St. Thomas, Ontario N5P 3V3; phone: 519/633–0031) monthly, $36.70/annual subscription. Most ten or so job listings under "Staff Wanted" are for Ontario Province.

Bulletin (Canadian Association of Municipal Administrators, 24 Clarence St., Ottawa, Ontario K1N 5P3; phone: 613/563–2590) quarterly, $35/annual nonmember subscription, free/members. Few job ads.

Civic Public Works (Maclean Hunter Limited, 777 Bay St., Toronto, Ontario M5W 1A7; phone: 416/596–5953) six issues/year, $36/annual subscription (Canada), $72/foreign (includes U.S.). Jobs listed under "The Market Place."

The Position Place (Canadian Institute of Public Health Inspectors, P.O. Box 5367, Station F, Ottawa, Ontario K2C 3J1; phone: 613/224–7568) bimonthly, $25/annual subscription, $40/U.S. About 15 to 20 openings for public health inspector and environmental health officers fill this jobs bulletin.

Canadian Journal of Public Health (Canadian Public Health Association, Suite 400, 1565 Carling Ave., Ottawa, Ontario K1Z 8R1; phone: 613/725–3769) bimonthly, $67.65/annual subscription, $82/U.S., $102.50/elsewhere. Jobs listed under "Employment." Five to 15 job ads in a typical issue.

Canadian Medical Association Journal (Canadian Medical Association, 1867 Alta Vista Drive, P.O. Box 8650, Ottawa, ON K1G 3Y6 Canada) biweekly, $82/annual subscription (Canada), $100/annual subscription (U.S.), $107/elsewhere. From 150 to 175 positions for physicians appear under "Classifieds" including some government positions.

Canadian Journal of Surgery (Canadian Medical Association, 1867 Alta Vista Drive, P.O. Box 8650, Ottawa, ON K1G 3Y6 Canada) six issues/year, $58/annual subscription (Canada), $63/U.S. and elsewhere. From 10 to 15 positions for physicians appear under "Classifieds."

Canadian Association of Radiologists Journal (Canadian Medical Association, 1867 Alta Vista Drive, P.O. Box 8650, Ottawa, ON K1G 3Y6 Canada) six issues/year, $110/annual subscription (Canada), $100/U.S. and elsewhere. From 12 to 15 positions for physicians appear under "Classifieds."

Plan Canada (Canadian Institute of Planners, 541 Sussex Drive, 2nd Floor, Ottawa, Ontario K1N 6Z6; phone: 613/233–2105) bimonthly, $58.85/annual individual subscription, $61.60/U.S., $65.91/annual institutional subscription, $77/U.S., free to members. Small number of jobs listed.

Canadian Institute of Planners (541 Sussex Drive, 2nd Floor, Ottawa Ontario K1N 6Z6; phone: 613/233–2105). CIP mails job notices directly to its members. Annual membership dues for Canadians are $110 plus provincial affiliate dues. International membership (yes, that includes the U.S.) dues are $150.

*Also see the **Public Welfare Directory** listed under "Social services" in Chapter 2. It includes Canadian provincial and federal social service agencies.*

Also see the publications listed under "Legal services and court administration" in Chapter 2 for several periodicals that carry a good number of notices for law and law–related jobs outside the United States.

Also see the listings under "Library services" in Chapter 2 for a number of job hotlines that identify vacancies with Canadian libraries.

Directories

Canadian Association of Municipal Administrators Membership Directory (CAMA, 24 Clarence St., Ottawa, Ontario K1N 5P3; phone: 613/563–2590) free/members only, published annually.

Associations Canada 1992 (Gale Research, Inc., 835 Penobscot Bldg., Detroit, MI 48226; phone: 800/877–4253) $175 (U.S.), 1,200 pages, 1992. Describes over 20,000 English and French language professional associations.

Canadian Almanac and Directory 1993 (Gale Research, Inc., 835 Penobscot Bldg., Detroit, MI 48226; phone: 800/877–4253) $145 (U.S.), 1,300 pages, 1992. Includes a list of major municipalities with direct phone and fax numbers of department directors. Also includes a list of registered lobbyists.

Canadian Environmental Directory 1992 (Gale Research, Inc., 835 Penobscot Bldg., Detroit, MI 48226; phone: 800/877–4253) $175, 760 pages, 1992. Includes federal, provincial, and municipal agencies active in environmental affairs.

Alberta provincial jobs

The Bulletin (Personnel Administration, Room 1101, 620 Seventh Ave., SW, Calgary, Alberta T2P 0Y8; phones: 403/297–6427; Alberta Government Employment Office, 4th Floor, 10011 109th St., Edmonton, Alberta T5J 3S8; phone: 403/427–7891) weekly. Copies are available at government offices

Canadian employment centers and post–secondary educational institutions throughout the province. Mail subscriptions are not available. Job descriptions and qualifications for about 15 positions with the provincial government appear in each issue. Includes application instructions.

HOTLINE for entry level clerical positions in Edmonton. For a 24–hour recording of job openings with the provincial government, call 403/427–8792. Recording updated every Monday.

rite Telephone Directory (Alberta Public Affairs Bureau, Second Floor, 44 Capital Blvd., 10044 108th St., Edmonton, Alberta T5J 3S7; phone: 403/427–4352) updated periodically. Contact for price. Complete directory of officials in all provincial departments and agencies. Listed by agency and alphabetically by location.

Nova Scotia provincial jobs

Nova Scotia Civil Service Commission Employment Opportunities (Civil Service Commission, P.O. Box 943, Halifax, Nova Scotia B3J 2V9; phone: 902/424–7660). Contact for information.

Saskatchewan provincial and local jobs

The Public Service Commission advertises provincial jobs in the Business Section of the Saturday editions of the daily ***Saskatoon Star Phoenix*** (204 Fifth Avenue, N., Saskatoon, Saskatchewan S7K 2P1 Canada) and ***The Leader–Post*** (Box 2020, Regina, Saskatchewan S4P 3G4 Canada). Municipal jobs are advertised in local newspapers.

The Government of Saskatchewan Directory (Central Survey and Mapping, 1st Floor, 2045 Broad St., Regina, Saskatchewan S4P 3V7 Canada; phone: 306/787–2799/6911) $7, price may change soon, published annually. Lists heads of provincial departments, divisions, personnel, Crown Corporations, and government agencies.

United Kingdom

The following items will assist the search for a government job in the United Kingdom. Because international currency exchange rates are so unstable, direct contact is advised to learn current prices.

In this section, prices are given first in terms of the country from which the publication or service emanates unless otherwise noted. Major U.S. banks can write checks for you in the currency of nearly every foreign country. For purposes of this chapter, U.S. citizens are the foreigners.

Job ads in print

New Scientist (IPC Magazines, Ltd., Freepost 1061, Hawwards Heath, England RH16 3ZA) weekly, £110/United Kingdom annual subscription, $130 (U.S. dollars)/annual subscription via air mail to the U.S., $170 (Canadian dollars)/annual subscription via air mail to Canada. Over 100 science positions in England are listed throughout, including government jobs. The publisher failed to respond to our request to update information from the 1992 edition of this book. If you reach them, please use the "Reader Feedback Form" near the end of this book to tell us the updated subscription and address information.

Municipal Journal (Municipal Journal, Ltd., 32 Vauxhall Bridge Road, London SW1V 2SS; phone: 071–973–6400) weekly, £59/annual subscription. Four to eight job ads on average per issue.

Planning Week (Haymarket Publishing, 38–42 Hampton Rd., Teddington, Middlesex TW11OJE; phone: 081–943–5046) weekly, £75/annual subscription, free/members. Includes four to ten planning positions in government and the private sector.

Job services

National Employment Register (Royal Town Planning Institute, 26 Portland Place, London, England W1N 4BE; phone: 071–636–9107, extension 30) free/members only. The job seeker completes a resume form which this service sends to potential employers who are then responsible for contacting the job candidate. This service is particularly well–suited to filling temporary positions with short notice.

Vacation Employment Register (Royal Town Planning Institute, 26 Portland Place, London, England W1N 4BE; phone: 071–636–9107, extension 30) free/members only. This service runs from April to August each year to find summer vacation employment for full–time planning students. The job seeker completes a resume form which this service sends to potential employers who are then responsible for contacting the job candidate.

Directories

The Municipal YearBook and Public Services Directory Volumes 1 and 2 (Municipal Journal, Ltd., 32 Vauxhall Bridge Road, London SW1V 2SS; phone: 071–973–6400) £140, published annually. Provides detailed information on county and district councils, and central government agencies, officials, and professional government associations.

Planning Directory (TPS Partnership, 13/15 Stroud Road, Glouscester, GL1 5AA) £19.95. Lists the public agencies in Great Britain concerned with town and country planning including the senior officer contacts of local authorities and information on adopted Structure and Local Plans. Central Government departments and other organizations such as the UDCs, EZs, and National Parks are also listed. The publisher failed to respond to our request to update information from the 1992 edition of this book. If you reach them, please use the "Reader Feedback Form" near the end of this book to tell us the updated subscription and address information.

Annual Directory of Planning Consultants (Royal Town Planning Institute, 26 Portland Place, London, England W1N 4BE; phone: 071–636–9107) free, published each January.

Directory of British Associations (Gale Research, Inc., 835 Penobscot Bldg., Detroit, MI 48226; phone: 800/877–4253) $250 (U.S.), 560 pages, 1993. Use this directory to find associations that include government workers so you can learn if they operate any job services or have advice on finding government jobs. It lists, by subject area, over 6,500 national, local, and regional associations based in England, Wales, Scotland, and Ireland.

Trade Associations and Professional Bodies of the United Kingdom (Gale Research, Inc., 835 Penobscot Bldg., Detroit, MI 48226; phone: 800/877–4253) $145 (U.S.), published in odd–numbered years. Its 575 pages give details on over 4,000 associations and professional bodies in the United Kingdom. You can use this to identify associations of government employees to learn if they operate any job services or have advice for finding government work.

New Zealand

These two items will assist the government job seeker in New Zealand. Since international currency exchange rates are so unstable, direct contact is advised to learn current prices.

In this section, prices are given New Zealand dollars. Major U.S. banks can write checks for you in the currency of nearly every foreign country. For purposes of this chapter, U.S. citizens are the foreigners.

Job service

New Zealand Planning Institute (P.O. Box 6388, Auckland: 156 Parnell Rd., Parnell, Auckland, New Zealand). Distributes notifications of planning (and some parks and recreation) positions. Write to request to be placed on mailing list for notifications of job openings.

Directory

Local Government Yearbook: The Handbook of Local Authority Management (TPL, P.O. Box 9596, Newmarket, Auckland, New Zealand; phone: 011–64–09/529–3000, fax: 529–3001) $30 (includes shipping), 184 pages, published each March. Includes city and district councils, central government departments and agencies, area health boards, regional councils, energy supply authorities, libraries, licensing trusts, and galleries and museums. Each entry includes names, addresses, and phone numbers, and in the case of government agencies, a list of positions, often with the names of the individual who holds the position, plus demographic information. The 50 or so professional institutes and associations it describes are potential sources of career information for anybody considering moving to New Zealand.

General notes on working overseas

Adapted from "Finding a Job Overseas," by J. Roy Saunders, Jr., originally published in Planning, July, 1980; copyright © 1980. Reprinted by permission of the American Planning Association.

The idea of working abroad is attractive to many government professionals. If you are not out to strike it rich, the public sector might be the place to start a foreign job hunt. Many public sector organizations offer internship positions for recent college graduates with limited experience. Their staffs, overall, tend to be relatively young.

Because so many qualified Americans are available, competition among Americans is stiff for positions with international lending institutions. Besides a sound knowledge of relevant skills, a government professional who wants to work for this type of agency should have some knowledge of other regions of the world as well as a foreign language. Good research and writing skills are essential.

Some international development banks view long–range planning as a luxury since most cities in developing countries simply cannot afford it. They are looking for quick solutions to immediate problems; their survival demands this approach. So, specialists are in greater demand than generalists.

Private foundations, volunteer organizations, and nonprofit agencies also provide jobs in foreign countries. The Peace Corps deserves special mention. While it offers a personally rewarding experience, it also serves as a training ground for later overseas employment. Unlike other overseas employers, the Peace Corps does not require previous experience in foreign countries. Hence, working for the Peace Corps gets your foot in the door for other overseas employment later on.

Note also that the Peace Corps offers many white–collar professional positions and is not exclusively for the young. A typical post–Peace Corps career pattern is a training program in administration at the School for International Training and then work with an agency like CARE. There are also permanent training, supervisory, and administrative positions within the Peace Corps itself.

Private consulting firms often have work in foreign countries. Some firms operate on contracts with bilateral or multilateral public–sector aid programs; others contract directly with foreign governments.

In most cases, a graduate degree and a strong record of experience are essential. Frequently, prior overseas work and knowledge of a foreign language are required, although a demonstrated facility for languages and a willingness to undergo intensive language training may suffice.

Be forewarned about the Catch 22 of breaking into the overseas employment market. Prior overseas experience does not, by itself, indicate an ability to adapt to foreign living and working conditions, but lack of it is a serious handicap in marketing yourself. The hurdle can be cleared, but it certainly can be a serious difficulty. To the job seeker, that first overseas job is like obtaining a union card.

Adapting to life without chocolate–covered Oreos, *Star Trek: The Next Generation* (which you'll have to do anyway since the 1993–94 season is its last), and David Letterman may be a real problem for many. Foreign employment can put substantial stress on family relationships, which can affect your performance as an employee. Some families thrive on new conditions and relish new experiences. Others wall themselves up in protective expatriate enclaves and fight boredom by complaining about the lack of conveniences. Being in a strange country, with a completely foreign language and set of cultural behaviors can be disconcerting and intimidating.

Frequently, a spouse is given a visa that prohibits employment. English language schooling is available in only a few cities. Transportation is difficult. Remote rural areas often lack western–style conveniences such as indoor plumbing, reliable electricity, telephone and mail service, but offer frequent exposure to such diseases as malaria, cholera, and hepatitis.

Insecurity is inherent in overseas consulting work. Most firms contract with people for particular projects which may last only a few months. If you relish financial security, overseas work may not be for you. Mobility is clearly an important aspect of overseas work.

General sources of jobs abroad

Advertisements for overseas employment frequently appear in the national publications listed in Chapter 2. Look in the Index of this book under "Foreign jobs" to identify sources in other chapters. Be sure to also check the classified and business sections of the Sunday ***New York Times*** (229 W. 43rd St., New York, NY 10036; phone: 212/556–1234) and the ***Washington Post*** (1150 15th St. NW, Washington, DC 20071; phone: 202/334–6000) where overseas jobs are often advertised. Frequently, though, you will have to contact foreign government agencies directly to learn of job openings as well as to obtain a job application and information on hiring and application procedures.

If you are interested in any social service jobs, see the ***Public Welfare Directory*** listed under "Social services" in Chapter 2. It identifies foreign social service agencies.

Each of the following publications and agencies provides some assistance to persons seeking government jobs outside the U.S. Most of these are available in public libraries. The first few publications or services are for positions with the U.S. government.

Job ads in print

Federal Employment Information Center (U.S. Office of Personnel Management, 300 Ala Moana Blvd., Room 5316, Box 50028, Honolulu, HI 96850) Write or visit for current listings of U.S. federal jobs overseas or listen to their job hotline described below under "Job Services." Theoretically, every FJIC should have listings for all U.S. government jobs. For the nearest FJIC, see the state–by–state listings in Chapter 3.

Peace Corps General Information Kit (U.S. Peace Corps, Public Response Unit, 9th Floor, 1990 K St., NW, Washington, DC 20526; phones: 202/606–3814, 800/424–8580 ext. 2293) free.

Peace Corps Staff Positions. For professional staff positions with the Peace Corps, contact the U.S. Peace Corps, Office of Human Resource Management (Suite 4100, 1990 K St., NW, Washington, DC 20526; phone: 202/606–3400).

Peace Corps Volunteers. To become a Peace Corp overseas volunteer, contact any of the Peace Corps' 15 field offices around the country (a list is available from the Washington office, call 800/424–8580, extension 2293) or the Washington office (1555 Wilson Blvd., Suite 701, Arlington, VA 22209; phones: 703/235–9191; if calling from the District of Columbia, Maryland, Virginia, North Carolina, or West Virginia, dial 800/551–2214).

International Employment Opportunities (Route 2, Box 305, Stanardsville, VA 22973; phone: (804/985–6444) biweekly, $29/two–month subscription, $49/four months, $69/six months, $129/annual subscription, $7.50/single issue. You'll find announcements of around 500 jobs in the U.S. and abroad with the federal government (as well as with non–profits, international institutions, and private companies) in foreign affairs, international trade and finance, international development and assistance, foreign languages, international program administration, international education, and exchange programs.

International Employment Gazette (Global Resources Organization, Ltd., 1525 Wade Hampton Blvd., Greenville, SC 29609; phones: 800/882–9188, 803/235–4444) semiweekly, $95/annual subscription (U.S.), $135/elsewhere; $55/six–month subscription (U.S.), $65/elsewhere; $35/three–month subscription (U.S), $45/elsewhere. This magazine contains over 400 advertisements for private sector, some government, and other jobs overseas.

International Jobs Bulletin (Southern Illinois University, Career Services, Woody Hall, Carbondale, IL 62901; phone: 618/453–2391) biweekly, $25/20 issues, $15/ten issues, $1.50/single issue. Write for free sample issue. The typical issue contains over 75 ads for jobs in government and the private sector for accountants, physicians, computer engineers and developers, economists, engineers, translators, teachers, physical therapists, horticulturists, etc.

International Employment Hotline (P.O. Box 3030, Oakton, VA 22124; phone: 403/620–1972) monthly, $36/annual subscription, $25/six–month subscription. Lists job descriptions (and to whom to apply) by country of assignment. Ads for jobs with foreign governments, U.S. Foreign Service, CIA, and other U.S. government overseas positions that do not require candidate to have pre–existing civil service status. Also included are jobs in the private as well as non–profit sector. Each issue is eight pages with two articles as well as job announcements. From 30 to 100 job descriptions are in a single issue, but usually towards the lower end of that range.

International Affairs Career Bulletin (Jeffries & Associates, 17200 Hughes Rd., Poolesville, MD 20837; phone: 301/972–8034) monthly, $95/annual subscription. Includes job listings for positions outside the U.S. with the federal government. Also includes listings for internships and fellowships.

United Nations Job News (Thomas F. Burola & Associates, Suite 7R, 6477 Telephone Rd., Ventura, CA 93003; phone: 805/647–7256, fax: 805/654–1708) bimonthly, $110/annual subscription, $55/six–month subscription, $39/three–month subscription. This newsletter compiles 50 to 100 job ads from other periodicals as well as current vacancy notices it receives for international positions with governments, the United Nations, and other international organizations.

Career Network (National Council for International Health, Suite 600, 1701 K St., NW, Washington, DC 20006; phone: 202/833–5900) $120/non-members, $60/members ($75 membership rate), annual. Anywhere from 30 to 40 positions in international health care.

The International Educator (P.O. Box 513, Cummaquid, MA 02637; phone: 508/362–1414) quarterly, $25/annual subscription (U.S.), $35/elsewhere. Lists around 100 teaching and administrative positions in privately–owned American and International schools in English–speaking countries.

TESOL Placement Bulletin (Teachers of English to Speakers of Other Languages, Inc., 1600 Cameron St., Suite 300, Alexandria, VA 22314–2751; phone: 703/836–0774) bimonthly, $20/members only (U.S., Mexico, and Canada), $30/elsewhere (air mail); annual dues range from $38 to $69 depending on category; contact TESOL for membership application; free if you subscribe to the *TESOL Placement Service* described below under "Job Services." Each issue features 60 or so ads for positions to teach English in the U.S. and abroad, and for curriculum developers and materials writers. Some of the positions are with government agencies.

OECD Economic Outlook (Organization for Economic Cooperation and Development, 2001 L St., Suite 700, Washington, DC 20036; phone: 202/785–6323) semiannual, $44/annual subscription, $25/single issue. Exclusively positions with the OECD's Paris office. Positions include economists, data processors, econometrics, fiscal policy, nuclear engineering and physics, public administration, education policies, statistics, and urban studies.

Internships and Careers in International Affairs (United Nations Association of the United States of America, 485 Fifth Ave., New York, NY 10017; phone: 212/697–3232) $10/prepaid, published in September of odd–numbered years. Lists overseas and domestic internships with U.S. government agencies, the United Nations, non–profits, and private organizations involved in international affairs. Explains the qualifications employers seek and names resources to find employment in international affairs here and abroad.

ODN Opportunities Catalog (Overseas Development Network, 333 Valencia St., Suite 330, San Francisco, CA 91401; phone: 415/431–4204) $7/students, $10/individuals, $15/institutions, plus $1.50 postage. Most recent revision: 1990. About 60 pages. Identifies employment and research opportunities, and internships for persons wishing to enter the international development field overseas. Presents job descriptions, qualifications, names and addresses of contacts, largely with non–profits and government–related positions.

Opportunities in International Development in New England (Overseas Development Network, 333 Valencia St., Suite 330, San Francisco, CA 91401; phone: 415/431–4204) $5 plus $1.50 postage. Lists domestic and international internship and employment opportunities with New England–based development organizations.

Job services

International Career Databank (Jeffries & Associates, 17200 Hughes Rd., Poolesville, MD 20837; phone: 301/972–8034) updated monthly, $275/first year subscription plus $5/shipping, $125/each subsequent year. This database works only on IBM–compatible computers with Microsoft Windows. It enables you to search its monthly listings for job openings, internships, and fellowships outside the U.S. with the federal government and the United Nations. It also includes positions in the private and non–profit sectors. The database also contains general information on working overseas, how to form your own business, and self–employment.

International Placement Network (Global Resources Organization, Ltd., 1525 Wade Hampton Blvd., Greenville, SC 29609; phone: 800/882–9188) $45/U.S., $50/elsewhere. Request an application form. Two to three weeks after submitting your completed form and check, you get a printout of foreign positions that fit your occupational interests and geographical preferences. Printouts come with four jobs per page. A typical printout runs 15 to 40 pages depending on your preferences and qualifications.

Talent Bank (TransCentury Corporation (1901 N. Fort Meyer Drive, Suite 1017, Arlington, VA 22209; phone: 703/351–5500) free. Obtain their "Professional Skills Registration Form." Submit a completed form with your resume. This service chooses consultants for international development jobs which are usually short–term and abroad situations. Occasionally, someone from another international development corporation will call asking for resumes and TransCentury will send those out. Resumes are kept on file indefinitely. Typical positions include accountants, agriculturalists, administrators, medical personnel, teachers, refugee affairs, engineers, project managers, forestry, and environment.

University Career Services (Southern Illinois University, Woody Hall, Carbondale, IL 62901; phone: 618/453–2391) $35/year, $25/year SIU students. Submit 15 resumes. Resumes are given to appropriate employers who submit vacancy notices. The employer is responsible for contacting the job seeker.

TESOL Placement Service (Teachers of English to Speakers of Other Languages, Inc., 1600 Cameron St., Suite 300, Alexandria, VA 22314–2751; phone: 703/836–0774) $20/annual member only registration fee (U.S., Canada, and Mexico), $30/elsewhere (air mail); annual dues range from $38 to $69 depending on category; contact TESOL for membership application. Complete the "Candidate's Registration Form" which enables you to specify your worldwide geographical preferences and your qualifications. When a match is made, the prospective employer contacts you for an interview. Teaching positions are with government agencies, units of higher education, public schools, international schools in both the public and private sectors.

Federal Employment Information Hotline (U.S. Office of Personnel Management, 300 Ala Moana Blvd., Room 5316, Box 50028, Honolulu, HI 96850) Call 808/541–2784 for a recording of U.S. federal jobs in Hawaii, Guam, Korea, Japan, and neighboring islands. For jobs specifically in Oahu call 808/541–2791.

Federal Job Information Center Hotline (See description beginning on page 230). Call 202/606–2700 with a touch–tone phone. Skip the often outdated introductory announcements by pressing "1" and then, after a few seconds, pressing "1" again. Then dial "110" to get *general* information on how the federal government hires people for overseas employment. This hotline tells you about applying for federal jobs overseas; it does not give out job openings. To receive a packet of material on applying for federal jobs overseas, dial "280". You're probably best off speaking to a real live job information specialist between 8 a.m. and 4 p.m. Eastern Standard Time. To do so, dial the number "000" during or after the introductory message.

Directories

Directory of International Careers (Jeffries & Associates, 17200 Hughes Rd., Poolesville, MD 20837; phone: 301/972–8034) $75 plus $5/shipping, 600 pages, published each March. Includes floppy disks with names, addresses, and phone numbers of organizations engaged in international employment in ASCII format which can be used with virtually any word processor to send mail–merged letters. In addition to describing how to approach virtually any type of international employment, this directory is filled with addresses and phone numbers for many U.S. government agencies that place employees in jobs overseas, the U.S. foreign service (and its examination requirements), international organizations, government agencies and private sector businesses that hire environmental positions worldwide, and information on grants, fellowships, and internships.

World Directory of Diplomatic Representation 1992 (Gale Research, Inc., 835 Penobscot Bldg., Detroit, MI 48226; phone: 800/877–4253) $375, 900 pages, 1992. Learn about 7,000 embassies and other diplomatic bodies throughout the world. Listed by host country, the entry for each embassy and consultate includes full contact information. This is a fine source for identifying embassy officials to whom you might wish to apply for a job.

World Directory of Environmental Organizations (California Institute of Public Affairs, P.O. Box 189040, Sacramento, CA 95818; phone: 916/442–2472) $47 plus 7.75 percent sales tax for California residents, foreign: $63/surface mail, $70/air mail, 1992, published every three years, 230 pages. Includes government agencies, research institutes, and citizens' and professional associations in the U.S. and around the globe. Divided into 50 topics with index, glossary, and bibliography of related directories and databases.

World Guide to Environmental Issues and Organizations (Gale Research, Inc., 835 Penobscot Bldg., Detroit, MI 48226; phone: 800/877–4253) $125, 400 pages, 1991. Includes about 250 international organizations, including national and regional government agencies and regulatory organizations, involved in solving environmental issues.

Directory of American Firms Operating in Foreign Countries (World

Trade Academy Press Inc., Suite 509, 50 East 42nd Street, New York, NY 10017–5480; phone: 212/697–4999) $195/three volumes, last published 1991. Lists some 2,600 American companies with 19,000 subsidiaries and affiliates in 127 foreign countries.

Directory of Foreign Firms Operating in the United States (World Trade Academy Press Inc., Suite 509, 50 East 42nd Street, New York, NY 10017–5480; phone: 212/697–4999) $145, published 1992. Lists more than 1,600 foreign firms and their nearly 2,700 subsidiaries and affiliates in the United States.

Directory of Consulting Firms to USAID that Hire Professionals (Thomas F. Burola & Associates, Suite 7R, 6477 Telephone Rd., Ventura, CA 93003; phone: 805/647–7256, fax: 805/654–1708) $85. We haven't been able to obtain a copy of this directory, but it presumably gives you just what its title suggests it does.

Directory of Consulting Firms to USAID that Hire Construction Professionals (Thomas F. Burola & Associates, Suite 7R, 6477 Telephone Rd., Ventura, CA 93003; phone: 805/647–7256, fax: 805/654–1708) $75. We haven't been able to obtain a copy of this directory, but it supposedly gives you just what its title proffers.

Directory of Only International Recruiters (Thomas F. Burola & Associates, Suite 7R, 6477 Telephone Rd., Ventura, CA 93003; phone: 805/647–7256, fax: 805/654–1708) $65. We haven't been able to obtain a copy of this directory, but it supposedly gives you just what its title proffers. This is a useful source for identifying potential recruiters to work for as well as to find recruiters to help you find a job overseas.

The Directory of European Business (Bowker–Saur; available from Reed Reference Publishing, P.O. Box 31, New Providence, NJ 07974; phone: 800/521–8110) $195 plus 7 percent shipping and handling, 512 pages, 1992. Included in the 4,500 business service companies and organizations are government agencies in 33 countries including former Soviet republics and Turkey. Covers political system and government along with: economic policies, business cultures, banking, legal systems, currency, taxes, trade regulations, incentives, accounting rules, sources of finance, and more.

Private schools with U.S. Department of State Affiliation. Although pretty independent of the U.S. government, these schools receive some assistance from the Department of State. Each school hires its own staff. A directory of these private and international schools is available from the Office of Overseas Schools, Room 245, SA–29, U.S. Department of State, Washington, DC 20522–2902.

U.S. Department of Defense Dependents Schools. Teachers in these U.S. Military Dependents Schools work for the U.S. government. Information on employment with these schools is available in the booklet *Overseas Employment for Educators*, available free from the Office of Dependents Schools, 4040 Fairfax Dr., Arlington, VA 22203; phone: 703/696–3068.

The Peace Corps and More: 114 Ways to Work, Study, and Travel in the Third World (Overseas Development Network, 333 Valencia St., Suite 330, San Francisco, CA 94103; phone: 415/431–4204) 1993, $8.95 plus $1.50 postage. Offers over 100 suggestions of organizations that allow you to gain Third World experience while promoting the ideas of social justice and sustainable development.

Pros & Cons of the Peace Corps (Overseas Development Network, 333 Valencia St., Suite 330, San Francisco, CA 94105; phones: 415/331–4204, 415/731–4205) $10, annual, last published February 1993. Listing of association members and nonprofit organizations by phone number and background of organization.

WorldWide Travel Information Contact Book (Gale Research, Inc., 835 Penobscot Bldg., Detroit, MI 48226–4094; phone: 800/877–4253) $175, 1,075 pages, 1993. Includes descriptions of over 25,000 international travel resources such including national and international tourism boards; national park, railroad, and wildlife departments; hotels, travel, and transportation associations; chambers of commerce; travel bureaus; and more.

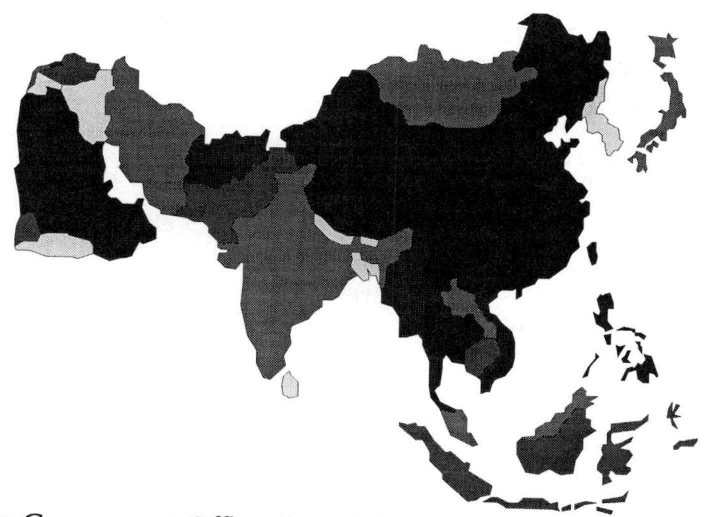

Foreign Government Offices in California (California Institute of Public Affairs, P.O. Box 189040, Sacramento, CA 95818; phone: 916/442–2472) $15 plus $2 shipping prepaid only, California residents add 7.75% sales tax, 1992, 30 pages. Lists full names, addresses, and phone numbers of some 250 foreign consulates, trade missions, official travel bureaus, and special offices of the over 90 countries represented in California.

General information on overseas work

Work, Study, Travel Abroad: The Whole World Handbook (available through Planning/Communications; see catalog at end of book) $13.95, issued in April of even–numbered years, 474 pages. Contains a short section on applying for foreign jobs with the U.S. government. Most of the book examines foreign countries and explains how to find jobs in them.

Looking for Employment in Foreign Countries (World Trade Academy Press, Inc., Suite 509, 50 E. 42nd St., New York, NY 10017; phone: 212/697–4999) $16.50/paperback plus $3.50 postage, 1990, 144 pages. Profiles employment situations in 43 foreign countries, including government jobs. Sample resumes and cover letters.

How to Get the Jobs You Want Overseas by Arthur Liebers (Pilot Books, 103 Cooper St., Babylon, NY 11702; phone: 516/422–2225) $4.95, 1990. Includes chapter on overseas jobs with the government.

Career Opportunities in International Development in Washington D.C. (Overseas Development Network, 333 Valencia St., Suite 330, San Francisco, CA 94103; phones: 415/451–4202, 415/431–9205) $10, annual.

Lists association members and nonprofit organizations by phone number and organizational background.

Evaluating an Overseas Job Opportunity by John Williams (Pilot Books, 103 Cooper St., Babylon, NY 11702; phone: 516/422–2225) $5.95, 1993. This book examines employer/employee contracts, family issues, financial factors, living overseas, taxation, and returning home.

Strategies for Getting an Overseas Job (Pilot Books, 103 Cooper St., Babylon, NY 11702; phone: 516/422–2225) $3.95, 1989. Identifies overseas job–finding associations, specialized employment agencies, and other foreign employment services. Special advice on resumes and interviews for jobs in foreign countries.

Resumes for Employment in the U.S. and Overseas (World Trade Academy Press, Inc., Suite 509, 50 E. 42nd St., New York, NY 10017; phone: 212/697–4999) $16.50/paperback plus $3.50/postage, 1990, 145 pages. Present special techniques to use when applying for foreign jobs including requirements for work permits in foreign countries.

Construction Employment Guide in the National and International Field (World Trade Academy Press, Inc., Suite 509, 50 E. 42nd St., New York, NY 10017; phone: 212/697–4999) $16.50/paperback plus $3.50/postage, 1990, 145 pages. Reviews government employment and how American civilians may apply for construction jobs. Standard Form 171 which is usually required for a government job is reproduced. Lists employment agencies that specialize in construction openings as well as more than 400 foreign contractors in 20 countries.

Directory of U.S. International Health Organizations (National Council for International Health, 1701 K Street, Suite 600, Washington, DC 20006; phone: 202/833–5900) $60/nonmembers, $30/members plus $3 shipping. Last published in 1992. A comprehensive listing of organizations working in the international health field. Information includes organization size, type, budget, area of specialty, contact person, address, and phone number.

Chapter 6

Cover letters and resumes

Once you've found the job openings, you still have to write an effective cover letter and resume to get the job — unless you are applying for one of those government jobs which requires submitting only a specified form. However, most professional positions in local and state government require you to submit a resume and cover letter; many federal positions do as well. And even if you only have to complete a form like the federal government's SF 171, the suggestions given in this chapter will help you better organize your responses.

The next step in the job search process requires you to persuade your potential employer that you are worth interviewing. That's where your cover letter and resume make the difference. Once you get the interview, it's up to you to make a good enough impression to be offered the job at the salary you want.

This chapter suggests ways to write an effective application letter to accompany your resume. Then it explains how to prepare an attractive and effective resume. For the student right of out school, these guidelines remove some of the mystery from applying for jobs. For the seasoned government worker, they offer a sound refresher course and debunk many of the myths built up over the years, particularly concerning the content of a resume.

Finally, Chapter 7 reviews ways to adequately prepare for your job interview and recommends productive interview behaviors that can benefit even the most seasoned professional.

Cover or target letters

Cover letters and resumes go hand–in–hand. A target, or cover letter explains why you are particularly well–suited to the specific job for which you are applying; it highlights the most relevant parts of your resume. The resume outlines your professional experience, education, and other related accomplishments in some detail and can be used for most any job to which you apply.

The purpose of the cover letter and resume is to market you to a potential employer well enough to get him to invite you to a personal interview. Because the person who does the hiring usually scours scores of applications (sometimes hundreds in today's job market), your cover letter should, in a persuasive, professional, polite, and personable manner, point out your specific qualifications for the job so well that the employer will carefully examine the resume your cover letter accompanies. As Dr. Krannich and William Banis put it in *High Impact Resumes and Letters*, "your letter should be the sizzle accompanying the sell." While the resume can, and should, be mass produced, the cover letter for each job application should be individually typed and targeted to the specific job.

Cover letter guidelines

Use your own personal stationery or blank paper and the appropriate business letter format for your cover letter. It is very bad form to use the letterhead of your current employer when applying for a job elsewhere. Use high quality white or light–colored bond paper.

If at all possible, the letter itself should be addressed to a specific person. If the advertisement or job announcement failed to name the person to whom you apply, it's usually worth a phone call to learn her name. Just ask the receptionist or secretary in the department that is doing the hiring. Sometimes you'll run into a brick wall where nobody will tell you to whom to write. One option is to consult one of directories described in chapters two through five of the *Government Job Finder* to identify the proper person. Then call the jurisdiction to confirm that the individual still works there (personnel do change after directories are published). Otherwise, make the

best of it and follow the style shown in the sample cover letter for an assistant village manager position at the end of this chapter.

Cover letter content

An effective cover letter is written with a professional tone and style. It should include the following items:

- ***Clearly identify the job*** you seek in the first paragraph or sentence.
- ***Indicate why you are applying*** for this particular position (if you feel a compulsion to state your career objective, *this* is the place to do it). Try to link your interests to the employer's needs.
- ***Describe your qualifications***. Explain why you are particularly well–suited for this specific position. Carefully review the job description, job announcement or ad to determine what skills are sought and how you meet them. In your cover letter, indicate how you meet these requirements. Refer to the highlights in your enclosed resume and emphasize your qualifications vis–a–vis the employer's needs. In a sense, you should re–write the employer's ad around the qualifications described in it. This approach is low–keyed, but assertive while not *appearing* to be boastful, hyped–up, or aggressive.
- ***Refer the reader to the enclosed resume*** for details of your experience and education.
- ***Request the next step*** in the hiring process: the interview, an answer to this letter, civil service exam, or a request for references (be assertive, but friendly). Make the employer an open–ended offer she can't refuse, as is done in the sample assistant village manager cover letter at the end of this chapter. This approach softens the request for an interview without putting the employer on the spot to say "yes" or "no" right away. A follow–up phone call lets you know whether or not you have any chance at all for the job. If you don't have a chance, you can move on to more promising job opportunities without waiting any longer.

Conversely, the employer may find you sufficiently interesting to invite you to an in–person job interview. Either way, you get results quickly. Alternatively, you can end the letter with the conventional, "Thanks for your time and consideration. I hope to hear from you in the near future." Just be prepared to wait since many government employers contact only job candidates they wish to interview and never even acknowledge receiving the application of someone they don't intend to interview.

- ***Provide any specific information*** the employer asked for in his job announcement or ad. If a job ad requests references, you should give their names, addresses, and phone numbers near the end of your cover letter or on a separate sheet. As the discussion on resumes urges, do not include references in your resume. If an employer requests your salary history, include that on a separate sheet, not in the cover letter.
- ***Thank the reader*** for her time and consideration.

If you are writing a so–called "blind" cover letter to learn of a job opening, you will want to adjust your letter accordingly. This sort of approach letter is designed for you to gain access to an individual who will either provide you with contacts, leads, and information on job opportunities within his agency or elsewhere. Be sure to learn the correct name of the person to whom you write. The various directories of local, state, or federal officials described in the first five chapters of the *Government Job Finder* will get you their names as will a phone call to their agencies.

Cover letter style

Your cover letter tells the employer a lot about your competency. No matter what kind of a job you seek, typographical errors suggest that you would be a careless employee. A poorly written cover letter suggests that you do not communicate effectively.

Instead, cover letters should be direct, powerful, and free of errors. Make like a good newspaper copy editor: eliminate unnecessary words; check grammar, spelling, and punctuation. Avoid using the passive voice ("should have been," "it was done by me" — it's suggestions like this one that make so many of us regret paying so little attention in high school English class.) Avoid pomposity and excessively long sentences. Don't try to be cute or too aggressive like the preceding parenthetical expression did. And do not use slang of any sort!

Keep the letter short and to the point. There's no reason to overwhelm the reader with a lengthy cover letter that repeats a lot of your resume.

Keep your letter positive. Highlight your past accomplishments and skills as well as your future value to the employer.

References

As mentioned earlier, the ad for the job for which you are applying may request references. You should identify your references near the end of your letter or on another sheet of paper. *Do **not** list references in your resume since you may want to give different references for different jobs.* In addition, it is prudent to let your references know to which positions you have submitted an application. If you know a potential employer is likely to contact your references, you would be sagacious to send your references a copy of your cover letter and the ad for the job so they can customize their responses to better fit the job.

Get permission to give each reference's name out as a reference. Use only references you are certain will comment favorably on your performance and ability to work with others. Be prepared to offer additional references if asked.

For each reference, be sure to give the person's correct name and title, and complete address and phone number including area code, so the reference can be contacted easily. If a reference's first name could belong to either sex (Chris, Leslie, Shelley), avoid embarrassment and use ''Mr.'' or ''Ms.'' before the reference's name. A fundamental principle of applying for a job is to make it as easy as possible for the potential employer to follow–up your application because some employers simply toss out an application if they are unable to reach references or obtain other relevant information about the job candidate. It's a buyer's market, and as the applicant, you are the seller.

The resume

Since the individual doing the hiring has to examine so many resumes, you are best off if you keep yours relatively short and sweet. Remember: your resume is both a sales pitch and a summary of your qualifications. Like it or not, those 60–second spots for political candidates nearly always have more impact than a five– or 15–minute commercial, Ross Perot notwithstanding. The same reasoning applies to resumes.

The recent college graduate isn't likely to have any problems keeping his resume down to one–page while the experienced professional may have a tough time limiting her resume to just four pages. The keys to making your resume stand out from the crowd—in addition to its substance—are to organize it well and produce an attractive, professional–looking document.

Resume content

By following several general guidelines you can make the content of your resume more effective.

- ❑ ***Include only pertinent information***. Do not include material unless it gives potential employers a reason to hire you.

  Include only information which will produce a favorable reaction. When in doubt, leave out the questionable information; don't gamble on adverse reactions. A resume simply is not the place to put anything negative about yourself. Remember, you are marketing yourself to the prospective employer as the best person for the job. Would the folks at Dow Chemical, so anxious to build a clean image today, advertise they manufactured the napalm used to burn and kill civilians in Vietnam. Would cigarette advertising voluntarily include warnings on the cause–and–effect relationship of smoking and cancer and other diseases?

- ❑ ***Be scrupulously honest***. For example, an Illinois municipality offered its village manager job to a man who appeared to have built a successful career in city government in California. Unfortunately for him, the local newspaper learned of his phony credentials when interviewing one of his past employers and exposed the rascal. It seems he failed to earn the degree from Purdue University that he claimed to possess and was ten years older than the 55 years he listed on his resume. He withdrew his name from consideration for the job before the city fathers and mothers could withdraw it for him. During the past few years, a number of high–level city employees around the country have lost their jobs, and in most cases their professional careers, for misrepresenting themselves on their resumes or job applications.

  Most resume fraud, however, does not become public knowledge. If a discrepancy is found during a job interview, the job simply is not offered. Fraud discovered after someone has been hired, usually results in the employer quietly asking the employee to resign with the not–so–subtle threat of dismissal hanging over his head. An executive of a credential verification service estimates that 30 percent of all resumes contain some fraudulent educational information. And with an increasing number of employers verifying this information, especially in the public sector, honesty and accuracy are essential for any resume or job application. Think about it, how could you ever trust somebody on the job, if he lied to get the job?

Dave reprinted by permission of Tribune Media Services. Copyright 1991. All rights reserved.

Like it or not, most employers still prefer a reverse chronological resume that presents your experience starting with the most recent job first. Even though many career books will urge you to write a functional resume, letter resume, or achievement resume, I'm going to focus on the reverse chronological resume for the simple reason that it still works the best. It cuts to the chase and gives the reader the sort of information she needs about you. If you want to learn how to write any of these other kinds of resumes, you should consult the many resume preparation books on the market, including those in the catalog at the end of the *Government Job Finder*.

There are a number of items of information that belong in your resume. An effective resume includes the following information in a clear, concise, and well–written style that uses the active voice:

- ***Applicant identification***. Your name should go at the top of the first page. If your resume is typewritten (and as is explained later, you probably should *not* just *type* a resume these days), underline your name. If produced on a word processor, place your name in a typeface and style that make it stand out. See the sample resumes at the end of this chapter. Be sure to include your home address, home telephone number (including area code), and work phone (if you want to be accessible during the day; but be careful, you probably don't want your current employer to learn you're seeking a new job). This is where you can indicate any preference for where you want to be contacted simply by writing: "Contact at [phone number]." If you think it will help you land the job, provide your birth date. For most job seekers, especially those over 40, you might be best off not revealing your age. You may want to produce an "age proof" resume that downplays your age and draws the reader's attention to your abilities and accomplishments. Two excellent books go into great detail on how to prepare an "age proof" resume: *The Over 40 Job Guide* by Kathryn and Ross Petra ($12.00, 352 pages, 1993), and *Resumes for the Over–50 Job Hunter* by Samuel Ray ($12.95, 216 pages, 1993) (for your convenience, both are available from Planning/Communications' catalog at the end of this book).

- ***Education***. Identify your college degree and any advanced degrees earned. Give the names of the schools that awarded your degrees and the years in which they were received. Include the city and state in which the school is located if that is not apparent from its name. Recent graduates may wish to list major scholarships or honors received. Also note relevant post–graduate education. Recent graduates may want to also list major extracurricular activities and organizational offices they held.

  The longer you've worked, educational information becomes less important to potential employers while practical experience becomes more significant. *For the recent graduate*, the education section should precede the section on professional experience, which is described below. The more seasoned professional will want to place the experience section before the education section. Job candidates who lack a college degree should indicate the highest level of education they have had, whether it was a high school degree, or some college or junior college education without receiving a degree.

  If you attended college, but did not graduate, give the name of the school and how many years you attended (Columbia College, 1991–1993).

  If you never attended college, don't leave out the education section. Omitting it will simply call attention to your lack of formal higher education. One option is to include the education heading and under it, print "Self–educated." Be sure to list any work–related courses or training you've had. Add a section to your resume entitled "Other Interests" or "Hobbies" where you can list items that show your intellectual activity or other interests that may help you stand out from the crowd.

- ***Professional experience***. Jobs in your professional field should be described under a heading such as "Professional Experience" or "Work Experience." Jobs should be listed in reverse chronological order with the most recent first. For each position, furnish the following information:

  Job title. Place your job title first. Use some emphasis to make it stand out: bold face, italics, borders, or boxing it if your resume is typeset or prepared on computer, underlined if prepared on a typewriter.

  Employer's name, address, and phone number. If there is even one former employer you do not want a potential employer to call, leave out the phone numbers of all past employers. Do not give the name of your supervisor here; just give the name of the company or government agency.

Period of employment. If you've frequently changed jobs, like every two or three years, you don't want to advertise it. Employers like to hire people they think will stay with the agency for a long time. It costs them time and money to train a new employee. So, if you've changed jobs frequently, place the dates of employment within the heading for each job as illustrated by the first sample resume at the end of this chapter. On the other hand, if you've generally held your jobs for four or more years, place the dates of employment in the left–hand margin as shown in the second sample resume at the end of this chapter.

Responsibilities, duties, and accomplishments. This may be the most important text in your resume. It is your opportunity to tell potential employers what you did in your former positions. Using short phrases rather than full–blown sentences presents this information concisely without appearing to be conceit or braggadocio. Unless jobs outside the profession in which you are seeking work reflect on your ability to perform your professional tasks, this list of jobs should concentrate on the professional positions you have held.

Organization memberships and honors. Identify the professional organizations to which you belong and offices you have held in them, professional certifications or licenses you have earned, and professional honors you have been awarded. Do not use abbre-

Maximizing resumes of recent graduates

For the student or recent graduate with no professional experience, it is appropriate to list nonprofessional jobs and part–time, summer, or volunteer work if you label the section something like "Work Experience." In addition, persons with little or no professional experience can list major school projects that resulted in a written product and projects they may have conducted with a citizen group or a planning commission. See the first sample resume at the end of this chapter for an example of a resume for an entry–level job candidate just graduating from school.

If you have no publications to list, you could label the publications section "Papers" and list selected papers you've written that you feel are pertinent and will generate a positive reaction from a potential employer.

Obviously, if you have no organization memberships, honors, or additional professional activities, leave these sections out of your resume. But again, I strongly recommend that you obtain a student membership in your fields' professional organization. Such membership helps illustrate your dedication to your profession.

viations nor acronyms. A potential employer feels pretty dumb when he doesn't recognize the acronym or abbreviation. One of the bonuses of providing this information is that if the person reading your resume belongs to these organizations, this will establish a common bond that will often enhance your chances of being hired. If you don't belong to the leading professional associations in your field, you may very well lose points. So, join your professional organizations. Many offer lower rates for student members and a few, like the American Planning Association, offer very low rates for unemployed members.

Do not include membership in political organizations — that's not any employer's damned business, especially a government employer! You can include germane civic and community organization memberships, particularly if you are, or have been, an officer or chaired an important committee.

- ***Publications***. Clearly identify major relevant publications such as books, plans, reports, budgets, and magazine or newspaper articles so the reader can find them if she wishes. Experienced workers should not include papers or projects from college or graduate school unless they were published. List publications in chronological order with the most recent last or in reverse chronological order with the most recent first.
- ***Additional professional activities***. List other professional activities such as participation in professional conference programs, guest lectures, commission memberships, courses taught, etc.
- ***References***. As explained earlier, never identify references in your resume. At the end of your resume, insert a line like "References available upon request." If the job announcement requests references, include their names, addresses, and phone numbers in your cover letter.

Correcting fallacies about resumes

Several common misconceptions about resumes continue to survive despite all the advice job counselors and career authors have given. Some items simply do not belong in a resume:

✘ ***Salary***. The purpose of your resume is to get you an interview. Don't undermine it! If your resume reveals your past earnings, it could scare a prospective employer into thinking you are too high–priced even if you are willing to work for less or the same as in your current position. Even worse, listing salaries might unwittingly lead the potential employer to reduce the salary she was prepared to offer. Salary should come up only at the end of the job interview after you've had a chance to demonstrate your value to an employer as well as learn about the worth of the position. You cannot realistically discuss nor negotiate salary if you prematurely mention it in your resume. However, if the ad for a job requests your salary history, submit it on a separate sheet, but not in your resume. Negotiating salary is a skilled art, advice on which can fill a book of its own. For sound advice on negotiating salary, see Ronald and Caryl Krannichs' *Dynamite Salary Negotiations: Know What You're Worth and Get It!* ($13.95, 1994, 164 pages; available from Planning/Communications' catalog at the end of this book).

✘ ***Career Objective***. If you have the insatiable urge to state your career objective in writing, describe it in your cover letter. This approach permits an applicant to express his career objectives in terms applicable to a specific job. *Do not place career objectives in your resume.*

✘ ***Military Experience.*** Your military rank and dates of service should be left out of your resume unless they have a direct bearing on the job you're seeking. If your military achievements and skills make you more employable or you achieved a high rank that looks impressive, include this information. If not, leave it out. On the other hand, many government jobs filled under a civil service point system award extra points for military service. If that's the case, be sure to include your military service on the job application or in your resume.

✘ ***Hobbies***. Most employers could care less about an applicant's hobbies or outside interests. Frankly, a list of hobbies and outside interests only clutters your resume with irrelevant information. There is also the danger that your hobbies may scare off a potential employer. For example, one Texas planner tells me that she is reluctant to hire anyone who lists skiing or other cold–weather sports on a resume because she thinks such people would vacation a lot on weekends and be unavailable for emergency weekend work. Other employers are reluctant to hire persons with a lot of outside interests because they think it will be hard to get them to do extra work at home or work late hours. Conversely, some employers like their employees to have outside interests.

There's an old story still circulating of the job candidate who won his position over equally–qualified applicants because the agency director wanted a fourth for bridge at lunch—admittedly not a sound hiring criterion. But nobody in good conscience can state that every agency director follows sound hiring procedures. *So, list hobbies and outside interests only at your own risk.* If your qualifications are any good, you'll make it to an interview where the interviewer can ask about these activities if they are really important to him.

As noted earlier, there is an exception to this rule. If you do not have a college degree, you can use a list of hobbies in your resume to establish some "intellectual" credentials.

Resume appearance and design

Although most employers are interested in the content of the resume rather than its appearance, design expectations have risen thanks to the accessibility of word processing and laser printers. Today well–designed, typeset–quality resumes are the standard. It used to cost a small fortune to produce a typeset resume. Today, typeset–quality can be produced by anyone with a word processing program and laser printer. Do not use a dot–matrix printer. The results look amateurish even in letter quality mode. Resist the urge to use them.

Nearly everybody can have access to high–quality resume design at a reasonable cost. Many resume preparation services will convert a one– or two–page typewritten resume into a classy–looking document for fee ranging from $30 to $200. Any resume preparation service that charges $100 or more for a two–page resume should include a major editing or rewrite and redesign of your resume for that price. Resume preparation services appear in the yellow pages under "Resume Service."

There are some really good computer programs designed specifically for easily producing beautiful resumes that grab a reader's attention (of course, once the appearance gets their attention, the content has to keep it). One of these programs is *WinWay Resume for Windows* ($69.95, 1993; available at computer software stores and in the catalog at the end of this book).

If you don't have a laser printer or good deskjet or bubblejet printer, there is still an alternative that is time consuming, but costs little. If you can prepare your resume on a personal computer, but don't have a laser printer, take a floppy disk with your resume file on it to one of the many photocopying shops that rents time on desktop computers and laser printers. If you can't find a copy shop that uses the same word processing program you have, find out if its word processing program can import your resume file. You'll probably have to do some reformatting using the shop's word processing program. Be sure to save a copy of the finished resume on your floppy disk so you can bring it back for easy, quick revisions.

Use the copy shop's laser printer to print one copy of your finished resume on high–quality white paper. Then photocopy additional copies on the shop's best photocopying machine. It's a lot less expensive this way since these shops tend to charge around a dollar for each page printed on the laser printer while photocopies usually cost less than 10¢ per page.

To assure an attractive, readable resume, type or print it neatly on 8.5–inch by 11–inch paper that is at least 20–pound weight. Unless you've got some very good reason to use bright colored paper, avoid it. Your best bet for a professional–looking resume is a conservative paper color like white, off–white, ivory, light tan, or light gray. Use a dark ink or toner such as black, navy, or dark brown. The exact format or design is up to you. Whatever you choose, keep it clean and professional looking. Two possible designs are suggested by the sample resumes that follow.

Sample cover letters and resumes

Two resumes and cover letters that illustrate these guidelines follow. The first shows a recent graduate who is seeking an entry–level position in public administration. The second shows an experienced planner applying for a top–level position. This resume is designed to show how to present your experience when you've risen through the ranks at a single municipality so it does not look like you simply changed jobs every 18 months.

Note that the job ad for the entry–level position does not include the name of the personnel officer. However, as noted earlier, you should call the hiring agency or check an applicable directory of officials to learn the personnel officer's name so you can address your letter specifically to her.

Both resumes are variations of the traditional chronological resume. I chose not to include samples of functional resumes or other trendy formats for the simple reason that *employers do not like them!* Despite all the rhetoric about resumes, employers still prefer to receive a chronological resume since it is the most straightforward presentation of a job candidate's credentials.

Entry-level position in public administration

Assistant Village Manager. Starting salary to $25,000 with fringe benefits. Requires B.A.; Masters of Public Administration with 0 to 3 years experience preferred. Responsibilities include risk management, budget analysis and support; staffing village board committees; assistant to Village Manager; requires computer skills. Deadline: May 1. Send resume to Personnel Officer, Village Green Civic Center, Village Green, Illinois 60068.

4321 Ocean Front Drive
Preservation Society, Indiana 46208
April 15, 1994

David Murphy, Personnel Officer
Village of Village Green
Village Green Civic Center
Village Green, Illinois 60068

Dear Mr. Murphy:

Your ad for an Assistant Village Manager in the March issue of PA Times captured my attention for several reasons. As my enclosed resume illustrates, my education, experience, and skills match the duties of the position you describe in your ad. Village Green has a long-standing reputation for sound and effective village management. I am seeking a position with such a municipality, that not only challenges me, but fully uses my talents.

My graduate work was so practice-oriented that it effectively constitutes more than the equivalent of a year's work experience. As a management intern with the City of Valparasio, Indiana, I was charged with developing the city's preliminary fiscal year 1993 budget of $5.2 million. The City Council eventually adopted this budget, written using a custom computer program I designed. In addition, several area governments are using my masters project, Analysis of Municipal Insurance Needs for the Tri-City Area, as the basis for their joint risk management insurance program. In all, my internship and masters project have provided substantial practical experience in the field of city management certainly equivalent to at least a year of work experience.

I would appreciate more information concerning this position as well as an opportunity to meet with you to discuss our mutual interests. I will call you next week concerning any questions we both may have and to arrange an interview if, at that time, we both feel it is appropriate.

Thank you for your time and consideration. I look forward to meeting you.

Sincerely,

Phyllis Quincy-Bach

Phyllis D. Quincy-Bach

Enclosure

Phyllis Denise Quincy–Bach

Current address:
4321 Ocean Front Drive
Preservation Society, Indiana 46208
317/864–8335

Permanent address:
40 del Lords Lane
Lakeview, Connecticut 06566
203/456–7890

Education

Master of Public Administration, University of Indiana, 1993
B. A. (Computer Science), University of Northern South Dakota at Hoople, 1989
Wahall Pembina Scholarship: 1988–90
Dean's list: 1986–87, 1990–92

Work Experience

Research Assistant, School of Public Administration, University of Indiana (1426 SE Hipple, Valhalla, IN 46211; 317/353–3537) Sept. 1991–June 1993

Developed introductory undergraduate course in public administration; developed computer applications in capital improvements programming.

Management Intern, City Manager's Office, City of Valparasio (1234 Bach Blvd., Valparasio, IN 46040; 317–635–8616) June 1992–Sept. 1992

Prepared and analyzed preliminary 1993 Fiscal Year $5.2 million budget; wrote computer municipal budgeting program; staffed city council budget committee

Program Designer, Union City Computations (869 W. High St., Union City, IN 46301; 317–541–9119) part–time during 1989–91 school years

Developed computer programs for financial management, investment counseling, Space Wars

Organization Memberships

International City/County Management Association
American Society for Public Administration

Major Papers and Projects

Analysis of Municipal Insurance Needs for the Tri–City Area, Masters Project, to be published as an article in *Journal of Public Administration,* May 1994

Valparasio Preliminary Budget, FY 1993, Sept. 1992

Computer Applications in Capital Improvements Programming, Jan. 1991

Systems Analysis Approach to Problem–Solving in City Government, Nov., 1991

References available upon request

Administrative-level position in city planning

Director of Town Planning. Responsible professional and administrative work directing technical and professional staff in planning matters related to community development, long-range master planning, and zoning. Requires degree in planning or closely related field, and considerable progressively responsible experience in the planning field. Population 125,000. Salary range $42,312 to $51,836. Send resume to Steven Van Zandt, Director of Planning and Economic Development, Town of Lucky, P.O. Box 3366, Lucky, FL 33479. Application deadline: Sept. 30, 1994

10 E. Shuffle Street
Asbury Park, New Jersey 08002
September 23, 1994

Steven Van Zandt, Director
Planning and Economic Development
Town of Lucky
P.O. Box 3366
Lucky, Florida 33479

Dear Mr. Van Zandt:

Your ad in JobMart for a Director of Planning immediately caught my eye as a potentially challenging and professionally rewarding opportunity. As my enclosed resume indicates, I have been working in community development, comprehensive planning, and zoning administration for so long that I've been accused of being born to plan.

In both my present and former planning director positions, I coordinated the preparation and implementation of grant applications and community development plans. I was chief author of the innovative, award-winning policy-oriented Comprehensive Plan 1978 for Jackson Cage. Throughout my professional planning career, I have administered and written zoning provisions. As indicated by the attached resume, my experience has involved considerably increased responsibilities each step of the way.

I have enclosed a copy of the Comprehensive Plan 1978 for your examination. If you would like copies of any of my other work products or publications, please do not hesitate to ask.

I would like to learn more about this position as well as have an opportunity to meet with you to discuss our mutual interests. I will call you next Friday about any questions we may both have and to arrange an interview if, at that time, we both feel it is appropriate.

Thank you for your time and consideration. I look forward to meeting you.

Sincerely,
Bruce Fallsteen
Bruce Fallsteen
Enclosures

Bruce Fallsteen

10 E. Shuffle Street
Asbury Park, New Jersey 08002

Work Phone: 201/807-5309
Home Phone: 201/501-5743

Professional Experience

July 1982+ Planning Director. City of Asbury Park, New Jersey (10 Freeze Out Ave., Asbury Park, NJ 08010; 201/807-5000)

Supervise four-person planning department; manage $2.3 million community development program; write and administer land-use regulations, prepare performance zoning ordinance; provide staff assistance to Plan Commission and City Council; initiate revision of comprehensive plan and economic development studies.

Village of Jackson Cage (Village Hall, Jackson Cage, MO 65106; 314/328-8800)

Nov. 1973–June 1982 **Community Development Director.** Aug. 1978–June 1982

Supervised 10-person staff including divisions of planning and community relations; managed $6.8 million community development and planning program; developed village's first capital improvements program; developed and implemented integration maintenance plan.

Chief Planner. March 1975–Aug. 1978

Researched and wrote innovative *Comprehensive Plan 1978*; wrote zoning ordinance revisions; reviewed zoning applications and proposed ordinances; supervised assistant planners; provided staff assistance to Plan Commission and Village Board.

Grants Coordinator. Nov. 1973–Feb. 1975

Identified funding opportunities; prepared grant applications and budgets for grants totaling over $1.2 billion.

June 1972–Sept. 1972 **Summer Intern.** Crosby, Stills, and Nash, Planning Consultants (4 Way St., Youngstown, Ohio 42351; 216/353-5555)

Designed and completed cohort survival population projections; input-output economic analysis, *Economic Base Study of Akron, Ohio*; and origin-destination transportation studies.

Education

Master of Urban Planning, Ohio State University, June 1973
Teaching Assistant, Sept. 1971–June 1973
B.A. (sociology), University of Chicago, June 1970
Dean's List, 1968–1970
Chairperson, Lascivious Arts Festival, 1970

Organization Memberships and Honors

American Planning Association, 1978+
National Award of Merit for *Comprehensive Plan 1978*
Ohio Chapter Vice–President, 1974–76
Metropolitan Housing and Planning Council (New Jersey):
Chairperson, Planning Committee, 1985+
Regional Finalist, White House Fellowship, 1980

Publications

"Roll of the Dice," in *Reckoning Day*, September 13, 1993, pp. 3–7.

"The River: You Can Look (But You Better Not Touch)—Time to Clean Up Our Waterways Before It's Too Late," in *Sunday New York Times*, Sept. 23, 1991, pp. 1,205–1,210.

"The Promised Land: Performance Zoning," in *New Jersey Planning*, May 1989, pp. 24–27.

"Backstreets: The Ties That Bind – An Analysis of Urban Subculture," in *Journal of Sociology*, Oct. 1986, pp. 521–548.

Meeting Across the River: Integration Maintenance Plans, Planning Advisory Service Report No. 1,749, American Society of Planning Officials, July 1981, 31 pp.

Comprehensive Plan 1978, Jackson Cage, Missouri, 1978, 621 pp.

"Economic Base Studies: Whole Lotta Nothin' Goin' On?" in Planning magazine, April 1975, pp. 17–19.

Additional Professional Activities

Speaker at American Planning Association National Conference:
"Diamonds on My Windshield: Economic Base Studies" (1979)
"New Coat of Paint: Revising the Comprehensive Plan" (1983)

Guest Lecturer: Rutgers University (New Brunswick), "Performance Zoning: A Lifetime of Trouble?" (1982)

Guest Lecturer: Rutgers University (Jersey City), "All That Heaven Will Allow: Preparing Comprehensive Policy Plans" (1983)

Guest Lecturer: Columbia University (New York), "Thundercrack: A Survival Course for Progressive Planners in Higher Education" (1985)

References available on request

Chapter 7

Performing your best at your job interview

In government's always competitive job market, a job ad often draws over 100 responses from qualified individuals. An invitation to appear for a personal interview indicates that your cover letter and resume interested a potential employer enough to make you a serious candidate. Now it's up to you to do your best at the job interview to clinch the job. Many highly–qualified, well–educated, and intelligent candidates lose jobs because they are uncomfortable in interview situations or fail to prepare adequately. Others just have a natural aptitude for personal interviews. Any well–qualified job candidate can improve his performance in job interviews by following the guidelines suggested here and in books on job interviewing such as the Krannichs' *Interview for Success* and *Dynamite Answers to Interview Questions* (both are available from Planning/Communications' catalog that begins on page 321).

Most professional positions in local and state government do not require a written examination. Instead there is an oral quasi–examination, more accurately called an interview. Some governments put you before a panel of two to four people who evaluate you. Others simply have the agency director interview you. Many small planning departments will have the most serious candidates meet with all the other professionals in the department to assure compatibility. When asked to come in for an interview, try to find out who will conduct the interview and who else will be present for it so you can be adequately prepared.

Preparing for the interview

A personal interview not only gives your potential employer an opportunity to evaluate you in depth and you a chance to sell yourself, but it also gives you the opportunity to learn much more about the employer and the agency for which she works. You want to be able to carry on a fairly intelligent conversation with your interviewer, even if he can't. By knowing what is expected of you and by undertaking a few simple preparations, you can make a more favorable impression and minimize any nervousness you may feel.

Interviewers will size you up in terms of the following qualities:

Initial impression
Past job performance
Analytic ability
Appearance and manner
Motivation
Ability to communicate
Initiative
Self–confidence
Fitness for the job
Maturity
Judgment and prudence
Leadership
Potential to grow in the job
Overall personality
Mental alertness
Compatibility with other staff

Some agencies maintain a standard rating form and use a point system to rate candidates. Prior to your interview, try to obtain a copy of the rating form from the Personnel Department so you can tell exactly on what qualities you will be evaluated.

This checklist of fundamental provisions you should take before you meet your interviewer will enhance your performance at the interview:

- ❑ ***Be certain of the exact time and place of the interview***. If you are uncertain how to get there, just ask. Write this information down and don't lose it. If you are really unsure of where the interview location is, check it out on a local street map or take a test drive there.
- ❑ ***Arrive at the interview on time or a little early***. There is no excuse for tardiness for a job interview. Innumerable jobs have been lost because the candidate was late for the interview. If it becomes obvious you are

going to be more than five minutes late, call and let the interviewer's secretary know. Try to arrive about five to ten minutes early.

- ❑ ***Know how to pronounce the interviewer's name correctly***. If in doubt, call in advance and ask her secretary how to pronounce it.

- ❑ ***Learn all you can about your potential employer and the position for which you are applying***. If you are applying for work in local government, you want to appear reasonably knowledgeable about the community. Drive around the town or county. Read its most recent comprehensive plan. Ask planners at the regional planning agency, if any, about it. Find out its population and socioeconomic composition. Find out what the employing agency actually does, how it functions, whom it serves, its size and budget, current issues facing the agency, with whom you will work, who your boss will be, and why there is a vacancy. Some of the directories described in chapters two through five provide details about government jurisdictions. There are also other directories available at libraries that provide census and economic information. Often a Chamber of Commerce publication will give the white–washed version of the jurisdiction.

  At least try to learn enough so your potential employer won't feel you are too much of an outsider to learn the vagaries of the community in which you would be working. And by all means try to learn all you can about the person or persons who will interview you and make the hiring decision so you can present the side of you which will appeal most to their sensibilities. It is possible that other people you know in your field may be able to tell you something about your interviewer and the jurisdiction for which she works.

Reprinted by permission from *Which Niche?* by Jack Shingleton, illustrated by Phil Frank. Copyright 1989. All rights reserved.

- ❑ ***Make a list of points you want to be sure to make in the interview*** at appropriate moments. You may have forgotten to make these points or facts about yourself at your last interview. Placing them firmly in mind before this interview should assure that you don't forget them. Even though you should never pull out such a list at the interview, the simple act of writing the list will help you remember the points.

Many interviewers will query you about your career goals. Whether or not you were once a Boy Scout, be prepared! Think this one out carefully because nearly every interviewer will ask it.

- ❑ ***Plan to bring several items to the interview***. Believe it or not, some interviewers lose a candidate's resume and cover letter just before the interview. So be sure to bring a clean copy of each with you. If requested, bring letters of reference and work samples. Students may substitute high–quality term papers or projects. Bring these materials in a folder or brief case and offer them only if asked or if they graphically illustrate a point. The interviewer's desk is probably cluttered enough as is.

Questions interviewers ask

Be prepared to answer the questions that inevitably surface in any job interview. According to the authors of *Interview for Success,* most of the following questions about your education, work experience, career goals, and yourself tend to surface in virtually every job interview. Obviously the first set of questions that deal with education are more likely to be asked of recent graduates than seasoned professionals who have work experience that will interest an interviewer more than the job candidate's education.

- Tell me about your educational background.
- Why did you choose to attend that particular college?
- What was your major, and why?
- Did you do the best you could in school? If not, why not?
- What subject did you enjoy most? ...the least? Why?
- If you started all over, what would you change about your schooling?

Recent graduates are likely to also be asked:

  - What was your grade point average? (The more work experience you have, the less likely this inquiry will be made.)
  - Why were your grades so high?... so low?
  - What leadership positions did you hold?
  - How did you finance your education?

- What were your major accomplishments in each of your former jobs?
- Why did you leave your last position? (If asked why you left any of your former jobs, give reasons that do not suggest you are a job shopper or jumper. Acceptable reasons include a return to school, better pay, new

challenges, more responsibility, and a desire for a different type of work.)

- What job activities do you enjoy the most? ...the least?
- What did you like about your boss? ...dislike?
- Which of your jobs did you enjoy the most? Why? ... the least? Why?
- Have you ever been fired? Why?
- Why do you want to work for us?
- Why do you think you are qualified for this position?
- Why are you looking to change jobs?
- Why do you want to make a career change?

Reprinted by permission from *Which Niche?* by Jack Shingleton, illustrated by Phil Frank. Copyright 1989. All rights reserved.

- Why should we want to hire you?
- How can you help us?
- What would you ideally like to do?
- What is the lowest pay you would take? (Always deflect this question. See the discussion on salaries later in this chapter.)
- How much do you think you are worth in this job?
- What do you want to be doing five years from now? (Working here with a promotion or two, obviously.)
- How much do you want to be making five years from now?
- What are your short–range and long–term career goals?
- If you could choose any job and agency, where would you work?
- What other types of jobs are you considering? ... other agencies?
- When would you be able to start?
- How do you feel about relocating, travel, and spending weekends or evenings in the office?
- What attracted you to our department?
- Tell me about yourself.

- What are your major strengths?
- What are your major weaknesses? (Never say you don't have any. Turn a negative into a positive with a response like, "I tend to get too wrapped up in my work and don't pay enough attention to my family. My wife keeps suggesting that I should join Workaholics Anonymous.")
- What causes you to lose your temper?
- What do you do in your spare time? What are your hobbies?
- What types of books and magazines do you read?
- What role does your family play in your career?
- How well do you work under pressure? ... in meeting deadlines?
- Tell me about your management philosophy?
- How much initiative do you take?
- What types of people do you prefer working for and with?
- How _____ (creative, tactful, analytical, etc.) are you?
- If you could change your life, what would you do differently?
- Who are your references? (Have a printed list with names, addresses, and phone numbers to submit.)
- How would you respond to a question from a reporter about the plan commission's decision to override your recommendation? (An increasing number of public sector employers are concerned with employees speaking to the press, especially on controversial issues. In developing your answer, keep in mind that when working for government, the public is your actual client and the public is represented by the people it has elected. Once the public's elected representatives, or appointed representatives such as plan commissioners, make a decision, you should not publicly criticize it, or criticize it on the record to a reporter, even if it runs counter to every sound principle of government.)

Stupid interviewer tricks: Illegal questions

Unfortunately, despite great strides over the past decade, illegal questions continue to arise in job interviews, even for government work. Sexism, in particular, is alive and well in the hearts and souls of many job interviewers. While equal employment legislation makes it illegal to ask certain questions during an interview, some interviewers ask them anyway. If you are prepared, you can fend them off effectively and still score points with the interviewer. If the questions don't get asked, you've got no problem.

Illegal or inappropriate questions include:

- What's your marital status?
- How old are you?
- Do you go to church regularly?
- What is your religion?
- Do you have many debts?
- Do you own or rent your home?
- What social and political organizations do you belong to? (Be wary if the interviewer steers the conversation to politics. Do not be evasive, but temper your remarks to camouflage radical or extremist views. Keep in mind that in some communities a traditionally "liberal" or "conservative" viewpoint is considered "radical." Your political views are really nobody's business but your own. But don't say that in an interview unless you have found an inoffensive way to express that view. Try to say no more than is necessary to answer the interviewer's broad line of questioning about politics.)
- What does your spouse think about your career?
- Are you living with anyone?
- Are you practicing birth control?
- Were you ever arrested?
- How much insurance do you carry?
- How much do you weigh?
- How tall are you?

If an interviewer spouts one of these illegal questions, don't go nuclear and shout "That question is illegal and I ain't gonna answer it!" You may be right, but this sort of reaction does not display any tact on your part, which may be what the interviewer is testing, albeit tactlessly. The authors of *Interview for Success* suggest that one type of response is humor. For example, if asked whether you are on the pill, you could respond, "Sure, I take three pills every day, vitamins A, B, and C, and thanks to them I haven't missed a day of work in three years."

Asked if you are divorced, you might respond, "I'd be happy to answer that question if you could perhaps first explain what bearing being divorced, or not being divorced, could have on someone's ability to perform this job?"

As you might have guessed by now, women are the main targets of these unjustifiable questions. But if you're prepared, you can neutralize them. For example, some interviewers will ask women with small children, "What if the kids get sick?" A sound response to this question goes along the lines of, "I have arranged for contingency plans. I have a sitter on standby, or my husband can take a vacation day." This sort of answer indicates to your potential employer that you are a professional (not that you should have to prove your professionalism just because you're a woman, but some guys never learn) and that you've anticipated the problem.

Married women with a family often get asked, "How can you travel?" An interviewer is trying to find out if the employer will have to pay for the woman's other responsibilities. An employer may be wondering if she is going to put her family before her job. A good answer would be, "Of course I can travel if it's important to my job. I'd be happy to do it. All I have to do is make the proper arrangements."

If an interviewer learns that your spouse works for a company that likes to move its employees around every three or four years, she may ask, "What are your plans if your spouse receives orders to relocate?" That's actually a reasonable question to ask of either partner in a two–income household, but for some mysterious reason it is rarely asked of the husband. A good answer is to say, "My husband and I have discussed this issue and we've decided that my work is important for my professional growth and we will work out a plan when and if that time comes." Once a woman has been working for an employer for a while and has proven her worth, she'll have a better bargaining position if spousal relocation threatens her job.

Try to decide how you will handle illegal or inappropriate questions before you go to an interview. With a little preparation, you can turn a negative into a positive when such questions are posed. Your answers to such questions could turn out to be your strongest and most effective of the whole interview.

Questions you should ask

Prepare questions before you go to the interview so you won't be speechless when the interviewer asks if you have any questions. You may want to inquire about the nature of the job and agency, opportunities to exercise initiative and innovation, chances for advancement, and status of the agency. Save questions about fringe benefits (health insurance, leave time, conference attendance) and salary for the end of the interview. As explained later in this chapter, you are best off if the interviewer raises these issues.

The authors of *Interview for Success* and *Dynamite Answers to Interview Questions* and other job counselors suggest that you be prepared to ask the following questions if the interviewer has not already answered them:

- What duties and responsibilities does this position involve?
- Where does this position fit into the organization?
- Is this a new position?
- What would be the ideal person for this position? Skills required? Background? Personality? Working style?
- With whom would I work in this job?
- Can you tell me something about these people? Their strengths, weaknesses, performance expectations?
- What am I expected to accomplish during the first year?
- How will I be evaluated?
- On what performance criteria are promotions and raises based? How does this system operate?
- Is this a smoke–free office?
- What is the normal salary range for such a position? (Assuming it was not given in the advertisement for the job.)
- Based on your experience, what types of problems would someone new in this position be likely to encounter?
- How long have you been with this agency? What are your plans for the future?
- What is particularly unique about working for this department?
- What does this agency's future look like?

Personal appearance

Face facts: clothes and grooming certainly do not reflect on how decent or qualified a person is for a job, or how well someone will perform on the job. Just look at Albert Einstein, or, at the other extreme, look at the immaculately–groomed gentlemen who brought us Watergate and the Iran–Contra scandal. But since the interviewer does not know you personally, your appearance can greatly influence his first impression of you—and first impressions count a lot at job interviews. You will make a much better first impression if you are well–dressed and well–groomed.

Don't take chances with appearance even if it means showing up better dressed than your interviewer. Research shows that women elicit a more favorable reaction from interviewers of either sex when they wear a dress or suit, the classic pump, nylons, and a bra. Jeans, shorts, culottes, mini–skirts, sandals, dirty or unkempt hair, an exposed middle, and flamboyant clothing evoke unfavorable responses. Carry a purse or attache case, but not both. It's hard not to look clumsy trying to handle both. If you opt for the attache case, keep a slim purse with your essentials inside the brief case.

Men should wear a suit and tie. Men make a less favorable impression with a sport coat, and a downright unfavorable one dressed in a sweater or boots. Shorts, T–shirts, jeans, or sandals turn off any interviewer. Some researchers insist that a maroon tie inspires confidence. Others have found that the shorter, more neatly trimmed the hair and beard, if any, the better the impression.

Whether or not your native culture places as much of a premium on cleanliness as the American culture does, be sure to bathe and use deodorant. On the job you'll be expected to be clean and relatively odor–free. Smelling like a locker room at your job interview *will* cost you the job no matter how ideal you are for it.

Whatever your everyday mode of dress and grooming may be, you've got to play the game when job hunting. Sometimes you will be better groomed and clothed than your interviewer, but remember that it is *your* appearance that counts. After you've landed the job, you can resume your normal work appearance if it varies from that suggested here and does not violate office standards.

For more information on how to dress for an interview, see any of the dozens of books on interviewing. They'll essentially tell you what you've just read—but they'll take 25 pages to do it.

Conduct at the interview

Common sense, above all else, should govern your conduct at a job interview. For example, be punctual and, if possible, arrive a few minutes early in case there are forms to complete. It only hurts your chances to keep an interviewer waiting.

Similarly, common sense dictates that you do your best to make a good first impression since, fair or not, first impressions are quite strong and seldom change later in the interview. A friendly, warm smile helps establish a good first impression that carries throughout the entire interview. A natural smile in the right places throughout an interview can mean the difference between a favorable and unfavorable response.

Greet your interviewer(s) with a solid handshake—something a bit softer than the Hulkster might use—no matter what your sex is. Most interviewers do not like a "wet fish" handshake.

Throughout the interview try to maintain good poise and posture; sit straight and avoid leaning on your elbow or talking with your hands over your mouth. Look alert and interested throughout the interview. Demonstrate that you can be a wide awake, intelligent listener as well as a talker. If nervous, hide it. Keep your hands still in your lap; do not tap your pencil or twist your purse strap. Don't fiddle with objects on the interviewer's desk or with your fingernails. Smoking without being invited to smoke, or chewing gum, usually makes a bad impression since both are generally regarded as signs of nervousness.

Naturally, you will want to establish and maintain good eye contact. Nearly every interviewer is conscious of eye contact. It is the surest way to convince her you know what you are talking about.

Above all else, be yourself and be honest. Since most interviews follow a simple question and answer format, your ability to respond quickly and intelligently is vital. Confused and contradictory answers can cost you the job. The best preventative against contradictory answers, logically enough, is the truth. An honest answer that seems a little unflattering to you is far better than a white lie that may tangle you up in a later question. If you don't know the answer to a specific question, the best thing you can say is, "I don't know." The odds are good that the interviewer knows the "right" answer to the question and a bad guess can only put you in a poor light.

Following several additional interview pointers will enhance your chances of winning the job:

- Follow the interviewer's lead. Most interviewers like to think they're in control. Some like to do most of the talking and judge you by your reactions. Because others believe it is your job to sell yourself, they hardly speak at all. When selling yourself, be modest about your accomplishments while getting your points across. Nobody likes, or hires, a braggart. Don't exaggerate your skills or accomplishments since most interviewers pick up on truth stretching very quickly and it hurts your chances for the job. Try to offer concrete examples of your better points.
- Do not take notes during the interview. A job candidate taking notes annoys and distracts some interviewers. If you must write something down, make a remark like, "That's very interesting. Do you mind if I jot it down?" Your best bet is to write notes of anything you have to remember *after* the interview.
- Job interviewers like candidates who are enthusiastic and responsive. Let the interviewer know you are genuinely interested in the job. If you are passive or withdrawn during the interview, the assumption can

easily be made that you will behave that way on the job. Some government employers want passive employees, though. So you will have to use your judgment to determine if your interviewer wants a passive or active employee.

- Don't let the interviewer know how much you need the job. Candidates who call attention to their dire straits are less likely to be hired. Hiring decisions are *not* based on your need, but on your ability, experience, and attitude.
- Be as complete and concise as possible in your answers since many interviewers can give only 30 minutes to an interview. Devote more time to answering important questions that require in–depth responses than to less significant questions. Some hiring executives recommend never spending more than one minute to answer a question. If the interviewer wants you to elaborate, he'll ask you to.

SYLVIA **by Nicole Hollander**

- Never denigrate a former employer. If you had difficulties, suggest that some of the blame must have rested on you.
- Since the last few minutes of an interview can sometimes change things, do not be discouraged if you have the impression that the interview has been going poorly and you have already been rejected in the interviewer's mind. Some interviewers who are interested in hiring you will try to discourage you just to test your reactions. Remaining confident, professional, and determined will help make a good impression.
- Salary is a sticky question. It is a subject best broached toward the end of an interview, preferably by the interviewer. Some experts believe an applicant should ask for as much money as possible to establish a bargaining position, and that employers offer as little as possible for the same reason. Ads for most government jobs, however, specify a salary range.

Other job announcements simply say, "Salary open." The interviewer may choose not to tell you the amount she has to offer and may ask how much you want. Indicate that you are more interested in a job where you can prove yourself than in a specific salary. If interested, the interviewer will usually suggest a figure. Try to find out in advance the standard or average salary for the type of position for which you are applying. Use the salary surveys described in chapters two through five of the *Government Job Finder* to learn what you should be offered. You should also know the salary level beneath which your needs will not permit you to go. For a whole book of detailed advice, see *Dynamite Salary Negotiations: Know What You're Worth and Get It!* ($13.95, 1994, 164 pages; available from Planning/Communications' catalog that begins on page 321).

- When given the opportunity, be prepared to offer a closing statement. This will be your last chance to mention any beneficial points you hadn't had an opportunity to raise during the interview and to summarize the positive contribution you can make to the department.
- A job offer is rarely made at the interview. The interviewer may want to discuss your application with other staff and may have other candidates to interview. Occasionally a job is offered on the spot. If absolutely certain you want it, you can accept it. However, it is best to ask for 48 hours to decide. But do not give the impression you are playing off one potential employer against another. You can easily lose both job offers that way.
- Since most interviews last a half hour or less, an inconspicuous glance at your watch will suggest when your time is almost up. Be alert for signs from the interviewer that the session is almost over, such as when he looks at his watch. Do not keep talking when the session appears to be ending. Summarize your thoughts and stop. Be sure to thank the interviewer for her time and consideration. Tell her to be sure to get in touch with you if she should have any further questions.
- With government jobs, there is usually no need to write a thank you letter after the interview. Of course, right after the interview you will note any further contact your interviewer may have suggested. Follow his instructions exactly, and don't muddy the waters by immediately sending unsolicited correspondence. If the interviewer indicated you will hear from him by a certain date and you don't, write a brief note to remind him about a week after you were supposed to hear from him. Express appreciation for the time and consideration he gave you, and briefly note your continuing interest in the position. You have little to lose at this point by refreshing his memory, and you might get a favorable response.

After the interview

If you don't get a flat rejection or the polite "know" that comes in the type of letter that says, "We will keep your letter and resume in our files and let you *know* if anything ...." keep in touch if there is anything in the letter that suggests you should. Unless you make a nuisance of yourself, you will be able to stay in the foreground if another vacancy opens.

It's a close call as to whether you should listen to the many job counselors who encourage writing a follow–up letter right after the interview. Most conscientious government employees barely have the time to conduct interviews, much less read your post–interview letter. You will have to use your impressions of the interviewer to determine whether a follow–up letter will help or hurt you.

Following these suggestions should, at least in theory, reduce the hiring decision to one based on qualifications. Not all employers make their hiring decisions the same way. So during your interview be sensitive to hints of what criteria the interviewer will use to make his hiring decision and temper your remarks to comply with them. In general, though, following the suggestions made in this chapter will place you in good stead with a potential employer.

When accepting a job offer, you should send the employer an acceptance letter in which you clarify your assumptions about the job (salary, training, fringe benefits, responsibilities) and indicate your expected date of employment. Once an employer has decided to hire you, you can usually get the starting date changed to one more accommodating to your needs as long as you are reasonable. Make certain that all conditions of employment are clear and that you have a job offer in writing before you give notice to your current employer that you are leaving. Try to give one month notice if possible, but certainly no less than two weeks.

When rejecting a job offer, you should send a letter as soon as possible that declines the offer and expresses your appreciation for the employer's interest and confidence in you.

When you get rejected, but would still like to work for that employer at some future time, it doesn't hurt to send a pleasant letter thanking the interviewer for her time and diplomatically expressing your disappointment at not being selected. Emphasize your interest in her department and ask to be kept in mind for future vacancies. Suggest that you believe that you would work well together and that you will continue to follow the progress of her agency. Such a letter shows your continuing interest, your recognition that you were not the only qualified applicant, and your genuine desire to work for that agency. Such a thoughtfully–written, brief two or three paragraph letter can leave a very favorable impression and enhance your chances should you ever apply there again or encounter the interviewer in another employment related situation.

The *Government Job Finder* helps you find the type of job you want in the location you desire, and gives you a leg up on other job seekers who are unaware of the procedures and sources the book suggests. Armed with the information in this book, you can identify government job openings that most job seekers will never know existed because they limit their job search to positions discovered by word of mouth, personal contacts, and only one or two publications that carry advertisements for jobs in government.

To find sources of job vacancies with non–profits, see the ***Non–Profits' Job Finder.*** To locate sources of job openings in the private sector, see the ***Professional's Private Sector Job Finder***. Both are available in bookstores or through the catalog at the end of this book. If you'd rather use a computer to find job sources, you might prefer ***The Ultimate Job Finder*** software. It combines all three job finder books into a search and retrieval program as described in the catalog at the end of this book. These books and software provide the same service for job seekers in the non–profit and private sectors that the *Government Job Finder* delivers for people seeking positions in local, state, or the federal government. For some occupations a few of the sources contained the *Government Job Finde*r also appear in one or both of these other books because these sources include job vacancies in two or more employment sectors. However, each book contains *many more* job sources for each occupation that do not appear in either of the other two job finder books.

Successful job hunting takes time and requires effort. But by using your common sense and the job–finding techniques explained in the *Government Job Finder,* it's quicker and easier — and your chances of finding satisfactory employment will soar even in the confusing and difficult economic times that face us all in the last decade of the twentieth century.

We'd like to make the next edition of this book even more helpful. You, our readers, are a source of valuable information and suggestions. So, please use this form to:

- Tell us if a job source you've tried to reach has moved or changed its phone number. If you can't reach it, chances are pretty good that we can track it down and send you the updated information.
- Tell us about any changed addresses or phone numbers you've found;
- Tell us how we can make the next edition of the *Government Job Finder* more helpful; and
- Let us know of any useful job sources that somehow escaped our attention or started operating after this book was written.

If you run out of space, just attach another sheet. Please send your comments to me at Planning/Communications, 7215 Oak Avenue, River Forest, IL 60305–1935. **Feel free to photocopy this page. Send any corrections or changes to me as soon as possible so I can include them in the free *Update Sheet* described on page 313.**

Thanks for your help and support.

Daniel Lauber

Daniel Lauber

____

____

____

____

____

____

____

____

Purely optional: Clearly print your name, address, and evening phone number in case we need to reach you for more information. **If you're asking us to find a job source you can't track down, please include a self–addressed stamped envelope and your home phone number.**

About the author

Author Daniel Lauber, AICP, worked for local and state government in Illinois as an award–winning city planner from 1972 through 1980. Since then he has served local and state governments as a planning consultant and, since 1985, as a land–use attorney.

He is the author of the ***Professional's Private Sector Job Finder, Professional's Job Finder, Non–Profits' Job Finder, Government Job Finder, The Compleat Guide to Finding Jobs in Government, The Compleat Guide to Jobs in Planning and Public Administration,*** and ***The Compleat Guide to Jobs in Planning.***

Mr. Lauber has explained how to unlock the secrets of the hidden job market on CNBC–TV's "Steals and Deals" program and on over 80 radio stations throughout the country. He is also a frequent speaker at job fairs and job clubs.

At age 35 he was elected the youngest president of the 26,000–member American Planning Association while attending the Northwestern University School of Law full–time. He is currently President of the American Institute of Certified Planners.

He received his Masters of Urban and Regional Planning in 1972 from the University of Illinois–Urbana, and B.A. in sociology from the University of Chicago in 1970. He received his J.D. from Northwestern University School of Law in 1985.

He has written dozens of articles on planning and law issues in professional publications and the popular press. He created the "Condo Watch" column for the *Chicago Sun–Times* in 1979. When not immersing himself in the preparation of this book, he spends most of his time as an attorney on zoning cases and on behalf of people with disabilities who wish to live in group homes. He also does computer consulting for a number of non–profits and edits and designs numerous monographs and newsletters.

Unfortunately, he can't follow his own advice. His resume runs a lot longer than the four page maximum recommended in Chapter 6. No wonder he's a consultant.

Free Update Sheet

As the *Government Job Finder* explains in Chapter 1, job sources are much like people and other businesses: they move, they change their phone number, they go out of business, and new ones spring up. It took a full year to identify and verify all the job sources described in this book. By the time you read this, a small percentage of them will have moved or gone out of business. A few new ones will have begun.

We're constantly monitoring these changes. We count on our readers to use the ***Reader Feedback Form*** on page 311 to let us know of changes in job sources they discover. We confirm any changes they report and add them to our ongoing ***Update Sheet.***

Books bought directly from Planning/Communications after June 1, 1994 will include the latest *Update Sheet,* assuming one is warranted. If you bought your book in a bookstore, you can still obtain a free *Update Sheet* by following these simple instructions.

Anytime **after June 1, 1994,** you can obtain your free *Update Sheet* by cutting out the coupon on the other side of this page and sending it with a self–addressed, stamped (one ounce postage) #10 business envelope to:

PLANNING/COMMUNICATIONS
7215 Oak Avenue
River Forest, IL 60305–1935

This offer ends when the next edition
of the *Government Job Finder* is published.

Coupon for free Update Sheet is on the next page

Updated information on the job sources in the 1994 edition of the

Government Job Finder

To get your **free *Update Sheet,*** cut out this wanted poster and send it along with a stamped (one ounce postage), self–addressed, #10 business envelope to:

PLANNING/ COMMUNICATIONS
Government Job Finder Update Sheet
7215 Oak Ave
River Forest, IL 60305

You *must* send this original page with your stamped, self–addressed envelope. No photocopies! If you don't follow these instructions, you'll get no response.

Do not send before June 1, 1994.

The first *Update Sheet* won't even be prepared until then. This offer expires when the next edition of the *Government Job Finder* is published.

Photocopies not accepted *Only this original coupon will be accepted*

Index

As explained in Chapter 1 (that's the chapter that told you how to get the most out of this book — which, naturally, nobody wants to read), this Index supplements the Table of Contents to help you find job sources for specialties that are not located in the chapter where you would intuitively expect them to be. When you locate a job source by using this Index, be sure to also look at the other entries in the same section of the chapter. There will often be additional job sources for that specialty there. So if you find a periodical for a particular specialty, be sure to also look at the entries under ''Job services,'' ''Directories,'' and ''Salary surveys.''

A

F

I

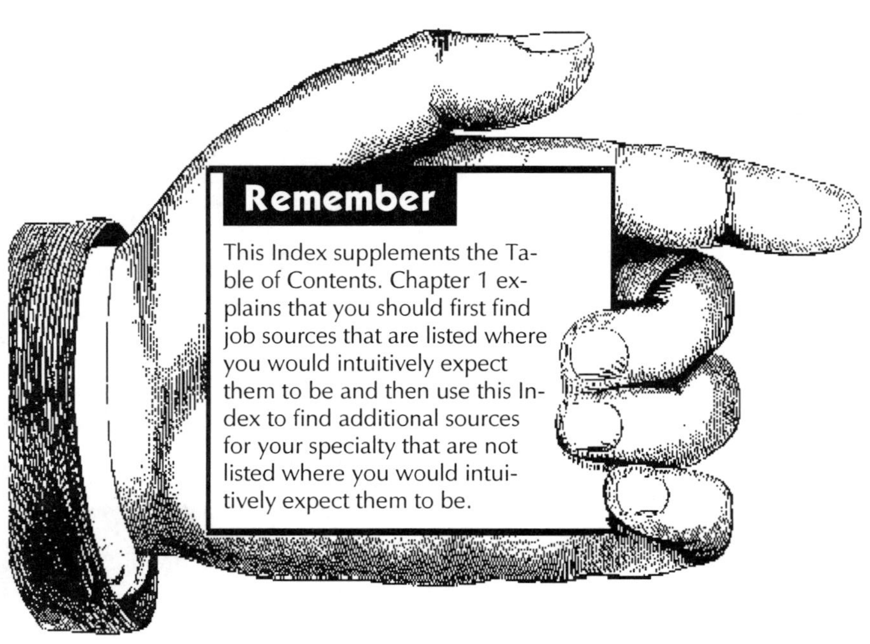
Remember
This Index supplements the Table of Contents. Chapter 1 explains that you should first find job sources that are listed where you would intuitively expect them to be and then use this Index to find additional sources for your specialty that are not listed where you would intuitively expect them to be.

Catalog of job-quest books and software

PLANNING/COMMUNICATIONS

7215 Oak Avenue
River Forest, Illinois 60305

Phone orders: 800/829-5220

This is the catalog at the end of the book. For your convenience, Planning/Communications carries this selection of the most effective career books and software to help you get a new job. Several of them are noted in the text of the *Government Job Finder*. Some are available in bookstores. But since most are hard to find in bookstores, we've made them available to you by phone and mail order.

Ordering information appears on the last four pages of this catalog.

America's Job Finders for the 1990s

Face it! You simply can't get a new job *unless you know where they are advertised*. Daniel Lauber's three job finder books and computer software get you to over 5,000 of the best places where job vacancies are advertised for all three sectors of the economy.

Government Job Finder, 2nd edition

$16.95, paperback; ISBN 0--9622019--7--9, 1994, 352 pages
$32.95, hard cover: ISBN: 1--884587--01--1

This is the book you're reading now. It will get you to all the best places where job openings in local, state, and the federal government are advertised or announced. For reviews, see the back cover and very first page.

Non–Profits' Job Finder, 3rd edition

$16.95, paperback: ISBN 0--9622019--8--7, 1994, 336 pages
$32.95, hard cover: ISBN: 1--884587--02--X

"**Recommended...invaluable, affordable...in–depth.**"
— *Library Journal*

"**Gold mine of job sources**...**superb** help to those seeking careers in the non–profit field."—*CEO Job Opportunities Update*

By the author of the *Government Job Finder,* this book offers over 1,201 sources of job vacancies in education and hundreds of other non–profit careers. New for 1994 are a chapter on sources of vacancies for jobs outside the U.S., 20 percent more job sources, and a free *Update Sheet.*

"I honestly can't believe that a quality, **comprehensive,** and entertaining resource like this doesn't cost more. I would feel comfortable recommending it on that basis alone, but here are three other reasons: (1) Even if you're not looking for a job yourself...the **foundation and grant directories listed here are alone worth the price.**... (2) The book **points you to the resources where the real job openings are listed**.... (3) It **makes the job search fun**....This is a very helpful reference; well worth the money." —*Job Training and Placement Report*

"**Excellent** resource for employment opportunities in the non–profit sector."
— *Community Jobs*

"**Great resource**. The book gave me lots of ideas and **pushed me to be more productive**. Great cartoons and non–sexist language." — *Sheryl Kaplan, user of the Non–Profits' Job Finder*

Professional's Private Sector Job Finder

$18.95, paperback: ISBN 0--9622019--6--0, 1994, 536 pages
$36.95, hard cover: ISBN: 1--884587--00--3

"A real powerhouse for job leads."
—Joyce Lain Kennedy, America's premier careers writer

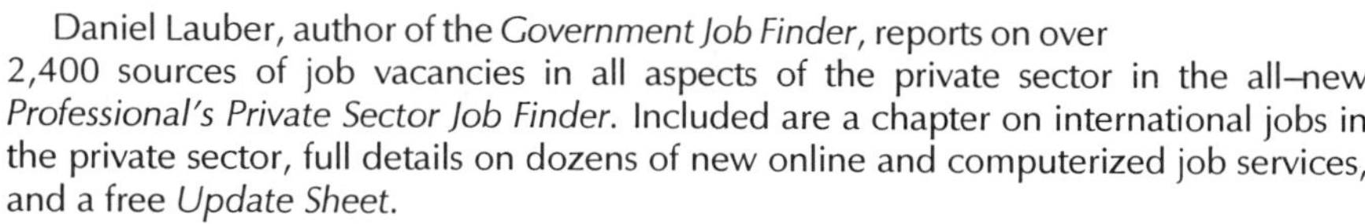

Daniel Lauber, author of the *Government Job Finder*, reports on over 2,400 sources of job vacancies in all aspects of the private sector in the all–new *Professional's Private Sector Job Finder.* Included are a chapter on international jobs in the private sector, full details on dozens of new online and computerized job services, and a free *Update Sheet.*

"**Excellent** reference book for job–hunters and career consultants....Unlike the scam artists who promise to provide job seekers lists of job openings in Alaska, **the author delivers** useful information on **where jobs are** advertised outside of the daily papers." — *Bloomsbury Review*

"**Exceptional**... In over 500 pages, the *Professional's Job Finder* describes more than 2,100 sources of job leads in the private sector.... This resource book is **one of the most complete sources** of information that I have seen." — *Search Bulletin: Career Opportunities for Executives and Professionals*

"This book is a little **different.** Leaving most of the motivational babble to other writers, [Lauber] steps beyond the local classifieds to mine specialized resources that can **give job seekers just the edge they need.... exceptional**..." — *Booklist*

"Handy, affordable reference for professionals seeking employment in the private sector. An **outstanding** compendium of resources....Additional sources include directories of businesses, corporations and agencies, and salary surveys....**clear, comprehensive....unique** and **valuable**..." — *Library Journal*

The Ultimate Job Finder

$49.95, comes on 3.5--inch floppies, 5.25--inch floppies available on request, requires Windows and 3 megabytes free space on hard disk drive. Write for availability of MS--DOS, Macintosh, and CD--ROM versions which should become available during 1994.

Harness the power of your personal computer to find sources of job vacancies in all sectors of the economy. *The Ultimate Job Finder* combines all 5,000+ job sources in Daniel Lauber's three job finder books described above into one search and retrieval software program. Just type in your occupation, and hit ENTER. You instantly get details on your screen for every job source for that occupation — from all three job finder books. Scroll through them and print out the ones you want to pursue.

"*The Ultimate Job Finder* **sparkles**...reasonably priced...**pleasant to use...remarkable**. Most other electronic employment databases cost thousands of dollars." — *Joyce Lain Kennedy,* author of the *Electronic Job Search Revolution*

Feel free to photocopy this catalog
To order: 800/829-5220 weekdays, 9 a.m. to 6 p.m. CST

Government Careers

The Complete Guide to Public Employment

$19.95, 1994, 528 pages

Called the "**seminal book** on public employment," this new edition is described on page 248 of the *Government Job Finder*. It's the **perfect companion to the *Government Job Finder*.** It helps you decide what career to pursue in government or with non–profits by providing in–depth information about career opportunities in all branches of government and the rest of the public employment sector.

The Complete Guide to Public Employment also helps people who wish to leave government learn how to shift their government skills into the related worlds of non–profits, trade and professional associations, contracting and consulting, foundations and research organizations, political support groups, and international institutions. By Caryl and Ronald Krannich.

The Almanac of American Government Jobs and Careers

$14.95, 1991, 392 pages

This book provides details on the educational and experience requirements for jobs with hundreds of federal agencies, Congress, and the judiciary. See page 249 for full details on this still very helpful volume. By Ronald and Caryl Krannich

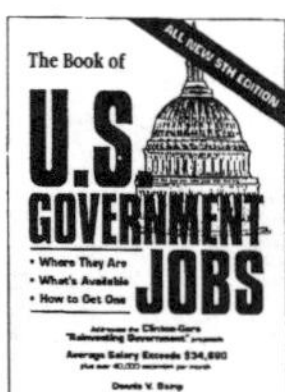

The Book of U.S. Government Jobs

$15.95, 1994, 224 pages

Called a "**treasure trove of information**" this book gives a thorough overview of the federal hiring process, civil service exams, veterans and military dependents hiring, overseas employment, the postal service, opportunities for people with disabilities, and federal occupation lists. Author Dennis Damp identifies the types of jobs available and how to get them. Includes sample civil service exam questions and answers. See page 249 of the *Government Job Finder* for full details.

"Extremely helpful and informative. I particularly like this author's gumption in ***dispelling the mystery*** of the generic federal employment application. The author lavishly supplies agency contact information."—*Small Press*.

Be sure to also see the *Government Job Finder* described on page 322 and *The Ultimate Job Finder* on page 323.

How to Get a Federal Job

$14.95, 1989, 186 pages

Still ticking after all these years, David Waelde's best–selling federal job preparation book remains the single best source for **unraveling the federal job application maze.** See page 251 for details. "**Essential reading** for anyone planning to work for the feds."

Find a Federal Job Fast!

$9.95, 1992, 196 pages

"A must for anyone committed to a federal job."
— *Midwest Review of Books*

"A great place to start the federal job search. A well–focused book that covers, but does not overkill, the subject of how to get a federal job."—*Career Opportunities News*. For full details, see page 251251 of the *Government Job Finder*. By Ronald and Caryl Krannich.

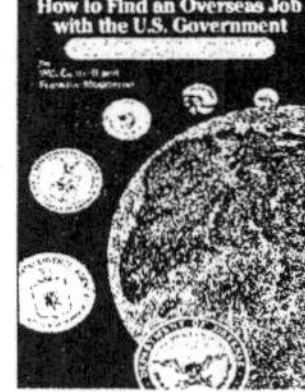

How to Find an Overseas Job with the U.S. Government

$28.95, 1992, 421 pages

This is *the* book for anybody seeking a federal government job outside the U.S. See page 258 for full details on this extremely valuable guide. By Will Cantrell and Francine Modderno.

The Right SF 171 Writer

$19.95, 1994, 209 pages

Two years in the writing, this book helps you prepare a much more effective SF 171 form for federal employment. For full details, see page 252 of the *Government Job Finder*. By Dr. Russ Smith.

The 171 Reference Book

$18.95, 1991, 162 pages

"Best of the best" according to the National Education and Information Advisory Committee. See page 252 of the *Government Job Finder* for full details.

Quick & Easy for the SF 171

$49.95 (single--user, call for prices on multiple--user versions), specify disk size and DOS or Windows version; hard disk drive required

Save time and money — write your SF 171 form on your personal computer. See page 252 for details on this software which lets you prepare different versions of your SF 171 form for federal employment. By Data Tech.

FOCIS: Federal Occupational and Career Information System

$49.95, available only on high density 3.5--inch floppies; requires hard drive

See page 234 of the *Government Job Finder* for a description of this software that enables you to search the federal government's database of current federal job openings and print the results on your computer at home. Also learn about over 600 federal occupations. You can take any of 300 federal employment exams at home on your computer. Requires a modem and MS–DOS, IBM–compatible personal computer.

Complete Guide to U.S. Civil Service Jobs

$10.00, 1991, 224 pages

Learn job benefits, conditions, qualifications, nature of work, and where jobs can be found for federal clerical, computing, accounting, law enforcement, health care, and postal positions. 10th edition. By Hy Hammer. ARCO .

Federal Jobs in Law Enforcement

$16.00, 1992, 288 pages

Learn about career opportunities with the FBI, CIA, EPA, INTERPOL, National Security Agency, and over 100 other law enforcement agencies. Includes complete job descriptions, qualification and application information, and famous cases for each agency. By John Warner., Jr. ARCO.

Civil Service Handbook

$10.00, 1992, 288 pages, new edition available May 1, 1994

Gives step–by–step procedures for applying for civil service positions with federal, state, and local governments, and the postal service. Explains eligibility requirements. Includes sample civil service exams with answers and detailed descriptions of the most popular jobs. Introduces you to the new exam for entry level administrative and technical positions filled through the federal Administrative Careers with America (ACWA) program. By Hy Hammer. ARCO.

The Book of U.S. Postal Exams

$13.95, 1990, 272 pages

Although a 70 percent score is considered passing, the Postal Service routinely selects only from among those applicants who score over 90 percent. A veteran of the Postal Service, author Veltisezar Bautista reveals his ***secrets for test taking and preparation that actually do boost scores!*** Get full details on page 250 of the *Government Job Finder*.

The Book of $16,000–$60,000 Post Office Jobs

$14.95, 1989, 186 pages

Learn where they are, what they pay, and how to get them with Veltisezar Bautista's unique guide to nearly 300 specific Postal Service job classifications. For a full description see page 250 of the *Government Job Finder*..

Order form is at the end of this catalog

To order: 800/829-5220 weekdays, 9 a.m. to 6 p.m. CST

Federal Government Job Winning Kits

#1: Books only

Every book you need (in addition to the *Government Job Finder)* to understand the federal system and get hired:

Almanac of American Government Jobs and Careers, Book of U.S. Government Jobs, Find a Federal Job Fast, The Right SF 171 Writer, and the Complete Guide to U.S. Civil Service Jobs.

Save 10 percent off the $70.80 retail price. Pay just:

$63.72 plus $7.75/shipping

#2: Books and Software

Every book plus the computer software to give you the edge for a federal job:

Almanac of American Government Jobs and Careers, Book of U.S. Government Jobs, How to Get a Federal Job, The Right SF 171 Writer, the Complete Guide to U.S. Civil Service Jobs,
plus software:
Quick & Easy for the SF 171
FOCIS software

Save 15 percent off the $175.70 retail price. Pay only:

$149.35 plus $9.75/shipping

The New Complete Guide to Environmental Careers

$15.95, 1993, 362 pages

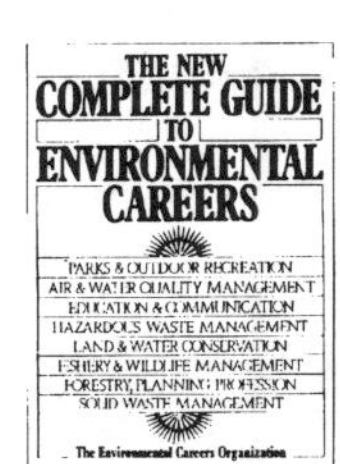

Get full details on environmental career opportunities with government, non–profits, and private companies in planning, parks and recreation, environmental protection, natural resource management, forestry, communications, air and water quality management, hazardous waste management, solid waste management, education, and communication. Also covers schooling required, internships, and career strategies. By the Environmental Careers Organization.

Job Opps 94: Job Opportunities in the Environment

$16.95, 1993, 224 pages

Learn about government agencies, non–profits, and private sector businesses likely to hire environmental personnel this year. See page 56 for a description of this very popular book. From Peterson's Guides.

Careers With Non-Profits

Jobs and Careers with Nonprofit Organizations

$15.95, 1994, 232 pages

Two years in the making, this book is the perfect companion to the *Non–Profits' Job Finder* described on page 322. It identifies major non–profit organizations that offer attractive job alternatives, job search strategies, and contact information on hundreds of domestic and international non–profit organizations. By Ronald and Caryl Krannich.

Good Works: A Guide to Careers in Social Change

$18.00, 428 pages, 1994 edition available June 1, 1994

Get details on over 800 non–profit employers: address, phone, director's name, purpose, budget, staff positions, number of staff openings each year, number of part–time employees, internships, where vacancies are advertised, and how to apply. Forward by Ralph Nader.

Great Careers: The Fourth of July Guide to Careers, Internships, and Volunteer Opportunities in the Non–Profit Sector

$34.95, 1990, 605 pages

Great Careers is *the* book that helps you decide which non–profit career to pursue. It's ***filled with details*** on types of jobs and many job sources for social services, legal aid, the arts, women's issues, consumer advocacy, environment, social change, research, philanthropy, foundations, disabilities, hunger and homelessness, animal rights, labor unions, children and youth, international non–profit organizations, and many other non–profit fields.

Jobs in Washington, DC: 1001 Great Opportunities for College Graduates

$11.95, 1992, 217 pages

"Must reading for anybody seeking a job in Washington, D.C." See page 156 for full details on this popular book.

Also be sure to see the *Non–Profits' Job Finder* described on page 322 and *The Ultimate Job Finder* on page 323.

International Careers

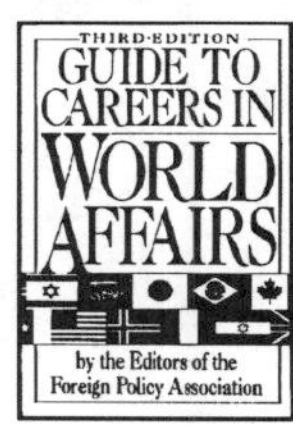

Guide to Careers in World Affairs, 3rd Edition

$14.95, 1993, 422 pages

Brand new by the editors of the Foreign Policy Association, this book tells you all you need to know about getting hired in many different aspects of world affairs. See page 257 of the *Government Job Finder* for full details.

The Almanac of International Jobs & Careers

$19.95, 1994, 348 pages

An all–new edition of the Krannichs' popular compilation of names, addresses, and phone numbers for over 1,000 key employers in the international arena. For the full scoop on this book, see page 257. It's the perfect companion to *The Complete Guide to International Jobs & Careers* described next. By Caryl and Ronald Krannich.

Complete Guide to International Jobs & Careers

$13.95, ISBN 0–942710–69–X, 1992, 306 pages

This book presents the **best approaches for entering the international job market** and describes, in detail, each of the different sectors of the international job market so you can decide which is best for you. See page 257 for full information about it.

International Internships and Volunteer Programs

$18.95, 1992, 233 pages

See page 258 for full details on this guide to internships and volunteer opportunities outside the U.S. By Will Cantrell and Francine Modderno.

Work, Study, Travel Abroad: The Whole World Handbook, 1994–1995

$13.95, 1994, 512 pages, available beginning April 1994

See page 275 for details on this popular book. By the Council on International Educational Exchange.

Finding the Right Job or Career

Change Your Job, Change Your Life:

High Impact Strategies for Finding Great Jobs in the 90s

$14.95, 1994, 363 pages

Loaded with **practical "how to" advice,** this highly acclaimed book covers everything from understanding today's job market and identifying the best jobs for the 1990s to assessing skills and mastering every step in the job search and hiring processes. It also includes unique chapters on relocating to another community, starting a business, and identifying useful job search resources. It's the **perfect guide** for anyone making a job or career change.

What Color is Your Parachute?

$14.95, 1994, 464 pages

The latest annual edition of Richard Bolles' perennial best–seller, this book really does help you find your calling in life with the most effective career and job–hunting methods.

Career Design Software

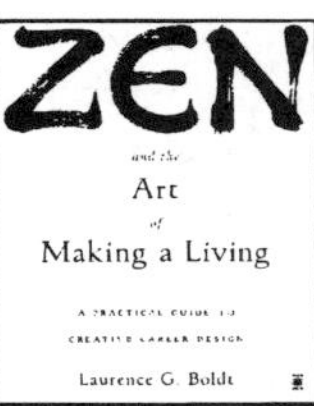

$99.95, specify 3.5–inch or 5.25–inch floppy disks, requires hard drive, MS–DOS single–user version; write for multi–user version price

Based on the career development system that is the foundation of *What Color is Your Parachute?*, this software lets you proceed at your own pace to uncover your interests and hidden skills, set goals, determine your career direction, negotiate, prepare for interviews, and much more. Includes automated resume preparation software.

ZEN
and the
Art
of
Making a Living
A PRACTICAL GUIDE TO CREATIVE CAREER DESIGN
Laurence G. Boldt

Zen and the Art of Making a Living

A Practical Guide to Creative Career Design

$16.00, 1993, 597 pages

The most innovative career guide since What Color is Your Parachute?, Laurence Boldt's book is not just about getting a job. The first part helps you discover what you really want to do and identify what work will be deeply satisfying. The second part furnishes practical action steps to finding or creating that work (including the very insightful advice to get the *Government Job Finder*). Over 120 worksheets help you find your way to a more rewarding job and career.

An Easier Way to Change Jobs

$14.95, 1993, 336 pages

Geared for people seeking professional, managerial, or executive jobs, this book is used by Princeton/Masters International as part of its executive outplacement and career management program. It completely redefines the steps you should follow to find a new job in the very different economic climate of the 1990s.

Also be sure to see the *Government Job Finder, Non–Profits' Job Finder, Professional's Private Sector Job Finder,* and *The Ultimate Job Finder* described on pages 322 and 323.

The Over 40 Job Guide

$12.00, 1993, 352 pages

So, you're part of the new bifocal generation and you're feeling the heat of Generation X on your heals. Kathryn and Ross Petras' book shows you how to beat age discrimination in every step of the job search process. Learn how to switch careers, deal with a lay–off, find self–employment, assess benefits and pensions (suddenly very important to us), write age–proof resumes, and handle age–related interview questions.

The New Relocating Spouse's Guide to Employment

Options & Strategies in the U.S. and Abroad

$14.95, 1993, 332 pages

The only way your spouse can stay employed is to accept that dread transfer to another city. This new fourth edition of Frances Bastress' classic helps you through one of the more traumatic times of your life and enables you to get your relocated career back on track. It's filled with practical advice, sources, and case studies that help you adjust your career and job when a move is in the air.

Graduating to the 9 to 5 World

$11.95, ISBN 0–942710–50–9, 1991, 195 pages

Here's one of the essential career books for everyone in Generation X (okay, so it's a lousy label, but the media insists we use it). This book will give you a real "Welcome to the Working Week" (with apologies to Elvis Costello). It's **every student's passport to the realities of the working week**. Prevent "9 to 5 shock" by learning what it's like to work in a structured world where office politics, productivity, and performance take center stage. Learn how to use your first 90 days on the job to greatly enhance your career.

Discover the Best Jobs for You!

$11.95, 1993, 185 pages

One of the best guides to finding the right job, this book helps you do first things first: assess skills, identify interests, and formulate a powerful job objective *before* writing resumes and letters, responding to job vacancy announcements, and interviewing for jobs. Complete with tests and self–assessment exercises, this book addresses **the fundamentals central to developing an effective job search.**

Internships 1994

$29.95, ISBN 1–56079–149–7, 1993, 424 pages

See page 30 of the *Government Job Finder* for a full description of Peterson's Guides' best seller.

Summer Jobs 1994

$15.95, 1993, 320 pages

Get the full scoop on this guide to mostly outdoor summer jobs on page 30 of the *Government Job Finder*. From Peterson's Guides.

Feel free to photocopy this catalog

To order: 800/829-5220 weekdays, 9 a.m. to 6 p.m. CST

Winning Resumes and Cover Letters

High Impact Resumes and Letters:

How to Communicate Your Qualifications to Employers

$12.95, 1992, 254 pages

Twice excerpted in the *National Business Employment Weekly*, this highly praised best–seller has set a new standard for resume and letter writing guides. This easy–to–follow guide walks you through the steps necessary to write resumes and cover letters with impact, ones that stand out from the crowd. It helps you "think out" your resume rather than simply imitate some model. ***"If we had money for only one book on resumes, this would be our choice."*** —*Career Opportunities News*

The Resume Catalog: 200 Damn Good Examples

$15.95, 1988, 316 pages

Yana Parker's classic set of resume examples includes tips on strengthening resume content. Other resume books come and go, but this remains one of the very best.

Dynamite Resumes: 101 Great Examples

$9.95, 1992, 137 pages

From the authors of *High Impact Resumes and Cover Letters* comes a unique guide for transforming ordinary resumes into outstanding ones that grab the attention of potential employers. Numerous examples illustrate the key principles for revising a resume. Included are two unique chapters that critically review resume guides and computer software used specifically for resume writing. By Ronald and Caryl Krannich.

WinWay Resumes for Windows

$69.95, 1993, requires Windows, includes both size floppy disks

All these resume books in this catalog give good advice, but you need WinWay Resumes for Windows to easily create the resume with the "look that gets hired." Choose from among 35 resume styles. Use any of the many fonts on your computer. Update your resume with ease. Includes a spell checker and action verb glossary.

Resumes for Re–Entry: A Handbook for Women

$10.95, 1993, 180 pages

Here's the definitive guide for women entering or re–entering the work force. Filled with examples and tips for navigating today's highly competitive job market, this book shows you how to use powerful language and present your interests, skills, and qualifications to grab the attention of potential employers.

Order form is at the end of this catalog

To order: 800/829-5220 weekdays, 9 a.m. to 6 p.m. CST

Resumes for the Over 50 Job Hunter

$12.95, 1993, 208 pages

Samuel Ray shows you how to turn your age and experience into an asset in the eyes of potential employers. Includes 95 sample resumes, tips for successful networking, how to follow up, and how to negotiate the best deal.

Electronic Resume Revolution

$12.95, 1994, 256 pages

If you've read the *Government Job Finder* carefully, you know there's an electronic revolution in hiring with hundreds of job–matching services and computerized resume and job databases becoming the new way to get a job. Premier careers writer Joyce Lain Kennedy teams up with Thomas Morrow to show you how to create a winning resume for this electronic resume revolution. Learn how to prepare your resume for electronic scanners and for computerized resume databases and job–matching services. The authors present over 30 sample resumes to get you past the computer and in front of the person who does the hiring. Also learn how to prepare a video resume.

Job Search Letters that Get Results

$12.95, ISBN 0–942710–70–3, 1992, 232 pages

The companion volume to *Dynamite Cover Letters,* this book includes 201 examples of the six most important types of letters every job seeker needs to write: cover, approach, thank you, rejection, withdrawal, and acceptance letters. By Caryl and Ronald Krannich.

200 Letters for Job Hunters

$17.95, 1993, 344 pages

Nobody does it better than author William Frank with his collection of over 250 types of job letters to cover every situation in the job search.

Dynamite Cover Letters and Other Great Job Search Letters

$9.95, 1992, 135 pages

A well–crafted cover letter is often more important than an applicant's resume. Learn how to write effective cover letters, blind approach letters, and thank you, negotiation, rejection, and acceptance letters. By Caryl and Ronald Krannich.

"A **really good book.** Filled with **common sense**...tells all the important things without forcing the reader to consume 350 pages....blends savvy with easy–to–read text with examples of all kinds of job search letters."
— *Career Opportunities News*

Interviews, Salary, and Networking

Interview for Success:
A Practical Guide to Increasing Job Interviews, Offers, and Salaries

$11.95, 1992, 218 pages

One of the most comprehensive and practical interview preparation books available today, *Interview for Success* is packed with solid advice on getting interviews and then using them to your advantage to win the job at the salary you want. The authors, Caryl and Ronald Krannich, present everything you need to know to do your best at your job interview, including how to handle stress. Included is a checklist of 54 interviewing maxims.

Dynamite Answers to Interview Questions

$9.95, 1992, 163 pages

"**No more sweaty palms**" —that's what the authors of this lively book promise. The perfect companion volume to *Interview for Success* (described immediately above), this book outlines the best answers to key job interview questions. Included are sample answers to hundreds of questions crafty interviewers are likely to spring. Learn how to turn negative responses into positive answers that can mean the difference between getting hired and being rejected.

Dynamite Salary Negotiations

$13.95, 1994, 164 pages

Praised by the *National Business Employment Weekly*, this book dispels myths and explains how to determine your true value, negotiate salary and employment terms, and finalize your job offer. It shows how to respond to ads that request a salary history or salary requirements and much more. By Ronald and Caryl Krannich.

The New Network Your Way to Job and Career Success

$12.95,1993, 188 pages

Pinpointing a practice often presented as merely a vague concept, this book shows you how to make the connections that get you to the jobs that aren't widely advertised. Learn to identify, link, and transform networks to gather information and obtain advice and references that lead to job interviews and offers. By Caryl and Ronald Krannich.

How to Order

Complete the order form on the next three pages, or call us toll–free at 800/829–5220 to order (call 708/366–5200 if you need more information before ordering), Mondays through Fridays, 9 a.m. to 6 p.m. Central Standard Time.

Be sure to include postage according to the formula given at the bottom of the page 337 and enclose your payment (check, money order, VISA, or MasterCard —individuals and private companies must prepay).

Call or write for special quantity discounts or resale prices. *Please note that prices are subject to change without notice.*

PLANNING/COMMUNICATIONS

7215 Oak Avenue
River Forest, Illinois 60305–1935

To order: 800/829–5220
For info: 708/366–5200
Weekdays: 9 a.m. to 6 p.m. CST

All orders from individuals or businesses must be **prepaid** by check, money order, VISA or MasterCard. **Purchase orders** are accepted only from libraries, universities, bookstores, or government offices.

The newest edition

At Planning/Communications, we always ship you the newest edition of a book or software program that is available to us. If the new edition costs more than the edition shown in this catalog, we will contact you first to see which edition you want.

Title	Price	x #	= Total
America's Job Finders for the 1990s			
Government Job Finder (paperback)	$16.95	x ___	= $_____
Government Job Finder (hard cover)	$32.95	x ___	= $_____
Non–Profits' Job Finder (paperback)	$16.95	x ___	= $_____
Non–Profits' Job Finder (hard cover)	$32.95	x ___	= $_____
Professional's Private Sector Job Finder (paperback)	$18.95	x ___	= $_____
Professional's Private Sector Job Finder (hard cover)	$36.95	x ___	= $_____
The Ultimate Job Finder (computer software)	$49.95	x ___	= $_____
Government Careers			
The Complete Guide to Public Employment	$19.95	x ___	= $_____
The Almanac of American Government Jobs and Careers	$14.95	x ___	= $_____
The Book of U.S. Government Jobs	$15.95	x ___	= $_____
How to Get a Federal Job	$14.95	x ___	= $_____
Find a Federal Job Fast!	$ 9.95	x ___	= $_____
How to Find an Overseas Job with the U.S. Government	$28.95	x ___	= $_____
The Right SF 171 Writer	$19.95	x ___	= $_____
The 171 Reference Book	$18.95	x ___	= $_____
Quick & Easy for the SF 171	$49.95	x ___	= $_____
Check disk size: ☐ 3.5–inch ☐ 5.25–inch Check version: ☐ DOS ☐ Windows			
FOCIS software (only on 3.5–inch disks)	$49.95	x ___	= $_____
Complete Guide to U.S. Civil Service Jobs	$10.00	x ___	= $_____
Federal Jobs in Law Enforcement	$16.00	x ___	= $_____
Civil Service Handbook	$10.00	x ___	= $_____
The Book of U.S. Postal Exams	$13.95	x ___	= $_____
The Book of $16,000–$60,000 Post Office Jobs	$14.95	x ___	= $_____
Federal Government Job Winning Kit #1 (include postage for 5 items)			
Disk size: ☐ 3.5" ☐ 5.25" Version: ☐ DOS ☐ Windows	$63.72	x ___	= $_____
Federal Government Job Winning Kit #2 (include postage for 7 items)			
Disk size: ☐ 3.5" ☐ 5.25" Version: ☐ DOS ☐ Windows	$149.35	x ___	= $_____
The New Complete Guide to Environmental Careers	$15.95	x ___	= $_____
Job Opps 94: Job Opportunities in the Environment	$16.95	x ___	= $_____
Careers with Non–Profits			
Non–Profits' Job Finder (paperback)	$16.95	x ___	= $_____
Non–Profits' Job Finder (hard cover)	$32.95	x ___	= $_____
Jobs and Careers with Nonprofit Organizations	$15.95	x ___	= $_____
Good Works: A Guide to Careers in Social Change	$18.00	x ___	= $_____
Great Careers: The Fourth of July Guide...	$34.95	x ___	= $_____
Jobs in Washington, DC	$11.95	x ___	= $_____
International Careers			
Guide to Careers in World Affairs	$14.95	x ___	= $_____
The Almanac of International Jobs & Careers	$19.95	x ___	= $_____
The Complete Guide to International Jobs & Careers	$13.95	x ___	= $_____
International Internships and Volunteer Programs	$18.95	x ___	= $_____
Work, Study, Travel Abroad: The Whole World Handbook	$13.95	x ___	= $_____

Finding the Right Job or Career

Change Your Job, Change Your Life	$14.95	x ____	= $_____
What Color is Your Parachute?	$14.95	x ____	= $_____
Career Design Software	$99.95	x ____	= $_____
Zen and the Art of Making a Living	$16.00	x ____	= $_____
An Easier Way to Change Jobs	$14.95	x ____	= $_____
The Over 40 Job Guide	$12.00	x ____	= $_____
The New Relocating Spouse's Guide to Employment	$14.95	x ____	= $_____
Graduating to the 9 to 5 World	$11.95	x ____	= $_____
Discover the Right Job for You!	$11.95	x ____	= $_____
Internships 1994	$29.95	x ____	= $_____
Summer Jobs 1994	$15.95	x ____	= $_____

Winning Resumes and Cover Letters

High Impact Resumes and Letters	$12.95	x ____	= $_____
The Resume Catalog: 200 Damn Good Examples	$15.95	x ____	= $_____
Dynamite Resumes: 101 Great Examples	$ 9.95	x ____	= $_____
WinWay Resumes for Windows	$69.95	x ____	= $_____
Resumes for Re–Entry: A Handbook for Women	$10.95	x ____	= $_____
Resumes for the Over 50 Job Hunter	$12.95	x ____	= $_____
Electronic Resume Revolution	$12.95	x ____	= $_____
Job Search Letters that Get Results	$12.95	x ____	= $_____
200 Letters for Job Hunters	$17.95	x ____	= $_____
Dynamite Cover Letters & Other Great Job Search Letters	$ 9.95	x ____	= $_____

Interviews, Salary, and Networking

Interview for Success	$11.95	x ____	= $_____
Dynamite Answers to Interview Questions	$ 9.95	x ____	= $_____
Dynamite Salary Negotiations	$13.95	x ____	= $_____
The New Network Your Way to Job and Career Success	$12.95	x ____	= $_____

Subtotal: $_____

☛ **Illinois residents only: Add 7.75% sales tax** + $_____

☛ Shipping: (**$3.75 for the first item plus $1 for each additional item; use next line)** + $ 3.75

☛ Additional items: _____ x $1/each = $_____

☛ ***Overseas orders: Add an** **<u>additional</u>** **$12 per book for air mail** (if actual postage is less, we will refund the difference to you) + $_____

** = Orders sent to U.S. possessions and military addresses do not require this additional overseas postage. They are shipped via Priority Mail.*

☛ **Total enclosed:** $_____

❑ Check here to get Planning/Communications' **free catalog** of 175 job–quest books and software

☛ Please continue on the other side.

Ship to:

Please print clearly or type.

Name ______________________________

Address ______________________________

____

For UPS delivery, give full street address and unit number. No post office boxes!

City–State–Zip ______________________________ GOV94

❏ **Enclosed is my check or money order for $__________ made out to:** ***Planning/Communications***

❏ **Please charge $_______ to my VISA or MasterCard**

Card number:

____

Expiration date: ____________________

Signature (if charging this order):

____

Please sign your name exactly as it appears on your VISA or MasterCard.

Home phone number:

___________/______________________

Payment terms

All checks must be in U.S. dollars drawn on an U.S. bank.

Orders from individuals or private businesses must be prepaid.

Purchase orders are accepted only from libraries, colleges, universities, bookstores, and government offices.

Send your order and payment to:

PLANNING/COMMUNICATIONS

7215 Oak Avenue
River Forest, IL 60305–1935

or call

Toll–free: 1–800/829–5220 (to place your order)
1–708/366–5200 (for information about books or software)
Monday through Friday, 9 a.m. to 6 p.m. Central Standard Time